ZIPPING MY FLY

ZIPPING MY FLY

Moments in the Life of
an American Sportsman

RICH TOSCHES

A Perigee Book

A Perigee Book
Published by the Penguin Group
Penguin Group (USA) Inc.
375 Hudson Street. New York, New York 10014, USA
Penguin Group (Canada), 10 Alcorn Avenue, Toronto, Ontario M4V 3B2, Canada
(a division of Pearson Penguin Canada Inc.)
Penguin Books Ltd., 80 Strand, London WC2R 0RL, England
Penguin Ireland, 25 St. Stephen's Green, Dublin 2, Ireland
(a division of Penguin Books Ltd.)
Penguin Group (Australia), 250 Camberwell Road, Camberwell, Victoria 3124, Australia
(a division of Pearson Australia Group Pty. Ltd.)
Penguin Books India Pvt. Ltd., 11 Community Centre, Panchsheel Park, New Delhi — 110 017,
India
Penguin Group (NZ), Cnr Airborne and Rosedale Roads, Albany, Auckland 1310, New Zealand
(a division of Pearson New Zealand Ltd.)
Penguin Books (South Africa) (Pty.) Ltd., 24 Sturdee Avenue,
Rosebank, Johannesburg 2196, South Africa

Penguin Books Ltd., Registered Offices: 80 Strand, London WC2R 0RL, England

Copyright © 2002 by Rich Tosches
Text design by Tiffany Estreicher
Cover design and illustration by Ben Gibson

PRINTING HISTORY
Perigee hardcover edition / November 2002
Perigee trade paperback edition / November 2004

PERIGEE is a registered trademark of Penguin Group (USA) Inc.
The "P" design is a trademark belonging to Penguin Group (USA) Inc.

ISBN: 0-399-52917-9

Library of Congress Cataloging-in-Publication Data

Tosches, Rich.
Zipping my fly : moments in the life of an American sportsman / Rich Tosches.—1st ed.
p. cm.
ISBN 0-399-52819-9
1. Fly fishing—Anecdotes. I. Title.

SH456.T67 2002
799.1'24—dc21   2002074817

PRINTED IN THE UNITED STATES OF AMERICA

10 9 8 7 6 5 4 3 2 1

CONTENTS

———

My First Fly Rod—More or Less

Thirty years ago I first laid my hands on a fly rod, lifting it gently from the red and yellow maple leaves alongside a small creek on a crisp autumn morning in New England. As my small hands felt the perfect balance of the most magnificent fishing rod I had ever seen, my heart began to race and my step quickened, young feet gliding now along the bank of the gentle stream.

Suddenly, as what would become for me a fascination with the art of fly-fishing had barely entered its infancy, I heard a voice coming from my head, a voice that would set the tone for a lifetime of marvelous fishing adventures:

"Hey, you little bastard! Get back here! Put down my fly rod!"

As it turns out, the voice wasn't coming from my head. It was coming from Porky Ferrara, who owned the fly rod and felt a very powerful attachment to it, judging by the way he dragged me down from behind, wrestled the rod out of my hands, and began to choke me.

When he wasn't delivering heating oil to the homes of our small town in Massachusetts, Porky was usually fly-fishing, perfecting the art through trial and error, casting endlessly, trying to master the movements of hand that could send the line and the tiny fly whistling through the air to a precise spot where he believed a wily brown trout or cunning rainbow lay in ambush. Judging from what I saw, he often believed this precise spot was a bush forty feet up on the bank. He would generally celebrate this event by shouting something in Italian that sounded like "Noah good sonamabeech!" which my father told me meant "My, isn't it great just to be outdoors!"

So I studied my mentor, hoping to gain some insight into the science of fly-fishing. And I learned much. I learned about the hatches of insects that send trout into a feeding frenzy. I learned about the importance of stealth when stalking the cautious fish. But mostly, I learned that if you take a clump of moss about the size of your fist and stuff it into your mouth, nobody could hear you laugh.

I've been fly-fishing ever since. The highlight came in 1990, when my employer, the *Los Angeles Times*, approved a sixteen-day trip to New Zealand, where I conducted extensive research into the sport and wrote a 10,500-word account of my trip, a story many literary experts said "contained only seven verbs." The trip ended up costing the newspaper—I am not kidding—$6,875.

It did, however, have a lot to do with my development as a fly fisherman.

On a less positive note, it also had a lot to do with the fact that I don't work for the *Los Angeles Times* anymore.

Nevertheless, in summarizing my three decades of fly-fishing and watching others who are even more proficient in the gentle sport than I am—a group of anglers I would call "all of them"— I can, in all seriousness, say this about my first teacher in terms of his skill, grace, and knowledge of aquatic insects:

Of all the fly fishermen I have met, he was the only one named Porky.

CHAPTER 1

The World Championship:
El Mucho Importante Evento

Jackson Hole, Wyoming, is a place of stunning beauty, a valley nestled at the foot of the majestic Grand Teton Mountains, a place of almost magical splendor that the Native Americans called, in very reverent terms, *totonka tanakawa*, or "land of $42 T-shirts."

In the summer, Jackson Hole—the gateway to Yellowstone National Park—beckons the adventurer. And they come in great, sweeping hordes to this land of elk and moose and grizzly bear, all of them hoping for that one special moment when the eyes capture a scene that most wilderness experts believe stays with a person for a lifetime: a guy from Houston in a Denny's parking lot, trying to put his rented, three-hundred-foot Winnebago in the space marked COMPACTS ONLY.

But the most spectacular time of year in Jackson Hole is the fall—when the air tingles with the coming winter and the geese gather for another migration and the aspen trees sparkle and the guy from Houston has now put his wife in the driver's seat as he stands behind the Winnebago with his hands over his head shouting, "OKAY, NOW CUT THE WHEEL TO THE RIGHT!"

And it was during a recent autumn that an event took place that the people of Jackson Hole are still talking about—the seventeenth annual World Fly-Fishing Championship, which attracted elite teams of anglers from eighteen nations, fishermen who spent their own money, leaving their homes in Germany and France and Wales and Denmark and Norway, traveling thousands of miles to this magnificent place with only one thought: "Oops. Maybe I should have told my wife where I was going! Oh well."

Seriously, the World Fly-Fishing Championship was very exciting, leaving the Jackson residents shaking their heads as they thought about Team England's casting skills, about Team Australia's delicate dry fly presentations, about Team Spain's gentle nymphing techniques, about Team Japan's breathtaking fly-tying skills, and mostly, about how they would ever get the smell of cigarette smoke out of Team Germany's hotel room.

The 1996 World Fly-Fishing Championship was held in the Czech Republic, with the gold medal going to the host nation, Team Czech Republic. Team members credited their victory to an intimate knowledge of the Czech rivers, which, during the actual fishing competition, helped them determine precisely where to *placuvas dyenomitovich* or "place the dynamite."

That was just a joke, of course. The World Fly-Fishing Championship is strictly catch-and-release, with no harm coming to any of the creatures involved. The exception would be the Germans' lungs.

For this 1997 World Fly-Fishing Championship, each team consisted of five anglers. There was also a reserve angler, entrusted with many important duties (keeping the cooler filled with beer is just one example), a nonfishing team captain, and a nonfishing team manager. Prior to the competition, the team captain is required to walk out to midfield for the coin toss, where he usually drowns. Then the team manager communicates with his players via a series of hand signals that could mean "cast upstream," "cast downstream," "use a dry fly," "use a sinking nymph," or "bunt."

Scoring was based on a formula involving the number and size of the trout caught, with an "impartial controller" measuring and recording each and every fish. The impartial controller—in more common fishing terms, "the guy who isn't drinking very much and can drive home"—was a professional fly-fishing guide. A professional fly-fishing guide is defined, in strict terms, as a guy who has successfully convinced his wife he is actually making a living and supporting the family in this pursuit. (An "excellent guide" is one who can come home at night, moan about how hard he worked that day, and talk his wife into giving "The Breadwinner" a foot rub.)

Also, the measuring of fish was done in centimeters, a decision made by the international fly-fishing people for two very good reasons. First, it allows a more precise measurement of the fish. Second, and more importantly, this metric system measurement causes the American anglers to blurt out such things as, "Uh, I caught a nice trout that was, uh, let me check my notes . . . 132 hectares. I think." This in turn allows the international fly-fishing people to laugh so hard they emit gas, which causes their rubber waders to expand.

Typical conversation:

> SVEN: Jean-Pierre, your waders look as if they may now burst. Was this caused by listening to an American try to figure out how large his fish was?
>
> JEAN-PIERRE: *Oui.* That and how do you say . . . *burritos?*

For more on the scoring system, let's go to the worldwide governing body of competitive fly-fishing, FIPS-Mouche (Fédération Internationale de Pêche Sportive Mouche, which is French and means "International Federation of Guys Who Like Joe Pesci with a Mustache"). Caution: Before you read this explanation of the scoring system, you may want to head for your most comfortable chair and settle in. Although no matter how comfortable you are, after—or perhaps midway through—reading this, you may want to shoot yourself.

Here now, as recorded at the Media Cocktail Party the day before competition began, is the FIPS-Mouche rules chairman, Mr. Jack Simpson:

> "You take one man from each team and put him in a group of eighteen anglers. All of the five team members are then distributed evenly and will therefore compete within their own group of eighteen, in that particular time period. So this is very critical. Then we'd be interested in how they change position in terms of

these cumulative placings. The team gets credit for each man's placing. If the team is very fortunate in the first round, say, and each of the five competitors places first in each one, the team now has a five and they would be the top team. In the second period they compete again and the individuals carry over their placings. So does the team. Tiebreakers are points and number of fish and finally, the largest fish, until the tie is broken. Those who are rewarded are those who show the greatest consistency. If one fellow gets 50,000 points in one period and no points in the others—or an eighteen—yet someone else had greater consistency in all five, he would win. Like a one and then an eighteen in four of them. He can't win. It's a very fair system. As for the wading portion, we're looking at the 200-meter beat plus the 20-meter buffer zone in which no one can fish. These will be physically marked with signs such as A, B, C, D, one through eighteen, and so on."

Some would say the oddest thing about this 6-million-word explanation by Mr. Simpson was that all stuff about the one and the eighteen and the 50,000 points.

Although if you ask me, the oddest thing about his long explanation was the fact that I had only asked him if FIPS-Mouche was handing out any free-drink tickets.

CHAPTER 2

The Grand Marshall Was a Carp

A s all anglers know, there are things to be done before any fishing can take place. For some anglers, there are worms to be dug up. This is best accomplished with a heavy shovel on a grassy area, preferably at night after your neighbor has gone to sleep and will not, in strict angling terminology, "be watching his front yard."

There are hooks to be sharpened, too, so that the barb will more easily penetrate a fish's lips and result in a higher catch ratio. More importantly, a sharp hook will be easier for your doctor to remove from your nose, thus freeing up more time for his more serious and life-sustaining work, such as golf. (That was just a joke. Doctors have far more important things to do than play golf. Keeping the office stocked with a complete set of 1973 *Reader's Digest* magazines and hiring a receptionist strong enough to hold you down and rifle through your wallet for an insurance card would be two examples.)

But no matter what type of angler you are, there is one thing that always precedes a day of fishing. That, of course, would be the parade.

The World Fly-Fishing Championship parade took place in downtown Jackson Hole, and at the risk of sounding melodramatic or elevating this event to some sort of mystical plateau, let me say this: Not only did it make me teary-eyed, but it also caused two of my ribs to snap and forced a huge mouthful of root beer to come out of my nose.

Heading up the parade was a band riding on a float, playing the emotional strains of the seventeenth-century French concerto *Behinez Bunchous Guylairre Fishez*, or "Behind Us Are a Bunch of Guys Who Are Going Fishing." As the parade kicked off and the band turned the corner onto Main Street, a roar went up from the several hundred onlookers, mostly residents of Jackson Hole who had long anticipated this moment. From the sidewalks they waved and cheered and hooted and hollered as the anglers drew closer, which gives you some idea of the magnitude of this event and, of course, the overwhelming loneliness that comes with living in Wyoming.

The first contingent of anglers to appear was Team Canada, its athletes marching proudly and silently, and their very appearance shouting out to the world, "We Are Canadian Athletes!" In other words, they were all wearing skates and cups and had no front teeth. I'm kidding. I love Canada. And, like most Americans, I fervently hope that one day they can break away from the United States and forge their very own country.

Behind Team Canada was Team France. Here I must caution you that I plan to bring into play all of my immense writing skills to conceal the highly suspenseful ending of this book, which will come, in literary terms, near the end. So I won't say very much at this moment about Team France.

Let's move on to the third group of fly fishermen in the parade, Team Italy, which marched right behind the eventual winners.

Damn.

Anyway, leading Team Italy was Edgardo Dona, a master angler who has developed his vast array of skills despite having only a few hours a week to practice. The rest of his time is spent in another pursuit, one he practices relentlessly, day and night, indoors or outdoors, in summer or in winter: laughing.

Edgardo Dona got off the airplane in Jackson Hole laughing. His baggage appeared on the airport carousel, which also made Edgardo laugh. During the week a member of Team Finland told a joke to his teammates and Edgardo laughed very hard, even though he does not understand a word of Finnish and believed the punch line of the joke to be, "And the uncle says, 'A carp? Not when I have two fields to plow with Bob's lamp!' "

With Edgardo were teammates Edoardo Ferrero, Mario Altora, Carlo Baldassini, and Pierluigi Cocito. Pierluigi, as you know, is a traditional Italian name which means, literally, "Let's take Luigi for a little walk on the pier." (That, obviously, was just a stupid joke and was not meant to offend any specific group of people. But just in case, I will now move to a new house and take different routes to work each day.)

Team Italy wore striking Armani suits for the fishing parade, the apparel reflecting all of the classic Armani trademarks: pleated trousers with cuffs and jackets with a full cut and gently falling lapels that accent the torso. And, of course, a four-by-four patch of unprocessed wool near the shoulder, where you can stick artificial flies.

As the parade continued through Jackson Hole, the passion we all shared for fly-fishing grew ever more evident even as the eight-hundred-foot-long Winnebagos on their way to Yellowstone were forced to stop and were backed up all the way to Utah. Near the Teton Kids Clothing Store (TODAY ONLY: T-SHIRTS $34.50 OR TWO FOR $85!) Team Belgium was strutting its stuff, its anglers looking sharp in their brown-and-white suits made entirely from the most well-known native Belgian fabric: waffles. Team members Marc David, Francis Lambinet, Alain Gigot, Alain Colonval, and Jean-Michel Grégoire smiled and waved behind their banner, which carried Belgium's national motto, which, loosely translated, goes like this: "We Know Our Names Are French. It's a Long Story."

Next came Teams England and Finland—the English looking magnificent in that typical English rumpled sort of way and the Finns shielding their eyes and cowering behind very dark glasses, almost as if they hadn't seen the sun in six months.

They were followed by Team Poland, led by master angler Marian Mozdyniewcz, who came to Jackson Hole with a lofty goal in mind: catching a trout longer than his name.

Next through the streets of Jackson Hole was Team Spain, its members—their instincts honed from years of similar street gatherings in their own country—looking nervously over their shoulders as they walked, wondering when parade officials would release the bulls.

Team Norway followed—the clear favorite should ice fishing break out. Then came the Australians—hopping, with all their fishing equipment in pouches on their stomachs. Team Slovakia was next, a group of men whose country has been torn by terrible conflict for the past decade but has now, thankfully, recovered to the point where everyone goes fly-fishing. Then came Ireland and Wales, two teams that with their mere presence signaled there would be some serious beer drinking.

New Zealand was next, whose members of the fly-fishing team accurately reflected that nation's population makeup. By this I mean the team consisted of one human and four sheep. Then came Team Germany, which, as previously mentioned, went through cigarettes like Michael Jackson goes through noses. The fly-fishing parade was no exception. It seemed odd, then, that placed directly behind—or downwind of—Team Germany was a U.S. Forest Service float containing Smokey the Bear, who today is still in counseling.

Second to last in the lineup was Team Japan, which would not perform all that well in what Fédération Internationale de Pêche Sportive officials refer to, in technical terms, as "the fishing part," but the Japanese anglers did look resplendent in their dark suits and matching red ties. And they have about forty-eight thousand photographs to prove it.

And finally came the Americans. The streets echoed with the roars of the crowd as Team USA lit up, faces aglow with the joy only a fishing parade can offer. And as the cheers grew louder, they walked slowly and soaked it up, from their cowboy hats to their cowboy boots, four men and one woman on their home turf now, five Americans who would, at the end of this competition—in the shadow of the inspiring Grand Teton Mountains—make the following statement in the international arena of fly-fishing:

We'd be dead last if Team Japan had not shown up.

CHAPTER 3

Hail to the Herring

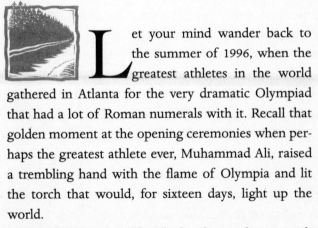Let your mind wander back to the summer of 1996, when the greatest athletes in the world gathered in Atlanta for the very dramatic Olympiad that had a lot of Roman numerals with it. Recall that golden moment at the opening ceremonies when perhaps the greatest athlete ever, Muhammad Ali, raised a trembling hand with the flame of Olympia and lit the torch that would, for sixteen days, light up the world.

Now whack yourself in the head several times with a heavy pot and try to forget it, because the opening

---

ceremonies of the seventeenth annual World Fly-Fishing Championship were not like that at all. For starters, Muhammad Ali was unable to carry the torch into the Jackson Hole rodeo grounds, having made a previous commitment in the area of choosing new linoleum for his huge kitchen.

To be honest, there was no torch at all for these opening ceremonies, which was somewhat of a disappointment to the fans and a huge disappointment to Team Germany, which had planned on using the torch to light their cigarettes and now had to settle for a more tedious method of lighting up: briskly rubbing two Frenchmen together.

This is not to say the opening ceremonies for the fly-fishing event were not dramatic. As a matter of fact, as the national anthems blared over the loudspeakers and the fly-fishing teams marched in behind their flags, I felt a lump in my throat. As it turns out, a hatch was taking place on the nearby Snake River and the "lump" was actually a giant mayfly. This in no way diminished the excitement of the opening ceremonies, although it did diminish my appetite for the next two days.

First to march into the arena was Team Slovakia, accompanied by their heart-wrenching national anthem, which I will now try to sing to you: "Da-da, da-da-da daaahhhh!" The anthem is entitled "Als Slovaken Wordsjk" or "We Think the Anthem Would Be Better If It Actually Had Words."

Slovakia was followed by the anglers from Team Spain, who entered the outdoor rodeo arena bearing centuries of tradition in the science of fly-fishing, traditions that at that moment had each member of the team thinking about just two things: When do we get to kill the bull, and who gets the ears?

Team Wales entered next, marching to their spirited anthem,

"Even Our Shorts Are Tweed." The rest of the nations followed then, Team Canada marching to its anthem ("O Canada"), just ahead of Team Australia ("O Australia"), Team Finland ("O Finland"), Team Norway ("Hail to the Herring"), and Team Italy (theme from *The Godfather*).

Anyway, when the teams were in place in the arena, the mayor of Jackson Hole stepped to the microphone and bellowed, "There you have it, folks. The very best fly fishermen on the whole dol' garned planet Earth! Welcome to Jackson Hole, Wyoming, and now I say, 'Howdy, pardners!' which is our way of saying welcome."

On a somewhat negative note, "Howdy, pardners!" sounds almost exactly like the Italian words for "I, personally, plan to sleep with each and every one of your wives while you are out fishing." The reaction from the anglers of Team Italy was swift and direct. That's right; they laughed so hard they blew the cameras out of Team Japan's hands.

"We are very pleased and excited that you have chosen our community for this competition," the mayor continued after allowing the Japanese anglers to retrieve their cameras and pound some of the dirt out of them. "If you haven't noticed it already, we are in a very unique and spectacular part of the world."

(Specifically, a part of the world in which during the nine months of winter, guys can get so lonely they begin giving human names to the elk. The most common one is Debbie.)

The mayor—who was now getting angry at all of my idiotic interruptions—went on to tell the international field of anglers, "What you probably don't know yet is that the people here are as warm and friendly as the scenery is beautiful."

(On a personal note, I imagine that if a bunch of tourists gladly

---

ZIPPING MY FLY

15

handed me $42 for a T-shirt with a picture of a moose on it—a T-shirt that came to my store at the cost of $1.39, thanks to a lot of hardworking eight-year-olds on the night shift in Malaysia, well, I'm guessing I'd be pretty damn warm and friendly, too.)

The mayor closed by saying, "And so, once again, I'd like to say 'Howdy, pardners!' and welcome to Jackson Hole."

The Italians laughed again.

Although this time, they were also keeping a pretty close eye on their wives in the bleachers.

The anglers then filed into the bleachers to watch a Wild West show. As they got to their seats, they demonstrated many different forms of resting on the seats. Highlighting this International Exhibit of Sitting Down were the anglers from the Czech Republic, who—I am not kidding about this—each spread one Kleenex-brand nose tissue on the metal seats and then rested their buttocks on this piece of paper. Feeling an explanation was in order, I asked master angler Jozef Lach to explain the tissue thing.

Here now, are his actual words: "Seats dat hat . . . or maybe I say *hot* . . . and we are not want hot pants for our suits. And they one seat . . . are dirty, either."

What Jozef was saying, obviously, is that the Czech Republic anglers, including himself, had sat on their hats, which didn't work out so good, so now they were trying Kleenex. Further, their behinds were hot for some unknown reason and at least one of them had had "an accident." This, in turn, forced the rest of the team to inhale ether.

Out in the arena—and here I will use the formal rodeo terminology, so please try to stay with me—a cowboy was chasing a small cow. He finally caught the cow by throwing a clothesline rope around its neck, and then, to make sure it did not get up and

---

run away before he could get the barbecue fired up, he used both of his hands to tie the little cow's feet together with more clothes-line rope.

At this, the anglers stood and roared their approval, the loudest roars coming from the anglers of Team Australia, who not only use this same roping method to tend their cattle, but also to get a wife. I am just kidding, of course. Australian men don't use *both* hands to tie a prospective wife's feet together. They need one hand to hold the ninety-eight-ounce can of Foster's.

And as the calf struggled to break free, the Japanese, the master fly-tyers in the international field, were on the edges of their seats, too. They seemed to sense they might never get a better opportunity than this to gather material for their special fly (a tan caddis with a Hendrickson wing)—the main ingredient of which is the hair from the ass of a small cow.

The ceremonies concluded with an emotional dance by Native Americans, members of the local Flathead tribe. Interpreting their dance as best I could, I surmised that the dancers were calling on the spirits to watch over the anglers, for the weather to cooperate, and for Jozef Trnka of Slovakia to buy a vowel.

The opening ceremonies came to an end and then, with the start of the tournament drawing ever closer, the best fly fishermen on the whole dol' garned planet Earth filed out of the stadium—the Canadians hopeful, the Americans confident, the Poles eager, and the Italians staying between their wives and the mayor.

CHAPTER 4

Das Fish—Big Wet?

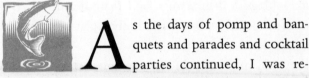s the days of pomp and banquets and parades and cocktail parties continued, I was reminded of an old saying in competitive international fly-fishing circles, one coined by the Germans: *Evn We Beeren. Ltesen Go Fasen,* which means, literally, "Even we can't drink any more beer. Let's go fishing."

And so, eventually, the best anglers in the world prepared for a day of angling. Officially, it was known as a practice day, with the results not counting in the Official Scoring System understood only by Einstein and, now, Jack Simpson of FIPS-Mouche.

———

The anglers would practice on the Greys River, some fifty miles from Jackson near the Idaho border. (During the actual tournament, the anglers would fish one day in Idaho, forcing officials to explain to foreign anglers the difference between a "brown trout" and a "potato.")

Anyway, the trip to the Greys River would involve loading the fly fishermen onto school buses for the long drive, which prompted the anglers to ask many questions. Examples would include "What is this Greys River?" (Team Slovakia); "How long does such a trip take?" (Team Spain); and "What is a school bus?" (Team Finland).

The loading operation was to begin at 5:30 A.M. in the parking lot of the Snow King resort, forcing the anglers to set their alarm clocks for 5 A.M. Except for Team Germany, which set its alarm clock for 3 A.M. so each team member could smoke a quick pack of cigarettes before climbing onto the bus.

At 5:15 A.M. the place was a zoo. By this I mean the Welsh were searching for their fishing rods, the New Zealanders were running around looking for their waders, and Team Poland was trying to get out of its room without waking the polar bear, the leopard, and the monkeys.

In the lobby of the Snow King, one-hundred world-class fly anglers milled about, all of them now wearing waders and carrying their fly rods, along with long-handled landing nets.

They drank a lot of coffee, too, forcing them to pile into the men's room in great waves. And not to get off the subject, but if you missed the fly-fishing event and want to see thirty or forty guys smoking cigarettes and standing around the urinals with their rubber pants and suspenders pulled down to their ankles as they hold fishing nets in one hand, well, quite frankly, you'll have to wait for the next Alabama State Fair.

RICH TOSCHES

At 5:30 A.M. the anglers had moved outside, awaiting their bus assignments. Volunteers with clipboards scurried about in the darkness, shouting out instructions in English, which was good news for the eight or nine anglers who understood English. For the others, there was a bit of confusion. Example:

BUS ASSIGNMENT PERSON WITH CLIPBOARD: Okay now, Olav Syversbraten, Norway; Jaroslav Barton, Czech Republic; and Bernard Marguet, France, please report within five minutes to Bus No. 6.

OLAV SYVERSBRATEN (in Norwegian): I am fishing with Clara Barton, the famous American nurse?

BUS ASSIGNMENT PERSON: No, that's JAROSLAV Barton. You are in Group P.

JAROSLAV BARTON (in Czech): No thank you. I just went.

BERNARD MARGUET (in French, with his mouth full): Anyone want a handful of snails?

This went on for about thirty minutes in the darkness—Finns talking to Spaniards, Italians talking to Germans, Poles talking to the New Zealanders, the Irish packing their waders full of potatoes in case another famine broke out.

In general, no one understood anything, which was in accordance with FIPS-Mouche Official Competition Rules Article 16, subsections 16.3–16.5, which clearly states: "Landing nets must not exceed one hundred and twenty-two (122) cm/forty-eight (48) inches in overall length, fully extended. Further, the competitor may only stand while netting the fish, but if he has asked the controller to net the fish, the competitor must remain seated."

This first subsection, standardizing the size of landing nets, was instituted to thwart all that "Mine is bigger than yours!" bravado so common among anglers. The second portion of the so-called Netting Article, the one regarding sitting down and standing up, prevents an angler from netting his fish while lying on his back, kneeling, squatting, or sitting down in the fast-moving river.

(Footnote: That rule is currently being challenged by attorneys for Fédération de Pêche Sportive Poland, the hardy Poles claiming a long tradition of netting large trout while bobbing up and down in a river, often three or four anglers at the same time, all of them floating in the deep water with only their hats visible. Although historians believe this may be not so much "tradition" as it is the result of "all of them reaching across the boat for a sandwich at the same time.")

Back in the parking lot, the carefully orchestrated division of groups or "Angling Units" was nearly complete, with anglers shuffling around in a smooth and orderly fashion, or as the Spaniards often say, *likez fumar drildejo las Chineze,* or "like a Chinese fire drill." Somehow, I found my way to one of the school buses and climbed aboard for the ninety-minute ride to the Greys River. My bus contained the following ancestry: French, Italian, Spanish, Slovakian, German, Irish, Welsh, Belgian, and Australian.

And that was just the driver.

Seriously, the bus contained twenty-six men from fourteen nations. And one woman, Team Canada's Kathy Ruddick. As the yellow school bus chugged toward the river, the men talked about all the things you'd expect from sophisticated, mature, international fly-fishing anglers. Topics included the latest fly rods and reels, the excitement of fishing a new river, and mostly, of course, who had the coolest lunch box and whether Hywel Morgan of Wales, who was sitting in the same seat as Kathy Ruddick, would catch "cooties."

I found myself sandwiched on a bus seat between Poland's Artur Raclawski (which means, literally, "Arthur should really trim his toenails") and Ulrich Schneider of Germany. Now, I don't know how many of you have ever been crammed onto a school-bus seat between a Pole and a German, but let me say this about my experience: I spent ninety minutes sweating profusely, waiting for some kind of invasion to begin.

This did not happen, of course.

Although at one point I complimented the German on his very nice fly-fishing vest.

He smiled and, in his broken English, said, "Tanks!"

And the Polish guy dove under the seat.

We arrived at the Greys River at 7:30 A.M., which was, on the bi-ological clocks of the anglers, 12:30 P.M. in France, 4:30 P.M. in Spain, and January in New Zealand. I got off the bus at the first stop along the river, partly because I wanted to watch the meticulous Japanese anglers, Junzo Ishino and Kunihiko Tsuzuki, but mostly because I had tired of the conversation between Raclawski and Schneider.

Actual highlight that I have on tape:

RACLAWSKI: I am have good fish maybe how?
SCHNEIDER: Das fish! Big wet.

Anyway, Ishino and Tsuzuki waded in and with long, sweeping casts began testing the water. The ninety-minute bus ride, com-bined with six cups of coffee, had me involved in some hydro-research myself. Although my research had brought me not so much into the Greys River itself but rather into the bushes about fifty feet away. (Startling scientific conclusion: Peeing into the wind can make your shoes wet.)

I emerged from the bushes and walked along the bank, stopping to watch the two master anglers. They caught a few trout and soon came ashore for a break. I showed them my notebook and tape recorder and then we introduced ourselves. After a lot of bowing, they smiled and gave me the nickname Mr. Jurinishoko, which I believed meant Mr. Journalism but later learned means "Mr. Urine Shoe."

When they stopped laughing—it was now about noon—Junzo said this: "I am the student. Mr. Tsuzuki is the teacher." This became apparent over the next few hours, as Junzo would set the hook too quickly on a gently rising trout and pull the fly away from the fish, or occasionally allow the line to hit the water with a hard splash, spooking the timid trout.

And each time Mr. Tsuzuki would walk over and smash Junzo's hand with a wooden ruler and send a note home to his mommy and daddy. Once, he made the trembling young man scratch out the words "I will not snag the shrubs!" one hundred times. In the hard dirt. With a stick. I am just kidding. It was only fifty times. With his finger.

Seriously, the two often stood side by side, the master showing the promising young fly angler the intricacies that separate world-class fly-fishing from, say, bass fishing. Example: Fly fishermen can recognize hundreds and perhaps thousands of insects in the pupal, larval, and adult stages. Bass fishermen, meanwhile, can sometimes recognize their own house. (Generally by the color of the propane tank in the front yard. If that doesn't work, they go to the next step in house identification—counting the number of wheels on it.)

Anyway, Mr. Tsuzuki had figured out that the trout were feeding on emergers that rise from the stream bottom toward the surface. And now, to emulate this movement with his artificial fly, he was skillfully raising his right arm high over his head along the pine tree–lined banks of the river. And I think you can imagine the result. That's right, Mr. Tsuzuki's right armpit was virtually moisture free and smelled like pine trees.

No, what really happened is that he hooked a trout on nearly every cast, the fish following the emerger from the bottom and attacking as it neared the surface—just like the classic movie *Jaws*. Except, of course, as I stood on the bank of the Greys River, I did not have to listen to actor Roy Scheider scream, "Get out of the water!" several thousand times.

Anyway, Mr. Tsuzuki caught about a dozen trout, and later, as the sun set behind the mountains, summarized his day: "I have good luck small fish, no big luck fish," he said, echoing my own thoughts. "Big fish, I think, other fish. Yes? Emerger is good today. Tuck cast. Emerger. Next day, who know? Much change. Small fish. Good."

And somewhere, Dan Quayle was smiling.

CHAPTER 5

Bite My Kiwi, Mate

The second most interesting thing about New Zealand is this: There are 3.3 million people in the country and 70 million sheep. (Here we will play a game of Make Your Own Joke. Although I strongly suggest a punch line containing the words "Wyoming" and "Sadie Hawkins dance.")

Anyway, the *most* interesting thing about New Zealand is the fly-fishing. As a staff writer at the *Los Angeles Times,* I was fortunate enough to convince my boss in 1990 to send me to the South Pacific at the *Times's* expense for fourteen days of spectacular fish-

---

27

ing. This played a major role in my development as a fly fisherman. On a slightly less positive note, it also played a major role in why I no longer work at the *Los Angeles Times*.

The journey began with a thirteen-hour flight from Los Angeles to Auckland, during which I had enough time to write down the entire list of highly successful Kevin Costner films. Then the plane actually took off.

Because of a complex series of time zones, we left California at 11 P.M. on Thursday and arrived in Auckland at 2 A.M. on Monday, a month before we had departed from Los Angeles, I think. I do know this for sure, however: We crossed something called the International Date Line. (Which is also what Woody Allen crossed when he began going out with his teenage Korean stepdaughter.)

After a sleepless night in an Auckland hotel (the hotel was fine, but because of my intellect and curious nature, I stayed up all night flushing the toilet and watching the water swirl around *counter*clockwise), I boarded another flight to the New Zealand capital of Wellington. This is where the government makes all its major decisions, such as whether the national anthem should contain words other than "baaaahhh."

From there, another short flight brought me and Bill Hoyt—a fellow fly angler from California whom I met in the Auckland airport—to the South Island town of Nelson, where we rented a car. From the car-rental agent: "You're in luck today, gentlemen. We've got you a Bluebird!"

I did not know what he meant by a bluebird, but I did know this: If history does indeed repeat itself, my brother was going to shoot it in the eye with a BB gun.

As it turned out, a Bluebird is a car—more or less—that is as popular in New Zealand as, say, our Ford Explorer. (The main difference is that when the road surfaces get above seventy-five degrees, its tires do not explode and Firestone lawyers do not come running out of the bushes.)

Soon we were off, me getting comfortable behind the steering wheel, which was on the right, or "wrong" side of the dashboard, and gunning the Bluebird down the left, or "wrong" side of the road. On my left, Bill knew he was in good hands and quickly settled into the passenger seat with visions of gigantic trout dancing in his head. And eighteen pairs of rosary beads wrapped around his fingers.

Just minutes into the drive, I swerved into the right lane, then swerved back into the left lane and panicked when I saw the enormous, bright headlights of a truck bearing down on us from the left. Fortunately, these "headlights" turned out to be Bill's eyes. (He must have been homesick and missing his wife and kid because right after that he kept mumbling "Sweet Mary and Joseph!" over and over again.)

Our first stop was the Lake Rotoroa Lodge, nestled in the Nelson Lakes National Park. As we approached the lodge we crossed a bridge over the Gowan River. We got out and Bill spotted an enormous brown trout resting on the gravel in the clear water. When we reported this to the lodge owner, Bob Haswell, he calmly replied: "Oh. That would be Trevor, the pet trout." (This made it much different than being in New Jersey, where, when you report seeing something huge resting on the bottom of a river, the typical reply is: "Oh. That would be Vinny, the rat-bastard.")

Trevor, we were told, had called the water under the bridge his home for a few years, and despite frequent attempts to fool him with a fly, he had never been caught. I even made a few skillful attempts myself, most of which consisted of kneeling on the bank, holding a net behind my back, and saying softly, "Heeere, Trevor!"

Anyway, for three days Bill and I fished with guide Zane Mirfin, a twenty-year-old New Zealander who had an uncanny ability to spot trout from great distances, often in fast-moving and riffled water. This made Bill and me think at times that he was, well, different from us. The sharp beak and the white feathers growing from his head only reinforced this feeling.

Seriously, we crept behind Zane along the majestic rivers for three days. When he spotted a huge trout he would stop, crouch lower, and back up toward us. Then, using his skill and experience with these wild and majestic trout, he would formulate a strategy to catch them, often starting with pinching out the burning fuse on the stick of dynamite I had just lit.

The first such stop came on the Rolling River, with a five-hundred-foot rock cliff on one side and a thick, tropical jungle on the other. Once in position, Bill made a perfect case to a six-pound brown trout, which moved to his nymph, inhaled it, felt the sting of the hook, and immediately headed downstream toward the, uh, the Straits of Magellan or Cape Horn, or maybe it was Cape Cod. (In school I was never very good in geometry.)

I kept casting as Bill worked the monster back toward us, his fly rod bent nearly double. After about ten minutes Zane slid a net under the massive trout and let out a shrill, piercing whooping sound—which I believed was some sort of New Zealand celebration whoop until Zane pointed out that my woolly bugger was stuck in his ear. (That, of course, was just a joke. It was a large pheasant-tail nymph that must have had quite a sharp hook, judging by the way Zane chased me into the jungle with a big stick.)

Day after day, Zane showed an amazing ability to spot giant trout where Bill and I saw only rocks and gravel. This made Zane laugh and mock us. Although he mocked us in that good-natured, I-would-still-like-a-big-tip sort of way customary among fly-fishing guides. At the head of one riffle he paused, and we knew he'd seen a trout. Because there would be many others—and also because it was another opportunity to mock us—Zane let us walk up to where he was standing and asked if we could see the fish.

Bill could not, even though his eyes were still pretty big, not having recovered yet from several of the so-called driving incidents on the way down. (Example: Because everything was opposite, I drove around and around a rotary on a highway so many times and at such a high rate of speed that when I finally stopped, Bill staggered out and tried to pin a tail on a donkey.)

I could also not see the huge trout, even though Zane kept pointing at a spot just behind a big rock and, in his funny accent, shouting "Roight thair!"—which is New Zealand, meaning "Great! I am guiding Ray Charles and Stevie Wonder!" Finally, Zane grabbed my fly rod, stuck the tip deep into the water, and suddenly a large pile of gravel, perhaps some thirty inches long, exploded and swam away. I felt ridiculous and looked sheepish. Being in New Zealand at the time, I think you probably know what happened next.

That's right, Zane apologized, bought me flowers and candy, and asked what my sign was.

We caught eighteen enormous trout in those three days and then said good-bye to many new friends and hit the road again. During the farewell, as we climbed back into the Bluebird, Bill had a lump in his throat. I thought it was the emotion of saying good-bye, but it turned out to be handful of Prozac and sleeping pills that he was trying to swallow. This appeared to make the passenger experience much more enjoyable for him. Occasionally he'd wake up and shout, "And I'll miss you most of all, Scarecrow!" then go back to sleep. But other than that everything went okay.

After a few hundred miles of driving we pulled into Cedar Lodge, north of Queenstown. There we met guide Owen King, who would later look at a fish and say, "Aye, now that's bein' a wee fat one, he was!"—which as best I could tell meant either (a) it was a small fat trout; (b) it was a fat small trout; or (c) Owen had gotten a plate of bad mutton and was now hallucinating.

In the morning Bill and Owen and I climbed into a helicopter piloted by lodge owner Dick Fraser. We soared just over the tops of the New Zealand Alps at 100 mph, twisting and turning in a heart-stopping flight as Dick laughed and made jokes about crashing. Still, Bill insisted this was a lot better than going around and around that rotary in the Bluebird.

After thirty minutes we landed alongside a gorgeous stream and began a memorable day of fishing under the shadow of Mount Awful, a towering mountain that got its name because when the sunlight hits it just right it looks like Rush Limbaugh in a Speedo. (Even when it becomes volcanic, it spews less hot air than the chubby radio guy . . . and I hereby vow not to make any more Rush Limbaugh jokes.)

Anyway, Owen operated the same way Zane had farther north—stalking large trout, then backing off and saying things to the anglers that they didn't understand because everyone in New Zealand sounds like Prince Charles on crack.

At the first stop, however, Bill connected with an enormous rainbow on a dry fly, the massive fish rising to the surface and inhaling the caddis like Rush Limbaugh sucking down a double cheeseburger.

Oops.

When Bill set the hook, the small stream erupted in spray as the fish took off, peeling the fly line and then much of the backing from the reel as Bill and Owen sprinted downstream after the trout. I followed as best I could with a notebook, jotting down important notes for my *Los Angeles Times* story, such as: "fish runs downstream; can't see legs; wonder if trout have knees? I'm spending $7,000 of someone else's money to go fly-fishing for two weeks! ha-ha-ha!"

During the battle I interviewed Bill, who was having one helluva time fighting this fish and running along a boulder-strewn bank while at the same time telling me to shut up and trying to kick me. I tried to interview Owen, too, but quickly became confused ("Aye roon, he roons . . . makes for woon eeeeepic bottle, now don't it?) and ran farther downstream, thinking it would be easier to interview the trout.

After twenty minutes, Bill had the monster near his feet and Owen netted it, although the giant trout still battled bravely even when he was in the net, desperate, it seemed, to disappear back into the waters of his native creek before Owen could say anything indecipherable to him. Trout, as many of you know, do not have hands and therefore are unable to scratch their heads, as Bill and I did whenever Owen said anything to us.

Later it was my turn, with Owen backing up toward me, pointing to a spot about fifty feet upstream, and saying, in an excited whisper: "She's a monster, and moight be fadin' on droys so we best jest be watchin' hare for a meenut!" I looked at Bill and he just shrugged his shoulders. (Then, when I turned my back, he

---

wrestled the Bluebird keys out of my pocket, threw them into the river, and laughed like a lunatic for fifteen minutes.)

Fifteen minutes later Owen allowed me to—and here I use the complex, scientific expression for this behavior—"actually try to catch a fish." On my first cast a twenty-five-inch trout rose to the fly and took it. I responded as I had done so many times in twenty years of fly-fishing: I panicked and jerked the rod back over my head in a savage, violent motion that broke the line. As he turned and walked away, Owen began quietly mumbling more New Zealand words, this batch sounding like "Aye, we got ourseeelves one doom-sheet heah, na' don't wee?"

About an hour later, on my next try at one of New Zealand's giant brown trout, I laid a dry fly fifteen feet upstream of a huge, dark shadow that Owen said was a "beeg brune," whatever the hell that is. This time, when the huge trout sucked the small caddis off the surface, I set the hook calmly and the battle was on! The trout ran upstream. He ran downstream. He ran through the briars where a rabbit couldn't go, although those might be song lyrics. The point is, this fish was huge and was giving me quite a beating.

Then—and I'm not kidding about this—the fish did the most amazing thing. It powered its way *into* the opposite bank and disappeared, with the line still screeching off my reel. Seconds later the fish leaped from the water, twenty-five feet upstream, the hook still in his jaw and my line still running straight into the bank. The fish, we discovered later, had gone into a water-filled tunnel under the bank, a tunnel worn by the flowing water, and had come out of the bank upstream. Owen was shrieking all kinds of things in what I believe was the native language of people from Denmark. What he wanted to do, I eventually understood, was get to the opposite bank, cut my line, grab it as the fish pulled it out of the upstream hole, and then *tie the two ends back together* so I could continue to fight the giant fish.

I suggested he hold the rod while I wade into the narrow creek and beat the fish senseless with a heavy stick and get my $1.25 fly back.

The debate became moot a moment later, however, when the line broke and the fish swam free.

"Neevah' seen enytheeng loik that!" Owen said. "He wint roight for that 'ole in the bink. Moosta knewn it was theere! Moight smart bloke he woos!"

I said "Right!" as I plucked a $1.25 fly out of the patch of wool on his vest and put it in my own.

More than a decade later, I still think about that day.

Specifically, I still wonder what the hell " 'ole' in the bink" means.

CHAPTER 6

515 Miles and No Trout (Let's Be Frank) Nightmares in Wyoming

You don't have to travel halfway around the world to get confused by fly-fishing. I can honestly say—and excuse me if this sounds like bragging—that I've been puzzled and bewildered by fly-fishing in Alaska, Colorado, Montana, Wyoming, and the Dakotas—North Dakota, South Dakota, East Dakota, and even West Dakota.

I think it's because I have not become really scientific about the sport, like, say Frank Plucinsky of Pennsylvania, who is featured in an ad in the February 2001 issue of *Fly Fisherman* magazine. In this ad there's a big photo of Frank. Under his chin are the words: "My diary has a record of every hatch I've fished for twenty-six years." This makes him different from me in the sense that under my chin are more chins.

The ad, for Sage fly rods, goes on to say: "If it flies, flits, or flutters, trout fisherman Frank Plucinsky knows it by name (in both Latin and English, of course). In fact, he knows life on Pennsylvania's Tulpehocken Creek so well, he can tell you when the caddis are on just by the blooming of Virginia bluebells that grow along its banks."

I do not even know what Virginia bluebells are. Although my cousin Tony, who lives in Roanoke, told me he once had a really bad case of Virginia blue *bal*—uh, let's just say he was single and lonely.

The point is, Frank has written down detailed descriptions of every insect hatch he has encountered in the past twenty-six years of fly-fishing. I, by way of comparison, cannot remember where I was last night or, at this moment, my middle name. So I cannot compete with fly fishermen such as Frank. (Which is why avid fly fishermen sometimes refer to dynamite and a heavy stick as "the great equalizers.")

I'm just kidding, of course. I am a big proponent of catch-and-release. Well, you know, I would be if I could ever *catch*.

Take a recent fly-fishing adventure I took with my equally inept fly-fishing friend Mike Anton. Like most Americans, we caught no trout during that particular six-day period in May. What made us different, perhaps, is that we drove 515 miles during that time period along some of the greatest trout streams in Colorado and Wyoming, often stopping, getting out, putting on our waders and vests, and *trying* to catch trout. We fished up to ten hours each day, stopping only occasionally to down a quick meal of

Prairie Dog McNuggets. (Did I mention we spent part of the trip in Wyoming?)

Anyway, here now, just like Frank Plucinsky's diary, is a summary of that particular trip.

Wednesday, May 10

2 P.M.: Stand near window in newsroom of newspaper where I work in Colorado and shout, "Look, it's Jimmy Hoffa!" When everyone runs to window, I sneak out back door, meet Mike, and leave on fishing trip. As we drive away, boss Cliff has sent team of reporters to ask the twenty-five-year-old sandwich truck driver across the street if he is Jimmy Hoffa.

6:30 P.M.: Arrive in Laramie, Wyoming.

7 P.M.: Check out Laramie cultural district.

7:08 P.M.: Depart Museum of Rodents.

7:30 P.M.: Stroll into Buckhorn Saloon, look at patrons, become frightened.

7:45–9 P.M.: Mingle nervously with locals. Gain valuable insight into technique for field dressing an elk using only your teeth and a bottle opener.

9:30 P.M.: Find cheap motel, go to sleep.

10 P.M.–7 A.M.: Have nightmares about Wyoming. In worst one, I am a sheep.

Thursday, May 11

10 A.M.: Arrive in remote Saratoga, Wyoming. Sign reads POPU-LATION 1969, which is, as it turns out, also the fashion year residents are stuck in.

11 A.M.: Wade confidently into famed North Platte River.

11:15 A.M.: Return to truck. Wring out pants and shorts. Put on waders.

11:30 A.M.–3 P.M.: Serious fishing in "Blue Ribbon" river. Catch nothing. Blame this on wind, inability to match the hatch, and unbelievably finicky trout. Local anglers we encounter believe repeatedly slipping on moss-covered rocks and falling into the river may also have played small role.

Friday, May 12

6 A.M.: Determine North Platte River has no trout. Set sights on nearby Saratoga Lake. Local fly-shop owner says lake contains lots of five-pound rainbows and browns. We ask how cold the lake water is and whether a man could "freeze to death if he repeatedly fell into it." He asks why that would concern us. We tell him to mind his own business.

6 P.M.: No trout in Saratoga Lake, either. Return to car. Wring out hats. See more local anglers, clutching their midsections, pointing at us and laughing in what appears to be some sort of "Wyoming welcome."

Saturday, May 13

6 A.M.: Return for another shot at Saratoga Lake. I am swayed by fishing partner's argument that it seemed "easier to swim back to shore in the lake than in the fast-moving river."

10 A.M.: Return to car. No trout. Crowd of local well-wishers now estimated at three hundred. They send up wild roar as we wring out our hats. We climb into truck and hit the road, vowing to return "when the fishing improves."

Noon: Leave Wyoming, cross into Colorado. Sign reads WELCOME TO COLORADO. PLEASE WIPE YOUR FEET BEFORE ENTERING.

2 P.M.: Arrive at famous Blue River. Desperate to do better, we take out insect screens, turn over rocks, and carefully examine the aquatic creatures we find.

RICH TOSCHES

4 P.M.: Sure beyond any reasonable doubt exactly which insects trout are not feeding on.

6 P.M.: Arrive at South Platte River near town of Hartsel, which combines Native American words *har* ("Who") and *tsel* ("took all the trees?"). In South Platte River, actually see huge trout rising to insect hatch that I'm sure Frank Plucinsky has made forty pages of notes about.

7 P.M.: No trout.

Hate Frank Plucinsky.

CHAPTER 7

The Drivel Runs Through It

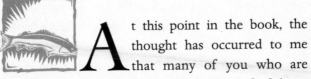

At this point in the book, the thought has occurred to me that many of you who are reading it might not know much about fly-fishing. Hell, I don't, and I'm writing it! So let's back up. First of all, when many people hear the word "fly," they think: "Zipper on a pair of trousers."

(Monica Lewinsky takes this sentiment so far that when she hears "fly" she starts whistling "Hail to the Chief.")

Anyway, if I wrote about an actual weekend I had in May of 1997 and began by saying I spent most of the time with my fly stuck in a tree, a lot of people would think I was somehow dangling by my crotch from the branch of a pine tree, screaming all day. This, of course, was not the case. It was a cottonwood, and I stopped screaming after the fourth hour, knowing I might need my strength when I "cut myself down."

And if I told you during that same weekend my friend Bill Vogrin kept getting his fly snagged on his own hat, you'd probably think: "Well, that's better than Bill Vogrin's fly getting stuck on YOUR hat."

Bill, Mike Anton and I were, of course, fly-fishing—a sport often defined as a jerk on one end of the line waiting for a jerk on the other. It is a sport every bit as frustrating as golf. The main difference is that in golf you don't spend all day in soaking-wet pants. Unless you start missing three-foot putts with $50 bets riding on them.

Anyway, the site of our adventure that weekend in 1997 was the Arkansas River near the Colorado town of Salida (town motto: "Don't Call Us Saliva.") We were there because of the hatch of the caddis fly, which sends the usually wily trout into a feeding frenzy—like Rush Limbaugh when he hears the buffet is closing in twenty minutes.

The secret to catching a lot of fish during this hatch is a stealthy presentation of the fly, the ability to "read" the water, and, of course, bringing enough dynamite. (The exciting part comes when the stunned fish float to the surface, or "rise.")

As a bonus, after about the fifth or sixth detonation you generally find yourself with a long stretch of river all to yourself, the other anglers—especially the ones without OSHA-approved BA-99826 hearing protection devices—having staggered up the riverbank, furiously pounding their hands against their ears.

(Director Robert Redford's decision to ignore this particular form of fly-fishing was my only real complaint with *A River Runs Through It.*)

Upon arriving at the river that day, we spent about thirty minutes rigging up our rods, a process in which a leader is connected to the fly line. The other end of the leader is then connected to a fly. This fly with its very sharp hook is connected to the tippet. And, as I remembered a moment later when I took a step backward and plummeted over a steep embankment, the thighbone is connected to the hipbone.

I was the "expert" of the group on this day because once, while fly-fishing in Alaska in September of 1982, I hooked a sixteen-pound rainbow trout. Technically I did not "catch" this gigantic trout because I was practicing my casts inside the lodge and the trout was mounted on the wall—although that in no way diminished the thrill.

(Alaska is a super-friendly place, but I sensed the lodge owner was becoming slightly irked after I "set the hook," yanked the fish off the wall, beat it with a heavy stick, and demanded he take a photograph of me holding it up.)

Back along the Arkansas River, I spent a few minutes with my friends and fellow journalists, going over the three key rules:

- Remove the hooks from your nose promptly, before tetanus sets in.

- If you actually catch a fish, you will be banned from any further fishing adventures with the group.

- The best defense against libel action is ignorance.

Soon we were actually fishing, waving the fly rods wildly over our heads like Florida voters trying to punch the hole near Al

Gore's name. And shockingly, we actually began catching trout. Bill, who is from Kansas, scored first, bringing a fourteen-inch brown trout into his net and shrieking, "Goll-eeeee! It are a swordfish!"

Then Mike caught one, which caused him to spew out an eighty-five-word sentence that included twenty-six words no one else had ever heard of. (Mike writes for the *Los Angeles Times*.)

The most memorable moment, however, came when I hooked a real whopper. After a lot of yelling and screaming, I got it onto the bank, removed the hook, held it, and posed for a quick photo.

Even today, when people come to my house, they almost always gaze toward the mantel above my fireplace and ask the same question:

"Is that a picture of your nose?"

CHAPTER 8

Dances with Morons

ow that we've covered the basics of the sport, let me tell you about one of the greatest fly-fishing trips I've ever been on. It was a trip to Montana, the state made famous in *A River Runs Through It*. In that movie, Brad Pitt is forced by his domineering father to try something he apparently doesn't like and is not any good at: acting.

Anyway, the trip took us to the Bighorn River, which required us to drive six hundred miles. It was a spectacular drive, except for one barren, treeless stretch called eastern Wyoming (motto: "The Land That Scenery Forgot").

Among the actual Wyoming highlights:

- The Interstate 90 exit for the towns of "Banner/Story." (In the Sunday edition, a gigantic headline trumpeted: CLYDE DRESSES UP SHEEP, AGAIN!)

- Montana has the famed Little Bighorn battlefield, but Wyoming—and I'm not kidding—has the "Fetterman battle-field." As I understand it, General Fetterman's cavalry battled valiantly but in the end lost all of their chicken soup and a third of their matzo balls.

- Chugwater, home of "Wyoming's Famous Chili." Chugwater—and trust me on this—allows you to get lunch AND gas all in one stop.

- The Crazy Woman River. The Crazy Woman runs through eastern Wyoming—then makes her way to Connecticut, where she keeps breaking into David Letterman's house.

Anyway, eventually we got through Wyoming and onto Montana's Crow Indian reservation. There we stopped and asked directions to the Bighorn. If you are lucky, as I was, you are given a proud American Indian name such as Soaring Eagle.

(Although that particular name was apparently already taken. So, after having to repeat the directions to the river to me seven times because my mind kept wandering, the woman in the store bestowed upon me another proud American Indian name: Dances with Morons.)

Fishing headquarters was the village of Fort Smith, an old cavalry outpost named for the former *Playboy* centerfold who married an eighty-nine-year-old Texas billionaire with heart problems. I'm talking, of course, about model Anna-Nicole Smith (Indian name: Digs for Gold).

For two days we drifted in a small boat that contained just the basics: oars, an anchor, and a bewildered Cuban boy named Elián González. No, really, we caught enormous trout from our drift boat. In one stretch of the river, near sunset, we watched thousands of big trout sipping midges. The last time anyone had seen that many things rise to the surface of a river was along the banks of the Hudson River in New York on April 14, 1974—three days after they had "squealed on Vinny."

Seriously, in one four-hour period on the Bighorn, I caught and released more than fifty large trout. It was a trip I will never forget. If you ever get up that way, stop in the general store.

And tell the woman that Dances with Morons sent you.

CHAPTER 9

Vail to the Chef

When you think of Vail, Colorado, you probably think of world-class skiing and rich people. And not just regular rich people, but the high-and-mighty kind of rich people, the kind who drink beer from a glass and have someone else wash their poodles for them. I, by way of comparison, drink my beer straight from the can—usually in a crowded bar when the guy who bought it turns away for a second. Oh sure, this method occasionally results in a mouthful of soggy cigarette butts, but I believe that's a small price to pay for free beer.

———

Also, I wash my own poodle. He seems to like that. And he usually does okay until the Kenmore Ultra Fabric Care Model 80 kicks into the spin cycle, at which time loud, screeching, whining noises emanate from the machine. (I think it needs a new drive belt.) Then, so the little guy doesn't get pneumonia, I take him out of the washer and get him right into the dryer. Making sure, of course, to first remove my cat, Fluffy.

The point is, Vail offers some terrific fly-fishing along with the famous skiing. Although you probably want to conduct these activities on two separate days, unless you're an idiot and like to be swept downstream in the Eagle River while clutching a fly rod in one hand and furiously trying to unbuckle your ski boots with the other, which CAN happen if you're in a hurry and not thinking. (On a more positive angling-related note, before I hit the deep pool, I managed to spear a fourteen-inch brown trout with my ski pole. I know what you "fly-fishing purists" must be thinking, but relax. I released him!)

Anyway, recently my thirty-year friend and fishing companion, Rob Bresciani, who lives ninety miles away from me in Boulder, Colorado, called. Rob and I have fly-fished together in tiny creeks in our home state of Massachusetts and in raging salmon-filled rivers in Alaska and in lots of places in between. This includes a place in Colorado called the Roaring Judy, although we were drinking a lot of beer that weekend and I don't recall if that's a river or what we called the bartender when she saw Rob relieving himself on the pool table. (I do, however, remember him yelling "Whoa! One-ball in the corner pocket!")

And the bond between us is a strong one, forged by laughter and time and, mostly, by the fact that no one else really likes us.

Anyway, Rob's wife and daughter were out of town for the

weekend, and he missed them terribly. The sadness in his voice was plainly evident on the phone when he shouted: "I've got the whole $%^&*# weekend to myself!"

That evening I somehow found myself in the town of Golden, home to the Coors brewery, which makes a terrific beer and, as a bonus, regularly dumps tens of thousands of gallons of beer sludge into a nearby river and kills all the fish. (Coors motto: "Making Everything Go Belly-Up, Including You After a Couple of Six-Packs.")

Anyway, coincidentally Rob showed up in the same parking lot at just about the same time, and after stuffing all of my fly-fishing stuff into his Suburban, we found ourselves headed west through the Rocky Mountains toward Vail and the Eagle River, two boyhood friends together once again, laughing and talking about the same silly, juvenile things we talked about thirty years earlier as teenagers. That's right: swollen prostate glands and erectile dysfunction.

We cruised into Vail and marveled at the castles nestled into the mountains, seasonal homes of people who have worked hard and achieved the American Dream. "Rich $%^&*(#@" was how we put it. Here is an actual story that tells you all you need to know about Vail:

If you're like me you've got an extra $45,000 in your pocket right now and are asking yourself the obvious question: "Do I make a long-term mutual-fund investment directed at the future educational needs of my children, or do I get that beautiful four-weight Orvis rod I've been looking at and a new sport-utility vehicle to put it in? (I've got my eye on that new, sixty-seven-ton Ford Exhibitionist.)"

And while I don't want to influence your decision, I spent four years at Marquette University in Milwaukee, Wisconsin, remember approximately six days of it, and have no intention whatso-ever of spending money so my kids can drink Pabst Blue Ribbon beer, bowl, and have as much sex as I did.

Okay, I lied. But I'm serious about the Pabst and the bowling.

Anyway, another way to spend that $45,000 would be—I'm not kidding—to purchase one of the fifty parking spaces in an exclusive underground garage in Vail. It's called the Golden Peak Passport Club, a name chosen during secret balloting by the members of Vail Associates, who narrowly rejected the other fine suggestion for a $45,000-a-space parking garage: Chuck's U-Park-It.

The $45,000 spaces are on Tier 1. Tier 2 parking is slightly less expensive and does not offer all the services you get on Tier 1—such as the glossy, just-licked-clean-with-my-own-tongue look the Tier 1 parking attendants give your tires.

The fifty spaces are just about gone now, and a price hike is being considered. From David Corbin, vice-president of development for Vail Associates: "We'll keep raising the price incrementally as we feel the market will bear."

Or, to paraphrase P. T. Barnum: There's a Golden Peak Passport Club member born every minute.

Oh, and this: Vail Associates will return the club members' $45,000 initiation fee to them.

In thirty years.

And I don't know about you, but I'd like to be there the day all those 110-year-old guys drive into the garage to pick up their checks.

So anyway, Rob and I cruised into—and out of—Vail, and as the sun began to disappear beneath the towering peaks of the Rockies, we pulled up alongside the Eagle River some forty miles farther west. The surface was alive as big brown trout feasted on a late-day caddis hatch, and we scrambled from the truck in an-

---

ticipation of a spectacular evening in the river. We rigged our fly rods, climbed into our waders, and—here I will let the magic of words paint the picture for you—"felt the cool water pressing against our big, middle-aged asses."

Then the storm hit. Bolts of lighting. Monstrous claps of thunder. Heavy rain and hail. The fish stopped feeding. And suddenly an evening filled with so much wonder and anticipation just moments earlier had been magically transformed into two idiots standing in a river, waving long graphite poles over their heads in a savage lightning storm, their waders starting to fill up with hail. I do not know if God is a fly fisherman. But if He is, I am guessing (a) He has some really nice clothing from the Patagonia company; and (b) He was up there that evening, looking down on two anglers and laughing so hard that holy water was coming out of His nose.

We squished our way back to the truck and headed for the nearby town of Edwards. We purchased a small bottle of tequila and two limes and talked about how much we'd grown up and matured over the past thirty years. (We used to buy a big bottle of tequila and no limes.)

Then we checked into a motel, talked about the meaning of life, and drifted off to sleep with that wonderful feeling in the pits of our stomachs, the feeling of anticipation fly fishermen get knowing a glorious day on a fly stream awaits them. Although the feeling in my personal stomach was mitigated somewhat by the large chunk of lime I had swallowed while gulping down tequila from a plastic Motel 6 cup.

The morning dawned crisp and clear, and we headed downstairs for the free continental breakfast. Thanks to me and the empty backpack I brought into the dining room, this also became free continental lunch and free continental dinner. Fact: The Columbia Sports Dayhiker Model 200 can accommodate fourteen bagels, six blueberry muffins, and five apples, with plenty of room on top for a large, fluffy Motel 6 towel.

Our first stop was the local fly-shop, where, in the finest tradition of fly-fishing, we handed over the obligatory $35 and walked out with a handful of flies the shop owner swore the fish were "really hitting." We got back into the truck and headed for the river; the morning air was so still and quiet we could hear the fly-shop owner laughing four blocks away.

We arrived back at the Eagle River shortly before 10 A.M., located a beautiful set of riffles and a deep hole Rob's friend had given him directions to, and kicked off what would be a memorable day that would involve the following phrases:

"Got one!"

"They're really on the prince nymphs!"

"That $%^&*# cow's face is coming back up on me!"

I will save the explanation for that last actual statement, made by Rob, for the end of this section, thus ensuring you will read through the next thirty or so pages.

Anyway, we positioned ourselves in some fast water and went at it. Rob nailed a nice brown on his third cast, a prince drifting near the bottom triggering a savage strike. I had my eyes on a rising trout about fifty feet downstream, thirty years of fly-fishing experience telling me a sizable fish was taking tiny emergers just below the surface, and that in all likelihood, I would fall into the river twice trying to get into the perfect casting position, and once I got there, the son of a bitch would be full and would go deep and begin a Gandhi-like fast.

Amazingly, this did not happen.

I only—I am not kidding—fell into the river ONCE.

RICH TOSCHES

After wringing out my shirt, I watched the big trout rise again. I laid a perfect forty-foot cast just upstream, and stunningly, he took the tiny fly and the war was on. And what a war it was. The most incredible part came when I pressured him into some quiet water, and he responded by invading Czechoslovakia.

Actually, I had the eighteen-inch brown whipped in about three minutes, the great fish indicating that he'd had enough by rolling on his side. Waving a small white towel at me seemed to confirm my belief. I released him with a flick of my forceps and he swam slowly into a quiet pool, where another trout joined him. The second one moved close and seemed to be taunting him about having been caught by an idiot carrying a backpack full of stolen muffins, but perhaps I was reading too much into the whole thing.

Rob was into a nice trout upstream, but lost the fish after he had eased it to within a few feet of his waders. He lost several other fish that way on this day, perhaps because of the tiny hooks, or his landing technique—which involved throwing his fly rod into the bushes, grabbing the silk-thin 6X leader, and shouting "I've got you now, you little bastard!"

By noon we'd hooked some twenty trout, releasing all of them either after the fight or, in Rob's case, during it. Then, despite the twenty pounds of free hotel food on my back, we decided to take a break and get something to eat up the road. We settled for the El Cantina roadside Mexican food truck, which is, as promised, getting us to Rob shouting "That $%^&*# cow's face is coming back up on me!"

I ordered a couple of pork burritos, and Rob, who is Italian, shook off the disappointment that came when a puzzled-looking Lupe told him they did not have lasagna. He pointed to the chalkboard menu and asked, "What's this?" She said something we did not understand, and moments later Rob had two of whatever "that" was on his plate. As it turned out—and I swear I am not kidding about this—he was eating tortillas filled with, according to a nice Hispanic man sitting next to us at a picnic table near the truck, "meat from a cow's cheek."

Rob said it was delicious.

However, an hour later, back in the Eagle River, he started looking funny.

Then he burped. It was real loud, indicating either gastrointestinal problems or a methane explosion in a nearby coal mine.

He solved the debate for me about ten minutes later when he lurched toward the riverbank and made the following announcement: "That $%^&*# cow's face is coming back up on me!"

Despite his medical problems, Rob stayed in the river, a fly-fishing warrior if there ever was one, a dedicated and driven man in the mold of John Wayne. And while I don't recall the great actor ever eating a cow-face burrito, I have to admit that I haven't seen all of his movies.

Anyway, we caught a dozen more trout over the next three hours, I with a No. 20 Adams and a No. 22 emerger behind it, trying to focus on the tiny flies while constantly glancing over at Rob, who kept belching and talking about the cow face. Similar things have happened to Rob and me for thirty years, evoking great howling laughing fits. I will write about other amazing adventures we've shared—like fishing in Alaska with a guide who saw a grizzly bear, pulled out a .44 magnum handgun, and promptly shot a hole in the bottom of his boat. But here I'd like to say this: I hope Rob and I have thirty more years of pounding the rivers together with our fly rods.

And if you're ever in Colorado and happen to see us fishing, drop by and say moo.

RICH TOSCHES

I'll Be Comin' 'Round the Mountain (When I Get This Hook Out of My Ear)—Pikes Peak

Among my favorite places on earth is a reservoir called North Catamount. Catamount means "mountain lion," so I guess one of my favorite places on earth is North Mountain Lion, whatever the hell that means. Anyway, the reservoir is nestled among towering pines and dazzling aspen trees at an elevation of ten thousand feet, on Pikes Peak in Colorado. Pikes Peak, as many of you probably know, was made famous in 1893 when Katharine Lee Bates climbed to the top, was overwhelmed by the sight of "purple mountains' majesty" and "fruited plains," and was moved to pen the lyrics to the classic American song "Me and Mrs. Jones (Got a Thing Goin' On)."

Okay, it was "America the Beautiful."

But the point is, none of that lovely history prepared me for my first—and only, barring some kind of miracle medical breakthrough involving an antiscreaming pill—trip to the summit of this beautiful mountain. The only good news from the trip is that it uncovered for me this gem of a reservoir teeming with large cutthroat trout.

Anyway, the trip to the summit of the 14,110-foot mountain began when I met Nick Sanborn, executive director of an annual road race to the top called the Pikes Peak Hill Climb. I climbed into his white Chevrolet Suburban for what I believed was a leisurely drive of about two miles, to a meeting place on the Pikes Peak Highway with another person who would take me the rest of the way.

Nick greeted me with these actual, comforting words: "I've raced this road so many times there's no thrill anymore in scaring myself. But I do like doing it with people like you in the car."

Then he laughed and stomped on the gas pedal. As we drove around hairpin turns on the side of the mountain, I asked Nick general questions about the race and the adventure it presented for the drivers, questions that went to the very heart of auto racing. An example would be: "Hey, Nick! Guess who?" as I clamped my hands over his eyes.

Midway up the mountain—and here I use the common Pikes Peak Hill Climb expression—"where the pavement ends and the years of intense psychiatric care begin," Nick turned me over to the man who would take me the rest of the way: veteran race-car driver Roger Mears.

Although Roger had raced this course many times, this one would be somewhat more difficult than usual because of many uncontrollable natural factors such as loose gravel, patches of ice, the passenger repeatedly diving over the console and leaning on the brake pedal with his hands, the passenger giving Roger quite a beating with his rosary beads. Things like that.

Let me say something here. I don't know exactly what mode of transportation Katharine Lee Bates utilized to get to the summit of Pikes Peak in 1893, but if Roger Mears had driven her there, we'd all be singing a very different "America the Beautiful" today, starting with these lyrics:

> O beautiful, for spacious skies,
> All I can say is 'Yowsers!'
> Roger drives like he is nuts
> And now I need new trousers!

Anyway, Roger was also driving a white Chevrolet Suburban.

(Footnote: If you're thinking of buying a white, 1997 Chevrolet Suburban, I'd strongly suggest not getting either of the white ones with the gigantic stains on the passenger seat.)

Suddenly we were on the actual racecourse. "Here's where A LOT OF PEOPLE GO OFF THE SIDE!" Roger shouted about a mile up the gravel road as he slid the Suburban sideways into a corner at 50 mph. Directly beneath us, at a distance of what I estimate was 1,458 miles, straight down, was the tourist town of Manitou Springs, Colorado.

My stomach tightened as I was gripped by the most common fear a person gets in this situation: plunging over the side and landing on a gift shop in a Chevrolet Suburban, smashing everything in the store except the "You Break It, You Buy It!" sign.

For the next seven minutes I was flung around in the vehicle like a rag doll, screaming and pulling on my own hair, which is bright red and made of yarn. As Roger slid the large vehicle to the edge of the cliff several hundred thousand times—I lost the actual count at 156,987 when I was struck in the head by my own foot—we had a lovely conversation about race-car driving and the thrill inherent in the sport. It went like this:

ROGER: I took the bark off the trees right there. I think it was in the '79 race!

ME: Oooooooohhhhhhhh!

ROGER: Right up here we . . . WE DROP THE RIGHT FRONT WHEEL OVER THE SIDE so we can line up for the straightaway!

ME: SWEET JESUS, MARY, AND JOSEPH! PLEASE FORGIVE ME. I THOUGHT SHE WAS EIGHTEEN!

ROGER: That drop there is about 1,400 feet. But you gotta' GET THE TIRES WITHIN SIX INCHES OR SO OR YOU'D HAVE TO BACK OFF THE GAS PEDAL!

ME: SANTA MARIA!

(I don't know why, but often, when I see death looming, I begin shouting out the names of Christopher Columbus's ships.)

On we went, though, sending up gravel and clouds of dust as we roared past actual areas called:

Devil's Playground: This was our lucky day: The recess bell had just rung and Satan was on the seesaw.

Bottomless Pit: Hikers say when the light hits this rock formation just right, it looks exactly like Oprah Winfrey in a buffet line.

Boulder Park: This one is named for the Colorado town made

infamous by the JonBenet Ramsey case. We were slowed here as the park ranger negotiated with our attorneys over taking a lie detector test, then made us give him handwriting samples.

Soon—and I cannot overemphasize just HOW soon—we made it to the summit. We got out, stretched our legs, and gazed at the exact same view that moved Katharine Lee Bates more than a century earlier.

Well, Roger did.

I was in the backseat, curled up in the fetal position, working my way through the names of Ferdinand Magellan's entire fleet. Which was pretty embarrassing. Although the real embarrassing part was the last mile of the ride.

Roger made me sit on newspapers.

However, as I may or may not have mentioned earlier, it was on this day that I saw water shimmering in the distance. Because we went by the sign at the turnoff to the reservoirs at what I estimated was seven hundred miles an hour, I knew the sign said either NORTH SLOPE RECREATION AREA or NOFT SBOBTH RIOPRECI ANIA.

One of the three reservoirs, NORTH HOUSECAT or whatever it's called, is a hidden gem, a mecca for fly fishermen. I say "mecca" because the first day I made this pilgrimage I watched in a solemn, respectful way as a man put down his fly rod, faced toward the east, dropped to his knees, and let out a low, religious-sounding wailing noise.

Turns out he'd hooked his ear with a No. 14 Parachute Adams.

But since that day I've spent countless hours walking the shoreline of the majestic reservoir, matching wits, as they say, with huge, cruising cutthroats. (Last week I took an eighteen-incher into the Bonus Round, finally bowing out when I failed to correctly answer the question "Who is on Mount Rushmore?" I got Millard Fillmore and Dan Quayle, but couldn't remember the other three.)

The first trip brought me and Dr. Jerry Thompson to the shores of the reservoir. Jerry was my brother-in-law back then. Today, he is not my brother-in-law. Because I'm a mature, forty-six-year-old man, I won't get into all the details of who did what to whom, or who got what in the divorce settlement, or in any way allow even a hint of bitterness to creep into a humorous book about fly-fishing.

Although I will say this: I bet when Stephen King slides back his "chair" and stands up after writing a book, he does NOT have milk-crate lines on his ass.

Anyway, Jerry and I hiked about a mile from a parking area, across the dam, and into the forest before finding a trail to the water. Immediately we saw large trout rising, sipping mayflies from the surface. I rigged both fly rods—Jerry is a pediatric surgeon and likes to save his hands for more important things than tying knots in tippet; an example would be cranking open a pickle jar when his wife hands it to him—and we started casting. In the clear mountain water we watched the trout come to the flies from a long distance, the anticipation building up, to use the old expression, "like Bill Clinton's blood pressure on Intern Interview Day."

For about half an hour the trout came to the flies and turned away, sometimes even bumping them with their nose before rejecting them. Then I dropped a tiny mayfly emerger about eighteen inches behind my dry and suddenly fishing was as much fun as watching a television news anchorperson when the TelePrompTer breaks down. A twitch of the dry fly would bring a trout in for a close look, and then they would gulp the emerger and the fight was on. After my fourth nice trout, Jerry, who had wandered about fifty feet down the shoreline, shouted, "What are they hitting?"

"The mayfly!" I shouted back with great excitement. "Right on top, just like you're doing. Just stay with it."

I like Jerry a lot. But frankly, I had no idea how many trout were in the reservoir and wanted to catch thirty or forty of them before giving away my secret. I'm like that. It's why hardly any of my friends will ever go fishing with me a second time. (The brightest ones don't even go the first time.)

Soon, though, I had added the emerger to Jerry's arsenal and the day became, to use one of his favorite expressions, "more fun than removing a child's malfunctioning spleen."

During the cutthroat frenzy, I began seeing an occasional larger fish cruising the shallow coves. Unlike the cutthroat, these fish had deeply forked tails and I knew I was looking at mackinaws, or lake trout. They weren't like those unbelievably huge lake trout of the Northwest Territory lakes of Canada, the kind the anglers have to shoot with a gun, whack over the head with a log, and then drag up onto the beach with winches (I loved that particular episode of *American Sportsmen* back in the early seventies, especially when Curt Gowdy got into a frenzy and accidentally whacked the guide on the head with the log), but these lake trout were big enough—twenty inches and more.

They weren't, however, interested in the mayflies drifting above them. I looked closer and began seeing small suckers hunkered down along the bottom. That's what the lakers were interested in. So I switched to a brownish streamer fly, added a split shot, and began bumping it along the bottom. The first lake trout came savagely to the fly, actually creating a wall of water with his snout—much the same way you figure Barbra Streisand does when she takes a dip.

I set the hook and line sizzled from my reel and I let out a tremendous whoop.

"What do you have?" Jerry shouted.

"Uh, just another cutthroat," I replied. "Nothing to see here. Go on about your business."

He's pretty smart, though, and walked right over and saw the twenty-four-inch lake trout at my feet, and I had to give him my last brownish streamer. Had to tie it on, too. Then I carefully revived the magnificent fish and watched him swim away.

Let's talk for a moment about this catch-and-release stuff.

I haven't eaten a trout. Ever. I don't eat fish of any kind, except for an occasional can of tuna. (Porpoise is good, too, but I hate all the squeak-squeak-squeak noises they make when you're trying to get them into the boat.)

Seriously, I think all fish taste, well, fishy. I mean, what other food do people talk about that way? "Try this kind," I've been told a hundred times. "It DOESN'T TASTE LIKE FISH." And I wonder what kind of an idiot, if he wanted something that didn't taste like fish, WOULD EAT FISH? Pork. Now there's something that REALLY doesn't taste like fish. Or a steak.

Or anything from McDonald's, including the filet o' fish, which is made from the employees' recycled paper hats.

And then I get this: "You go fishing all the time, BUT YOU DON'T EAT THEM?"

Then I ask them if, when they go bowling, they have a great desire to EAT THE SMELLY RENTAL SHOES, ready to draw the obvious correlation as to why I don't need to eat the fish I pursue.

RICH TOSCHES

Unfortunately, when I ask that last question, most of the people I hang around with indicate that they DO enjoy eating the rental shoes, and my argument is shot to hell.

The point is, I am a true catch-and-release guy.

Although once in a while, if a friend knows I'm heading for the river again and asks me to bring back a big trout for his barbecue grill, I will almost always return to town, drive directly to his house, open my Coleman cooler, and hand him a bowling shoe.

Jerry and I must have caught sixteen or seventeen trout that day, a few lakers but most of them brilliant cutthroats—"the lawyers of trout," as they're known. There have been perhaps fifty more trips back to North Pussycat Reservoir over the years, mostly resulting in terrific memories of action-filled days.

But every once in a while, for reasons known only to God and Bill Gates, who thinks he's God, I get shut out. Blanked. Skunked. (Twice I've returned and had to give myself a bath in tomato juice. Then I tried to cross the road in front of my house, got flattened by a truck, and stank up the entire neighborhood for three days.)

Okay, that last part never actually happened.

But I've had days on this reservoir in which the fish are cruising and eating vorashus . . . vorraciou . . . A LOT, putting away mayflies, caddis flies, and even pop flies, although I may be thinking of a New York Yankees game I watched on TV last night. Anyway, on some of these days nothing artificial seems to interest them.

Which is, by the way, the same reason Michael Jackson doesn't get a lot of dates these days.

I'd gone to twelve-foot leaders and 7X tippet. I'd changed flies as many as two dozen times, searching for a single fly or combination of tiny dry and nymph that might trigger a strike. But each attempt brought the same result. A trout would rise to the bug, hesitate, and turn away. It was maddening. On one of these days, I had perfectly matched the small callibaetis hatch—and if you're a devoted fly angler you've had this happen to you, too—and was staring like a madman at my artificial fly, surrounded by the real insects being plucked from the surface by feeding trout, when suddenly, and quite startlingly if you're really focused, the artificial fly FLEW AWAY. And you realize you were NOT watching your fly, which is no longer floating and has disappeared in a gigantic swirl three feet to the right.

And it is at this time, and only this time, that respected clergy members—including Pope John Paul himself in the Vatican's monumental Fly-Fishing Edict of 1994—agree that it is okay to shout "Goddammit!"

CHAPTER 11

The Painfulliness of It All

The rematch.

I spent two weeks preparing to resume my battle with the trout of North Catamount Reservoir. I'd read articles in fly-fishing magazines, checked and rechecked my equipment, and even dropped the obligatory $35 on the counter of my local fly shop. (I think the guy gave me a strike indicator for my $35, but I'm not sure and, frankly, don't care anymore.)

The magazine article I studied during this two-week training program was in the September 2001 issue of *Fly Fisherman*. It's the one with the cover photo of President George W. Bush fishing with his father off the coast of Maine. The president has a striper fly embedded in his earlobe and, in the accompanying story, talks about the "painfulliness" of the incident.

Anyway, here's what the actual article, entitled "Fishing Small Dry Flies," had to say:

> During most small-fly hatches, trout position themselves just below the surface and eat the minute insects like whales eating plankton.

Which explains why once, in 1994, I hooked a twelve-inch brook trout that stripped all the fly line from my reel, then all the backing, then blew air out of a hole atop its head, and beached itself, after which a crowd of screaming and crying Greenpeace people tried to push it back into the water. I'm not kidding!

Anyway, the actual story goes on to say:

> Holding near the bottom and rising to the surface when an insect enters their window isn't efficient enough. This would be like sitting in your living room, having a bowl of popcorn in the kitchen, and for each piece of popcorn you ate, having to get up and make the journey to the kitchen.

I have often caught trout that were feeding in this manner, using a method I pioneered myself. First, I leave a large Coke and a box of Milk Duds on the shoreline. Then, when the trout come out of the water and grab the snacks, I leap out of the bushes dressed as an usher and step on them before they can get back into the movie theater.

RICH TOSCHES

The article continues with a section called "Playing the Fish." Caution: If you confuse this with Playing the Violin, you're going to kill a lot of fish. And, of course, get a lot of strange looks when you try to hold the trout under your chin. This section of the actual article says you should set the hook if "the pod of fish scatters. One fish has felt the hook, spooks, and the others take the warning and run like a bunch of toddlers at bathtime."

I used this information just the other night when it was time to give my own toddler a bath. I can now report that I got him into the tub more quickly than ever before. On the downside, it took about forty minutes to get little Billy untangled from the net. And while I was toweling him off, he threw up a couple of caddis flies.

The article then says this (I swear I am not kidding):

Often the trout will ignore the duns and focus on emergers as they struggle on the underside of the surface film, or meniscus. For tiny mayflies, breaking through the meniscus's rubbery barrier is akin to a human trying to dive through a swimming-pool cover.

The difference, generally, is that the trout is not drunk and isn't leaping off a motel balcony during spring-break week in North Dakota.

Anyway, armed with all of the knowledge gained from reading that *Fly Fisherman* article, I headed back up the mountain for the rematch. About an hour after I arrived, the surface feeding frenzy began, fish rising to my left, to my right, in front of me, and behind me. That last one surprised me because I was standing on the shore. As it turns out, it was a chipmunk—and a fierce one, too, as I found out while trying to unhook him.

But the point is, the feeding frenzy had begun, and this time I was ready. On my very first cast with a No. 22 emerger, a trout rose and sipped it off the surface, just like a whale, except quite a bit smaller.

I hooked another trout, a sixteen-inch cutthroat, about five minutes later and was feeling pretty darn good about myself. Then, as my fly lay motionless on the surface, a much larger fish approached, made a rush at the fly, and I yanked it away. Yanked in the sense that the fly, the leader, and about twenty feet of fly line came racing off the water and landed in an area that many leading fly casters would call "my face."

(The first time that happens to you, you scream and drop your fly rod. Fortunately, this was my 424th time, and I simply gathered up the line and continued casting a moment later, pausing occasionally to rub my face where the fly line had left welt marks, which are, as you might imagine, very painfulliness.)

During that marvelous day, I hooked and landed about a dozen dazzling trout. I missed about the same number of fish because, well, because let's just say it's hard to concentrate on fly-fishing when a chipmunk with a sore lip and a grudge is repeatedly attacking your ankle.

But I had, with the help of *Fly Fisherman* magazine, conquered the tough trout of North Mountain Lion Reservoir in Colorado. The only one who caught more fish than me on that lovely day was the guy fishing about fifty feet to my right. He must have caught a hundred! He said his name was Orville Redenbacher.

CHAPTER 12

My Eyes Adore Ewe

Fact: The Arkansas River flows through Colorado.

Fact: The Colorado River does NOT flow through Arkansas.

This may seem somewhat unfair to the beautiful state of Arkansas. However, I would point out that life is not fair, and if the people of Arkansas feel cheated in any way, they may find some solace and comfort in the old Latin saying *Alestus wei non livum nei jirsei* ("At least we don't live in New Jersey").

Anyway, the Arkansas River is a marvelous eighty-mile stretch of trout water that gurgles from the

---

Rocky Mountains and flows through the old Spanish settlements of Buena Vista ("Ben is visiting") and Salida (town motto: "Don't Call Us Saliva"). It cuts through rugged canyons lined with cactus, yucca, and cows. You can differentiate between these three by patting them roughly on the head. The cactus and yucca will make you scream in pain, whereas the cows will moo.

As a bonus, several herds of Rocky Mountain bighorn sheep live in the canyons, and it is not unusual to see gatherings of male and female sheep as you fish the river. These sheep have even inspired many great songs, such as "My Eyes Adore Ewe" and "Ewe Are the Sunshine of My Life."

I am truly sorry for both of those stupid jokes, vow never again to stoop so low, and will now get on with a serious discussion about fishing the Arkansas River.

My introduction to this river came in the spring of 1995 when my good friend Karl Licis, who is a terrific outdoor writer for the *Colorado Springs Gazette,* invited me to accompany him for a day of fishing. The deal involved me doing all the driving, paying for all the gas, and buying lunch for him. In return, Karl would serve as the guide. Being a guide on this day turned out to be pretty easy, in the sense that once we got to the river, Karl pointed to a spot about a mile downstream and said, "Why don't you go way down there," and then vanished for the next five hours, leaving me, to use the old saying, holding my rod.

Fortunately, on this day I brought all of my extensive knowledge of entommol . . . entumology. . . . entamallog—bugs, and quickly matched the hatch. It helped that the air above the river was filled with what I would estimate to be 600 trillion jillion caddis flies. Further, after about an hour I noticed that when a caddis fly would ride on the surface of the water for even a few seconds, a trout would rise and pounce on it with a great big splash. (For the first fifty-five minutes I thought some asshole was throwing rocks into the water and I kept shouting for him to stop it.)

As I learned later, when it was getting dark and my good friend Karl dropped by and said he had to get home, it's known as the Mother's Day caddis hatch and happens every single year around Mother's Day, which I thought was pretty ironic.

Billions and billions of these insects hatch from the bottom of the river and make their way to the surface, where they dry their wings and then form huge flocks and fly south to their wintering grounds unless they are shot along the way, although I may be confusing the caddis fly with the Canada goose.

Here's all you need to know about fishing the caddis fly hatch on the Arkansas River: I caught—and I am not kidding about this—more than one hundred trout that day! I had not caught that many trout in the preceding thirty years of fly-fishing combined, unless you count that almost freakish incident in 1988 involving my cigarette lighter and that stick of dynamite on the famed Yellowstone River. (I netted one "whopper" that now hangs above my fireplace, and allowed the other eight hundred or so beautiful trout to drift back downstream, except for the few dozen that were up in the field and the one that went flying over the ranger's house.)

Seriously, I actually caught more than one hundred trout on the Arkansas River that day, most of them browns of thirteen to sixteen inches, all of them crashing the surface and gulping down a No. 16 elk-hair caddis. I had tied about thirty of these flies in preparation for the big day, which left me exhausted. Not so much from the actual tying of the flies, but from all the careful stalking through the Colorado mountains followed by all the running that

I was forced to do every time I yanked a clump of hair out of the elk's ass.

During one stretch, I caught fifteen trout in fifteen casts, all from a fifty-foot-long riffle, the fish rising savagely to the caddis. The presentation was very important. I found that I only caught a trout when I made a perfect cast, with the fly actually landing IN THE RIVER. (Although once, it landed about five feet up on the bank and a trout broke off an overhanging willow branch and began beating the fly with the branch, then dragged it back into the water. Okay, I made that part up.)

The casts were upstream, downstream, across the stream. It didn't make much difference. The trout sometimes hit it with even more vigor when it was being dragged across the surface by the current, a skittering move that imitated the natural movement of the struggling insects.

The fish gorge themselves outlandishly. Trout caught early in the morning are sleek and relatively thin. By the end of the day, almost all of the trout are fat, their stomachs swollen with food. If you can't make it to Colorado for this memorable few weeks of fishing, you can see pretty much the same thing in your own town—by following people for a few days after they walk proudly out of their last Weight Watchers class.

Since that unforgettable day with my friend Karl, I've brought many other friends to the caddis hatch on the Arkansas, beginners mostly, people who started the day with only the rudimentary skills of fly-fishing. By the end of the day, however, with me there to guide them, many of them were hooking branches and their own hats at nearly the same rate as "the master."

Mike Anton caught thirty-five trout during one day of the hatch in 1997. Prior to that day, his grand total of trout subdued by a fly rod was zero. We packed away our rods in the evening and headed for the town of Saliva. Oops, I mean Salida, where we got a motel room and celebrated with fairly expensive beer and cigars, two men reveling in the thrill of fly-fishing and, more importantly, the fact that we'd found yet another way to get away from the house for a few days and behave like idiots.

We went to sleep after midnight, having depleted the supply of beer and cigars, and got back into the river the next morning with great eagerness, a burning sense of anticipation, and two unbelievable hangovers. At one point I started fishing deep with a nymph because the constant, loud *slap-slap-slap* of the trouts' tails on the surface felt as though it would make my head explode.

Mike was worse, though. He kept shouting "Jesus Christ, do they have to bang their wings on the water like that?" whenever a caddis fly tried to take off.

It was a bad day. We caught only forty or so trout between us. Which wasn't bad, considering I spent two hours on the bank, curled up under a bush, sleeping.

And that day I made an important decision about my health and my way of life: no more cigars!

So prodigious is the Mother's Day caddis-fly hatch on the Arkansas River that towns along the banks actually have celebrations. Most of these are sponsored by the chambers of commerce and celebrate the fact that fly fishermen tend to drop gigantic wads of cash wherever they go. The town of Canon City, for example, has a huge Caddis Fly Festival each spring, with music and dancing and booths selling T-shirts honoring the caddis fly.

Only one other fly in history has received so much attention.

That, of course, was President Bill Clinton's fly.

My fondest memory of caddis-fly-fishing, however, is the hatch of 2001. I brought my friend Susie, whom I'd introduced to the sport of fly-fishing just a few months earlier because of my feelings for her, my desire to see her enjoy nature as I do, and the mere pleasure of her company.

Okay, it was so I could go fly-fishing more often without having to beg.

Nevertheless, Susie took to fly-fishing like a duck to *l'orange* sauce. And it was during the caddis-fly hatch of 2001 that she became a devoted angler, catching and releasing nearly twenty brown trout in a day, and in just two days reaching a level of fly-fishing proficiency that took me more than ten years to attain.

This, she correctly pointed out, was because I'm an idiot.

Then she made me put out my cigar.

And made Mike get his own room.

In summary, the spring caddis hatch on the Arkansas River is nothing short of fantastic.

But just as the hatch and the feeding frenzy reach a peak, spring brings a wave of warm weather and the Rocky Mountain snows begin to melt. And quickly, the Arkansas River turns into a frightening, churning, dangerous body of rolling brown water, bringing with it the inevitable hordes of people in gigantic rafts, and for most anglers signaling the end of some of the most incredible fishing to be found anywhere.

Although I've found that some really wild action can continue well into the rafting season.

Especially if you make accurate casts, use about sixty-pound test tippet, and hook the rafters in that really sensitive area right under their nose.

CHAPTER 13

The Early Years, for Chrissakes

I 'm thinking this might be a good time to tell you a little bit about the beginning of my fly-fishing life, sweeping you back to a time before my best friend made himself sick by eating a couple of cow faces, and before a World Fly-Fishing Championship entrant from Belgium looked me straight in the eye and said, in an excited way, "Mine fish dat small fish . . . neeeemph!"

It began, as I may or may not have pointed out at the start of the book, in Massachusetts. I grew up in the town of Hopedale in the southeast part of the state. Hopedale had about three thousand residents and my public-high-school class had sixty-eight graduates. I was an excellent student and would have been the class valedictorian and also would have been officially ranked number one in my class if not for a technicality: about fifty-five of my classmates kept showing up at school (they were smarter than I).

So the teachers were left to tell my parents that I had "potential," which combines the French words *potent* ("powerful") and *ial* ("urge to screw around and disrupt class").

What none of them knew, however, is that by my twelfth birthday I had become possessed. Not in the satanic way. (Although once, in tenth grade, Vicki MacLean bent over to pick up some pencils while wearing a really short skirt and my head turned completely around—and the word *Yipes!* appeared on my stomach.)

No, I was possessed by fly-fishing. As I said a bit earlier, my father bought me my first fly rod that year—1967—and guided me through the early stages of my development as a fly fisherman. By this I mean every time he drove me to a nearby lake or stream, he'd shout, "For chrissakes be careful you're gonna close the car door on the damn rod and if it breaks so help me I am not getting you another one for chrissakes!"

I walked into the house one day and said: "I got a ride home, but Andy closed the car door on my fly rod and it broke."

Dad: "For chrissakes I told you . . . dammit to hell, dumb bastard closed the door on your fishing rod for chrissakes you shoulda been more careful! For Chrissakes!"

I told him I was just kidding and I think he laughed. Although it was hard to tell because he was breathing really hard as he chased me through the house swinging a mop handle. Later he calmed down and I heard him tell my mother, in a soft and gentle voice, "The kid's pretty fast. Dammit to hell, for chrissakes."

Anyway, my very first outing with my new fly rod was at nearby Louisa Lake, which was stocked with trout. As far as I could tell, perhaps two of them. Weeks went by without a single strike, as I clumsily tied knots and changed flies and untangled the fly line from around my head and my feet and tripped over my brand new hip boots. Eventually I got out of the car.

But finally, on a Saturday morning that in my mind seems as though it was yesterday (see Chapter 42: The Pot-Smoking Years), I caught my first trout. It was a rainbow, about twelve inches long, and it struck a wet fly that I'd been twitching along near the bottom of Louisa Lake. The strike was shocking to a young boy who had made hundreds and hundreds of casts without any response. Oh sure, I'd had plenty of firm tugs on the line during previous outings, but this one was different. Mostly because there wasn't any blood coming from my ear and I wasn't crying "Someone, please, get the hook out of my ear, for chrissakes!" as I'd done so many times in the past.

No, by golly, this was a trout and my heart raced with excitement. It struggled valiantly, but I soon landed him, using a technique I still enjoy today that involves stumbling backward and dragging the fish about fifteen feet up onto the shore, then dropping the rod and sprinting toward the fish while yelling "Got one!"

I let that trout go on that sparkling day, as I've done with virtually all trout I've caught in the many decades since. Catch-and-release, I feel, is the most critical aspect of this sport, a gentle nod by the angler to our Creator as we say, "Thank You for giving us such special creatures and the magnificence of the natural world they live in, but now, God, I shall return it to battle yet another day with another angler."

And, of course, because trout taste like fish, and frankly, I'd rather eat a sweatsock.

Anyway, I released my first trout, watching in wonder as he swam back out into the lake, where I'm guessing he took quite a ribbing from his friends. ("You were caught by WHO?") And then I sat on the shore, breathless, realizing at the age of twelve that I'd found something magical.

My next great experience in fly-fishing came about a month later, at a nearby pond at the Nipmuc Rod and Gun Club, of which I was a junior member. And, without sounding as though I'm bragging, I was probably the most amazing junior member the rod and gun club ever had. I've been told that old men still gather at the skeet range and talk in hushed tones of the day the spring-loaded launcher broke and they gave a kid $2 to run across the range, holding clay pigeons over his head.

Anyway, the Nipmuc pond held a lot more trout than Louisa Lake, and one day, after my father had dropped me off near the shore and wished me well ("Don't fall in, for chrissakes!") I saw something that made my heart thump: a large trout rising to the surface for insects. I didn't even know trout did that!

I had about five or six dry flies that I kept in a plastic film canister, and picked out one that looked like a moth. After a long struggle to tie it to the leader—in those early days, tying knots often involved all ten fingers, a couple of toes, and a stick—I began my approach. The fish was rising steadily near the dam, a concrete structure that rose about four feet off the ground. I scrambled onto the dam and began making beautiful, graceful twenty-foot casts out onto the lake, which was terrific for a kid my age. Unfortunately, the fish was rising about forty feet out onto the lake. Suddenly, however, the fish moved closer. *Splash*. He rose within casting distance and I set the giant moth down about five feet from him.

I remember everything being blurry. A fluffy cloud went by. I was no longer looking at the trout or even at the pond. I was looking straight up. And having a great amount of difficulty—to use the formal fly-fishing term—"breathing." From the account given to me by my friend Kevin Smith, who was about twenty feet away at the time, here's what happened:

My giant moth had just settled onto the water when *bang* —the big trout struck. I vaguely recall seeing that. I'm told I reacted by pulling quite forcefully on the line and the rod, along with making a frighteningly loud sound like Yaaaaaeeeeeooohhhhhhh!

Then I fell off the dam. Backward. Onto my back. Needless to say, I didn't hook the trout.

Today, after thousands and thousands of hours in some of the most breathtaking places on earth in search of the elusive trout, I know that when a big trout crashes a dry fly like that, you have to be patient, waiting one or two seconds for him to engulf the fly and turn back down with it firmly in his mouth.

Then, and only then, do you lift the rod, smiling with that great feeling of accomplishment as the fly comes out of his mouth and you fall backward off the dam.

CHAPTER 14

My First Giant Rubber Pants

I'd fly-fished the lakes and ponds around my home for about two years before venturing into moving water. The debut of my creek-fishing skills came in Muddy Brook, a meandering stream that went through our town and neighboring villages, often cutting across cow pastures. I'd stare at the flowing water and wonder what array of insects the trout were feeding on and how I'd drift a fly down into the pools where they lurked. My friend Rob, who also grew up in Hopedale, would usually lag behind on these outings, staring at the cows and wondering how their cheek meat would taste rolled up in a flour tortilla.

Transportation on these adventures generally consisted of bicycles, the cool ones with the banana seats and the really high handlebars. As I'd set off on my journeys, holding my fly rod across the handlebars and clutching a sack of flies and spools of monofilament line that would serve as leader, my father would stand on the porch, watching his little boy growing up, and offer words of encouragement.

"For chrissakes, you're gonna fall off and break your neck!" would be one example.

This would usually be followed by: "And don't get that rod stuck in the spokes or you'll break the goddamn thing. For chrissakes!"

I'd pedal furiously to my destination, often a pasture in the nearby town of Mendon, where Muddy Brook grew deep and wide and fifteen-inch trout lurked behind the rocks. Sometimes I'd spend half an hour just watching, sitting in the grass, hoping the cows would not move any closer. I was afraid of cows back then. Of course I was just a kid. Now, at the age of forty-six, I am also afraid of goats and sheep.

Anyway, I'd sit in the grass in the early morning and wait until the air warmed and a few insects would appear. They were mayflies, I think, and as the sun rose higher they would come in small clouds from the water, followed by the trout. I'd spend hour after hour drifting tiny flies into the pools but never, ever caught a trout off the surface in those early years. I'm guessing the leader was too heavy and perhaps the fly dragged across the surface. But later, when the surface activity would stop, well, that's when I'd catch trout. A small nymph drifted deep would do the trick, the leader giving a telltale twitch at the strike.

I'd caught three or four small trout one day, the largest being about thirteen inches, when suddenly the leader darted violently to the right and I set the hook on Moby Trout. My heart raced as the fish roared downstream, the fly line tearing through my hands as I ran alongside, sometimes stepping in "meadow muffins" the cows had left along the stream.

When I was done fishing on those days I'd meet up with my friends, who had usually spent the day playing baseball or basketball. They knew where I'd been, my reputation as a fly fisherman having spread from one end of town to the other, a distance of exactly three miles. They'd look at me on those quiet summer evenings and I'd sense a bit of envy in their eyes, knowing I had stepped beyond the normal boundaries of youth and was, day by day, teaching myself the art of fly-fishing. Sometimes, this jealousy would show itself in their quiet whispers as I approached. An example would be: "Here comes Tosches. I bet he's got cow shit on his shoes again."

Back at Muddy Brook, the huge trout had taken me about two hundred feet downstream before I could turn him, adrenaline racing through my veins as I gently brought him toward me. And then, standing knee-deep in the water in my blue jeans, I slid him onto a sandbar near the shore and let out a shout of glee, a boy crying out in sheer joy at the wonder of it all. Although to the cows, it may have sounded like "Shit! It's a carp!"

It was a lovely carp, though, perhaps eight pounds of puckered lips, beady eyes, swollen stomach, and slimy scales. And I'm not sure why, but some thirty years later the memory of that moment came racing back to me.

I think it was the day I met Jeffrey, my ex-wife's divorce attorney. Muddy Brook wasn't my only special place, though. Another was the West River, which required about a five-mile bike ride, uphill. Both ways.

The West River was a classic tail water fishery, although that term had not yet been invented and I just called it "fishing under the dam." By then I had my first pair of waders, allowing me to get into the right position to make my casts and probe all parts of the nearby streams and river, opening up a whole new aspect of fly-fishing. And the whispers of my friends changed, too. ("Here comes Tosches. I bet he's wearing those giant rubber pants again.")

But these giant rubber pants put me in position to make long drifts with a nymph along the bottom of the West River where the water emerged from the dam, and this, I'd found, was where the trout waited for their food. I didn't know about nymph indicators back then, which now consist of polymer yarns and fluorescent cork and dozens of other high-tech tools that allow you to detect the most subtle strike. I used—I'm not kidding—pieces of wood carved from the branches of nearby trees, held to the fly line with thread. It worked just fine. And when you've got a three-inch piece of rough wood whistling by your face all day, well, it taught me a lot about concentration and proper casting techniques.

And, of course, it taught me a lot about ducking.

But I caught trout this way, and that's all that mattered. The small, floating piece of wood would twitch or pause in the current and I'd set the hook and feel the gentle tug of a trout, and at that moment, to a young boy alone on a trout stream, the world was a magical place. I say "magical" because for about five years, my time-consuming obsession with fly-fishing somehow caused my schoolwork to vanish. Although amazingly, I was still able, once in a while, to pull some decent grades out of my a . . . uh, out of my *sleeve*.

RICH TOSCHES

CHAPTER 15

Alpha Chi Cheese

I left Massachusetts in 1973, bound for Marquette University in Milwaukee, Wisconsin, a nice city tucked against the shore of Lake Michigan. I brought my fly rod, of course, and it didn't take me long to figure out what I'd be doing for the next four years. That's right: drinking beer.

Once in a while, though, I'd step over the cases of empty Red White and Blue brand beer bottles that littered the house I shared with seven other guys, and I'd head past the campus and down to the lakefront, where the people of Milwaukee would gather with friends and family to breathe the fresh air and marvel at the expanse of water stretching to the horizon.

Okay, they were all at the lake's shore drinking beer and throwing up cheese.

But the point is, I would often board a city bus for the thirty-block ride to Lake Michigan to throw a fly into the deep, clear water. The first few trips were disappointing. I'd occasionally see a fish rise to the surface, but they showed no interest in the dry flies I offered. The shoreline in the fall and again in the spring was patrolled by big brown trout, I was told, so I eventually switched to a sinking line with big streamers and woolly buggers and began getting thumped by monstrous trout.

And nearly flunked out of college.

By the midsemester mark of my freshman year, I'd been summoned to the office of the dean of the journalism college and shown my grades. I had a C-minus in an English class, D's in civics and science, and an F in a math class.

As much as I loved fly-fishing, it was obvious that something was wrong with the way I was allocating my time.

Clearly, I was spending too much time on the English class.

So I vowed to make some adjustments and begged the assistant dean not to send these midsemester grade reports to my parents. They were spending about $10,000 a year to send me to this fine school and I didn't want them to worry needlessly. And, of course, I was having enough problems without the thought of my angry father jumping into his 1970 Mercury and driving a thousand miles to Wisconsin while mumbling "I'll give the little bastard some fly-fishing goddammit to hell wasting my damn money for chrissakes!"

Which would, I believed, be followed by me spending weeks of valuable study time trying to get a nine-foot, six-weight Shake-speare fly rod out of my ass.

So I tucked the fly rod away for a while and brought the grades up to a respectable level.

I slept through most of the winter, when temperatures would drop to thirty degrees (Fahrenheit) below zero, which was either 1,566 degrees Celsius or six cubic hectares. (My struggle with science continued.)

But then spring came to this lovely land, and the people celebrated by rubbing their noses together in greeting and dancing around the seal carcasses. I celebrated by taking out the fly rod and heading to the lake. On that first outing of the year, in April of 1974, I hooked six huge browns on a streamer fly, the wild fish tearing fly line and backing from the reel until I would eventually work them up onto the beach. People would gather around during the battles, swearing excitedly in a way that made me homesick.

And then, when I'd release the huge trout, they'd ask the question I'd been hearing since I began fishing:

"Aren't ya gonna eat them?"

No, I'd say to these fine, God-fearing people of Wisconsin, I was not going to eat the fish. I'd try to explain the catch-and-release concept—conserving valuable resources, the joy I felt in watching a fish return to its habitat—and would then make the explanation understandable by comparing a wild brown trout to cheese.

Cheese, they'd nod in agreement, is seldom released.

The exception to that rule involved my roommate, George Mc-Cullough, a big, lovable farm boy from Chesterfield, Missouri, who would often "release the cheese." Always in the middle of the night, when we were locked in our airtight dormitory room.

(I'm just kidding, of course. Sometimes George would release the cheese during a class. Or during a date.)

In four years of fly-fishing the shoreline of Lake Michigan, I only kept two trout. Let me tell you the story.

On my twenty-first birthday, my buddies took me out to celebrate. We laughed and drank beer and then they shoved my head into a disgustingly filthy public men's-room toilet in the Avalanche Bar, which was a big hangout for homeless people, and flushed it. This was called a "swirly" and was meant to convey their affection. What it actually did was force me to stagger back to our house and wash my hair nonstop for two hours, with dish soap. When I finally emerged from the shower, I'm proud to say that my hair contained only a very faint aroma of a homeless guy's ass.

I don't want to get into a long-drawn-out discussion of the word *revenge,* so let me get to the point. A week later I caught a pair of twenty-two-inch brown trout. I kept them. We cooked them that night and my dear old pals thanked me for the fine meal.

Three nights later Jim "Wild Bull" Bristol returned home around midnight. Jim, or JB, is a big, rugged, manly man who scared us. Anyway, he went into his very dark room that night, reached for the light chain dangling from the socket over his bed—and grabbed a handful of brown trout head that had somehow tied itself to the chain.

Today, some twenty-four years later, I can still hear the sissylike sound of "eeeeeeeeeeee!!!!!" that came out of JB's room that night. When he emerged a moment later his testosterone level had returned to normal and he strutted around for a while ("I saw it. I didn't touch it!") before slipping into the bathroom to wash his hands with bleach.

RICH TOSCHES

And we were all still laughing about it the next morning, when suddenly, the voice of Tom Murphy—I think he had been holding my feet when my head went into the toilet—echoed from upstairs: "Jesus Christ! There's a #$%^!@# fish head in my $%^&*(@ underwear!"

I told him that was disgusting, and he might want to start changing his shorts a bit more frequently.

I miss my college buddies.

The bastards.

CHAPTER 16

Vince Lombardi Didn't Fly-Fish

In the spring of 1977, with my degree in journalism all but assured thanks to four years of diligent study—-and, according to my doctor, with nearly 15 percent of my liver still functioning—I took a three-day weekend, which was quite unusual. Most of my weekends in college were five or six days.

Anyway, needing a break from all the hard work, I packed up my fly-fishing gear and boarded a Greyhound bus, heading for the wilds of northern Wisconsin. The bus stopped in lovely towns such as Sheboygan (a Native American word meaning "the chief is dressing up in women's clothes again") and Manitowoc ("screw Manny, let's make him walk") and on into the famous town of Green Bay—where legendary Packers football coach Vince Lombardi would often stand and, in a voice choked with emotion and filled with the love he had for his players, say proudly, "How the hell did I end up here?"

After about a twenty-minute stop at the Greyhound station, which gave the passenger sitting next to me time to grab a cup of coffee before returning to his seat and resuming talking to himself, we were off again. Soon we'd reached my destination: the tiny town of Fish Creek on the sixty-mile-long peninsula separating Lake Michigan from the waters of Green Bay. I got a decent motel room for $19 a night—today, of course, the same room goes for $21.99 a night—and began hiking the trails of Peninsula State Park with my fly rod.

What I saw remains forever etched in my mind: gigantic chinook salmon, cruising the deep, clear waters along the shoreline at the mouths of tiny creeks. Concealing myself in shrubs along the creek banks, I could creep within a couple of feet and watch the fish, some I estimated at fifteen and twenty pounds, shoot past me in three and four feet of water. It was breathtaking. Soon I was actually in the creek, plunging my head into the icy water and emerging with a huge, thrashing salmon in my mouth, part of which I ate myself and part I gave to my young cubs, although I may be confusing my own personal experience in the Wisconsin north country twenty-four years ago with a Discovery Channel special I watched last night.

Have I mentioned that my friends and I drank a lot of beer during the college days?

My attempts to catch one of these monster salmon was a real

---

hoot. For a few hours I cast a bright orange streamer into the bay, where I could see the fish cruising, waiting for that biological trigger that sends them up the stream, according to wildlife biologists, like Bill Clinton heading for the Oval Office rest room. Only once did a salmon show any interest in the gaudy streamer, following it nearly to the shore before turning away. I recall making loud shouting noises and having to sit down because my knees were weak.

So I moved one hundred feet up the stream, switched to a small egg pattern, and waited. You could see the salmon come over a gravel bar and then into the pool where I crouched. After a dozen or so casts, a huge salmon nailed the egg and headed upstream, with me sprinting behind. I ran through the bushes and I ran through the brambles. I ran through the briars where a rabbit couldn't go—which I predict will someday become lyrics to a hillbilly country song.

The stream was no more than ten feet wide, and the salmon cut straight up the middle, tearing into my backing as I stumbled through the shrubs. I have never—before or since—felt such an indescribable rush of pure excitement, which tells you a lot about fly-fishing and, perhaps, why I've been married and divorced twice.

I never caught that giant salmon. He just kept going. Eventually, with thirty yards of fly line and perhaps twenty more yards of backing separating us, the line simply went slack and began drifting back downstream. I reeled it in and sat, shaking, in the lush green forest.

In the Adam Sandler movie *Happy Gilmore*—which is considered a film classic by not just me but many, many other idiots— Happy's golf instructor teaches him to relax by remembering a good time in his life, or as it is called, "going to his happy place."

Fly-fishing has given me a dozen or more happy places, sun-dappled streams or glistening lakes that are so firmly burned into the memory that I can still smell the wildflowers in a New Zealand meadow, still see the trout rising to my dry fly on my hometown trout pond when I was just a kid. And I can still feel the heart-pounding thrill of that wonderful spring day in Wisconsin when a monstrous salmon left me dazed and breathless.

The bastard.

CHAPTER 17

Goin' Hollywood

In 1977 I found myself getting off an airplane in Los Angeles, where I would live for the next fifteen years, first as a reporter for United Press International and then for the *Los Angeles Times*. Los Angeles offers a lot of things. I had lunch with Bob Hope, for example. Just Bob and I, dining on pork chops and talking about college football, sitting at the table in his Toluca Lake neighborhood home, which had a three-hole golf course in the backyard. By way of comparison, my backyard had an assortment of homeless people who would occasionally charge at me before toppling

———

into the shrubs and peeing in their pants. Bob Hope's house was a lot nicer.

I covered earthquakes and raging wildfires and once, about six weeks into my career, answered the phone in the L.A. bureau of the UPI wire service and the man on the other end said, "Hi. This is John Wayne."

It sounded sorta like the great actor, too, but I was busy writing the regional weather summary for the day, and as we got perhaps a hundred calls from loons each day, I replied, "Right. And I'm Roy Rogers." And I hung up.

Five minutes later the bureau manager, John Lowry, emerged from his office with a gigantic vein protruding on his forehead. "YOU JUST HUNG UP ON JOHN WAYNE, YOU STUPID SON OF A BITCH!" he said. Back then it was okay to talk to your employees that way. Today, of course, with labor lawyers and political correctness and workplace sensitivity, a thing like that would never happen because, well, mostly because John Wayne is dead.

I also covered three Super Bowls. After one, Dan Marino of the Miami Dolphins removed white athletic tape from his ankles, balled it up, and after I kicked off the locker-room interview session by throwing out the ceremonial first stupid question, Dan threw the ball of tape at me and hit me in the eye. I'm not kidding. He then apologized and said I could ask another question. I went with "If you were a tree, what kind of tree would you be?" The great quarterback came at me with scissors.

I also covered three World Series, highlighted by the 1981 series between the Los Angeles Dodgers and the New York Yankees in which Reggie Jackson called me an asshole and walked away from an interview. And I hadn't even gotten to the question about the tree.

Rich Tosches

The most memorable moment of my baseball-writing days, however, came in the Dodgers locker room after a game in the early 1980s when Dodger outfielder Pedro Guerrero, who was from the Dominican Republic, walked past manager Tommy Lasorda's office, which was filled with about a dozen writers. Pedro was naked. Seeing his star slugger, manager Lasorda—and I swear to God I am not making this up—shouted, "Hey, Pete! Come on in here and tell these guys about that time in Mexico when you f#%^&*# that goat!"

Guerrero, standing naked in the doorway, laughed and replied, "Oh, 'Sorda, that was a long time ago!" and walked away, scratching his ass.

Yup, I've been to the mountaintop!

Oh, and I also covered boxing for three years. For an in-depth study of the brutal sport I climbed into the ring, in 1987, with then world middleweight champion Michael Nunn. He beat me senseless for three rounds, leaving my eyes swollen, my lips swollen, and my nose swollen. When it was over he came to my corner and asked if I was okay, to which I replied, "Ghafgth bahagamoof, thampghs."

Did I mention that my lips were swollen?

All in all, it was a hoot.

What Los Angeles didn't offer, however, was much in the way of fly-fishing. Everything was more or less paved. The exception, of course, was the ocean, which the city of Los Angeles could not pave because, as I understand it, Johnny Carson owns it. But we could still use it, and within a few months of my arrival I found myself standing at the harbor in the nearby town of Redondo Beach. The surface of the water was being churned white as fast-moving fish slashed through schools of baitfish no more than twenty feet from the rock jetty I was standing on. My fly-fishing instinct kicked in and I did exactly what you'd figure a guy would do in that situation. That's right, I stared at the blonde with the roller skates and the gargantuan fake breasts until drool covered the entire front of my shirt.

About a week later I went back to the Redondo harbor, this time armed with my fly rod and an assortment of saltwater streamer flies I'd picked up at a tackle shop. The fish, I was told, were bonito. What I was not told was that bonito are like trout on steroids, and trying to stop one with a six-weight fly rod is not easy. Especially when the reel you own has an intricate drag system that basically consists of the handle smashing into your fingers as it goes around at about 4,500 rpm and you shouting "Holy shit!" over and over again.

I got into position on the rock jetty. The water was still. About twenty minutes later, however, I saw the bonito crashing the surface and moving in my direction. A long cast dropped a white streamer into the middle of the frenzy and then I just hung on as a fish struck and—despite my repeated cries of "Holy shit!"—headed straight out into the Pacific Ocean toward Holland or Wales or whatever's on the other side of the Pacific Ocean. (I wasn't very good in geometry.)

Somehow, though, the bonito eventually turned and I wrestled it back toward the rocks, sliding it into a space between two boulders and unhooking it. At which point it slammed its powerful tail against my hand, which in turn crashed into a rock. It hurt so much I staggered backward and fell on the slick, seaweed-covered rocks, banging my right hip on a jagged boulder. So there I lay, my hand bleeding, my ass going numb, twisted into a tiny pathetic little heap on rocks covered with seagull poop.

I was the happiest guy in the world.

You know, if you don't count Richard Simmons.

In this strange new land that I would call home for a decade and a half, I had found my little place, my happy place, a place that would sweep me away from the mad life I was living just a few miles inland, a place called Redondo Beach—home to seals and sea lions and blondes with huge artificial breasts and, of course, bonito, which had regular, normal breasts. I think.

CHAPTER 18

Maggie Meets Mr. High Jumpy Guy

Eventually, though, the lure of the wily trout had me exploring streams around Los Angeles. There were very few places. One was called Piru Creek, about fifty miles to the north, although Piru lost some of its appeal for me when seven Vietnamese refugees—I am not kidding—were arrested for blowing up trout in the stream with sticks of dynamite and netting the fish as they floated downstream. The men seemed quite puzzled by the whole legal mess, scratching their heads during a court appearance and saying over and over again, in sad, plaintive voices,

"Tam won hangue guanade" ("Next time we'll use hand grenades like everyone else").

My quest for trout fishing eventually brought me to the Sierras, a stunning chain of mountains that runs through Yosemite National Park about a five-hour drive north of L.A.—unless gang members believe you have cut them off in traffic on the Hollywood Freeway and begin chasing you, which allows you to cover the 275 miles in fifty minutes. (Gang members don't seem real interested in fly-fishing, despite the obvious connection: a pair of extra-large breathable Orvis waders look exactly like the gigantic trousers they enjoy wearing, pants apparently stolen from their grandfathers.)

An early discovery for me was the Kern River, which held a fair number of browns and rainbows. On my first outing along this river, I watched a grasshopper fall from the streamside brush and immediately disappear into the swirl of a good-sized fish. I quickly tied on a hopper imitation and, well, I don't think I have to tell you veteran fly anglers what happened next. That's right, my first cast caught the bush on the opposite bank and I snapped the leader trying to get the grasshopper out. Unfortunately, it was my only grasshopper, so I spent the next two hours using a lot of foul language as I went through about two dozen other flies in my box without a strike.

Then, perhaps out of frustration, perhaps because I'm an idiot with few principles, I caught a live grasshopper, pinned him to the hook of a No. 10 Adams, which looked like a moth, and tossed the whole mess out into the middle of the Kern River.

A brown trout came to this odd combination in a hurry. I don't know why, although my extensive knowledge of entomology tells me that the trout believed the giant moth was going to carry the grasshopper off, and dammit, he was going to get a bite of *something* before the buffet table flew away.

The trout was released unharmed, and I suddenly felt terribly guilty about having resorted to the use of live bait. This nagging guilt haunted me for the rest of the day, hanging on to me like a heavy weight that, I believe, slowed me down as I raced around in the grass and threw myself onto more grasshoppers, trying not to let the little bastards bite me as I stuffed them into a vest pocket and went sprinting back toward the river.

I'm just kidding, of course. I sent my daughter, Maggie, who was three, after the grasshoppers.

Maggie held a small cardboard box as she lurched around in the tall grass, a squeal of delight echoing through the valley with each capture. When she'd bring the 'hopper to me, I'd say things such as "We'll name this one Mr. High Jumpy Guy and he can be our new pet." Then she'd return to the grass fifty feet away and I'd have Mr. High Jumpy Guy drifting down the middle of the Kern River, attached to his new friend, Mr. Moth.

When Maggie returned with another grasshopper, I told her the first one had jumped back into the grass, probably to be with his family, whom he loved very much, and we'd keep this *new* grasshopper as a pet and name him Mr. Leap High Into The Air Guy. He, too, would later "escape"—as would each and every one of the dozen or more grasshoppers little Maggie brought to her daddy that day.

Today, I've matured a lot and promise that I will never, ever again do anything so despicable. These days I pursue the trout fairly, using only the artificial flies that I keep on my fly-fishing vest, on that little patch of wool that hangs over the left pocket.

Just above the hand grenade.

CHAPTER 19

Oh No! Not the Cows!

After a few years in L.A. it occurred to me that to do any
real fly fishing I'd have to get
on a plane. Luckily, my boyhood friend Rob had settled in Boulder, Colorado, and had mistakenly given
me his phone number and address.

In the early 1980s I began making annual journeys
with Rob and other friends through Colorado ("The
Lone Star State") and neighboring Wyoming ("I
Swear I Was Just Helping the Sheep Through the
Fence!"). We called these events "elk-hunting trips"
and would usually go as far as to purchase an elk li-

cense and actually bring rifles along. In twelve years of these alleged hunting trips, the closest I actually came to an elk was in 1984—when a gust of wind along the North Platte River in Wyoming caused a No. 16 elk-hair caddis to become embedded in my right earlobe. As you might imagine, this was unbelievably painful and I spent the better part of the afternoon screaming and falling into the grassy field along the river, trying to pull the fly out of my ear.

Back at the cabin that night, Rob and I swapped tales of our day in the great outdoors. I told him about having the elk-hair caddis in my ear, but he topped that one. Apparently he had an elk in his crosshairs several times during his hunt—but claimed that every time he was about to pull the trigger, the elk would disappear into the tall grass.

And he'd hear a man scream.

The destination during those years was the Wyoming town of Saratoga in the Medicine Bow National Forest. I'd fly from Los Angeles to Denver, and often the trip from the Denver airport to Wyoming was the highlight of the journey. In 1980, for example, the three-hour drive in Rob's small Toyota pickup took place during a pounding rain-and-sleet storm, with passing vehicles throwing up a relentless spray of brown water and mud from the road. Rob had prepared for just such an event by draining the windshield-washer-fluid reservoir in his truck and disconnecting the hose. That trip was a lot of fun.

As a bonus, I now know the thrill Stevie Wonder must get when he gets a sudden rush of independence, sneaks past the servants, fires up the Mercedes, and heads down to Burger King.

Another memorable trip from Denver to Wyoming came in 1982, when Rob's International Scout blew both headlights on the last leg of the trip, which was down the side of a mountain in the Medicine Bow range. At midnight.

This—I'm not kidding—is how we navigated the final eight miles of that trip: me sitting on the hood of the truck, shining a flashlight on the roadway, trying to dig my fingernails into the paint to keep from sliding off as Rob sent the truck hurtling downhill at 50 mph. It was fifteen degrees at the time, and using the National Weather Service conversion chart, I can tell you that on that night some twenty years ago, the combination of the temperature and the man-made 50-mph wind created a windchill factor somewhere between "Pretty Damn Cold" and "To This Day I Still Have Not Gotten Much Feeling Back in My Testicles."

But that was a long time ago and I've forgiven Rob and no longer dwell on the incident.

And the presence of the North Platte River made the epic struggles worthwhile. One of the last great freestone rivers in the West, the North Platte meanders through lush forests and meadows, with as many as five thousand wild trout per mile, most of them smart enough to (a) Never hold a flashlight and sit on the hood of a fast-moving truck being driven by an idiot; and (b) Keep their testicles safely tucked away inside their warm body so, in the event they ever needed them, they could ACTU-ALLY USE THEM!

Sorry.

I will now tell just four stories culled from hundreds of interesting moments during a long love affair with the area around Saratoga, Wyoming, and the North Platte River. (I would tell more, but all the other stories involve whiskey, livestock, and women's clothing and would be horribly embarrassing to Rob, who is now the chief probation officer for Boulder County.)

———

The Nice People on the Deck

I met the nice people on the deck in 1988. I had hiked about four miles from a parking area along the North Platte, fighting my way through bushes and briars, fishing each likely hole, and catching a few nice trout. Then, through the forest, I saw a cabin. It was built on the river. And the deck actually hung over the river.

Here I will cite Wyoming law, specifically Chapter 43, Subsection IV, Paragraph 14: "If a resident of a rural region of the state attends a 'moving picture show' prior to 4 P.M. on days designated as *weekdays,* said resident shall be admitted for $2, and the sheep shall be admitted free."

Oops. Wrong law.

The one I'm talking about deals with ownership of river property. It says that a landowner may own half of the river. In other words, if you drew a line down the middle of the Platte River, well, your pen would get wet and you'd probably drown, you damn fool!

No, what it means is that if you drew an *imaginary* line down the middle of the river, the landowner owns the half bordering his land and no one may step upon the bottom of the river on the landowner's side!

Which is one of the reasons you seldom hear the expression "good ol' Wyoming wisdom."

You can, however, fish on the landowner's side by making long casts. Which brings us back to the nice people on the deck. As I approached the cabin and the lovely, swirling pool of trout in front of it, I was welcomed by a hand-painted sign hanging from the deck. The actual sign read:

YOU'VE GOT THE WHOLE RIVER TO FISH IN. DON'T FISH HERE!

———

RICH TOSCHES

As I understand it, the cabin's owners went with that particular wording because they didn't have enough paint for:

HEY DICKHEAD! WHY DON'T YOU STICK THAT FLY ROD UP YOUR ASS? OR WAIT, I KNOW . . . MAYBE WE COULD JUST SHOOT YOU! WE HATE EVERYBODY! WE WERE DROPPED ON OUR HEADS AS BABIES AND FRANKLY, WE'RE THE ONLY TWO PEOPLE ON EARTH WHO CAN STAND EACH OTHER. (AND JUST BETWEEN US, ABOUT TWICE A WEEK I EVEN THINK ABOUT THROWING *HER* INTO THE GODDAMN RIVER!) YOU BASTARDS!!!

Anyway, I did what anyone would do when confronted with such a message, telling me, in no uncertain terms, that I was not wanted. That's right; I switched to a No. 16 blue-winged olive, stripped out about forty feet of line, and started nailing some huge rainbows in a nice little seam against the opposite bank.

This brought the nice people onto their deck. Even though I was fishing legally, from the other side of the river, the woman began screaming at me. She called me a son of a bitch, a term I had not heard since, well, since about eight that morning when I grabbed my sack lunch—and my friend Rob's—off the front seat of his truck and sprinted into the woods.

The man rolled out onto the deck in a wheelchair and I immediately felt sorry for him. Not because he was in a wheelchair but because he was trapped, probably for the rest of his life, in a small cabin with this bitch. I figured not being able to walk probably wasn't even on his top-ten list of Things That Make Life Unpleasant.

I told the woman, in a calm voice, that I was fishing legally. That Wyoming law allowed me to make casts from the opposite side of the river. That the fish in the entire river belonged to the state of Wyoming. That there was currently a fine hatch of blue-winged olives under way, and that I would release all of the trout unharmed and would not make a peep or leave so much as a gum wrapper as I fished for the next thirty minutes or so before heading upstream.

"Get out of here now, you son of a bitch!" she screamed.

At that moment a huge rainbow rose to my fly, gulped it in, and the battle was on. It stripped line from my reel on this fine October day, slashing through the two-hundred-yard-long pool nearly beneath the feet of Cuckoo Woman as I stayed firmly planted on my side of the river. Eventually the trout—twenty-four inches of trout—came to my net beneath a towering cottonwood tree of yellow leaves.

And I realized that for those five minutes I'd been immersed so deeply in my own world, a magnificent world of fly-fishing and giant trout on a wild river in Wyoming, that I had blocked out the unpleasantness that was attacking my ears and now had only a vague recollection of a babbling, nagging woman hovering over me and screaming at me.

And I had this thought: "If fly-fishing isn't good training for being a husband, what is?"

The Cows Are Trying to Drown Me

It was on a warm October day in 1979 that I found a stretch of the North Platte River that was bordered by farmland, the flowing water sparkling in the autumn sun, the kind of water that seems to be begging to be fly-fished by a moron. Recalling bumper stickers I had seen, I had my kid beat up your honor-student kid. Oops. Wrong bumper sticker. The one I mean says ASK FIRST!— and so I tracked down the landowner and asked permission to fish on his property.

He gave his approval and then added these words: "Be careful of the cows."

Be careful of the cows?

First of all, I couldn't see any cows. I had seen two white-tailed deer off the in distance as I walked along a road near his ranch-land, and I wondered now if the amiable fellow thought they were cows. This is what can happen to you when you spend endless hours sitting on a horse in the hot sun, worrying about all the things ranchers worry about—mostly why your three sons insist on living in your house despite the fact that they are in their forties, and one of them calls himself "Hoss" and eats so goddamn much that your cook, Hop Sing, has tried to poison him, and the fact they never seem to have any girlfriends, which makes you wonder if maybe all three of them are gay!

Sorry.

Second, I wondered just how careful you have to be with cows when you're armed with nothing more than a five-weight St. Croix fly rod and a boxful of dry flies? I mean, even if you accidentally hook one, I'm sure the 6X tippet would break before the cow got into your backing—unless you were using Rio-brand leader material with superb abrasion resistance plus high knot and tensile strength.

I bet that will get me a big fat sponsor contract! I can see the new advertisement series now, featuring me saying: "Use Rio leaders and tippet. It can stop a cow!"

Anyway, I thanked the man and headed downstream and found a spectacular looking pool at the tail of some riffles. I sat on the bank for a few moments and saw heads popping up, heads of big rainbows slurping Tricos. I tied on my favorite, a parachute Trico, which is like a regular Trico except just as it hits the water a man leaps from an airplane, pulls the rip cord, and lands safely on the tiny fly.

No, a parachute has a tuft of hair that you can actually see from more than twelve inches away, making it the ideal fly for those few people who cannot see a fly the size of a pinhead floating thirty feet away with the sun in their eyes—the losers.

On my fifth or sixth cast, the fly made a nice drag-free float and a trout sucked it in and we battled then under the warm fall sun, a sixteen-inch rainbow eventually sliding onto a gravel bar at my feet. I released the fish and caught four more in the next half hour, a thrill that made me lean my head back, gaze at the deep blue sky, and say out loud, "Mooooo!"

Turns out that wasn't me. It was a cow that had, along with perhaps twenty-five of her friends, snuck up behind me in that stealthy, leopardlike way that cows have. I turned and admired the cows—huge creatures with brown hair covering their entire bodies, enormously large asses, and big eyes and eyelashes—and I thought, "I wonder what my high-school prom date is doing these days?"

The cows kept inching closer to the river, looking—and here I use the old expression—"thirsty as cows." I moved a few feet downstream, but three of the cows moved, too, and cut me off. Then a few stepped down off the upstream bank and held their ground as the main attack force of cows lurched off the bank toward me.

There comes a time in a man's life when he's forced to ponder the meaning of life. This generally comes after about eight beers, and sometime around midnight we settle on this: "Thank the Good Lord Jesus Christ that that I am not married to Martha Stewart!"

———

RICH TOSCHES

I had not had any beers on this fine day in the wild lands of Wyoming, but I pondered the meaning of life anyway and came up with this: I am about to die a bizarre death that will involve cows, a fly rod, and a lot of swearing.

The cows kept coming now, coming in waves off the grassy bank. They had no fear of humans, particularly of one who was shouting "Bad cows! Get away! Shooooo, goddammit!"

I even tried yelling "How now, brown cow?" but that didn't work, either.

They just kept mooing.

And coming.

And suddenly, with my arms extended and my hands actually pushing on the head of what appeared to be the Queen of the Cows and my fly rod tucked under my right armpit, I was pushed gently off the gravel bar.

And into the North Platte River.

The pool where the trout were still rising—you have not really seen big trout rising until you've seen them rising at eye level as you float past them—was about eight feet deep, I estimated. I estimated my personal height at, well, less than eight feet. And so I floated. Right up to my chin. The cows drank madly from the very spot where I'd been standing just moments before, seemingly oblivious to the floating, screaming human now headed downstream.

I dragged myself out on another gravel bar on the opposite side of the river about thirty feet downstream, gasping for breath because the cold water had rushed in through the chest region of my waders and had reached all the way to the testicle region. I stripped off the waders and my socks and my long underwear and stood there for a moment, thankful that I had not joined that small list of people who have been killed by brown cows.

———

I was also thankful that the gravel bar I was now standing on contained several baseball-size rocks which—I wish I was making this up, but I am not—I began launching at the cows while shouting "You sons of bitches!"

Maturity has not always been my strong suit.

The third rock hit a cow squarely on the side of the head and it mooed in what seemed like some pain, and then, standing in my wet boxer shorts alongside a wild river in Wyoming, I felt terribly, terribly sorry.

Specifically, sorry I wasn't able to kick the cow in the ass as she scrambled up the bank and went lurching through the field with her mooing gang of sons-of-bitches friends.

It's been more than twenty years since the cows tried to kill me in Wyoming, and I cannot begin to tell you how much steak I have eaten since then. I'm guessing it's been a ton or two. And wherever I go, I ask for Wyoming beef.

I should probably grow up.

The Fourth-Best Day of My Life

The fourth-best day of my life occurred on October 5, 1987.

The three best days were November 28, 1985, March 3, 1989, and May 28, 1992—the days my children were born.

(If I had to list my fifth-best day, it would probably be that giddy day in June of 1978 when, while working as a reporter for United Press International, I was standing in a crowded Los Angeles County courthouse when actress Farrah Fawcett walked by and accidentally brushed against my ass. And if my older son's grades don't improve pretty soon, his birthday could be replaced by what I like to call the "Farrah Fawcett ass incident.")

Anyway, back to the fourth-best day of my life.

It began about thirty miles east of Saratoga, Wyoming, when I shot a huge mule-deer buck. I hadn't "bagged" a deer or elk in a decade, in part because after spotting them in the woods, I'd almost always trip while sprinting toward them with the Wal-Mart shopping sack.

Anyway, I had the big deer in the back of the truck by 10 A.M. and by noon found myself standing knee-deep in a remote section of the North Platte River, fly rod in hand and not a cow within ten miles.

And for three hours I caught wild rainbows and browns, perhaps fifty or more, all of them full of a majestic fight and spirit that said, "We are native Wyoming trout, and it's not out of the question that someday one of us could be elected governor!"

I think that's what they said.

But the point is, the trout hit dry flies at a breathtaking rate, sometimes on consecutive casts, never more than a half-dozen casts before a fish struck, rushing at the Tricos and baetis and even caddis with amazing energy. In one memorable incident, I was changing flies when a gust of wind blew the line and newly attached Trico out of my hands. It landed about three feet upstream and was dragged quickly downstream by the leader, making it appear that the fly was water-skiing. And a fifteen-inch brown chased it almost to my leg and inhaled it. (I mean the Trico. I still have my leg.)

For about thirty seconds I had to fight this fish with the fly rod tucked under my arm as I struggled with my magnifying-reading glasses sliding off my nose and simultaneously trying to get my fly box closed and back into a vest pocket.

Somehow, I eventually netted what I'm guessing was the brown-trout version of Dan Quayle.

Rob and my other hunting/fishing friends had gathered along the riverbank at some point and were watching as I connected with trout after trout after trout as tens of thousands of brilliant gold cottonwood leaves rustled along the banks.

And for one day, one magical day that all fly anglers dream of, I was the "Lord of the River."

This should not be confused with either *River Dance* or *Lord of the Dance*—those show in which popular Irish dancers slap their feet around in such a frenzy that eventually the bottles of whiskey *and* the potatoes fall out of their pants and go sliding across the stage.

(That, of course, was just a stupid stereotype joke and I hereby issue this apology: I am sorry for my insensitive comment. Not all Irishmen carry potatoes in their pants.)

And Then There's Saratoga Lake

(Note: I would have come up with a catchier title for this final story about the fantastic fishing around Saratoga, Wyoming, but frankly, I used up nearly all of my creative talent on "The Cows Are Trying to Drown Me" and am now struggling just to slap a name on these stories.)

Saratoga Lake sits just on the edge of the town, nestled among tall grasses and juniper bushes and high-desert sage. We'd been directed to the lake by the owner of the Great Rocky Mountain Outfitters fly shop in town. We gave him the prerequisite $35 each, grabbed the flies he forced us to purchase, and headed for the lake.

The flies were tiny mysis shrimp. The fishing was amazing. Huge trout cruised the weed beds edging out from the shoreline, occasionally making themselves known with gigantic splashes and swirls as they moved through clusters of the shrimp. Sometimes we'd see them moving along under the surface, browns and rainbows of five and eight and even ten pounds. My hands shook as I tied on my first fly, partly because of the presence of the giant, startling fish but mostly, I believe, because of the enormous amounts of George Dickel whiskey we had consumed in the cabin the night before.

I laid out about thirty feet of line on my first cast and began a slow, twitching retrieve that perfectly mimicked the natural movement of the shrimp. Which was a good thing, because "slow and twitching" was all my hands were capable of. With all due respect to the George Dickel distillery and what I'm sure is its battery of lawyers, it's a fine whiskey unless you have any plans for the following day—such as getting up.

Anyway, I had retrieved the fly perhaps five or ten feet when the fish struck, a heavy, surging tug that stripped line from my hands and had me making loud, whooping noises. The five-weight rod bent heavily and from my left someone shouted, "Keee-rist! What is that?"

(Turns out it was one of my cabin mates and George Dickel drinking partners on the shore who had coughed up something, something that had apparently been dislodged from his small intestine by the whiskey, and he was now staring at it.)

The battle went on for almost ten minutes, long screeching runs followed by heavy, sulking head shaking as the monster trout tried to get rid of the fly. When he appeared on the surface about ten feet away, I greeted him with the magical words a fly angler saves for these moments of complete and utter exhilaration:

"Holy shit!"

I had about half of the fish in my net a few moments later, stumbling backward toward the shore as I gently dragged him along on the surface, a rainbow trout of astounding proportions. My rear end plopped down on a clump of grass on the shore, and after removing the tiny shrimp from the corner of his mouth, I held him for a moment on the lake surface. I took out a tape measure and gasped at the number at the end of the fish's tail—twenty-seven inches—and carefully held him in the water as he regained his strength.

When the giant trout swam back into the depths, I could feel my heart pounding like it hadn't pounded in years. (See *Farrah Fawcett ass incident*.)

There would be many more fish that pounded our flies in Saratoga Lake over the years. The shrimp patterns were consistent winners, but I also took dozens of big fish on drys and small pheasant-tail nymphs. I never caught another to match that first one, but many were over twenty inches and some measured twenty-three and twenty-four inches—giant, fat, healthy trout.

A year after the initial adventure I brought some older friends from Massachusetts, Bill and Butch and Billy, who is now deceased, to the shores of Saratoga Lake. One day we caught a dozen or more big trout in an hour. Bill Meaden, who had spent a lifetime fly-fishing, called it the greatest day he'd ever had on trout water. Bob "Butch" Butcher smiled nonstop for three hours as the trout crashed his shrimp pattern.

And Billy, who was in his seventies, laughed out loud at the sheer joy of the whole thing.

Billy died a few years later. I can still see him standing on the shore of Saratoga Lake. And I can still hear his laugh that day.

RICH TOSCHES

When it's at its best, and sometimes even when it's not, fly-fishing can stamp a permanent memory like that. Days can live forever. For example, I'm betting that today, somewhere in the majestic ranchland near Saratoga, Wyoming, a cow is telling her calf about the day Grandma made a man in big rubber pants go for a swim in the river.

CHAPTER 20

Pontoon Boat Envy

Where Lunkers Lurk

 Wading in the creeks and streams and rivers and wading into our lakes and ponds and reservoirs, however, apparently is not enough for the avid fly angler. Many years ago, according to fly-fishing historians, a man, probably named Chuck, stood on the shore of a lake, gazed out at the water, and spoke these prophetic words:

> "Someday we'll find a way to be out there, away
> from the shore, our gigantic asses submerged as we
> float around in some kind of tube."

———

And the float tube was born.

Today, it is not uncommon on many trout lakes to see dozens of people bobbing around out there, propelling themselves by kicking swim fins that are attached to their feet, their behinds wedged into an inflated truck-tire tube that is marketed as a "belly boat." We gladly pay $200 or $300 for the privilege of climbing into this contraption so we can float around with the fishes. Although in parts of New Jersey you get to do the same thing for free—as long as you're willing to talk to the FBI and rat on Vinny.

And because we are America, we have taken this concept of floating around in a truck tire to astonishing heights. At the top of the line, they are called personal float craft or pontoon craft and can cost $1,000 or more. My personal favorite is the Dave Scadden Pontoon Craft. I am now looking at an advertisement for this fine product that appeared in the September 2001 edition of *Fly Fisherman* magazine. Let's review this ad.

At the top, the ad screams: HOT, NEW! REVOLUTIONARY! NEW!

(Modern marketing, as you know, is 1 percent new ideas and 99 percent exclamation points.)

Under this herd of exclamation points in the ad, we find the actual name of this "Hot, New! Revolutionary! New!" device.

It is called: Cardiac Canyon.

This name was chosen by the Dave Scadden Co. marketing department over two other fine suggestions: Massive Stroke Craft and Complete Kidney Failure Boat.

Here now, more of the actual wording in what I stress is a fine, well-made fly-fishing pontoon craft that you and your fly-fishing friends will use and enjoy right up until you drown.

"It's revolutionary, eight-piece frame and 49 lb. weight store easily in our 28x28x12 boat pack!"

I believe the first word of that sentence should have been "its," without the apostrophe.

But frankly, as a fly fisherman, if I have to choose between (a) a company that does not dwell on grammar but chooses instead to concentrate its efforts on making a highly dependable personal pontoon boat; or (b) a company that spends its resources on fancy marketing departments and copy editors who produce perfect grammatical advertisements, yet also produces personal pontoon boats that will explode and send me screeching across the lake and over the dam, well, I say you go with that first company.

It's just the way I am.

The ad for the Cardiac Canyon pontoon boat also makes this claim: "Revolutionary 11 ft., 6 in. length."

As you know, for centuries our personal fly-fishing pontoon craft have been either eleven feet long or twelve feet long. The guys with the smaller ones would invariably suffer from what psychiatrists call "pontoon boat envy." The guys with the twelve-footers would walk around with a big arrogant smile on their faces—right up until word got around the bar that they were having trouble "inflating the pontoon," if you know what I mean.

Anyway, we grappled with this monumental problem for a long time before finally someone at the Dave Scadden Co. blurted out this idea: "Hey, I know! Let's make a pontoon boat that's bigger than eleven feet and smaller than twelve feet!"

This caused Dave Scadden himself to jump out of his seat during the board meeting—toppling forward, of course, because he was wearing swim fins—and shout, "Sweet Mary and Joseph! That's revolutionary!"

Another note in the ad proclaims the Cardiac Canyon pontoon

boat, which includes a seat that extends a couple of feet above the pontoons, has "zero wind resistance."

Because I was skeptical of this claim, I contacted the chairman of the physics department at esteemed Harvard University. I asked him whether a personal pontoon boat used by a fly fisherman so he could get away from the shore and thus wouldn't keep getting his woolly bugger stuck in the shrubs and have to lurch around on the shore trying to retrieve the $1.99 fly could, possibly, be designed so as to offer "zero wind resistance."

Being an intellectual, the professor responded with a rhetorical question: "How the $%^* did you get my phone number?"

Then he called me an asshole and hung up.

But the point is, if the Dave Scadden Co. has come up with a design so unbelievably thin and streamlined that it offers absolutely *no wind resistance,* I believe what they have created is swimsuit supermodel Elle MacPherson.

Now there's something I'd like to ride across a lake!

Anyway, most of the guys I know have simple float tubes or belly boats that do, indeed, consist of a truck tire tube. This allows us to get out onto the lake where the lunkers lurk. As a bonus, the truck-tire tube will eventually burst, which causes us to go skimming across the water at breathtaking speeds in a final act of manly thrill seeking before we drown or, as mentioned previously, go flying over the dam.

The float-tube experience begins near the shoreline. Step number one involves pulling on your waders. If you forget this crucial step, you will find yourself sitting in a lake while wearing pants. After the waders are on, you put swim fins on your feet. If used correctly, these will propel you quickly across the water at speeds reaching one-one-hundredth of a mile per hour. As a bonus, they also put an unbelievable amount of stress on the ligaments and tendons in your knees, eventually crippling you and thus keeping you from skiing, which is a *really* stupid sport.

After you've put on your waders and rubber swim fins, you climb into the tube and begin the graceful walk toward the water. There are two popular methods for doing this. The first is to walk forward. This allows the tips of your gigantic swim fins to catch the ground, toppling you face first into the lake. The more preferred method, of course, is to walk backward. Using this approach, the modern angler is able to stumble over something he cannot see and topple into the lake with the back of his head leading the way.

For the few anglers who ever actually get into the lake without having their lungs fill with water, the next step is to kick the swim fins in a manner that allows you to go around and around in circles until it's time to go home. This, as I understand it, is called "whirling disease" and is a big problem on many trout waters.

My favorite experience in one of these float tubes came in 1997 on an outing with my outdoor writer friend, Karl Licis, who, as I mentioned earlier, apparently doesn't like me. The trip brought us to Spinney Mountain Reservoir some sixty miles west of Colorado Springs, Colorado. On the way up Karl mentioned that the place tends to get a "little breezy."

As I was to find out, this was like saying former President Bill Clinton tends to get a "little horny."

After waddling around the shore for a while with my ass wedged into the float tube, picking myself back up a dozen times after tripping over the swim fins and then taking both the tube and the fins off so I could hike back to Karl's truck, where I had left my fly rod, I somehow found myself drifting away.

I caught a nice rainbow, Karl hooked and landed a huge pike, and then the wind came.

The wind came over the mountains and, to borrow a phrase made popular by Kansas trailer-home owners being interviewed on TV after watching their house take off, "sounded like a freight train."

Suddenly I found myself in a tire tube that was riding up the front of four-foot waves and down the other side, into troughs so deep I expected to find Rush Limbaugh feeding in one of them. The wind was howling at 40 and 50 mph, I would learn from the National Weather Service the next day—after I was done choking Karl.

And it was blowing parallel to the shore. No matter how hard I kicked the swim fins, I could not close the gap between myself and land. I was screaming and flailing my arms and kicking as hard as I could as I went past the spot on the shore where he was standing, having apparently anticipated the "little breeze."

As I went sailing past him frantically waving my hand at him, Karl responded by waving back.

I washed up on a point that extended well out into the lake, some one and a half miles from where I was when the typhoon hit. When I crawled out of the float tube, I tried to stand up and went lurching sideways for about thirty feet, my knees aching and my thigh muscles burning and unable to hold my weight. I lay on my side on the gravel for about fifteen minutes thinking about what a wonderful experience this float-tube thing had been.

And wondering if Karl's proctologist would return my landing net.

RICH TOSCHES

130

CHAPTER 21

Tying It All Together

If you become an avid fly angler, you go through a lot of flies. You lose them in all the typical ways.

Snagged in a bush.

Snagged on a log in the river.

Snagged in the side of that guy's neck after he tried foolishly to move into the pool you were fishing.

At about a buck and a half each, losing flies can get expensive. Eventually, most fly anglers tire of shelling out their hard-earned cash. The exception would be attorneys, who simply pad the billable hours sheet and buy more flies—which they display proudly on a patch

———

of wool they keep on their dorsal fin and go on catching fish the usual way: in their three rows of razor-sharp teeth.

And so now we venture into one of the oldest, most traditional and enjoyable aspects of fly-fishing, a much more enjoyable way to fill our fly box. That's right, during a streamside lunch we take a handful of flies out of our friend's fly box while he's off in the bushes taking a leak.

No, actually, we begin the art of fly-tying.

And instead of *buying* flies, we create our own flies—right after we buy $200 stainless-steel vises, delicate feathers plucked from the groin area of Peruvian mountain sparrows, fur yanked from a cheetah's rump by a swift African tribesman, hooks handmade in Sweden by a man named Sven, who can, in a good week, make two of them, and fly-tying desks made of a certain type of birch that only grows on one hill in a very-hard-to-get-to part of Newfoundland.

By doing that, we will, if we live to the age of 214 and tie flies six days a week, have saved approximately forty-five cents.

Here's just one of hundreds of desks you can purchase to begin tying flies, a desk handmade by the terrific Chilton Co. in Freeport, Maine, and advertised this way:

A FLY TYER'S DREAM

Imagine my surprise when the advertisement went on and on and nowhere did it mention getting a back rub by the Dixie Chicks.

Anyway, the ad says: "Keep things organized and neat with this handsome birch desk and cabinet. Eight large drawers are lined on the bottom with red cedar to naturally protect your wool, fur and feathers from moths."

Nothing displeases me, personally, as much as having hundreds of moths in my wool. Never is this more true than when the wool is my long-underwear bottoms and I am wearing them when the cloud of moths descends from the sky.

This fine fly-tying desk is available, we are told, for $799, plus shipping and handling.

In other words, after you've tied your 350th blue-winged olive, which should take you no more than ten or fifteen years if you have other interests such as A JOB, the damn thing has paid for itself!

Another option is the wonderful fly tyer's desk made by the equally terrific George D. Roberts Co. of St. Louis, a desk available "in three sizes in oak, cherry, walnut or the wood of your choice." (My favorite is the wood from the rare Ply tree.)

This ad says your family will be proud to have this desk prominently displayed in the home and asks: "Why tie alone in a cold, damp basement or back room?"

Why, you might be wondering, would anyone tie flies alone in a cold, damp basement?

I'll tell you why.

Because your wife just found out you spent this kind of money on a friggin' fly-tying desk while her 1986 Dodge Dart keeps sending up a billowing cloud of orange smoke every time she steps on the gas pedal, her best shoes are held together with a tube of Goop, and a month ago you told her that new spatulas are too expensive and she can just turn the kids' pancakes with that broken yardstick that's in the closet.

Anyway, in an effort to make this section on fly tying more realistic, I will now clamp my own high-tech fly-tying vise to my computer desk and actually try to create some of the flies listed in a fly-tying book.

My vise, by the way, is an expensive English-made model hand-crafted and designed to hold even the tiniest hooks in a firm yet delicate way so as not to stress the fine metal of these hooks.

Oh sure, it may look like a clothespin glued to a sheet of wood from the Ply tree, but is NOT.

Okay, the first fly we will tie is called, I am not kidding, the "PMD Cripple." This fly imitates the pale morning dun and, as a bonus, gets those really good parking spaces right in front of the grocery store.

(Yipes. Was that insensitive, or WHAT?)

First, according to the book, we will tie the tail and body from pheasant tail. I will do this as soon as I get Max, my Labrador retriever, to stop shaking it.

Okay, now we'll make the thorax of the insect out of yellow Haretron dubbing. Haretron, as you might guess, is made from a rabbit, or hare.

(Dubbing is what they do to make Britney Spears's voice sound a little less like a cat getting its tail stuck under a rocking chair.)

The wing of the PMD Cripple is where things really get interesting. According to the book, the only material suitable for the wing is "coastal deer hair."

I am not kidding.

And I'm not sure how one gathers coastal deer hair. Although I'm guessing you might just wait on the beach and hope one washes up after being hit by a ship.

So I have made the tail and body from pheasant tail, lightly coated with dog spit, and tied to a No. 14 Tiemco TMC 100 hook, which is made in Japan by a sissy-guy who apparently couldn't hack the twenty-one-hour days in the Toyota factory anymore.

Then I wrapped the yellow Haretron dubbing and finished it

off with the coastal deer hair and voilà . . . I have created what appears to be a good-sized moth.

Perhaps that one was a bit too difficult. I'll try a "Hi-Vis Parachute."

Let's see here. This one—I swear I'm not kidding—will require a Tiemco TMC 101 hook, gray 8/0 thread, and . . . "hackle fibers from a grizzly bear."

(And I thought wrestling that pheasant out of my dog's mouth and yanking a feather out of the bird's ass was a big deal.)

I am reading this fly book, and frankly, I can't seem to find a single fly that can be tied without some degree of danger. The Iso Compara-Nymph, for example, calls for "mallard flank fibers dyed amber." I don't know what kind of company you hang out with, but frankly, I don't want to risk the good-natured ribbing I'd get if any of my friends caught me out in the swamp, rubbing amber dye or, to be honest, rubbing ANYTHING between a mallard's thighs.

Here's the Royal Double Wing, which requires brown elk hair (make sure not to use the *blue* elk hair that is commonly found on older elk, especially the ones living in Miami) and the following material for the wing: "belly hair from a white-tailed deer."

As I understand it, the accepted way to get this wing material is to dig a shallow hole, about six feet long, in a well-marked game trail. Lie down in the hole, facing up. Keep your hands ready. Then, at some time during the fall or early winter, when a white-tailed deer walks over you, reach up quickly toward the belly, grab a handful, and hang on.

(Important Footnote: If it's a big buck and you grab this handful after most of the deer's underbelly has passed by, especially during the rutting season, you'll *really* need to hang on.)

Finally, here's another fly, one that I have actually tied. It's called the Love Bug, a small bead-head emerger created by a noted fly angler and fly tyer who goes by the actual name of Trapper Badovinac. (Legend has it he got his name during college, when he actually chewed off his leg to get away from a blind date.)

Anyway, the Love Bug is tied on a tiny, No. 18-22 Tiemco hook and calls for a wing made of partridge feather. (I nearly killed myself when I fell out of the pear tree.)

And the thorax is made from beaver.

As I said, I've tied this fly. I actually used it once, on a stream near my Colorado home. I caught two nice rainbows in the first half hour. Then a knot broke and the fly was free from the tippet. Later that day, however, it came out of the river, gnawed down forty aspen trees, and built a huge dam.

I'm not kidding.

CHAPTER 22

In Which a Fish Flips Me the Bird

After you've been fly-fishing for a few decades, you start thinking you're pretty good at this sport.

You are not.

If you need proof of this, travel to famous tailwater fisheries such as Colorado's Frying Pan River or Taylor River. Stand at the big pools closest to the dams, put on Polarized sunglasses, and peer into the water. You will see trout that have reached stunning size by feeding on a steady diet of shrimp. (After twenty years of marriage, actress Rhea Perlman, who is married to four-foot-ten-inch actor Danny DeVito, also complains of a "steady diet of shrimp.")

Anyway, I've stood at these fly-fishing meccas and seen the beasts that lurk beneath the water. Rainbows mostly, outlandish trout of five and ten and fifteen pounds. Feeding. Constantly feeding. Moving back and forth in the current to inhale the tiny mysis shrimp that have been sucked from the reservoir and are now rushing from under the dam.

It's October of 1988. Having spent three days hunting elk, I need a break. Mostly, a break from listening to the damn elk bugling or "laughing" as they run away from me. So I find myself along the banks of the Frying Pan, which empties from Ruedi Reservoir, which is named for Ruedolph, the Red Nosed Reindeer. I think.

I start about a mile downstream of the dam and am having quite a good day, hooking and landing eight rainbows before noon, nice fish between fifteen and eighteen inches long. The aspens are a brilliant gold, the air is warm, and life is good.

Then a no-good son of a bitch named Lee shows up. He seems like a decent guy at first. We talk. Then he says if I really want to see some big trout, I should walk up to the pool just beneath the dam.

So I do.

I'm an idiot.

In the pool are trout that are so big it makes you gasp. Thirty inches long and more. Fat. Gigantic tails. And they're feeding. Slashing at things I cannot see, huge mouths opening and closing as they move back and forth in the current. Mysis shrimp, Lee the no-good $%^&*# had told me. White mysis shrimp. I had several in my fly box. Got to use light leaders, Lee had told me. My spools of tippet went all the way down to 8X, which, for those of you un-familiar with things such as line diameter and tensile strength, is the number-one choice of tippet among those who do not want to ever, ever land a fish because they make their hands all stinky.

I began by tying on shrimp-pattern fly to a section of 5X tippet, which is the lightest I generally use. It breaks if you sneeze too hard while casting. But on this river, at this pool, I might as well have been using clothesline rope.

The massive trout—I could seem them clearly; they fed vora-ciously within ten feet of me—actually swam *around* the leader to inhale more live shrimp. It was like stepping around your sleeping dog to get to the refrigerator—and then suddenly he awakens and bites you right on the back of the leg to get to the plate of ham you're carrying.

Sorry. I made that last part up.

Anyway, it was obvious the fish, which see hundreds and hun-dreds of idiots just like me every year sneaking around in L.L. Bean waders, were not interested in anything tied to 5X tippet. So I went to 6X, which the human eye cannot actually see, forcing us to pretend we are tying a knot and then hope for the best.

The trout ignored that, too.

So I went to 7X. On about the fiftieth cast, a monster I figure weighed ten pounds rose from the depths, moved to the shrimp pattern . . . and turned away. About fifty or so casts later, another, slightly smaller trout—probably a child of six pounds or so—did the same thing. They seemed interested—if two fish in one hun-dred casts can be called "interested"—in the dead-drifting shrimp I was offering.

But that leader . . .

I sat down for a while. I had the pool to myself on this weekday during a splendid Colorado elk season, so didn't risk losing my prime spot. I took out my spool of 8X tippet and laid it down on the ground beside me. I glanced at it, then looked away.

What kind of complete, utter, slobbering, stupid, brain-damaged moron, I thought, would attempt to hook and land one of these huge trout on 8X tippet?

Well, this far into the book I think we all know the answer to that question.

About fifteen minutes later, Dumbo waded back into the Frying Pan.

Trailing behind my fly rod was a long leader. At the end was a No. 18 white-mysis-shrimp fly pattern. Somewhere up ahead of that shrimp was three feet of 8X tippet, which I had tied to the rest of the leader by putting on a pair of thick magnifying eyeglasses and holding the two ends within about an inch of my nose as I fashioned the knot.

As I went back into the river, no matter how I squinted, I could not see the tippet that was attached to my small fly.

I had been trying to hook one of these trout for nearly three hours now.

And then, suddenly, a rainbow rushed at the shrimp. She came from about five feet away as my shrimp approached, her massive tail flicking in the clear water. Her mouth opened. My fly disappeared. I set the hook.

Often, it's hard to measure time. I recall watching Neil Armstrong poised on the final step of the *Eagle's* ladder after it had touched down on the moon in 1969. It seemed like Neil stayed on that step for a long, long time. It was about ten seconds.

My second marriage lasted fourteen years. It seemed like 1,500.

And I believe I had that trout on for about a minute that warm autumn day in the Frying Pan River in 1988. It was probably five or ten seconds. She moved to the left, and my five-weight rod bowed and strained. She moved back to the right and a bit upstream, and my reel sang. She came back downstream, to within maybe ten feet of me.

Then—and I'm pretty sure about this part—I think she gave me the finger.

The next thing I knew, some twenty feet of line had been stripped from my reel and then the weightless, slack line was drifting back downstream. She was gone. I never had a chance. None at all, really. It was like tying kite string to the back of Senator Ted Kennedy's belt, holding on to the other end, and pointing him toward an open bar.

So convincingly beaten was I that I did the same thing, with the same mysis-shrimp pattern and the same three-foot length of 8X tippet, *only five more times that day.*

Did I mention that I'm an idiot?

All five ended the same way the first encounter had. I'm sure the tiny barbless flies were easily dislodged from the gigantic trouts' lips when they returned to the bottom of the pool and gave a few shakes of their big heads.

That night, back at our elk-hunting cabin, I opened a bottle of whiskey and had a long drink. Then I started a grand blaze in the fireplace, put my feet up on a table, leaned back in my chair, and let out a contented sigh.

Then I threw that $%^&*# spool of 8X tippet right into the fire.

CHAPTER 23

Dave, the Dress, and the Brown Midge

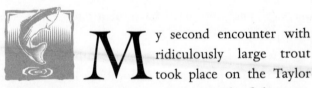y second encounter with ridiculously large trout took place on the Taylor River, below Taylor Reservoir just north of the town of Gunnison, Colorado. It was even worse, in the sense that it was exactly the same as the encounter on the Frying Pan River eight years earlier, except it lasted two days instead of just one.

It was the autumn of 1996. Once again, elk hunting was the excuse for a few days of fly-fishing. The Gunnison elk herd was elusive, running just barely ahead of me in the forest and, through some uncanny knack

---

honed by centuries of being hunted, leaving behind piles of four-week-old droppings.

So after three days I quit and picked up my fly rod. I knew of the pool of monster trout beneath the Taylor Dam. After a few years of living in Colorado, I had heard the quiet, muffled whispers in my local fly shop.

Rainbow trout.

Fifteen pounds and bigger.

Dave the night sales guy sometimes dresses in women's clothes.

Perhaps I heard too much. Nevertheless, I decided to go to the pool and have myself a good look-see, as they say in some rural areas and, of course, all of Arkansas.

The pool was deeper than the one on the Frying Pan, and the fish weren't as easy to spot. But if you sat high on the bank above the pool, they'd emerge from the darkness once in a while. I saw rainbow trout larger than any I'd seen on the Frying Pan. If you don't believe me, the same September 2001 issue of *Fly Fisherman* magazine that I have mentioned earlier has, on page 60, a photo.

The photo shows a man, perhaps in his early thirties, kneeling near the bank in the pool on the Taylor River. In his right hand is a rainbow trout's tail. In his left hand, which is about twenty inches away from his right hand, is a rainbow trout's stomach. Well beyond that left hand is the rest of the trout's stomach region, along with the gills and the head. It is, apparently, the same trout, very much alive and about to be returned to the water, the caption tells us.

The man is not identified in the caption. This is because of his desire to stay out of the spotlight and, of course, because he knows the rest of us who fly-fish would find him and try to choke

---

him. The caption reads: "Tough trout, such as this 10-plus pound Taylor River rainbow, are seldom easy to catch."

The magazine editors chose that carefully worded sentence because the word "Duh!" would not have filled the white space beneath the photo.

Back to October of 1996.

Having watched my spool of 8X tippet burn in the fireplace of the elk-hunting cabin eight years earlier—I would have thrown that $%^&*@ Lee into the fireplace, too, but he had the sense not to come around—the lightest tippet I now carried was a spool of Rio-brand 6X, which has a breaking point of 3.2 pounds.

Although I think it's good stuff, several years ago they made a feature-length film about a guy who kept snapping off nice trout with this brand of leader material and because he was a whiny, yuppy kind of guy, refused to believe it was his fault. The film was called *Blame It On Rio*.

Sorry.

So I got into the Taylor pool and watched these submarines rising to the surface, feeding not on mysis shrimp but apparently on, well, on nothing. No matter how close I got to the surface of the water, without an insect screen to capture and analyze the bugs, I could not see anything that would be causing these giants to sip from the surface.

Midges?

Here we will take a brief side trip into the world of midges. In fly-fishing magazines, midges are often photographed lying on coins as a way to show the smallness of them, if that's a word. You can fit dozens of them on a dime.

I've tried many times to fish with these midges, but on the first cast the dime always sails off into the shrubs.

Okay, enough of that side trip.

My fly box contained dozens of midges, red ones and black ones, all so small I had to pick them out with the tip of my forceps, which are delicate stainless-steel pliers used by fly anglers to remove hooks from fish and by surgeons for the obvious purpose: to pick a golf tee out of their bag on the first tee as you sit in their office miles away, reading a 1968 edition of *Reader's Digest*.

Anyway, I picked out a red midge I believe was a size 24, which is really small. For the rest of that day the huge rainbows in the Taylor River alternated between totally ignoring the red midges and totally ignoring the black midges. They were feeding on something, though. As the sun dipped below the mountains, another angler stopped by.

"They've been hitting brown midges," he said.

I wondered if anyone would find out if I threw him into the river.

Then I wondered if he was related to that $%^%&*# Lee over on the Frying Pan River.

I came back at about 10 A.M. the next day. I had a dozen brown midges that I'd purchased the previous evening in Gunnison, about twenty-five miles away.

I hooked two trout before noon.

One stripped nearly all of my fly line from the reel, sulked across the pool near the opposite bank for about forty-five seconds, and then the fly came loose. He jumped once on the way over. I'd guess he weighed seven or eight pounds.

Energized by this roaring success of having a trout on my line for nearly minute, I began making more drifts with the tiny brown midge. At about 11:30, all hell broke loose.

The fish took the fly just under the surface and a large area—a

RICH TOSCHES

146

very large area—of water turned white. He ran upstream into the heaviest flow of the river, then back to the other end of the pool some fifty yards away. This took approximately one second.

Then the fish headed back upstream and jumped. Drool actually escaped my mouth and ran down my chin. I no longer wanted to catch this fish. I just didn't want him to hurt me. If the first fish weighed seven pounds, well, this one was bigger. Much bigger. Maybe twice as big.

He kept making great spurts back and forth from the front of the pool to the back and from the opposite bank to within fifteen feet of my shaking knees, at which time I'd stand perfectly still because I was afraid he would notice me and attack me.

The tiny fly came loose after a while. The line just went dead and that was that.

My first thought? I looked at the net dangling from my vest, and I smiled. If the fish had stayed on, if somehow he had been subdued on this 6X tippet—my best hope seemed to be that maybe he'd have a heart attack—the net was a bit too small anyway. I think I might have gotten part of his head into it.

So now, speaking to you as a fly fisherman who has stood in some of the West's most prolific waters and come away with nothing to show for it except some vivid memories, snapped leaders, and a fear of large trout, I can say this:

6X.

That's the ticket.

CHAPTER 24

Snuggling with Misty Fiords

Eventually, this itch that is fly-fishing must be severely scratched, leaving you with quite a rash and a lot of ointments from the pharmacy, although I may be thinking of poison sumac.

The point is, after a while, if your blood runs thick with a love for this sport and your spine is made of graphite, your fly-fishing thoughts turn to the Big One.

I'm talking, of course, about Alaska—our thirty-fourth state, if you don't count West Carolina or East Dakota and I, personally, do not.

———

I was still living in Los Angeles when the first urge struck to fish in Alaska. I began planning a trip using three important criteria: the quality of the fishing, knowledgeable guides, and of course, finding someone else to pay for the entire thing.

I cannot stress enough the importance of that last one. A week at a decent lodge in Alaska will run you anywhere between $5,000 and $1.5 million, depending on whether or not you bring Ivana Trump with you. My first trip to Alaska or "America's Dairyland" was funded in part by *Sports Illustrated* magazine, which paid a handsome sum for an article on my adventure. As I understand it, the nation's premier sports magazine had quite a bit of money left over that year because of a high-level executive decision that said, basically, instead of hiring expensive experts as they'd done in the past, from now on the anemic swimsuit models would be responsible for brushing the sand out of their *own* butt cracks.

Anyway, the first of my three trips to Alaska brought me and my friends Larry Mascari and *L.A. Times* photographer Mike Meadows to the southern Alaska village of Ketchikan, which is a native Inuit fishing term and means, literally, "I have caught a can." We landed shortly after noon at the Ketchikan International Airport, which consists of a sandbar and a gift shop, and soon found ourselves at our lodge alongside the Misty Fiords National Monument. Misty Fiords, ironically, was also my high-school girlfriend, and while she was not an actual "national monument," I found out years later she was a "local treasure"—at least among about forty other guys in the senior class.

We walked down to the docks beneath our lodge, and as we gazed out across Alaska's famed Inland Passage—a maze of islands, seals, and majestic bird-poop-covered rocks—a group of killer whales surfaced no more than a hundred yards offshore, sending sprays of water high into the air by blowing air out of the holes in the tops of their heads, just the way Dan Quayle does when you force him to try to spell "potato."

The killer whales, we were told, were chasing salmon, which they would herd into big schools and then devour. I'd come a long way and was spending quite a bit of someone else's money to catch these salmon, so I began cursing and throwing large rocks at the whales before Larry and Mike wrestled me to the ground. In a tribute to this bravery in the face of the killer whales, a local Inuit elder who had been watching the whole thing said, in his native tongue, *"Terifik weik e mo, lare kirlaa"*—which I later found out meant, "Terrific, we get to spend a week with Mo, Larry, and Curly."

On the first day we set out onto the sound in an aluminum boat in search of the salmon. This was going to be quite difficult because, due to pollution and overfishing, there are only about 987 trillion salmon that swim into Alaskan waters each year. We were after king salmon, which look different from the dozen or so other species of salmon mostly because of the crown on their heads. And the British accent.

It didn't take long for us to hook into the powerful fish, with the three of us whooping and hollering as the thirty- and forty-pound salmon streaked across the calm sea. I was the only one using a fly rod, an eight-weight fiberglass rod that bent and shuddered with each screeching run by a salmon. It would often take as long as twenty minutes to subdue a big king on this rod, with Mike and Larry using spinning gear, reeling in each fish and then taking a nice nap while they waited for me.

But if you've ever hooked a big fish, a really big fish such as a striped bass or big bluefish or a king salmon, on a fly rod, you know why I was using this equipment and not spinning gear for my battle with the streaking fish.

That's right: I believed I was better than my two friends.

The highlight of the trip for me came a few days later when we boarded a float plane known as a Beaver—I tripped over the two big front teeth as I was climbing in—and headed into the remote bush country of Alaska, where, we were told, we'd find hungry trout in a pristine lake. The pilot was Charlie Ward, who was seventy-four years old and said he shuttled anglers into this remote country all the time, which made me confident. Making me a little less confident was the fact that the seventy-four-year-old Charlie also claimed he had, earlier that morning, dropped off President Millard Fillmore at the same lake.

The trip went well, though, Charlie swooping his Beaver low over the endless green forests before banking sharply and settling the pontoons onto the surface of a place he called Salmon Lake. I asked what kind of fish were in Salmon Lake and he said, seriously, "Trout."

I grinned and asked him what kind of fish we'd find in "Trout Lake."

He said he didn't know any place called Trout Lake and then he ignored me for three hours.

Alaskans are funny like that.

Charlie guided the plane toward the shore and we all hopped out in our hip boots. Charlie told Larry to "hold the plane for a minute" and handed him a long rope that was hooked to one of the pontoons. About ten minutes later—after I was pretty much done crying and screaming about how the bears would eat us and we'd never see our homes again—Charlie reappeared along the shoreline, carrying a very large rock.

He came back through the shallow water with the rock, plunked it onto one of the pontoons, grabbed the rope, wrapped it several times around the rock, and then dropped the boulder into the lake.

"The thing about float planes," said old Charlie Ward, who was not smiling at all, "is they never stop until you tie 'em to something."

We were speechless in the presence of such a wise man, so we just shut up and started fishing.

We had come to a stop near a gravel bar that extended perhaps two hundred feet into the lake, with deep water on both sides. I tied on a bright orange streamer, added a split shot to get it down a bit, and began casting.

And caught twenty-six trout on my first twenty-six casts. I am not kidding.

The trout were called dolly varden, a brightly colored species common in extreme northern waters such as in Alaska. (Dolly varden can be differentiated from Dolly *Parton* quite easily: when Dolly Parton heads upstream on her annual spawning run, she leaves two enormous trenches in the gravel on the river bottom. At least that's what the old Inuits say.)

If fly-fishing can be too easy—and it cannot—then this would have been that day. I caught trout with a fast retrieve and a slow retrieve. I caught trout when I just let the fly sink. I caught them deep and near the surface. For about fifteen minutes, I actually switched the rod to my left hand, made a series of feeble, awkward casts of about twenty feet, and caught trout that way, too. It was fun, but after a few hours I longed for a good, old-fashioned skunking, at least a cast or two without getting a sharp jolt from trout that had, apparently, not had anything to eat in about two years.

I wanted to catch nothing!

But I couldn't.

By noon, I estimated I'd made 150 casts and caught perhaps 125 trout. We released them all, so I began thinking that maybe there were only two or three trout in Salmon Lake, but they were *really* aggressive. I suggested this to Charlie Ward and his brow furrowed as he thought about it for a few seconds. Then he walked about thirty feet farther away from me and never said another word.

To my right, Larry and Mike had been catching trout, too, on their spinning rods. Larry was now making casts backward, over his head, and reeling the lure in that way and hooking a trout on most every cast. Mike was casting sideways, staring at the lush shoreline and a Forest Service cabin nestled in the woods, and was catching fish without looking.

Eventually we took a break and headed for the shore and the cabin, just to check it out. This plan was aborted as we got to shore and saw, in the soft muddy beach, footprints that were made either by a grizzly bear or Los Angeles Lakers' center Shaquille O'Neal.

(If it was indeed the great NBA basketball star, I'd really suggest he start trimming his toenails more often.)

The bear tracks were enormous, each one the same size as if a man had put his hands together, fingers to wrist, and pressed them into the soil. I know this because I did just that. As I stood there in the Alaskan wilderness, gazing in awe at the tracks in the mud, I had just one thought: "Man, I've got to wash this shit off my hands."

With a creepy feeling that perhaps I was being watched from the dense, dark forest by a thousand-pound bear, I scurried back into the lake toward the plane and tried to get over my uneasiness by catching about six hundred more trout before Charlie said it was time to go.

The Beaver shook as it roared across the lake and suddenly we were in the air again, headed for the lodge. Before I knew it I was back in Los Angeles. But even today I smile with the knowledge that on the final day of my first trip to Alaska, on one marvelous day in the bush of Alaska, I was almost as good a fisherman as those Vietnamese guys with the dynamite.

CHAPTER 25

Father and Son Share a Moment at the Dump

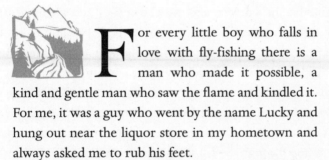

For every little boy who falls in love with fly-fishing there is a man who made it possible, a kind and gentle man who saw the flame and kindled it. For me, it was a guy who went by the name Lucky and hung out near the liquor store in my hometown and always asked me to rub his feet.

No, really, for me it was my father, Nick. He never fly-fished a day in his life, looking at the delicate nine-foot rod and thinking "Now there's something you're gonna slam in the damn car door, for chrissakes!"

But my father was always behind me. In my pursuit

of sports and my pursuit of writing and, frankly, in my pursuit of anything. He was a newspaper editor in Massachusetts for four decades and gave me my first job, which consisted of scraping the sticky paper off the composing room floor with a putty knife. That was thirty-eight years ago.

He still owes me $24.75.

Today he's retired, spending part of each day reading several newspapers, clipping out articles, and sending them to me in the fervent belief that I might find a way to change a word here and there and turn them into my own columns for my newspaper in Colorado Springs so I could be out of the office by noon every day.

He is a wise, wise man.

And when he did indeed purchase that $15 fly rod from his friend Porky Ferrara—okay, I didn't steal it—he backed up the gesture by looking at his goofy twelve-year-old kid the next day and asking "So now what?"

And then he'd drive me to the lake or the pond where I learned how to catch bluegills on a popper or perhaps fall off the dam when the trout struck the dry fly, and later to the West River, where he'd drop me off with my fly rod and my waders and offer words of encouragement such as "Don't drown, for chrissake!"

Sometimes he'd stay and watch—mesmerized, I think, by the sight of his young boy and the graceful motion of the fly rod, the line slicing through the air alongside a New England stream. You could sense the emotion in his voice when he'd shout, "For chrissakes, you're gonna put your eye out with that thing!"

And then he'd leave, probably heading back to the newspaper office for a few hours of work as I stayed and learned the graceful art of fly-fishing.

———

RICH TOSCHES

158

And most of the time he'd remember to come back and pick me up.

The summer that I got the fly rod, my father asked if I'd like to take a trip with him. Maybe we'd drive up to Maine, he said. And so he bought a huge blue-and-white canvas tent, stuffed it into the trunk of his 1967 Mercury—the fly rod had a safe spot on the backseat—and the two of us left on a ten-day road trip, an adventure that still lingers in my mind today, a magical journey of a young boy and a father who didn't know it when they set out that first day, but who were linked by a powerful bond: Neither of them had any idea how to put up a tent.

The trip brought us north out of Boston along the rugged coast and into Portland, where we turned inland through Lewiston to the town of Mexico—yes, there is an actual place called Mexico, Maine—where we stopped for lunch. We both had the special: moose burritos.

It was right after lunch that we came upon the most exciting thing I had ever seen that did not have a centerfold stapled into the middle of it. It was the Androscoggin River, which combines the native Maine Indian words *Andro* ("land") and *scoggin* ("that L.L. Bean hasn't purchased yet").

The Androscoggin was wider and deeper and faster than any river I had ever seen. It was wide enough that I could not throw a stone across it, although I kept trying until the guy fly-fishing on the opposite shore yelled, "Hey, you little bastard!"

I had no clue whatsoever as to how to fly-fish such a place, a river fast enough and deep enough that I knew only one thing: If I even tried to put my waders on, signaling that I was going to enter the water, my father would have tackled me and thrown me into the trunk with the tent.

———

ZIPPING MY FLY

So I left the waders in the car and rigged up my fly rod, choosing a large black woolly bugger and adding a couple of split shot. I cast and cast for more than an hour without a strike, and then, suddenly, as the streamer swung toward the bank in the heavy current, the rod doubled and nearly came out of my hands. A huge fish moved out into the current and headed downstream, and because I had never felt anything so powerful, I clamped my fingers onto the fly line and heard the eight-pound test leader snap.

It had all happened so fast I hadn't even yelled. I walked back to the car, where my father had a map opened on the hood and told him I'd lost one.

"Yeah?" he asked, looking up. "You probably horsed him."

Ah, "horse this" I was thinking, although I did not actually say that to him. I know that because I am still alive, writing this book.

But as I took the fly rod apart and set it on the backseat and climbed back into the front with my dad, my hands still trembled from that brief encounter with a big trout. As we headed out of the town of Mexico and turned onto Highway 142, passing through the small Maine towns of Carthage and Madrid, I remember having this thought—a powerful thought that would lead me into a lifetime of passionate fly-fishing: "Mexico? Carthage? Madrid? Where the hell are we?"

Anyway, we drove on in the Mercury, which was so big we could have pitched tent in it before we'd left the house. Turns out that wouldn't have been a bad idea. In the late afternoon we pulled into the town of Rangeley, which my dad said he'd found earlier on the map and had actually been *trying* to find. I believed him, which was quite a milestone in our relationship.

I'd doubted him on all travel-related matters since a few years earlier when, on a car trip to Florida with three kids stuffed in the backseat, he ran out of gas on a Georgia cotton plantation. After walking quite a distance to a house and finding no one home—he let me walk along with him despite the fact I was only eight, probably in case they had a big dog—he left a five-dollar bill under a rock on the doorstep and filled a big can with gasoline from a pump near the barn.

After the long walk back, he poured the gasoline into the tank and cranked up the Pontiac. I can still remember turning in the backseat to watch the billowing cloud of black smoke that poured from the exhaust pipe as he drove away that day—and reminding myself that when I got big and had my own car, I would never, ever pour two gallons of diesel fuel into it like my daddy had just done.

I told him later that I saw the word *diesel* handwritten on the pump by the barn, but didn't know what it meant. My dad, kind and understanding at all times, was even more so in critical times such as this. When I told him about seeing that "diesel" word on the pump, I remember him looking at me with those understanding eyes and saying "Jesus Christ, you coulda said something, for chrissakes, dammit to hell!"

Somehow, we made it to Miami, where we spent two terrific weeks, a million memories tucked away in the mind—although for me, about 900,000 of those memories are of watching my father walk along the beach dressed in shorts, black shoes, and black socks.

Anyway, we were in Maine now and pulled into the town of Rangeley during the late afternoon. We stopped at the general store in the little town and bought a couple of sodas. Dad explained to the man behind the counter that we were on a fishing and camping trip. Dad inquired about nearby campgrounds and then asked what there might be to do around town.

"Well," the old man said from behind the counter. "You could go out to the dump and watch the beahs!"

This was Mainese, and meant "bears."

I thought this was a great idea: Let's take the twelve-year-old awkward kid down to the dump to play with the bears.

First, however, there was the simple matter of pitching the tent. So we worked together, both of us huffing and puffing and pulling on this and pulling on that, and surprisingly, within half an hour we had the tent out of the trunk.

We spread it on the ground at the campsite, turning it so the door faced the picnic table. Then dad looked at the gigantic pile of aluminum poles on the ground. Then he looked at me. Then we both looked back at the pile of tent poles. If we had any sense at all, we would have stuffed everything back into the trunk and gone home.

We started messing around with the poles, which slid in and out of other poles and went through Flap A and connected to Center Pole D and Awning Support F—although a lot of that information came the following week when we got home and read the instruction booklet, which *someone* had left in the basement.

I still have that blue-and-white tent. It's in my garage, in the original box. And almost every summer my kids make me take it out and we set it up in the backyard and they sleep in it.

I've told them the history of the tent, and now, whenever we begin setting it up, one of my two lovely sons will say, "Look, I'm Grandpa!" and then he'll kick the pile of poles across the yard and yell, "Dammit to hell!"

Oh, how we laugh.

———

RICH TOSCHES

Anyway, somehow my dad and I got the tent set up. It took about three hours. And at dusk, with camp set, we got back into the car and headed for the Rangeley Town Dump, which was about five miles up a dirt road. And within ten minutes of our arrival, the black bears came out of the woods. Six of them.

My father, Mr. Newspaper Guy, reached into the backseat and pulled out his always ready camera, which did not have any type of telephoto lens, and said I should get out and take some pictures.

I am not kidding.

Once I was outside, with the bears some fifty feet away rifling through the garbage, my father, who stayed in the Mercury, actually said this:

"Get closer!"

A few weeks later, the *Milford Daily News* ran a photograph of bears at a dump in Rangeley, Maine. The credit line read *"Daily News* photo by Richard Tosches." In the photo, one of the bears was very close and you could see it holding its head up, sniffing the air.

Almost as if he had caught the scent of urine in a twelve-year-old kid's pants.

We stayed near Rangeley for three days and discovered gigantic Rangeley Lake. I caught a few trout on my fly rod, Dad caught a few more with his spinning outfit, and we ate trout over the campfire at night. I do not like the taste of trout. I have not eaten one since that night in Maine in 1967. In the years since, we've had a lot of conversations about this idea of catch-and-release. Dad still keeps a trout or two when he fishes and I'm okay with that. But he cannot understand why I release every trout I catch.

"They're good eatin'," he'll say. "Why the hell would anyone go fishing if they won't eat 'em?"

I tell him I do it because I love being in the water, that I love the feeling of being in pristine places where wild trout swim, that I love watching a big trout rise to the surface and sip the tiny fly, perhaps one I have created myself, and feeling the thrill of the fight on the delicate fly rod. I tell him I love knowing that if I do everything just right, I get to watch a large rainbow slide into my net.

"Yeah," he'll say, in that kind and caring way. "I guess I know what you mean.

"Although you could still eat him."

CHAPTER 26

Call Me Ishmael

I would like to pick up the telephone each and every day for the rest of my parents' lives and call them so I could thank them for all they've done for me, and for kindling the fire that became my passion for this sport called fly-fishing. Although quite frankly, after about a month of this, I'm guessing my father would get his phone bill and shout, "Where'd all these collect calls come from, for chrissakes?"

But on my first trip to Alaska with my friends Larry and Mike, I thought about how much my mom and dad meant to me. And I sat on a rock in the majesty that surrounded me and I had the following thought:

"Good God, grizzly-bear scat tastes awful!"

Then I spit it out and looked around to see if anyone had been watching me.

Seriously, another thought I had on my first trip to Alaska was that somehow, someway, I had to bring my father to that stunning land.

A few years later I did.

Although technically, if you're the kind of person who has to factor in who paid for what, he took *me*.

He arrived in Los Angeles after a flight from Boston and we left the next day, headed for Anchorage on Alaska Airlines. My father is not what you'd call "crazy" about flying, in the sense that he believes every plane he ever gets on will "crash" into a remote part of a "forest" where he, as the only survivor, will be eaten by "squirrels."

But as we looked out through the airport terminal window and saw the gigantic face of an Eskimo painted on the tail section of the Alaska Airlines jet, I could tell his confidence level was at an all-time high by the way he said, "What the hell kind of picture is that to put on an airplane?"

We got on anyway, and in a few hours the plane began its descent into the Anchorage airport, which is surrounded by towering mountains, a descent that basically involves the pilot turning off the engines and allowing the plane to drop faster than the pants of a former president who we will just call Bill.

Dad loved this part of the trip.

Today, some fifteen years later, I'm guessing the FBI crime-lab people could still find Alaska Airlines seat fibers under his fingernails.

———

RICH TOSCHES

But the best part was yet to come. This was the part in which we had to crawl through the door of a tiny airplane for a forty-five-minute flight to the lodge, the plane zooming over the spectacular Kenai Peninsula as the giant rubber band unwound and spun the propeller.

The pilot had put Dad and me in the two backseats of the nine-passenger jet, aware of the need for perfect weight balance on the light craft and, of course, instinctively knowing that if we were seated anywhere near the door, my father would, at some point, try to open it and leap out.

But everything went just fine and soon we arrived at the airport in a town called Homer, which was named for the ancient Greek writer Homer and philosopher Ulysses.

We were greeted at the airport by a representative of the Ninilchik Lodge and soon found ourselves in a van, passing lush forests and breathtaking views of Cook Inlet, which was named for the explorer who discovered the area: Homer.

I cannot begin to write the words that could possibly describe the setting of the Ninilchik Lodge except to say it sits right on the beach at the edge of a forest of towering pines, the gentle waves of the inlet lapping rhythmically on the gravel-lined shore as eagles soar overhead. It evokes a feeling of great serenity and yet at the same time an adrenaline rush of adventure sweeps over all who have ever set foot in this amazing spot.

Anyway, my father and I stood there for several moments without saying a word, taking in the most incredible view either of us had ever seen—if you don't count a black bear chasing a kid through a dump as his father shouts, "Don't drop the goddamn camera!!!!"

This would be our home for the next five days. Beyond the beach, out there in the emerald-colored waters of Cook Inlet, swam tens of thousands of king salmon—fish that had spent three or four years growing to outlandish size in the rich waters of the Pacific and had returned in a remarkable display of determination to the place they were created, thirty- and forty- and fifty-pound fish which now had only one thing on their minds: avoiding getting a mouthful of cheap ashes flicked relentlessly over the side of a boat by this strange creature who kept saying "Look, it's another eagle, for chrissakes!"

We made our way to our room and stowed our gear, which included the fiberglass Shakespeare Wonder Rod that my father had purchased for me some twenty years earlier. The Wonder Rod had seen many remarkable things in those two decades—from a salmon from hell in a small creek that emptied into the waters of Green Bay, Wisconsin, to the furious bonito of Redondo Beach, California.

The Wonder Rod, however, had never seen anything quite like what it was about to see in these waters of Alaska.

(Here I briefly considered writing the rest of the book from the perspective of the Shakespeare Wonder Rod, but was dissuaded from this approach by my literary agent, Chip MacGregor, who said in his calm and soothing way, "Are you a moron, or what?")

Later in the evening, after watching more than a dozen eagles land on the beach, we gathered at the dinner table at the Ninilchik Lodge with a few other guests and learned about the history of the place. Ninilchik, we were told, is a native word meaning, well, it means something. I should have paid more attention, but the history session made me flash back to my carefree days of high school and I found myself looking out the window and daydreaming—a daydream that ended suddenly when the lodge owner shrieked, leaped out of his seat, pulled a thumbtack out of his ass, and spent the rest of the meal staring pointedly at me.

We would be fishing, we were told, from large aluminum boats. We would troll and drift mostly, which was the accepted way of taking these heavyweights. But there would be opportunities to cast a fly, too, and I was excited by that prospect.

Not as excited, I would find out, would be the other guys in the boat—who didn't much care to have a gigantic, brightly colored streamer fly with a huge hook whipped back and forth just over their heads by a guy who had, during the wildlife discussion at that first dinner, asked, "So, like, do the birds that *have* hair make fun of the bald eagles?"

Turns out there would be no fly-fishing from the boats, but the Wonder Rod would have its moments.

Anyway, after dinner we stood on the beach and watched the midsummer Alaska sun try to set, but it never really did. To the west, across Cook Inlet, stood two active volcanoes named Iliamna and Redoubt. Iliamna had been spitting smoke for months, and each night the sun would briefly dip beneath the chain of mountains and the volcanoes, the fading sunlight turning the volcanic smoke and sparkling water into an unforgettable painting of red and gold light.

At noon the next day—we slept a bit late; it was still light out when we finally got to bed at about 1 A.M.—the rod jerked violently and then bent nearly double and my father held on for dear life as line screeched from the reel and he said, I'm not kidding, "Christ, I think I've got one!"

We reeled in the other lines as this battle unfolded and I sat there watching my father in the fish fight of his life, a huge smile on his face, and at this moment a son who was now thirty gazed upon the sight of his father sitting beside him in a boat in this marvelous land called Alaska and wondered if he had ever found the beer cans and the condom wrappers I left under the seat of his Mercury when I was in high school, which I thought was an odd thought to have at that moment.

The salmon fought hard in the ice-cold water, tearing off fifty feet of line in seconds and then grudgingly giving some of it back before making another run, and another. My father's smile had turned to a grimace as I offered all the usual words of encouragement fishing partners give each other:

"Keep the rod tip up!"

"He's getting tired!"

"Don't horse him!"

"Your cigar ash has fallen onto your shirt, which is now smoldering!"

After beating out his chest fire, Dad worked the fish closer and closer to the boat and then the guide slid a huge net under the fish and hoisted him from the water, a silver giant of thirty-five pounds or so that posed for a picture with my again-smiling dad and then was released to continue his epic journey to the stream of his birth, where he would find a mate and complete the amazing cycle of a salmon's life. (See *beer cans and condom wrappers* above.)

"Christ, that's a big fish!" my father said. According to my records, this was the 845,987th time in my lifetime that my father had invoked the name of our savior, with 223,346 of those involving his attempted use of a hammer. (Another 1,092 times involved his inability tear a piece of duct tape from the roll.)

We headed south a bit and soon saw a flottill . . . flotila . . . floatyla—a big bunch of boats, perhaps fifty or more, from thirty-footers to inflatable rafts. The bunch of boats was gathered about a half mile offshore, where a river named Deep Creek emptied into the inlet. Deep Creek, we were told, was the birthplace of millions and millions of salmon, and now the tough ones that had survived their long stay in the ocean were coming home.

The incredible salmon are able to smell and identify the fresh water that was their birthplace—detecting even a drop of the fresh water that has been diluted in billions of gallons of salt water, according to biologists. And so they gather at the threshold of their homes and wait until the right moment, when the urge to spawn has become uncontrollable, before suddenly making a mad rush into the river.

This is not entirely unlike the way President Clinton used to wait outside the Intern Break Room in the White House—and I hereby vow not to make another joke about Mr. Clinton unless I think of one.

Alaskan fishing regulations prohibit anglers from getting too close to the mouth of some of the prime spawning rivers—the guide said the no-fishing zone at Deep Creek extended out five hundred yards—to offer the majestic fish a final bit of security on their long journey. So we stayed outside the zone and began the most incredible three hours of fishing imaginable, as giant king salmon slashed at baitfish near the surface in their final feeding frenzy before they entered the river. At that point they would stop eating, begin blindly chasing complete strangers around so they might have sex, and then shrivel up in a pathetic sort of way and slowly die.

(For more information on that subject I suggest the new book *Hugh Hefner: The Autumn Days.*)

Anyway, we hooked ten salmon in those three hours, three of them twenty-pounders and half a dozen that weighed more than thirty pounds. And then I hooked Moby Salmon.

The strike nearly tore the rod from my hands, a stunning, crashing attack that brought me out of my seat and nearly into the frigid water before I steadied myself and watched the line disappearing from the reel. The guide shouted an obscenity and turned the boat and began to give chase. For twenty minutes the battle raged, with the enormous salmon sounding deep beneath us and then suddenly surging away in a display of raw speed and power. He came slowly to the boat in the final minutes of the battle and the guide somehow got most of the fish into the huge net. He was forty-eight inches long. He weighed, the guide said, fifty-five pounds or more.

And even though I hadn't gotten the chance to battle such a monster on a fly rod as I would have liked—I'm sure the battle would have been brief, but I was okay with that—I got to do something just as exciting. I got to let the monstrous king salmon go. I removed the hook, wrapped both hands around his tail, and waited until the oxygen in the cold water had revived him. Then he slammed his massive tail against the side of the boat, sending a wall of water over my father and me, and he was gone.

The fishing seemed less important after that. We caught a few more but nothing to rival the Big One. As the evening sun crept across the sky toward Mount Redoubt and Mount Iliamna, another sight brought a memorable ending to our first day on this marvelous trip.

A man alone in a twelve-foot inflatable raft had hooked a big salmon. And on the calm waters of Cook Inlet, the fish began swimming west, away from the shore, taking the man and his raft on what I'm sure was an unforgettable trip, moving the craft steadily, relentlessly, toward the middle of the thirty-five-mile-wide inlet. Forty-five minutes after we watched the man hook into the giant, his raft had become just a small red dot on the western horizon.

And through my binoculars I could see that it was still moving.

CHAPTER 27

The Salmon Smoked Me

 mentioned earlier that I got a few
opportunities to unsheathe the
Wonder Rod during this trip to
Alaska with my father. After determining that it was
too dangerous to use in the small boat, a guide said
that often, right in front of the lodge, the king salmon
would cruise the shoreline in search of the herring
that would fill their bellies for the final time.

So I sat on the deck with the guide one night and
asked if anyone had ever tried pitching a big streamer
fly at them from the shore. He said there had been only
one guy in his four years at the lodge who had tried it.

————

175

"He'd come back at night looking pretty beat up," Tom the guide said. "He never actually caught one, but he had a helluva time trying."

I wanted a helluva time.

The next evening, after yet another meal that made my own personal ass about three inches wider, I took the Wonder Rod out of its case, which consisted of a five-foot tube of heavy plastic PVC pipe. Before the trip I had loaded 150 yards of twenty-five-pound Dacron backing onto the huge, heavy Pflueger reel. Now I fashioned an eight-foot leader of fifteen-pound test monofilament, tied on a four-inch silver-and-white streamer, and headed down to the beach.

The sun was perched between the volcanoes on the opposite shore, beginning its breathtaking nightly dance of colors. About a hundred feet to my left a pair of bald eagles were squawking over a fish carcass. I sat down on the gravel beach and took it all in, gazing at the eagles for a while and then letting my eyes wander back out to the shimmering water.

Which suddenly exploded.

Some hundred yards down the beach and maybe fifty feet offshore a great burst of water had broken the placid scene. There were seals in the area, and killer whales, too, so at first I didn't know what had caused the commotion. And then a huge silver shape crashed through the surface and came back down with a great splash. Salmon.

I lurched to my feet, moving quickly now toward the splashing, which was coming toward me. I stopped, stripped off as much line as I felt I could throw and double-hauled the line and the giant streamer as far as I could, and waited. When the salmon moved closer I stripped the line back toward me. The water boiled where I knew my fly was skimming under the surface. I stripped again and another monstrous boil surged up behind the fly.

With my heart beating wildly I began stripping line madly, hoping the salmon would be enticed by the sight of the fur-and-feather herring trying to escape. And as I stripped the line a wave came up behind the fly, a wall of water maybe a foot high that began picking up speed. A wave generated by a big salmon as he rushed toward the fly. And then half of his body came out of the water and he struck.

Remember the day when I was kid and was floating a dry fly on the pond at the Nipmuc Rod and Gun Club and the trout came after it and I fell off the dam? Well, that had been two decades earlier, and now, with uncountable hours of experience, I am proud to report that I did NOT fall off a dam.

What I did do was jerk the big streamer away from the monstrous salmon in an adrenaline-laced seizure, stumble backward over a chunk of driftwood, and fall on my back onto the gravel. I looked up in time to see the two eagles, the symbol of America, beating their wings wildly and taking flight to get away from what they probably believed was a seal on crack flopping around on their beach, making the usual sound that a seal on crack makes, a call of nature which sounds like: "Soonoofabitch . . . soonof-faBITCH," as the big mammal struggles to stand up.

The fly line was piled in a heap to my right, the big fly was about fifteen feet farther up the beach, and as you might have guessed, I did not hook that salmon.

Another school of salmon cruised near the beach about forty-five minutes later and I made a few feeble casts, but frankly, my heart wasn't in it anymore. Something told me that when the next salmon made one of those frightening rushes at my fly, I would once again panic, stumble backward, and fall heavily to the ground.

Although, avid fly fisherman that I am, something deep in my soul also told me it would sure be fun to keep trying.

So I thought I'd ask around at the lodge and see if I could borrow a fly-fishing helmet.

The days at Ninilchik Lodge passed much too quickly, even with an extra day that Dad and I got by strategically missing our scheduled flight from Homer to Anchorage. And much too soon the trip had come to an end. It could not have been a better journey.

And I could not have picked a better partner.

CHAPTER 28

Alaska: Even Our Mosquitos Have Pontoons

 ow that I'd made two trips to Alaska, including one with my father, who will always be my number-one fishing partner, I began thinking of a third trip. This one, I thought, should involve the guy I've fished with since childhood, the guy who ate the cow's face near Vail, the guy who now works in a very high-profile law-enforcement capacity in Colorado and would be quite embarrassed to read in this book about a certain someone being arrested in 1972 for having what turned out to be fourteen stolen pumpkins in the trunk of someone's 1965 Ford Mustang.

———

But I would never do that to him.

Anyway, in 1988 I'd talked to my friend Rob about making a trip to Alaska and he actually frothed at the mouth. The big day finally came in August of 1989. I flew from Los Angeles to Seattle and he flew from Denver to Seattle.

Boy, were our livers tired.

The trip would take us about a hundred miles northwest of Anchorage to the tiny, remote, water-bound village of Skwentna (town motto: "Even Our Mosquitoes Have Pontoons"). I had secured another magazine job to pay for this trip, and the editors allowed me to bring my friend Rob along because of his reputation as an outdoor and wildlife photographer. Though he had never actually, in technical photojournalism terms, "taken a picture while outdoors," I knew he'd be a fast learner and that, more importantly, we'd laugh our asses off for a week in Alaska.

Rob met me as I entered the Seattle-Tacoma airport, and as we walked I knew he was taking this job as photographer seriously because of the way he was mumbling under his breath, "Shiny glass thing is called the lens. Lens points toward the thing you're taking a picture of. Shiny glass thing is the lens . . ."

When we were younger, Rob and I often had what we called "laughing fits"—great, racking uncontrollable bouts of laughter often brought on by nothing. The fits could last thirty seconds or thirty minutes, two kids gasping for air as the fit took on a life of its own, causing its own laughter like a nuclear fission reaction.

Anyway, it was just a childhood thing long ago forgotten as we headed to our next flight with our fly-rod cases tucked under our arms. Soon we'd found our seats on an Alaska Airlines jetliner for the trip to Anchorage, and as we settled in, I mentioned to Rob that perhaps when we got to Alaska we should shoot a grizzly bear in the ass with a tranquilizer dart and then humiliate him by putting things on him such as sunglasses, and then have our pictures taken with him.

But we were adults now, the silliness of youth long abandoned for lives of raising children and paying mortgages. So imagine our surprise when the other passengers began staring at us. Some even moved away.

"And after we drug him we could put his fat ass in a lawn chair . . ."

A flight attendant stopped by to see if we were okay.

"And put a beer in his paw."

"I bet we could get pants on him!!!!"

The howling subsided somewhere over Canada, and we slumped into our seats with sore ribs and watering eyes and stuff coming out of our noses.

We don't know why we laugh this way. We know from years of experience that few other people believe that whatever we are laughing at is funny. We have been criticized for this behavior by friends and family. "For Christ's sake, when are you two gonna grow up?" is the one we hear a lot. (Once I answered that question by saying, "Personally, I believe it will be Thursday"—and we laughed for twenty-six minutes.)

Anyway, I cannot imagine two people who have ever laughed as hard and as long for so many years as Rob and I have.

Unless, of course, you count the two doctors who had treated Monica Lewinsky for carpet burns and then heard President Clinton declare, under oath, "I did not have sex with that woman!"

Somehow the pilot had refrained from joining Rob and me in

this roaring fit, opting instead to continue flying the airplane toward Anchorage. At some point we caught our breath and looked out to see the mountains and glaciers of Alaska. The glaciers were the most impressive. When something is carrying tons and tons of ice and is moving at the speed of one inch every twelve hours, marching relentlessly toward the ocean, you know you are in Alaska. Although it's also possible you are watching Senator Ted Kennedy walking out of the family compound on Cape Cod with another gin and tonic.

The plane began a steep descent into the Anchorage airport, and before we knew it we were in a cab, headed for a nearby airstrip named Merrill Field, where we'd arranged to catch an early evening Cessna flight to Skwentna. Plans had changed, however, and we were told by our pilot that we wouldn't be leaving until the morning. I feared the magazine had conducted a background check and discovered that of the nine photographs Rob had taken in his entire life, six contained the image of his thumb, and that the deal was off.

Turns out it was just a mix-up between the pilot and the lodge, and we'd leave at 7:30 the next morning.

So we got back into the cab and spent that night in Anchorage, at the lovely Voyager Hotel. We had a lovely meal in the evening. Rob had Alaskan halibut, which he said "didn't taste like fish," and I had prime rib, which also didn't taste like fish. We got back to the hotel at about midnight and Rob actually said he'd go to sleep with "visions of salmon dancing in my head."

I had to settle for visions of the seven Moose Head beers I had at dinner dancing in my bladder.

We were out of the hotel by 6:30 A.M. and met our Cessna pilot, Lois, at Merrill Field. Neither Rob nor I had ever flown in a

Cessna before, so we had a lot of questions for Lois. I opened with, "So, Lois, how the hell could you not have figured out that Clark Kent was Superman?"

No, really, we asked about the plane and the flight, learning that we'd be flying in a Cessna Cardinal. (The giveaway was that the safety information cards in the seat pockets were written in Latin, and the plane itself had a big red hat.) We would be traveling at about 140 miles per hour, Lois told us, and the flight to Skwentna would take "just thirty-five minutes, or less." Lois then added that "less" would be the case if the plane crashed before it got to Skwentna. Alaskan pilots joke around like that. Rob and I, who have laughed about such varied topics as shooting bears in the ass with darts and eating a cow's-face burrito, found no humor whatsoever in Lois's comment.

The talk then turned to mosquitoes and Lois laughed. "I start slapping myself when I even think about Skwentna," she said.

By way of comparison, I start slapping myself when I even think about ever getting married again.

Lois continued the comedy routine a few minutes later when she pointed out the left side of the plane and said, "There's the airport." Beneath us, in the dense spruce forest, was a tiny strip of land where the trees had been removed, apparently by beavers. A Skwentna mosquito wouldn't be able to land on it, never mind this Cessna airplane, and Rob and I laughed along with Lois right up until she jerked the steering wheel to the right, dropped the plane out of the sky like a rock, and thumped down on the beaver clearing and said, "Welcome to Skwentna!"

Rob was frightened, speechless, and bug-eyed, but not me. I am much tougher and more rugged than Rob, and so I laughed a long and hearty laugh—and would have laughed even louder and longer, but at this point the urine had soaked through my shorts and pants, and one of my boots.

When the plane rolled to a stop we stumbled out and began removing our bags and fly-rod cases, our minds filled with a million questions. Rob looked at me and posed the first one.

"Did . . . did . . . did we just *crash*?"

Turns out we hadn't, that it was a very typical landing on this patch of dirt that served as the Skwentna airport. We'd been waiting for about ten minutes—Rob looking at his camera and wondering where the film went in, me blowing on my boot to dry it out—when Skwentna Roadhouse lodge owner John Logan showed up, accompanied by two guides, Ray Douglas and T. W.

They had roared through the woods on three all-terrain vehicles carrying three fishermen from Switzerland who had spent the week at the roadhouse and would now be leaving on Lois's plane. We spoke for a few moments with the departing Swiss anglers, not long enough to get to know them but long enough for us to ask them a few critical questions. Rob went with, "So, you guys have those army knives? Can I play with the toothpick and the scissors?"

Being the more intellectual of the two, I apologized for my friend's stupid questions and inquired as to whether they had "brought their own cheese."

The Swiss men climbed into the Cessna then, leaving Rob and me with what I assume was a warm Swiss farewell word ("arsehools") and Ray and T. W. began tossing our stuff onto the four-wheelers. They looked around as they worked, and before we sped off, Ray explained their nervousness.

"Grizzly ate a fisherman two weeks ago, about forty miles from here," he said. "Ate him. They found a sock."

Having some expertise in this area, I told the men the bear had probably spit out that one sock because it was, in all likelihood, the sock the man had peed in during the flight to the fishing camp.

I went on to tell them that if the searchers looked hard enough, they'd probably find the man's pants and shorts not too far away.

They just stared at me for a few moments. In the rough bush country of Alaska, admiration and respect must be earned.

I had struck quickly.

CHAPTER 29

Dick Butkus Smells Like a Fish

The Skwentna Roadhouse was charming, a two-story structure made of logs hacked from the nearby forest and painted red, apparently so you can find it easily when a bear is chasing you. Inside we met John's wife, Joyce, who would cook for us for five days and, in this land far from our homes, become somewhat of a mother figure to us. One night, for example, I didn't finish my vegetables and she sent me to bed early despite my whiny, childlike protest. "For chrissakes, Joyce, I'm thirty-six!" were my exact words.

Then she washed my mouth out with soap and said I couldn't keep the puppy.

We gathered that morning at the breakfast table and were told of the great salmon runs that sweep up the Skwentna River and a dozen smaller rivers and streams nearby. Hundreds of thousands of salmon, all of them in a spawning frenzy and eager to attack anything, according to Ray, "bright and flashy and gaudy and cheap looking."

And boy, was he right! On the first day I tied on an eight-by-ten color photograph of Britney Spears and caught 1,456 salmon before noon.

Skwentna, we were also told, is a stop on Alaska's famed Iditarod dogsled race, with thousands of dogs racing up the frozen river and often stopping here for food and a brief rest on their monumental journey. Then, in the spring, as the stunningly cold winter begins to break and the ice begins to thaw, another monumental Alaskan journey takes place: tons of Siberian husky crap washes down the Skwentna River a hundred miles into Anchorage. As I understand it, the fumes from this four-month-old floating dog crap creates gas clouds that float high above the city, creating an eerie nighttime illusion known as the "Northern Lights" or "Aurora Borealis" or "Sasquatch."

Our fishing journey would begin by traveling up the Skwentna River, a magical place of pools and eddies and fast-moving currents, a special river where, according to native Alaskan legend, *salmas tas dogj paap* ("the salmon taste like dog poop").

We piled onto a four-wheeler for the short trip from the roadhouse to the river and then found ourselves in a sixteen-foot boat, screaming across the raging Skwentna River, the boat powered by a Yamaha-brand jet outboard motor as Ray expertly guided the craft between gigantic logs and floating trees torn from the shore by the surging river. The Skwenta was full of salmon, he told us, but the volume of heavy, brown water roaring down the two-hundred-foot-wide river made it unfishable. So we'd use the Skwentna as our highway, traveling to dozens of tributaries where the water flowed clear and cold.

The temperature was about 42 degrees that morning, and combined with the speed of the boat, this created a pleasant windchill factor I estimated at 1,786 degrees below zero—using a complicated mathematical formula that includes temperature, wind speed, humidity, and how many minutes go by before you can no longer feel your testicles.

As we zoomed along I sat in the front of the boat, bravely serving as a windbreak for my friend Rob, who huddled behind me in the middle seat deftly ducking the snot-cicles that were breaking off the end of my nose and hurtling back toward him.

After about half an hour Ray slowed the Hypothermia Express and slid the boat into a seventy-five-foot-wide river that emptied into the Skwentna. Soon, after determining that at least one of my testicles was still in the boat, I picked up my fly rod and began casting a bright orange streamer toward the bank.

When a trout sips a dry fly floating on a placid stream or creek, it is a wonderful thing, the gentle rise of the fish as the fly disappears in a small splash. It speaks of the serenity and peace that we all long for in this ever-changing world of ours. When, on the other hand, a salmon hits a fly, it's like Hall of Fame Chicago Bears' linebacker Dick Butkus crashing into you, except in this case Dick Butkus is silver, smells like a fish, and has been interrupted while trying to have sex in the gravel at the bottom of a river—which I'm sure did not actually happen to Mr. Butkus more than a couple of times in his entire NFL career.

Anyway, that's what it was like when the first silver salmon struck on the first day, a thud that jolted my arm and ran all the way up to the bones of my shoulder blades or "spatulas." The spot was a tributary of the Skwentna River, a place called Eight-Mile Creek that was perhaps twenty feet wide at the point where our guide, Ray, had eased the big flat-bottomed boat. The fly was a bright orange streamer, and as I stripped it slowly back toward the boat, the salmon rushed at it from twenty-five feet away. And in the clear water I reacted the way I always do in these situations: I made a pathetic, whining, sissy sound and tried to pull the fly away from the rushing fish.

This time, however, even my bad habit was no match for the speed of the fish, and he crashed into it with all the fury of Richard Simmons attacking a pie when no one is looking. I set the hook and the fish streaked away and the rod nearly came out of my hand. Ray, who had seen this sight perhaps a thousand times in his years in Alaska, remained eerily calm as he lurched to feet and shouted "Keee-rist almighty!" and scrambled for the net.

About fifteen minutes later we had our first salmon in the boat. Ray unhooked the fly and lowered the net back into the stream, and the fish, thirty-two inches long and perhaps fifteen pounds of silver power, exploded from it, racing back to the gravel bottom, where he would, as hundreds of generations of spawning salmon before him had done, get lucky. Then he would smoke a cigarette before being asked to leave, although I might be confusing him with me.

I collapsed back onto the seat of the boat, nearly crushing the three sack lunches Ray had prepared for us earlier that morning—

each bag containing a huge, manly sandwich made of a delicious native meat they called *slosledpooch,* which I later learned means "slow sled dog."

As I sat there trying to catch my breath, I noticed a large metal plate welded to the bottom of the boat, covering what might have been a big hole. I asked Ray about this.

"Couple years ago, about a mile up this creek, a grizzly came out of the bushes and stood up," he said. "I carried a .357 magnum and the son of a bitch kept coming, like he was going to get into the boat with us. So I stood up in the boat and took out the gun to fire a shot in the air to scare him. I was pretty nervous. And I accidentally shot a hole in the bottom of the boat. We almost drowned.

"I don't carry guns anymore when I'm fishing."

This was, as you might imagine, a comforting thought, reminding Rob and me of the National Rifle Association's famous saying: "Guns don't kill people. Grizzly bears kill people by standing up and making the people pee in their trousers and then shoot a hole in their boat."

For the rest of the trip we found great peace knowing that while we were in the capable hands of superb guide Ray Douglas, there would be no tragic firearm accidents. The trade-off, of course, was that it remained possible there would be a tragic having-your-ass-chewed-by-a-grizzly-bear accident, with our guide valiantly trying to save his clients by repeatedly striking the thousand-pound bear on the head with a net.

Or a *slosledpooch* sandwich.

Eight-Mile Creek was filled with salmon on this day, thousands of fish that had already made a brutal journey of some sixty miles up the Skwentna River from the Gulf of Alaska and had now found their birth stream by using a miraculous sense of smell honed by thousands and thousands of years of instinct. Although a few of them, the so-called yuppy salmon, had used handheld GPS locators. They were generally shunned by the rest of the school.

Rob and I stood in the boat and peered into the clear water and shouted with excitement as the salmon swam by, sometimes alone, sometimes in small "packs" or "herds"—their powerful tails propelling them with lightning speed into the current. I would make a second cast and hook another salmon a moment later, this one leaping clear of the water and landing with a splash as Rob stood behind me, his shaking hands trying to tie a fly to his leader as he shouted encouragement to his longtime friend, encouragement that sounded like "You bastard!"

Ray had netted this second fish and returned it to the water before my slow friend was ready to make his first cast. He brought the fly back with slow twitches, mostly because his hands were still shaking, and just ten feet from the boat a big silver charged and struck and the line began peeling from his reel. Rob, who swears more than any person on earth, was only able to shout three "holy shits" and one "sonofabitch" before the fish rushed back toward him. The line slackened and the salmon shook the fly free from its mouth.

It is at these times when friendship is most important, when a man needs to know that despite a bit of bad luck he is still admired and appreciated by the man standing next to him in the boat, that a friendship born some thirty years earlier is still alive and well.

So I shouted, "What a loser!" and made my third cast, hooking yet another salmon and bringing him to the net as my friend looked on in admiration, turning away only briefly to open my sack lunch and spit into the bag.

Eventually, Rob hooked another salmon and battled it skillfully. Near the boat it jumped from the water, its silver sides flashing in the Alaska sun before Ray slid the net under it and Rob pumped his fist in celebration. I had videotaped the entire battle, putting aside my own fly rod when Rob had set the hook and capturing my friend's battle with the strong fish so that someday his children could sit in the living room with their father and watch as their hero fought a large salmon in the Alaska wilderness, their hearts filled with pride and wonder as they asked, "Dad, what does 'son of a bitch big bastard goddammit' mean?"

We caught fifteen more silver salmon, magnificent fish between eight and eighteen pounds, fish that had two grown men mumbling and stammering and exchanging excited glances just as they did decades earlier—first when they hooked bass and bluegills in the small ponds of Massachusetts and in later years when a police officer opened the trunk of a Mustang and asked, "Where'd you get all the pumpkins?"

Our first fishing day in Alaska had been a stunning one, filled with joy and laughter and excitement and breathtaking battles with tremendous fish. We were exhausted, beaten into a happy fatigue by the drama.

It was noon.

Ray turned the boat down Eight-Mile Creek and back into the raging Skwentna River. We regrouped at the roadhouse for a few hours, sitting on the porch in the warm rays of the sun and babbling about the morning we'd had as we tried to digest the dog sandwiches we'd eaten.

Note: I am making up the dog sandwiches stuff. However, I am not making up any of the following: The meat in the sandwiches was, I swear, moose! It was my first-ever moose sandwich and it was good.

Then, after lunch, I lowered my head and attacked a sled dog and was shot to death by roadhouse owner John, who then mounted my head over his fireplace.

CHAPTER 30

Rob Gets to Drive the Boat

After lunch and a nap Ray said it was time to go to his cabin, which was not in what you'd call an urban setting, like the house owned by my friends Doug and Caryn in the Los Angeles area. Their house was in the seaside town of Hermosa Beach. On Super Bowl Sunday in 1982, we gathered there to watch the big football game, which pitted the Miami Dolphins against the Brooklyn Dodgers, I think. We drank a lot that day.

Anyway, just before kickoff I plopped my large behind into a chair in their living room. Suddenly the sound of gushing water hit my ears. It sounded as if a pipe had broken. I was alarmed. Doug stuffed another handful of salsa into his mouth and just sat there. I couldn't believe he wasn't dashing madly around the house searching for duct tape like a normal guy. Finally, I got out of my chair and said, "Doug! I think a pipe broke. Don't you hear that water?"

He stopped chewing for a moment, listened, and then announced, "It's the guy next door. He's peeing."

Doug's house was separated from the neighbor's house by a distance I would estimate to be, oh, two feet. As I was sitting there, beside an open window—January in L.A. can bring bone-chilling temperatures such as sixty-eight degrees—what I was listening to was not a broken pipe. It was, indeed, his next door neighbor urinating in his own bathroom, into, hopefully, the toilet, which was twenty-four inches from the window in Doug's house.

So I settled back into my chair to enjoy the Super Bowl, hoping for a close, exciting game in which the Dolphins and Dan Marino would triumph and the guy next door would not accidentally pee on me.

By way of contrast, if you sat in Ray Douglas's home and heard the loud sound of urinating outside the window, it would not be his next-door neighbor. It would a moose. Or a raccoon with a healthy prostate gland.

We climbed back into the Skwentna Roadhouse jet boat and set off on the river again, roaring along for one hour at a speed of twenty miles per hour. How far had we traveled?

(a) 20 miles
(b) The train from Chicago.

———

RICH TOSCHES

(c) Trains A and B would meet in Peoria.

(d) Go on with the damn fly-fishing book, you Attention Deficit Disorder poster boy!

The correct answer is (d), of course, and soon Ray had turned the boat into an area called Donkey Slew. This was either a shallow swampy lagoon or an odd-looking animal created when famous racehorse Seattle Slew screwed a donkey.

Anyway, we raced through Donkey Slew and then up Donkey Creek toward Ray's cabin. Along the way we saw an interesting thing: a black bear crashed into the narrow, ten-foot-wide creek about a hundred feet ahead of us, looked at us briefly, and then crashed through the willows and ran away. I was glad to have seen such a spectacular show of nature. I was also glad I'd brought forty-five pairs of underwear on this trip because when we got back to the roadhouse I was going to need at least one clean pair.

I failed to mention earlier that one week prior to the Alaska trip I had sprained an ankle playing softball. I was wearing a soft cast and was limping badly throughout the adventure. So when this brief confrontation took place with the black bear—which are, they say, less dangerous than a grizzly bear, although much more dangerous than, say, a chipmunk—my childhood friend Rob reminded me of one important thing: If we should be attacked by any sort of bear, he and Ray would have nothing but nice thoughts about me as they ran away and left me to be eaten.

After pausing to let the bear go on his way, Ray cranked up the jet boat again and we roared past the spot where the large beast had trampled small trees along the creek and we continued upstream for another hour or so. Eventually the creek widened and we skimmed over a gravel bar and onto a lake, which was not, surprisingly, named Donkey Lake. Several hundred yards up Not Donkey Lake, Ray rammed the bow of the boat into the shore and said, "We're here!"

I was crying and refused to get out of the boat. Eventually, however, they coaxed me out and we strolled—well, they strolled; I limped—a mile and a half up a trail. And somehow found ourselves at Ray's home, which he and his wife built from cutting down trees. It took them three years to build the sixteen-by-sixteen cabin, where they would raise Raymond Jr. and Holly—perhaps the only two kids in America who believe Nintendo is an intestinal disorder you get from drinking from a stream that a bear has pooped in.

The scene was surreal. We had flown a hundred miles from Anchorage into the Alaskan bush. Then we had traveled some forty miles via boat up a big river, through a slew, up another creek, and halfway down a lake with no real name before staggering for another hour up a steep forest trail. And someone lived here!

I was speechless, in part because of the realization of just how far we were from any semblance of civilization, but also because my bad ankle had now swelled up to the size of a watermelon.

And then Ray told us a story:

As they were building the cabin, on forty acres of wilderness land the state of Alaska had given them, they looked down from their hillside and noticed one day that across the huge lake was a tiny speck on the opposite shoreline: another cabin. It was, they figured, about a ten-mile walk around the lake to get there and they didn't have any extra time or energy, so they never made the trip. But one summer day an old man approached them as they sawed logs, Ray said. They had seen him walking along the opposite shoreline in a bright red coat earlier in the day, and now he appeared from the forest.

They were thrilled to have some company and couldn't wait to sit down with him and talk.

The old man, perhaps seventy, Ray said, did all the talking.

"You've got the whole goddamn state of Alaska," he told Ray and his wife, "and you gotta come build your cabin *right on top of mine?*"

And then the old man turned and walked back into the forest toward his own cabin. Ray and his wife never saw him again. About a year later, Ray said, he trekked over to the old man's cabin and found it abandoned. The old man, clearly sensing that the area was about to become a subdivision and that he'd be listening to his neighbors peeing during the Super Bowl, had packed up all of his belongings and left. Ray said he'd probably gone deeper into the forest and built another cabin, away from all the hustle and bustle.

In this setting, fifteen-year-old Ray Douglas, Jr. and his sister, Holly, sixteen, seemed stunningly happy. At the Skwentna High School—she stayed with friends in the village during the week— Holly was ranked number one in her senior class. Nobody was number two. She was the only member of the senior class—making it pretty hard to blow a spitball at the teacher and then look innocent. On the plus side, Holly had clearly locked up the Most Likely to Succeed award.

Seriously, Holly was just like any sixteen-year-old American girl, except for little things, such as having once shot a moose through her front door. She and Ray Jr. were delightful and never once said, "Uh, like, hello, like, you know?" like most teenagers. Rob and I liked them a lot.

And Ray's wife was terrific, too, exuding that fierce, independent spirit that comes from having to stoop over to pick her husband's underwear up off the floor—underwear that she had lovingly made for him out of a snowshoe-hare pelt.

Which explained why whenever Ray would scratch himself, his nose began to twitch.

Soon, all of us headed down the trail—including me, who Ray Jr. had given the proud native nickname *berbaet* ("bear bait")—and we climbed into the boat for the wild and furious ride back to Skwentna, where the Douglas family would pick up some supplies before heading back the next day to their little paradise in the Alaskan woods.

Along the way we came upon another fishing boat that had run aground on a sandbar. We climbed out and spent about an hour—to use the technical waterway navigational term—"unsticking it" and sending our fellow anglers on their way.

"Up here you stop and help," Ray said. "Otherwise people die."

We had another great dinner at the roadhouse that night. Salmon and a pot roast. We had kept one fish from our first day on Eight-Mile Creek, a seven- or eight-pound fish that would serve the entire gang of guides, along with Joyce and John. I don't eat fish. As a boy in New England, I wouldn't even eat seafood. My father and brother ate clams all summer, but I couldn't fathom the idea of eating any creature that made its home between two ashtrays. So everyone thought I was strange. Not so much because of the seafood thing. Mostly because I liked to wear lipstick.

Just kidding.

Rob and I stayed up until after midnight talking about this incredible experience. At 1:00 A.M., John shut off the generator and the lights went out. We settled into our beds, which John had made from the trees of the forest. The light from the full moon shone . . . shined . . . shinyed . . . came through our window, and because I was now a grown-up, I only made hand shadows on the bedroom wall for about twenty minutes instead of three hours like I did when I was in my late twenties. The morning would bring us twenty-five miles up the neighboring Yentna River, which flows out of Denali National Park, and up a tributary called the Talachilitna ("I think we are lost").

It would turn out to be even better than our first day.

We finally went to sleep with visions of huge salmon on fly rods dancing in our heads.

Although Rob kept saying it looked like a wolf and said he'd kick my ass if I didn't stop making the damn hand shadows.

By 9 A.M. we'd settled into our usual positions in the boat. Ray fired up the jet outboard and we were off, roaring up the Yenta River at 30 mph. Without slowing, Ray shouted that he had to untangle some line and switched seats with Rob, who was now piloting the boat. Here is an actual entry from Rob's journal, a diligent and detailed account of our trip that I borrowed for this book. My own journal was, uh, eaten by the big, hairy half-man, half-monster that roams these north woods: "Aurora Borealis."

Anyway, here's Rob's account of what was clearly the most exciting moment of the entire trip:

We're at full speed/Ray says 30 mph/I'm driving. I think I feel Ray grab the controls again, so I let go.

Here's my account of what happened next:

———

Ray had NOT, in fact, grabbed the outboard throttle handle back from Rob, who was apparently delirious. So when Rob released the throttle handle, the outboard pivoted all the way to the left, sending the craft into a 30-mph snap turn to the right and directly toward the riverbank, which was roughly one inch away. Rob had actually stood up to return to his seat when he'd felt "Ray grab the controls" and was now hanging over the edge, perilously close to a dive into the thirty-five-degree raging river in the out-of-control boat.

Ray leaped from his seat, lunged at the outboard motor as we missed the shoreline by one-one-hundredth of an inch or less, and got us headed back up the river.

"Keeee-rist!" Ray said. "What the hell happened?"

Rob babbled about "feeling" someone grab the controls and about wolf shadows on the bedroom wall and some other shit, and Ray told us how close we came to dying.

I sat in the bow, unflinching, staring bravely ahead, lost in my own thoughts. These thoughts centered around how forty-five pairs of underwear didn't seem to be nearly enough for a trip like this. About twenty minutes later, as we approached the Talachilitna and I had calmed down enough to be able to let out a series of shrill screams, we eased into the most awe-inspiring scene I'd ever witnessed. The tributary was clear, about a hundred feet wide, and as it flowed into the Yentna, great billowing clouds of mist rose from the surface and hung just above the river. The stunning Alaska range loomed in the background, a dense spruce forest crept up to the banks, the rays of the sun were filtered through the misty air, and amid it all, enormous salmon seemed to be flying from the river—giants of twenty and thirty pounds, hanging for a moment in the pristine air before smacking back down onto the water with a loud *crack*.

Just as Aldo Leopold and John Muir and John Audubon before me, I became entranced by the vision stretching before me and summoned up the eloquence only such majestic scenes can inspire, declaring, in a loud and emotional voice: "Hooolllly shit!"

Rob: "Holy shit is right! Look at this $%^&*# place!"

The salmon came at our flies then in a frantic way, thumping the streamers with a vengeance that spoke directly to their unhappiness at being kept from having sex. We caught a dozen or so, and lost a few that were, simply, too big and too strong to handle on our six- and seven-weight fly rods. We didn't much care. It was one of the few times in my three decades of fly-fishing that the scenery defeated the actual fishing and earned a place in my permanent, unending memory—a day so vivid that nothing could ever erase the images.

Did I mention the part about Rob letting go of the $%^&*# outboard throttle and nearly killing everyone?

That night, Rob walked from the roadhouse and sat among the nineteen sled dogs that were being kept and trained on John's property. In his journal he wrote: "I really felt like I was in Alaska when I was sitting with those dogs. What a great feeling!"

(In their journal, the dogs wrote: "Visited this evening by the knucklehead who 'felt' someone else grab the outboard motor throttle, causing him to let go. What a dipshit!")

The next day we were met at the breakfast table by the other guide, who went by T. W. or just plain T, (who would take us out today because, well, I think because after two days with us Ray had an appointment with a psychiatrist.)

———

T, who was a funny guy, took us back up the Yentna River to a tributary called Johnson Creek. The highlight of the day came when I hooked what I believe was either a king salmon or a seal on methamphetamines. I set the hook and within seconds was down to the backing on the reel. Within thirty seconds the creature had all my fly line and the backing stripped from the reel. I grabbed the final three feet, wrapped it around my hand, and was dragged about five feet across the gravel before I felt the sixteen-pound test leader pop some 150 yards downstream.

T, who had watched the whole thing with a smile on his face, said, "Did someone have a bite?"

Another night of good food, great stories, and a spectacular hand-shadow show followed. It would be our last night in Alaska.

The final day of fishing would be the best.

CHAPTER 31

The Meowing Sissy Boy

T had us back in the boat at 9 A.M. We believe T is insane. A good kind of insane. He often laughs for no apparent reason, laughs harder when something is the least bit funny, and laughs so hard stuff comes out his nose at the real funny stuff. Rob and I liked him.

It rained hard as we raced a mile down the Skwentna River and turned up the Yentna River. It was about sixty-five degrees and the rain felt good. We're headed back to Johnson Creek. I am holding a grudge against whatever the hell it was that I'd hooked the day before.

Rob had watched my brief, one-sided battle with that fish and began this day with a heavy spinning rod. Being an avid fly angler, I looked down my nose at him. He made his first cast and his heavy lure snagged the bottom. He gave a mighty tug and the spinning rod snapped, the top two feet dangling like a . . . well, like something that dangles.

God is a fly fisherman.

Today, T says we should try drifting egg-pattern flies near the bottom in hopes of enticing the giant salmon that are surging out of the Yentna River and into Johnson Creek. Unlike the streamer fly-fishing we'd been doing, this approach involves making long casts upstream and then watching the floating fly line to detect a strike.

Because I've nymph-fished for years in this manner, watching the indicator for the slightest twitch that might suggest the subtle strike of a trout, I was able to detect my first strike quite easily.

This was because the fly line suddenly straightened out and made a loud hissing sound as it sliced through the water. I set the hook and hung on as a monstrous salmon headed, it seemed, back toward the ocean. But this time I applied heavy pressure from the start of the fight and turned the fish, which now ran upstream and passed within ten feet of my legs. It was gigantic. I made a noise that sounded like "Eeeeiiiiiyip!" as the fish, some forty inches long, I thought, streaked past.

T said, "Does someone have another bite?" I said, "Bite ME!" and we all laughed.

Twenty minutes later I slid the fish onto the gravel bar, a massive king salmon that stretched out at forty-three inches and weighed twenty-five pounds or so. I released the big male, and as I held him by the tail in the river, he thanked me by spraying me with quite a bit of white, milky fish semen.

RICH TOSCHES

Quite frankly, a handshake or even a nod would have been enough thanks.

For three hours Rob and I and our new friend T stood in the clear waters of Johnson Creek as salmon jumped all around us. Rob's journal says: "Rich and I were about thirty feet apart and a huge salmon began jumping right between us. Then it headed straight at me and came completely out of the water within five feet of me! It scared me a little bit. I thought he might hit me! He didn't, but his splash soaked me. Rich laughed as I started swearing at the fish."

The swearing, however, had hardly begun.

After we took a lunch break—T started a driftwood fire on the gravel bar and cooked cheeseburgers—we waded back into Johnson Creek for our final few hours of fishing. I began catching a big salmon on every cast, the powerful fish attacking the egg-pattern fly along the bottom.

Then, standing twenty feet downstream of me, Rob sets the hook and his reel begins screeching. I turn just in time to see him start hopping up and down in the river, obscenities echoing off the Alaska range. As the monstrous salmon began a roaring downstream run, Rob had reached awkwardly for his fly reel to slow the fish and the handle, which was going around at roughly 467,000 rpm, slammed into his right, or nose-picking, hand.

The nail on his middle finger was torn completely off. The nail on his thumb was smashed and purple. T and I raced over and did what we could. That's right, we make a $10 bet, with me insisting the salmon will actually kill my childhood friend in the next five minutes. A $5 side bet says the salmon will then eat Rob.

Fifteen minutes later I lose the bet, narrowly, as the fish appears to feel sorry for Rob and comes to the net.

From Rob's journal: "My hand hurts but it doesn't matter. I've learned to keep my fingers out of the way."

He was thirty-nine years old at the time. I was just glad I hadn't done anything that stupid.

My big fish came about half an hour later, a salmon as powerful as the previous day's giant slamming the fly and heading downstream. The reel screamed and the handle whirred around like the propeller on my beanie, and then the fish turned suddenly into an even heavier current, where Johnson Creek emptied into the raging Yentna. A moment later the salmon raced to the right and sulked in the shallow riffles far, far away.

T was just a blur then as he sprinted past me in his hip boots, net in hand, racing toward the fish. About a hundred yards downstream he waded into the heavier water, plunged the net into the river, and pulled it back out with my fish in it. It was a king of about twenty-six pounds, he figured. He pumped a fist in the air, I did the same, and he released the giant in a calm stretch of water where it could catch its breath.

We fished late into the afternoon and then into the evening, the sun still high in the blue Alaskan sky but our wristwatches telling us that, well, telling me that Mickey's little hand was on the eight and his big hand was on the six, so I think it was about five minutes past noon.

We got back to the roadhouse late that night. Joyce helped me wash out a deep gash on my right index finger and bandage it up. Rob said I had actually stuck the finger into my reel, between the frame and the spool, during the last fight with the big salmon. He said the cut bled for twenty minutes and turned the edge of the river red and left my shirt spattered with blood and that I actually made a sissylike meowing sound like a hungry kitten.

RICH TOSCHES

208

Joyce worked on the cut as I looked down at my shirt, which appeared to be covered with ketchup, probably from the lunchtime cheeseburgers. And as the sun faded over the Alaska range on the final night of one helluva fishing trip, my dear friend finished telling his tall tale ("The Big Salmon and the Meowing Sissy Boy," he called it) and I just laughed.

Stuck my finger into my reel. Right. Like I'm some kind of idiot.

As Joyce finished wrapping my finger in about fifteen feet of gauze and tape, I wondered how Rob comes up with stuff like that.

CHAPTER 32

So That's What Trouties Look Like

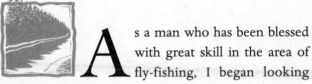As a man who has been blessed with great skill in the area of fly-fishing, I began looking early for the telltale signs that my offspring had, perhaps, inherited this remarkable trait—a special gene that would allow them to spot a rising trout, select just the right fly, move quietly into position, and snag a giant willow shrub behind them on the $%^&*@ bank.

Maggie came first, a large bundle of joy born on Thanksgiving Day in 1985. I can still see the look on the doctor's face as the miracle of childbirth was completed and I grabbed her chubby little leg and shouted, "Ohhhhh, I got the drumstick!"

I didn't introduce Maggie to fishing right away, of course. She was just a baby and would need time to grow and develop before stepping into this world of rivers and streams and wild trout and the dangers associated with this sort of thing. So I waited until she was three.

Our first trip together brought us five hours north of Los Angeles, along the Owens River, where she would catch the pet grasshoppers and hand them to her daddy for safekeeping. But then it was time for bigger things, so it was on to the eastern edges of Yosemite National Park, to a place called June Lake, nestled high in the Sierras. Because she was just three, I knew I could not spend nights in the great outdoors the way I usually did— curled up in the fetal position on the cold ground near a smoldering fire made of wet wood, a pine branch my blanket and an empty bottle of Jack Daniel's my pillow.

No, on her first trip the princess would need a tent and a sleeping bag. So on that April day I set up camp just like a Boy Scout, capturing the essence of scouting later in the afternoon by accidentally shooting an adult in the eye with a BB gun.

We would fish in the morning, but now it was time for sleep. So we crawled into the tent, snuggled into our sleeping bags, and listened as two owls serenaded us. It was a special time, that first night in the wild with my princess. And we talked.

"Da-da," little Maggie asked. "Why do owls say 'who'?"

"What?"

" 'Who.' Owls say 'who.' Why?"

"When?"

"Now, da-da. Why 'who'?"

"Why who *what?*"

"Owls who. Why?"

"Uh, I think I hear a bear outside, Maggie! Bears eat little girls if they hear them talking."

Today, Maggie is sixteen. And sometimes I regret having told her that little fib about the bears. Never is this more true than when she walks into the room while I'm watching my favorite TV show. As soon as she sees Yogi or his pal, Boo-Boo, she begins shaking and screaming until I can wrestle her to the floor and give her the medication.

I don't blame her, of course.

I blame those $%^&* owls.

Another memorable thing happened that same night. It took place long after the owls had suddenly shut up, almost as though someone had lurched out of a tent and thrown a Jack Daniel's bottle high up into the tree at them and would then pick the bottle up the next morning because I, I mean they, didn't want to be known as a litterbug.

Anyway, around midnight it began to snow.

It was a heavy, driving snow that quickly built up on our tent as Maggie slept in her sleeping bag. I wondered if the tent might collapse, leaving a father and his three-year-old daughter to stagger around in the wilderness until we could find a member of the Donner Party who might still be wandering around in these California forests and be willing to share his leg of Al with us.

Then I dozed off to sleep, only to be awakened a few hours later by the loud screaming of a child. It turned out to be Maggie, who had, in her sleep, climbed out of the sleeping bag and then climbed back in—headfirst.

In the near-total darkness I reached for where her head had

been, but found only two small feet. I climbed out of my own sleeping bag, found her head by beating around the tent with my hand until something shouted "Ouch!" and then somehow dragged her back out. She was crying, so I held her for a while and told her what had happened. Then she laughed, we climbed into the sleeping bags feet first, and slept until morning as the snow kept coming down.

In the morning it was twenty-five degrees outside, so I packed up all the camping gear and rented a nice warm cabin for the next three days.

During one of those days, Maggie caught her first trout.

She squealed.

(It was a different squeal from the one she made a dozen years later, when her first boyfriend came to the door and I gave him a little advice: "I have a shotgun, a shovel, and three acres out back. Have her home before ten.")

After another day or two on that first fishing expedition in which I showed her how Daddy fly-fishes ("Da-da, how come you never catch any fishies?") we headed for home, stopping along the way at the Lone Pine trout hatchery near Mount Whitney. We fed the trout ("So that's what trouties look like!") and then Maggie sat on the grass, pulled out a piece of paper and her crayons, and drew a map showing how we would get out of the hatchery and make our way back to Los Angeles.

She believed the map was our only hope of finding our way home, and I, of course, went along with the whole thing, asking her all the way back to L.A. where I should turn and which road we should take next.

We laughed the entire way, a father and his little girl enjoying a precious day together.

———

I didn't stop laughing until we saw the sign that read WELCOME TO EUGENE, OREGON.

Nick came along next, in 1989, the cutest little guy you could ever imagine. Nick greeted me in the hospital delivery room—I am not kidding about this—by peeing directly into my eye within forty-five seconds of his birth. I was holding him at the moment the fountain erupted, and after I regained my composure, I smiled an awkward smile and then hugged my son.

You know, right after I'd picked him up off the floor and kissed the big lump on his head. The doctor said the little guy probably traveled about seven feet across the room and I had to take his word for it because I had staggered out into the hallway shouting, "I'm blind! I'm blind!"

Three years later Nick and Maggie and I went back to June Lake, where Nick made his fishing debut. I rigged a fly behind a plastic bubble and would cast it far out onto the lake for him and let him reel it back in. And on this very day, he caught a trout!

But more importantly, it was during that outing that little Nick, who had only known the congestion and urban ways of Los Angeles, learned to pee in the woods instead of in a toilet or my eye.

The discovery thrilled him and he spent endless hours that week wandering around the lake and nearby streams, urinating like there was no tomorrow. Or if there was a tomorrow, it was going to be yellow and wet. Wherever he was when the urge came, he'd drop his little tiny trousers and pee and laugh.

But all too soon the trip ended and we found ourselves back in L.A. I dropped Nick off at his preschool on Monday morning and returned around 2 P.M.

"Uh, Mr. Tosches, we need to talk," said his teacher, Miss Shelley. "Nicholas peed in the sandbox today while the other children were playing in it."

As I understand it, the little guy nearly filled the moat in someone's sand castle.

"Do you have any idea why he'd do a thing like that?" a highly concerned Miss Shelley asked.

Knowing the bond between a parent and teacher is based on trust, I told her the truth: His evil sister had bet him $5 he wouldn't urinate in the sandbox.

I told Miss Shelley I'd have a stern talk with both of them over this incident.

Back home, I sat Nick down and explained that he couldn't pee outside anymore, that we were back in civilization now and all bathroom functions would once again have to take place in a bathroom, not on someone's sand castle.

He hugged me and said Okay. Then he added, "Daddy, I think I washed out the drawbridge."

I don't think I have to tell you how proud I was.

Three years later the third and final addition arrived. John was the fearless one, the one I could not scare by leaping out from under the kitchen table and shouting "Boo!"—as I had done with Maggie and Nick and as my father had done to me. (He stopped doing that when I was thirty-four because, frankly, it had just become stupid. And, of course, because Dad was then in his sixties and would sometimes get tangled up under one of the chairs and we'd have to help him out.)

Anyway, by the time John turned one, we had moved to Colorado and the fishing trips were now more frequent. He'd caught his first trout before he was three and seemed to love this outdoor life. Once, on a blustery winter day high in the Rockies, I brought the kids onto the Antero Reservoir and introduced them to ice fishing, which is sometimes what we do as we await the return of spring and the fantastic fly-fishing it brings.

I have an ice-fishing hut, a black tentlike structure that stays toasty warm inside as you stare through the hole in the ice waiting for a trout to bite. I had been waiting like that for five winters. Once, I thought I saw a trout swim by, but it turned out to be my own foot twitching after my leg had fallen asleep.

So one day I left John and Nick inside the warm ice-fishing shelter and told them I'd be back in a minute. I paused outside for a while, but they apparently thought I had walked away. I know this because suddenly, in a voice that ripped through the tent and echoed off the mountains, John, who was four at the time, shouted (I am not kidding about this):

"HOLY SHIT!"

I shouted, "Hey!"

John shouted, "Uh-oh!"

That kind of language is not what you want a four-year-old using, and so I unzipped the ice hut to deliver quite a lecture on the use of foul language. Inside, I saw little John standing up, his ice-fishing rod doubled over, engaged in a death struggle with some type of monster lurking beneath the ice. So I yelled, "Holy shit!" and began coaching him, screaming at him to relax and take it easy and not to horse the fish or he'd break the line.

Suddenly the head of the largest rainbow trout I'd ever seen in my life appeared down inside the hole. I plunged my entire arm into the frigid water and slowly eased the giant through the ice and onto the floor of the hut.

I took a photo of John holding the monster of some twenty-six inches, then we slipped the fish back into the water.

———

A few moments later John and I talked about swearing and how it's not okay and that I didn't want him to use that kind of language anymore—unless he hooked a huge trout like he'd just done and then it was okay as long as, like, he wasn't fishing with a priest or anything.

I wanted Nick to hear this little talk, too, but he was outside.

Peeing his initials into the snow.

Maggie, Nick, and John are my all-time favorite fishing companions.

CHAPTER 33

The Children and the Elk Droppings

I bought my kids their own fly rods and waders in 1998. I told them how their grandpa had bought me my own fly rod when I was twelve. John looked puzzled and then asked, "Did they have trout back then?" I told him we did, but often, as we reeled them in, gigantic screeching pterodactyls would swoop down from the ash-filled sky, which is how the sky was back then when the earth was still forming, and grab the fish away from us.

Today, whenever John hooks a trout he quickly looks up at the sky. Last summer, as he battled a trout on the Taylor River, I snuck up behind him and let out a loud, prehistoric-sounding *screech*, which made his brother, Nick, pee all over his own boots. Maggie dove headfirst into her sleeping bag.

Our first outing with the new fly rods came on Pikes Peak, the stunningly beautiful mountain that rises out of Colorado Springs, Colorado. We drove about halfway to the summit and then hiked about a mile, cutting off a trail and heading down to North Catamount Reservoir, with someone pausing briefly to scoop up a handful of dried elk pellets and toss them at someone else. When we reached the shoreline I washed my hands in the water and we continued around the reservoir to a secluded spot where big, cruising cutthroat rose steadily amid a hatch of small caddis flies. I rigged up their fly rods and we began the long, slow process of learning the basics of casting, something that took me nearly five years of relentless practice.

They had it down in about fourteen minutes, throwing tight loops thirty feet out onto the water and then waiting for the trout to come. And they did, slashing at the artificial caddis in big swirls. This is where fly-fishing gets tough, I told them, when the fish rise and your heart pounds and invariably you yank the fly away before the fish actually has it because the fish are so smart.

"This one isn't!" said Maggie, her fly rod bent as she slowly backed away from the water and eased a fifteen-inch trout gently onto the gravel.

"Wow, that's great, honey! Way to go. Sometimes the fish just hit so hard it's easy to hook them. I'm so proud of you. And if you miss a few, don't feel bad."

She hooked the next five trout that rose to her fly, hesitating perfectly at the strike and then setting the hook just as her dad learned to do after only twenty-five years of fly-fishing.

RICH TOSCHES

Nick, however, had his dad's yippy nerves. After watching him set the hook too early on his first two strikes, I told him to count "one Mississippi, two Mississippi" before setting the hook on the next fish that rose to the fly, and soon he began getting results. That's right; he was wearing overalls, missing his front teeth, and hauling in one catfish after another.

Actually, this hesitation trick worked and he nailed a nice cutthroat a while later, letting out a loud "Yes!" as the line tightened and the trout jumped from the water about fifteen feet from the shore.

John caught on quickly also, his small arms working hard to move the rod between the ten o'clock and two o'clock casting positions and laying down a fine cast. The trout didn't seem too interested in his fly, and when you're just seven, a minute without a strike seems like an eternity and you get fidgety and start looking around and not paying attention to the fly, and then you put the rod down and start tossing rocks into the water.

Eventually the kids told me to knock it off because I was scaring the fish away.

John hooked his first trout on a fly rod that morning. This came after he had been sternly cautioned by me not to shout out any obscenities unless the fish was eighteen inches or longer.

The late-spring day was warm and sunny as we fished in the shadow of majestic Pikes Peak, and I knew fly-fishing had grabbed them like it had grabbed me some three decades earlier. We walked slowly on the way back, enjoying the smell of the forest, the majestic scenery, and the memory of big trout rising to their flies.

Then someone reached for another handful of elk droppings and the only mature member of the group whacked him on the back of the hand with a long stick and said, "Don't even think about it!"

Sometimes Maggie really ticks me off.

———

ZIPPING MY FLY

221

CHAPTER 34

The Kids and Ol' Sonuvabitch

As my kids' interest and skill in fly-fishing increased, I started taking them farther and farther from home, to some of the great trout rivers of the West. I was unable to catch anything in any of those places, though, so the kids unhooked *their* fish and decided we should go someplace "where Daddy can catch something, too." Then they'd laugh.

The ungrateful little @#$%^&s.

So in the early summer of 2001 we packed up the 1989 Chevy Suburban and headed for Taylor Reservoir, just north of Gunnison, Colorado, for a week of camping and fly-fishing along the shoreline where we'd caught many trout over the years. Taylor is about a four-hour drive from our home and we made ten stops along the way.

"I have to go to the bathroom!"

Twenty minutes later: "I have to go to the bathroom again!"

And again. And again.

It was infuriating.

Especially when Maggie yelled, "Geez, Dad, we want to go fishing. You should have your prostate gland checked."

Actually, the frequent stops were mainly for gasoline because someone at the fine General Motors Corp. decided years ago that it would be funny to make a vehicle that gets two miles to the gallon. Sometimes, as I drive around in my Suburban, crowds of Saudi Arabian-Americans stand on the sidewalks and cheer as I roar by, all of them waving, many with tears of joy streaming down their cheeks as they scream, *"Alulla Guccha!"*—which means "Thanks to you, even our camels wear Gucci loafers!"

Somehow we arrived at Taylor by midafternoon and began setting up camp. This became somewhat more difficult when we discovered that I had forgotten the tent poles in the garage. My kids, as you'd guess, were very understanding.

"Oh, way to go, Dad!"

"Way to show us about responsibility, Dad!"

"Way to be organized, Dad!"

"Now what are we going to do, Dad?"

(That fourth kid had just wandered over from the camp next door. The little $%^&*# is lucky he ran away because I was just about to smack him with the . . . empty . . . uh, nylon tent-pole bag.)

I managed to put up the tent without the poles, using a brilliantly engineered system involving what I estimated to be 143,500 feet of clothesline rope. When I was done, our tent stood proudly among the towering pines, fully prepared for any onslaught nature might throw our way, unless the onslaught included something like rain or a breeze.

As a bonus, our campsite looked like, well, it looked like the web built by a hundred-foot-tall spider in that famous 1966 Japanese horror film *Gadtzaki*—which means "spider that spins clothesline rope out of his butt, which has to be uncomfortable."

By early evening we were ready to head to the reservoir and rig up the fly rods, where I hoped to get another glimpse of the grandest trout I had ever seen, a stunningly huge and majestic brown trout that I'd seen at Taylor twice in the past few seasons, a fish so fine and so grand that I was left in awe.

I first saw him in the spring of 1998. I was wading the north shoreline, casting tiny emergers at rising rainbows in the clear water amid a submerged field of boulders and having a great time. And then he swam past, a behemoth of a fish, a trout I figured might be thirty-five inches or longer, and as fat as a pig. A moment later he came to the surface and oinked, and I ran back to the shore, crying.

Okay, he didn't oink. I made that part up. But the fish that I guessed might weigh fifteen pounds or more turned when he got within ten feet of my waders and I saw the golden-yellow sides and the distinct spots on the brown trout, spots the size of silver dollars. I never even made a cast, settling that day for the simple pleasure of watching this gigantic trout—ruler of his domain, lord of his kingdom.

I named him with the first words that came out of my mouth when I saw him that day.

I call him "Sonuvabitch."

A year later I saw him again, I think. I was in a rented boat with my sons and their friend Spencer, moving toward the same boulder field from across the lake. When we got within a hundred feet of the spot, he came out of the water and I shouted "Sonuvabitch," as you do when you see an old friend. Spencer saw him, too, and while he didn't curse he did allow his mouth to open and a small bit of drool to run down his chin. Spencer is my friend Jim's son, and his father had obviously passed along this family trait: being speechless and drooling on yourself in disbelief when you actually see a fish.

"Did . . . did . . . you see that FISH?" Spencer shouted a few moments later, his eyes still as wide as cheap paper plates. (Sorry. I lost my saucers in the divorce, forcing me to come up with brand-new metaphors.)

"Oh yes, boy," I replied. "Indeed I did. I have seen this most imposing creature once before, this magnificent trout, and today we have encountered his lordship yet again. Rejoice, young man, in this moment!"

Although my boys and Spencer later insisted I'd only screamed "Sonuvabitch" and blew half a can of diet Pepsi out my nose.

Anyway, we would challenge the trout of Taylor once again on this late-summer afternoon, my kids and I casting to rising trout and catching five cutthroat along the rocky shoreline. We fished for only an hour or so on that first day of our camping trip before the sun faded behind the snowcapped peaks and we hurried back up the trail, me leading the way and my kids scurrying along behind in the gentle evening breeze. And as we moved through the golden light of dusk, four fly anglers filled with contentment, Nick spoke the hushed words that I can still hear today:

"I bet the tent blows over."

———

RICH TOSCHES

CHAPTER 35

Maggie the Cloven-Hoofed

ith the clothesline rope holding up well in the face of this fierce three-mile-per-hour wind, the tent was not blown over. We cooked hot dogs and hamburgers and marshmallows over the fire that night, and then we slept, fifteen-year-old Maggie leading the way by saying good night and crawling headfirst into her sleeping bag.

The next morning was brisk and sunny and we caught a dozen or more trout before noon, rainbows and cutthroat that were feeding on a hatch of blue-winged olives. We'd take a break whenever any of us

---

felt like it, which is, I think, the key to fishing with kids. We'd head back to the truck, drive to the store for a doughnut, or head back to the camp for a cup of hot chocolate.

John would use these breaks to feed the chipmunks around the camp, tossing sunflower seeds toward them and seeing how close he could get them to come. The first time he did this I began ranting and raving, sternly lecturing him about the dangers and telling him about the sign posted at the entrance of the campground warning us NOT to feed the chipmunks because of the great threat of injury, and that chipmunks had been seen foraging in this campground for more than a month.

Turns out the sign said BEARS, not CHIPMUNKS and we all had a good laugh.

Then I handed Nick a camera and pushed him out into the forest to get a picture of one of these bears—carrying on yet another proud Tosches family tradition, one passed from father to son for many generations. The lone break in this tradition came in the late 1800s, when little Nunzio Tosches was eaten. My great-grandfather said it happened near a dump.

The third day at Taylor would be our best. We'd found a point jutting out into the deeper water, and the trout were feeding close to the shore. This would allow the children—who did not yet have the technical casting savvy their father had long ago honed to a science—to make shorter, simpler casts and still reach the cruising fish. I explained all of that to them as I walked to the small, lone shrub behind me to retrieve the sixteenth fly I had snagged in its branches.

I rigged each of their rods with a large caddis that would float high on the water. Two feet beneath it would drift a small hare's ear, a common fly created with the fur of a rabbit, a fly that is relatively easy to tie. You know, if you can pry the rabbit out of the beagle's mouth.

Thirty feet offshore, large trout began a steady feeding pattern and the kids' excitement grew. Nick was the first to shout, his fly rod bending mightily as he set the hook after the dry fly had disappeared, tugged down by a trout that had taken the nymph below.

The fish ran left and then right and then Nick eased it onto the shore. He gently unhooked it, wet his hands before touching the fish so as not to rub away the delicate protective layer of slime on the fish, and then set it free. He had performed a difficult task, from detecting the strike and setting the hook to playing the sixteen-inch trout and releasing him, perfectly, as if he'd been doing it for twenty years.

This is the same kid who has a list of 435 excuses why his homework wasn't turned in on time. (No. 237: "A bat flew into my bedroom, lodged itself in my hair as bats will so often do, and I spent the entire night trying to get him out. Frankly, I'm lucky to be alive!")

John figured it out, too, making delicate casts and then watching intently as the big caddis bobbed in the gentle waves of the lake. When the fly disappeared, John would raise the rod and let out a hoot. "It's a big one!" he'd shout every time, although he knew none of these trout would make it into the prestigious "holy shit!" category. This was somewhat disappointing for the little guy.

A highlight came around 11 A.M. when Nick, staring intently at his large floating caddis and waiting for it to submerge, was greeted by an enormous splash as a very big trout rose from the water and slammed the dry fly. "Oh! Oh! Oh!" he yelped, setting the hook and stumbling backward as the fish ran toward him. Then it turned and fought doggedly—in the sense that at one point it came onto shore and bit Nick on the leg and then the fish sat down and licked its groin area.

Okay, it didn't, but the fish did fight hard and gave Nick all he could handle. But this kid was getting good, and with just the right amount of pressure he turned the battle and soon had the fish in the shallow water at his feet. It was a lake trout, the only one we'd catch on this trip, and stretched out to an impressive twenty-two inches.

But it was Maggie who turned in the all-star performance on this day. She had wandered away as we began fishing, seeking a bit of solitude, showing me that me she was starting to understand the heart of this special type of fishing. And quickly, she began hitting trout, the rod arcing overhead as a big rainbow or cutthroat slashed at the nymph, Maggie delicately setting the hook and quickly forcing the fish into submission. She would kneel at the water and remove the hook with a flick of her wrist, guide the trout back into the deeper water, stand for a moment and gaze out onto the water with a big smile, and then check the fly and begin casting again.

Watching Maggie fly-fish that day was sort of like looking at myself.

Except, of course, she's stunningly beautiful, doesn't have a potbelly or a giant behind, and has never, to my knowledge, shouted "Sonuvabitch!"

Although I have seen her shoot a soft drink out of her nose.

Late that afternoon, the wind and rain that had so perfectly stayed away for three days suddenly came hard, sweeping over the mountains. It made a mess of our campsite. Somehow, the clothesline rope didn't hold up as well as I'd imagined and the roof of the tent began collecting a bit of water, "bit" in this case meaning several hundred thousand gallons.

So we broke camp during a lull in the storm, packed everything back into the Suburban, and rented a cabin about a mile up the road, trading in the prospect of a night in wet sleeping bags for a warm, cozy cabin with real beds and a shower. As you might imagine, we were deeply saddened.

The storm passed at about 6 P.M. The kids had taken warm showers, changed into dry clothes, and were dancing in the cabin to a CD being played on a boom box that one of them had somehow hidden in the truck, probably under my six-foot-high mountain of clothesline rope. They were warm and happy and were not about to let that change.

So when I asked them if they wanted to go back out and fish the evening hatch, all three of my kids and their friend Spencer, who had stayed with us after his father had to return home, stared at me like . . . I don't know . . . like I had a bee on my forehead or something.

After I stopped screaming and got some ice onto the sting, I asked them if it would be okay if I went back to the lake to catch the evening hatch.

"Okay," Maggie said. "One hour. You've got one hour. Eight o'clock. Then come back and make us dinner. At eight o'clock! Right?"

I agreed and headed out the door for one hour of solitary fly-fishing. The fish dimpled the surface like raindrops, hundreds of rising trout on a mirror-slick surface, their snouts breaking the water and their dorsal fins emerging as they sipped at blue-winged olives. I had the perfect imitation, a No. 22, and began one of the greatest hours of my fly-fishing life.

ZIPPING MY FLY

231

I caught three trout on my first three casts, all fat, healthy rainbows between fifteen and eighteen inches. I'd rub the wetness from the fly, blow on it to dry the wings, and set it back down about thirty feet out. The wait generally lasted only a moment or two, with a fish rising in the slow, deliberate way to inhale the imitation.

Out in front stretched the Rocky Mountains, a golden light shimmering through the valleys as the summer sun set. And the trout just kept coming at the little blue-winged olive. I would occasionally glance down the shoreline and could see the tiny cabin, about a mile away. Even though Maggie was fifteen and was sickeningly responsible, I was a bit concerned because I knew that in that cabin were two things that should not be together:

Nick and matches.

From the age of two, Nick had been fascinated by matches and fire. He'd always ask if he could start the campfire, and then spend hours staring into the blaze and tossing things onto it. Sticks. Pinecones. Leaves. Charlie, my ex-mother-in-law's Yorkshire terrier.

Oops. That last one was just a lovely dream I had once.

But Nick had, indeed, been born with this love and fascination for fire, so I worried about him being in the cabin.

However, as we discussed earlier, God, in his infinite wisdom, had also given Nick a love of peeing on everything. I figured the two just sort of canceled each other out.

So I relaxed as I made a few more casts and then I checked my watch to see how close it was getting to the 8 P.M. deadline and saw that it wasn't close at all.

It was 9:20!

I snapped the fly off the leader, stuck it into my hat, reeled up the rest of the line, and sprinted across the gravel point. At about nine thousand feet in the Rockies, sprinting up a steep hillside isn't all that much fun in the sense that it often makes you throw up. But sprint is what I did, realizing that I was going to be facing the Wrath of Maggie, which is, as her brothers will tell you, not something you should take lightly.

I flung myself and the fly rod into the truck and sent gravel spewing across the landscape as the tires spun and I headed for the cabin. I drove way too fast on the mountain road and screeched to a halt in front of the cabin, quickly going over the explanation I would offer for my tardiness. (I had settled on the bat-in-the-hair thing, and thought I would dazzle them further by using the word "guano.")

I never got the chance. On the other side of the cabin door—the locked cabin door—stood Maggie, her brothers, and Spencer.

"If you want to come in," she shouted through the glass, "here's what we've decided you will do. You will run around the cabin two times, like a chicken. You will make loud clucking sounds. And you will flap your wings. Twice around the cabin."

Then we all laughed, my laughter echoing off the mountains and theirs muffled but still joyous inside our small cabin.

"You guys are too funny!" I shouted through my laughter. "A chicken! That's good. Let me in now and I'll start dinner."

Maggie's voice came back through the door like that of a fanged cacodemon from the Outer Darkness, the chilling sound of the archfiend of Gehenna himself, a voice booming from the fiery flames of Abaddon.

"Twice," the voice cracked. "Around the cabin. Like a chicken."

"Uh, no, really," I said, my voice wavering now, a forced half grin on my face. "In. Me. Start dinner. Eat now?"

ZIPPING MY FLY

233

"Flap your wings!" the voice of Beelzebub boomed from inside the cabin.

And the next thing I know I'm halfway around the back of the cabin, hopping, making really loud chicken sounds, my hands tucked into my armpits and my elbows flapping like, well, like a $%^&*@ chicken!

I was forty-five years old!

The kids followed me from inside, running from window to window to make sure I was clucking and hopping, their laughter filling the cabin. I got back to the door in about thirty seconds, paused, looked in at the glaring face of Maggie the Cloven-Hoofed, and just kept going, clucking and hopping and flapping my way around the outside of the cabin for the second time, which was just like the first lap except for the elderly couple who had now moved out onto the front porch of their cabin about fifteen feet from ours and were, well, "staring" is a good word.

"Are . . . are you okay?" the older man asked, his head cocked to one side like he'd never seen a middle-aged man racing around in the dark behaving like poultry.

"Oh yeah," I said, the stupid half grin reappearing on my face. "It's just my kids . . . inside the cabin . . . I fished too late . . . big hatch . . . kids won't let me in. Ha-ha."

As I talked to them and tried to explain the whole thing I realized that I had not stopped hopping. Up and down, up and down I hopped, just feet away from the startled couple.

Oh, and I was still flapping my "wings."

I couldn't think of anything else I could possibly say to the couple—I offered a weak "good night"—and I turned and then hopped and flapped my way off into the darkness around the corner of our cabin.

RICH TOSCHES

When I got back to the door, Maggie was smiling. "Did we learn a lesson?" she asked.

I was gasping for breath and I was shivering and I said that I had, and that I'd never fish too long ever again. And then my daughter let me in.

When we got home the next day we were still smiling about the chicken incident. After putting away the wet tent and the clothesline rope, I went inside and spent two hours putting old photographs—little Maggie taking her first bath, little Maggie having her diapers changed, little Maggie stumbling naked into the backyard on her first birthday—into an album.

And labeled it: "Show to boyfriends."

CHAPTER 36

A Tear and a Long-Tail Deer

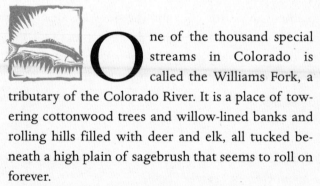One of the thousand special streams in Colorado is called the Williams Fork, a tributary of the Colorado River. It is a place of towering cottonwood trees and willow-lined banks and rolling hills filled with deer and elk, all tucked beneath a high plain of sagebrush that seems to roll on forever.

In October of 2001 I found myself crouched near the Williams Fork with Nick and John, miles from the nearest dirt road and huddled beneath the low branches of an enormous spruce tree as an autumn storm with snow and sleet and pounding wind battered the Rockies.

It was part of my annual elk-hunting trip, which had over the years become about 10 percent elk hunting and 90 percent fly-fishing. I'd hunt for a day and then put away the gun and take out the fly rod and begin a four-day adventure, fly-fishing alone from dawn till dusk.

But this year, for the first time, my sons would come along. I shot an elk, too. Nick and I dragged it out, about a mile, mostly downhill, and then collapsed. John had sat on a rock about twenty feet from the animal, at the age of nine not yet interested in the glamorous field-dressing aspect of hunting.

And the next day, with the elk hanging in the camp and the hard work completed, we went fly-fishing. The walk from the truck across the sage plain and down to the Williams Fork had taken most of an hour, and now, twenty feet from the water, we huddled under the spruce tree. Nick was shivering badly, complaining about the cold and the sideways sleet and saying that he felt weak. So I thought I'd take his mind off things by telling the lovely tale of the ill-fated Donner Party ("A long time ago in California, on a day just like this . . .") and the interesting way some members of the party managed to stay alive.

(I don't want to give away the ending for those of you who've not read about that exciting expedition, but I will give you one of their menu entrées: "Fillet of Saul.")

Anyway, telling the story was a good idea. When I finished, Nick said he was a lot warmer, felt much stronger than he had a few moments earlier. He even began whistling.

John was quiet and passed the time by tapping a stick rhythmi-

---

RICH TOSCHES

cally against the tree's trunk and casting an occasional glance at the meaty part of his brother's leg.

It was cold under that tree, despite the thick pine cover. The wind howled and the rain dripped from the branches onto us. But then the storm broke. The wind died and the sun poked out from the fast-moving clouds, and suddenly a cold, nasty, miserable day showed some promise.

We rigged our fly rods and headed through the willows to the river.

Brown trout of bragging size vaulted from the water, their red spots glistening in the sun before they came back down with frightening splashes, which caused one of us to swear. The boys had limited swearing privileges on this their first elk-hunting trip. I'd also taken them out of school for three days after both had knocked out some pretty good grades in the fall quarter.

I had thought I'd wait longer to introduce them to elk hunting. Some of my friends had already brought their sons, but with Nick and John at twelve and nine I figured there was plenty of time. But then September 11 came.

And by October, well, it just seemed like the right time to bring them a bit deeper into a world of smelly cabins and wood-burning stoves and long walks along rivers. And out of a world that was filled with images of hijacked airliners crashing into skyscrapers. And war. And anthrax.

So we loped along on the sagebrush plateau and then headed down the trail to the Williams Fork, where we shuffled through the fallen leaves. Once, we stopped to watch a white-tailed deer bound up a ridge to our left, pausing for a moment before she disappeared into the woods. I told Nick and John that the whitetail is common in the Eastern United States but somewhat rare in the

West, and that they have a much longer tail than our mule deer. They just kept walking. I wasn't sure they were listening.

We walked for another fifteen minutes or so, the stream rushing alongside our feet, and then John stopped, looked at me, and said, "Dad, do you think we'll see any more *long*-tail deer?"

Soon we settled near the big spruce and alongside a pool where a beaver dam had collapsed, a large structure of some fifty feet that had now given way in the middle. In the pool were a hundred or more big brown trout, I guessed, dozens and dozens of them rising at small insects and others vaulting clear of the water in eye-popping shows. It was the spawning season, so I talked to the boys about fishing clean and not injuring the trout, keeping our feet mostly on the bank so we wouldn't step on any of the beds.

And we caught trout. Oh, did we catch trout! A hatch of small duns had the big browns on a binge.

And Nick and John had this club in their bag, making gentle casts and letting the No. 20 duns float back to a spot where a trout was steadily rising. Their screams echoed through the canyon as I stood behind them, moving in to pop the tiny hooks free when the fish came in, Nick and John pausing only for a moment to watch the fish return to the pool before they cast again and again, nailing perhaps ten or twelve of the big fish. Yellow aspen leaves floated by on the river, the air turned warm, and geese flew overhead.

We released all of the trout and then began the long walk back to the truck. For about a mile none of us spoke. Then Nick stopped, looked around, and said, "Dad, this is great. Thanks."

I stayed ahead of them for the next mile, moving along in part because I knew the darkness was coming but mostly because I didn't want them to see the tears on their old man's face.

Two days later we were back home, back in a different world, a world of war, a world in which people were afraid to open their mail because they might inhale anthrax.

I hope my kids always remember which one is the real world.

CHAPTER 37

Undimmed by Human Tears

I'd like to tell a final story about North Catamount Reservoir. It will not be a funny story. (Here many of you are asking, "And how does that make it different from the rest of the book?")

Anyway, it's about a fishing excursion that I made a few days after the terrorist attack on the World Trade Center in New York and the Pentagon in Washington in September of 2001. I needed to get away. From the TV. From the newspapers. From the heartache. I tried to get away from an America that was hurt, saddened to the soul by the loss of thousands of mothers and fathers, sisters and brothers, and children.

So I grabbed my fly rod.

It's what I always do when I need to leave the world for a while. I've fly-fished through the deaths of friends. I fly-fished through a divorce, too. (The settlement went well: I got to keep one hip boot and half of my lucky hat.)

So on that day when the world became too sad, I decided I'd walk the shoreline of a lake near my home high in the Rocky Mountains. I wanted to forget. But on this day that I wanted to forget the sorrow, I had chosen the wrong lake. And the wrong mountain. I picked North Catamount.

On the side of Pikes Peak.

The same Pikes Peak where, in 1893, Katharine Lee Bates sat down and wrote "America the Beautiful."

I knew I'd made a mistake when I came to the stand of yellow aspens where, a few Septembers earlier, my children and I stopped to gather leaves and to rub the white "paint" from the bark onto our faces. The Indians did that, my little Maggie told me that day, to keep from getting sunburned.

I thought of that day, and I smiled.

But I stopped when I remembered that the next day, a not-so-little-anymore daughter would be bused to and from her high school, which is located inside the boundary of the United States Air Force Academy, which, in the wake of the attack, was cloaked in the highest level of security.

They said that week that we were at war.

I eventually got to my spot near a cove on the lake, and as I made the first few casts I looked up at the peak towering just over my head.

RICH TOSCHES

O beautiful for patriot's dream
That sees beyond the years.
Thine alabaster cities' gleam,
Undimmed by human tears.

I wondered if Katharine Lee Bates could ever have imagined that many tears.

The sun climbed higher and a rainbow trout rose to my fly. As I released him I thought about my father, who despite not knowing fly-fishing from flypaper, saw his son's eagerness and bought him a fly rod when he was twelve. And at some point, as I stood high in the Rockies, it occurred to me that someday we'd all climb out of that hole we were in during that horrific time, and that life would go on. And that I'd get to spend another day fly-fishing with my kids.

And that two thousand miles away, they may have hit the World Trade Center and they may have hit the Pentagon.

But they had missed America.

And that on this brilliant September day, I hadn't chosen the wrong mountain at all.

About the Author

A former UPI and *Los Angeles Times* writer, **Rich Tosches** was nominated for a Pulitzer Prize for his Olympics coverage. He has also written for *Sports Illustrated, Modern Maturity,* and other national magazines. Rich and his family live in Colorado Springs, Colorado, to take advantage of excellent fly-fishing and other outdoor activities. Named Colorado's Journalist of the Year by the state's Press Association, and once called "one of the funniest men in America" by Steve Allen, Tosches has been the humor columnist for the *Colorado Springs Gazette* since 1993.

MOST OF ME

Surviving

My Medical

Meltdown

Most of Me

ROBYN MICHELE LEVY

GREYSTONE BOOKS
D&M PUBLISHERS INC.
Vancouver/Toronto/Berkeley

Greystone Books
An imprint of D&M Publishers Inc.
2323 Quebec Street, Suite 201
Vancouver BC Canada V5T 4S7
www.greystonebooks.com

Cataloguing data available from Library and Archives Canada
ISBN 978-1-55365-632-6 (pbk.)
ISBN 978-1-55365-633-3 (ebook)

Editing by Nancy Flight
Copyediting by Lara Kordic
Cover design by Naomi MacDougall
Text design by Heather Pringle
Cover photograph by Angela Wyant/Getty Images
Illustration on page 60 by Robyn Levy
Lyrics on page v are by Leonard Cohen, "So Long, Marianne,"
Songs of Leonard Cohen, Columbia, 1967.
Lyrics on page 39 are by Feist, "1234," *The Reminder,* Cherrytree, 2007.
Lyrics on page 49 are by Marvin Gaye, "I Heard It through the Grapevine,"
In the Groove, Tamla, 1968.
Printed and bound in Canada by Friesens
Text printed on acid-free, 100% post-consumer paper
Distributed in the U.S. by Publishers Group West

We gratefully acknowledge the financial support of the Canada Council for the Arts,
the British Columbia Arts Council, the Province of British Columbia
through the Book Publishing Tax Credit, and the Government of Canada
through the Canada Book Fund for our publishing activities.

"... it's time that we began to laugh and cry and cry and laugh about it all again."

LEONARD COHEN, "So Long, Marianne"

Songs of Leonard Cohen (debut album, 1967)

To my parents
And in loving memory of my auntie Glenda

Contents

Acknowledgments

I AM FOREVER GRATEFUL to my husband and daughter, who together bore the burden of responsibility for keeping me sane while I wrote this book. Bergen has been my sounding board, in-house editor, computer whiz, administrative assistant, bread baker, biggest fan, and best friend—with "benefits." Naomi has been my inspiration, memory bank, compassion guide, in-house masseuse, vegetarian cook, and loyal listener.

I am also grateful to my mother and father for their constant love and support and to my sister and brother for their love, compassion, and friendship.

A world of thanks to friends, family, and neighbors who played starring roles in my dramatic decline and comeback: Lisa Kelner, Ruth Tal, Bonnie Beecher, Hildi Weiman, Gloria Macarenko, Diana Kjaer-Pedersen, Brian and Gillian Campbell, Joey Mallett, Betina Albornoz, Linda Low, Teresa Goff, Terrye Kuper, Simca Kuper, Marg Meikle and Noel MacDonald,

Christine Dolling and John Kilburn, Helen and Will Rosebush, Mahima Mathur and Amitava Chattopadhyay, Corry Hunter, Yvonne Gall, Sheila Peacock, Sue Black, Cheryl Dundas, Susie Seidner-Katz, Cicely Bryce, Lourdes Davenport, my e-mail update group, the men's cooking club, and the women's no cooking club. And to the special women no longer with us who loved life and continue to inspire me: Zoë, Chantal Jolly, and Dawn Jones.

I would also like to thank my health care community: Adrienne Mahaffey, Dr. Elliot Mintz, Dr. Penny Smyth, Dr. A. Jon Stoessl, Dr. Allan Young, Dr. Chung, Dr. Mona Mazgani, Jessica Whidden, Dr. Hagen Kennecke, Dr. Caroline Lohrisch, Carl Petersen, Peggy Spears, and Nora Soriano.

And finally, heartfelt gratitude to Rob Sanders for inviting me to submit a book proposal based on a collection of my quirky e-mail health updates he received from a mutual friend, and to my radiant editor, Nancy Flight, for her enthusiasm, sensitivity, and support.

MOST OF ME

Prologue

I N A WAY, this is a love story. Not the classic kind, with the fair-haired delusional damsel in distress, who is rescued by the handsome narcissistic prince, and then they live happily ever after. This is a medical love story, with the dark-haired middle-aged dame in distress, who is rescued many times— first by the chivalrous neurologist, then by the petite surgeon, followed by the spiffy oncologist and, finally, by the other, younger surgeon. And although none of them live together, the dark-haired middle-aged dame survives and limps happily ever after.

As with many medical love stories, the beginning is hard to pin down. Diseases are cunning creatures—they can incubate and mutate for years. Mine certainly did—both of them. Although I'll never know the exact moment that Parkinson's penetrated my brain or cancer invaded my breast, I know in my heart I was sick during the five years leading up to my

diagnoses. I know, because that's when things began to change for me and my family. That's when the stranger surreptitiously moved into our lives. I was thirty-eight years old.

At first, we only caught fleeting glimpses of the stranger. Her tiny intrusions into my happiness were easily missed or misconstrued. Back then, she was still unpacking her belongings and just getting to know us. She had yet to unleash the full fury of her rage and the depth of her despair. But she dropped hints: brief bouts of depression, flashes of anger, hurtful accusations, petty resentments. And it only got worse with each passing year, no matter what measures I took to evict her.

This stranger had a stranglehold on my family, affecting each of us in different ways. I was trapped in her tyranny and riddled with guilt and self-loathing. Bergen was compassionate, accommodating, and fiercely protective of Naomi. And although Naomi tried to deflect and appease the stranger, she fell into a protracted funk—weighed down by the discord and dejection and a secret she kept locked away.

I hate thinking about that time in my life—what was happening to me, who I was becoming. But most of all, I hate that I hurt people I love. Which is why, if dementia ever begins devouring my mind, I hope the first memories to go are of the Bad Old Days.

I

The Bad
Old Days

I WASN'T ALWAYS LIKE THIS: so moody, so anxious, so volatile. I used to be just a little moody, a little anxious, a little volatile. And only when I was premenstrual, overworked, or overtired. But now things are getting worse. My mood swings are growing more frequent and more severe. The flashes of anger ambush me anytime, anyplace. I'll be at the grocery store, happily picking out vegetables; then, for no apparent reason, my blood starts to boil and my hands reach out to rip the broccoli heads right off their stalks. Or I'll be sitting at my desk at work, and a colleague will absentmindedly leave his empty Tim Hortons coffee cup next to my phone, and suddenly I feel violated and vengeful and imagine that I am a cannibal, ripping him to shreds with my razor-sharp teeth, devouring his flesh and guts, then washing it all down with gulps of his double-double-infused blood.

In the interests of keeping my job and shopping privileges, when I am out in public I struggle to keep it together. I put on a pseudo-happy face, complete all my assignments on time, keep

my angry impulses bottled up inside, waiting until I get home to explode, eat my young, then blame my man.

When I walk in the front door, anything can set me off: clutter in the hallway, a stray sock on the floor, dirty dishes in the sink. Tonight it's a basket of clean laundry. At least, that's what it was earlier this week, when I washed and folded everything and lugged it upstairs to my eleven-year-old daughter's bedroom. Or should I say bedlam? What a mess.

"Naomi! Come upstairs right now!" I yell from the top floor down to the kitchen.

I only came in here to turn down her music. If I'd seen her room like this, there's no way I would have allowed her friend to come over. Or even allowed her to have a friend.

"Naomi! I said right now!"

There are clumps of clothes everywhere—all over the floor, the bed, the desk, the chair. And the laundry basket is exactly where I left it, next to the wardrobe. Nothing's put away. Everything's crumpled up with dirty clothes and half-eaten sandwiches and expired school memos.

"What is it?" Naomi asks, running up the stairs.

"Your room is a pigsty! You promised to put away your laundry! That was two days ago! Two days ago! I washed and folded everything. Now it's filthy. What the hell is wrong with you?"

"I'm sorry. I'll clean it after Denise leaves," she mutters sheepishly.

"No! You'll do it now!" I scream, slamming the door.

"But she's downstairs, waiting for me."

"I don't care. You have a mess to clean up. Now!"

Naomi's eyes well up with tears. We hear a knock on the door.

"What's going on? Can I help?" Bergen steps inside, then stands between us. Father Teresa to the rescue.

"No. Stay out of it, Bergen."

Nothing can extinguish my rage once it becomes inflamed. I feel the hate smothering my self-control and civility. Bergen bends down and picks up a dirty sock. I hear my shrill voice barking out orders, insults, accusations, ultimatums:

"Don't help her! Naomi needs consequences, not help. Why do I always have to be the bad cop? She made this mess all by herself; she can clean it up all by herself. And from now on, she can do her own laundry. Her friend can wait. Or you can drive her home. I don't give a shit! Naomi! Clean up this room!"

Fear floods my daughter's eyes as she jolts into action. Her tears begin dribbling down her cheeks as she frantically gathers up her jeans and T-shirts, socks and underwear, loose papers and magic markers. I walk down the hall to my room, slam the door, and force myself to lie down. Later, way past Naomi's bedtime, I crouch on the dark stairway outside her room and listen to her sobbing and Bergen consoling. I feel sick to my stomach. I am a cesspool of self-loathing; I am drowning in regret. I think that if only I could say the words "sorry" and "forgive me," I could escape from the fury. But I can't. I'm paralyzed with shame, and so I watch until it burns itself out, turns into cinders, then ashes. I'm such an ash-hole.

In the morning I wake up with exactly what I deserve—a pounding headache and explosive diarrhea. On my way to the shower, I see Bergen and Naomi at the kitchen table. They're both eating cereal and oranges and reading the comics. Our Yorkshire terrier, Nellie, is asleep by their feet. Only Bergen makes eye contact with me.

"Good morning," he says, quietly.

His warm voice slides under my skin, inviting me toward him, toward Naomi, toward contrition and reconciliation. As if it's still possible. But my heart is shackled with grudges and resentment, and I'm afraid of trying, of failing. But most of all, I'm afraid of facing myself and my deteriorating relationship

with Naomi. So I keep my distance, exhale a feeble "hi," and carry on getting ready for work.

TODAY, I AM the first one at my desk. I like getting here early, before everyone else. It's dark on these November mornings. It's quiet. I can collect my thoughts—at least the ones I can locate. They are so scattered that searching for them is like going on a scavenger hunt. I find them wedged between my worries, hiding beneath my habits, scrawled on sticky notes. Slowly, I cobble together my day's to-do list: book band for pretaped interview, write script for live on-air interview, edit items for radio broadcast and website, attend music committee meeting, produce guest host program, ask boss about extending my contract, possibly go to lunch-hour yoga class. That's what I really need—deep breathing and inner peace. Something to take the edge off, to ease the stress. This new job—producer at Radio 3, Canadian Broadcasting Corporation—is killing me.

Radio 3 is the most laid-back work environment there is at CBC. It's like a dingy basement hangout for teenagers. The lights are dim, the dress code is casual, and the focus is music—new, independent Canadian music. Here, we play songs, talk to musicians, and cover concerts, festivals, and other music-related events. Fun stuff. It sure beats slugging it out in the pressure-cooker newsroom or on current affairs programs—chasing politicians, filing numerous stories, racing against the clock. Which is why I can't understand what's wrong with me, why I'm so frustrated and anxious.

I'm starting to wonder if something is *really* wrong. More than just premenopause, which is what I suspect I have been going through these past few years. I'm only forty-one, but it's possible. I have many classic symptoms: irregular periods; trouble sleeping at night; muddled thinking and problems

concentrating; inexplicable aches and pains, muscle and joint stiffness, and fatigue; and terrible mood swings and bouts of depression. I've been taking vitamins and Chinese herbs to regulate my hormones. They seemed to help in the past. But not anymore. Now, the only thing that really helps me cope is sleep. Thank goodness I have no trouble napping in the daytime. At home, I just crawl into bed, pop in a pair of earplugs, and doze right off. At work, I sneak away to the yoga room when it's empty, assemble a makeshift bed with yoga mats and blankets, turn off the lights, and disappear. As far as career coping mechanisms are concerned, it's a real skill, which I'm proud of—it ranks right up there with secretly throwing tiny tantrums in the soundproof room or crying my eyes out alone in the ladies' washroom.

By the time my coworkers trickle in, I have written the script and left a copy of it on the host's desk. Later, he takes me aside and says, "Thanks for the script. It's great. Could have used it last year, when the band came in to promote their previous album. I guess you didn't notice they have a new release?"

"Oh, shit. I'm sorry. Do you want me to rewrite it?"

"Nah, I already did."

He walks away. I am crushed by the weight of my ineptitude and slump down into my chair. I am torn between needing to scream and needing to cry. But there's no time to do either— the boss is about to give his morning pep talk. So I take some deep breaths, swivel in my chair, and suck it up, all the while saying to myself, "Things will get better. Things will get better."

The next two months are a blur of work and sleep. My thoughts are becoming more agitated and jumbled; my body is starting to feel battered and shaky. Like I'm being bounced around in a rock tumbler. I'm also dropping things. Pens. Cutlery. A coffee cup. And today at work, I stumbled on the

stairs. Something is definitely wrong. Or maybe I'm just going crazy. I should probably go see my doctor again. Maybe I'll call him later.

First, it's time to call my dad. We speak on the phone every day. He hasn't been feeling well for a while—he's been slowing down, having difficulty walking, and losing his balance. And even though I know he's been undergoing tests and seeing specialists, I am shocked when he tells me he has just been diagnosed with Parkinson's disease. After I hang up, the thought that he's afflicted with this devastating illness is too much for me to bear. Whatever flimsy mechanism is holding me together suddenly snaps. I take refuge in a private recording booth and cry me a river of turbulent tears.

I HAVE A CONFESSION: I have a Cry Lady living inside me. She makes me choke up anywhere, anytime, with anyone—at the drop of a hat, the stub of a toe, the hurl of an insult, or the hint of bad news. Fortunately, I'm one of the few middle-aged women who look attractive with puffy red eyes, blotchy skin, and a snotty nose, so my public outbursts don't bother me. They don't seem to bother my colleagues either—at least not the ones that scuttle away like cockroaches when my lower lip starts quivering and my eyes start leaking. This has been going on for weeks now, ever since my dad told me he has Parkinson's.

I've never cried so much in my entire life—though I have had plenty of practice. I've cried over broken toys, broken bones, broken hearts, broken dreams. It helps that I've been blessed with PMS and an artistic temperament. It's no wonder my repertoire of tears is so extensive—ranging from infantile to crocodile and everything in between. I was built to bawl. I was built to do a multitude of other things too—laughing being one of them. But I can't even crack a smile these days, let alone

laugh. I'm afraid my joy is in jeopardy of becoming extinct. I need help. I need therapy.

DEPRESSION DESERVES DISCRETION—that's why there's no sign on the clinic door. Just the address. I appreciate this gesture as I walk, unnoticed, inside. I also appreciate the steep staircase and what it offers—a hopeful climb toward a new beginning, or perhaps a hapless fall to a hopeless ending.

I'm here tonight to meet Theresa, a cognitive behavioral therapist who specializes in treating depression. She finds me in the waiting room, leafing through a *Reader's Digest*.

"Are you Robyn?"

I nod.

"I'm Theresa. Come with me."

I follow her around the corner, along the hallway, into a tiny office. We sit down opposite each other, me on the couch, she on the swivel chair. She smiles, takes a deep breath, then exhales slowly, loudly. Without intending to, I smile, inhale deeply, then exhale slowly and loudly too.

"Would you like to spend a few more minutes breathing together?" she asks.

I nod and follow her lead, and as we inhale and exhale in unison, a comforting intimacy overrides the awkwardness between us. Relaxed and alert, I take in her features: oval face, straight nose, stormy blue eyes, intelligent mouth, pale complexion, shiny shoulder-length auburn hair. She looks like she sprang from the same gene pool as Jodie Foster—a half-sister perhaps, or a first cousin. She probably thinks I sprang from the gene pool of a cosmetically challenged, hirsute cavewoman— given my frizzy brown hair, dark-circled bloodshot eyes, thick bushy eyebrows, and bleached mustache sandwiched between a runny nose and chapped lips. But we keep our first impressions

to ourselves. After all, it's not the physical we're delving into, it's the emotional—that temperamental realm where once a week, in a tiny office, my Cry Lady confesses her life problems and emotional turmoil to a therapist with a compassionate heart, an intuitive intelligence, and an endless supply of Kleenex to mop up an endless supply of tears.

Thanks to Theresa's perceptive and skillful direction, our first therapy session is grueling—a real emotional workout. It starts with my telling her my abbreviated life story:

I grew up in Toronto in a typical dysfunctional middle-class Jewish family. I felt like the black sheep—the disobedient daughter who dated non-Jewish boys, who left the nest before getting married and moved to the other side of the country. My mom is fiery and flashy, spontaneous and demanding; my dad is laid-back and refined, cautious and accommodating. They have been married for forty-four years, and while learning to love one another they perfected the fine art of arguing, carrying grudges, giving each other the silent treatment, and blaming the other. They taught their children well. All three of us—me, my younger sister, and my baby brother. We spent much of our childhood embroiled in battles, tearing down trust, building up walls. It drove my parents crazy. Especially my mom. She had a short fuse, and her conflict-resolution techniques were often framed as questions. Sometimes she'd wait for an answer, like a TV game show host waiting for the contestant to make up her mind.

"Will it be curtain number 1? Or would you rather have what's behind curtain number 2?"

"Are you going to stop that crying, or do you want me to give you something to really cry about?"

"Will you apologize to your brother, or do I have to teach you a lesson that'll make you really sorry?"

"Can you and your sister stop that fighting, or should I bang your heads together and knock some sense into the both of you?"

Choices, choices, choices. It never really mattered who decided what—we usually got what we didn't want. And for me, the only thing worth getting was *away. Far, far away.*

I made my escape in 1986, when I was twenty-two. I moved to Vancouver, to study at the University of British Columbia. One year shy of completing my undergraduate degree in psychology and fine arts, I left school and started my own successful art business, Robyn Levy Studio. I sold my original paintings, greeting cards, and T-shirts across Canada and the United States and even in Japan (where my company name was advertised as Lobyn Revy Studio). In 1991, I met Bergen; in 1994, our daughter, Naomi, was born. Six years later, I started working at CBC, in radio.

"And why are you here to see me?" Theresa asks.

"Because I can't stop crying. I've never been so depressed in my life."

"Do you have any idea what might be causing your depression?"

"Probably lots of things," I sob. "Wonky hormones from PMS and premenopause. Stress at work. Stress at home. Naomi is depressed. We're fighting a lot. And she's having trouble at school. You know, girl culture; girls can be so mean. She's different, and it's hard to fit in when you're different. Then there's our house. It's unfinished. Bergen is slowly fixing it up in his spare time, but it's taking forever. There are always power tools and messes everywhere. I hate it. But the worst thing is my dad was just diagnosed with Parkinson's disease."

"Are you close to your father?"

"Very close. Always have been. I am so sad that he's sick, and I'm so far away. I wish I lived closer so I could be there, to help him."

"How is he coping?"

"Not well. He's incredibly depressed and anxious. Can't sleep. Can't work. Losing weight. Slowing down. He can barely talk on the phone. He's having all sorts of adverse reactions to meds. It's like my dad has disappeared."

Theresa nods, then says, "It sounds as if you are in mourning."

"But my dad didn't die. He's still alive."

"Of course he is. But given your dad's health, he may never be quite the same as the dad who raised you, the person you are used to. It's possible you're mourning the loss of your pre-Parkinson's dad."

I let this idea sink in. Images of him from photos taken over the years flash through my mind: playing tennis, driving his vintage red convertible, hugging his three kids, napping on the brown couch, napping on the white couch, napping at the Blue Jays game.

Then a memory I'd long forgotten surfaces.

"I was in my early twenties, and my dad and I were walking on a path in a park. I had picked up an ordinary stick from the ground and was shifting it back and forth between my hands as we chatted. After a while, my dad wanted to see the stick. So I handed it over to him, and he casually asked, 'Do you mind if we share it?' It was an odd but sweet request, and I must have nodded yes, because he snapped it in half, passed me one part, and kept the other for himself. Then we continued walking, neither of us mentioning the stick again."

Theresa says, "Maybe nothing needed to be said. It sounds like the sharing was complete."

Suddenly I feel my chest tighten, and I begin gasping for breath. Theresa crosses her arms, places her hands flat against her upper chest, and says, "Try doing this with your hands. And breathe deeply."

I do, and within seconds I am overcome by grief—Theresa a witness to my weeping, my wailing, my Cry Lady crescendo, and the first of many mournful farewells to my aging, ailing father.

When I eventually calm down, I complain of a pounding headache and tingling in my left hand and left foot. The same tingling sensations that I've been experiencing on and off for weeks now.

"Would you like to do something to help relieve your headache and get rid of the tingling?"

"Are you offering me heroin?"

Theresa smiles. "Nope. Sorry, I'm all out of heroin. But I can teach some exercises that will help you feel better."

So for the last part of the session I mirror Theresa's movements: self-massaging my temples and jaw and neck, deep breathing while moving my head from side to side, raising my arms up over my head and then flopping them down at my sides, and stomping my feet. Surprisingly, my headache disappears, and the tingling in my hand and foot is almost gone. But not quite.

Our time is up, and Theresa says, "You worked really hard tonight. Drink lots of water when you get home; your body needs it."

After scheduling next week's appointment, I walk carefully down the steep staircase, out into the drizzling rain, and drive myself home—exhausted and cranky and thirsty as hell. I am thankful that Bergen and Naomi instinctively stay out of my way the rest of the night. Only Nellie, with her squeaky toy, dares to approach.

COME SUMMERTIME, work conditions are perfect for a TV sitcom but pitiful for real life: poor management, tight deadlines, big egos, and hot tempers, and to top it all off, the entire CBC

building is under construction. It looks like a war zone. The grounds are a wasteland of rubble and dust. Trees and shrubs lie wounded in piles. Parking lots are tunneled into massive graves—out of which will eventually rise the TV Towers con-dominiums and a world-class broadcast center—with an integrated multimedia newsroom, state-of-the-art technology, a performance studio, public spaces, and more. It's all part of CBC's Vancouver Redevelopment Project, which will take three years to complete.

Month after month, season after season, we toil away at our desks, despite the nerve-racking noise of dynamite blasting, pneumatic drilling, and jackhammering. We write scripts and edit tape in workspaces speckled in drywall dust and demolition debris while breathing in noxious fumes from paint, cutting oil, and glues. We conduct live on-air interviews with guests while construction workers make a ruckus above our not-so-soundproof studio.

By early spring, our laid-back Radio 3 office has been laid to rest, and our team is transplanted into the brand-new corporate cubicle farm. Ergonomic specialists tweak our workstations—adjusting table heights and chair angles, computer monitors and keyboard positions, bending over backwards to make us comfortable and productive. My chronic back pain makes sitting difficult, so they give me three chairs to try. My left hand gets tingly and clumsy while typing, so they buy me a special keyboard. But no matter what they change, replace, or adjust, I'm Goldilocks from hell; nothing feels just right. Still, I do my best to settle in to this new workspace—not just for me but also for my Cry Lady, who now accompanies me to meetings, answers my phone, and replies to my e-mails.

This morning, my supervisor e-mailed me the most soul-destroying, nitpicking, inconsiderate critique of an assignment

I've been working on. Her words crush my Cry Lady and trigger a waterfall of tears. Somehow, my Cry Lady manages to write this response:

> Dear supervisor across the room,
> Am I correct to assume your ass is glued to your chair?
> And that is why from over there, you e-mailed me your
> carefully composed criticisms and slyly missed this
> lovely vision of all my tear ducts in a row? Because if
> this is really so, then fuck you!

Just as my Cry Lady is about to hit *send*, I intervene and press *delete*. Why stoop to my supervisor's level with an impersonal e-mail, when I can take the high road, go over my supervisor's head, and talk face-to-face with her boss? I muster up my courage, stomp across the room, and lay it on the line:

"Enough is enough! I deserve to be treated with respect! Give me constructive—not destructive—criticism! There's too much work piled on my plate! Assign this project to someone else! Supervisors aren't always right! Some supervisors are never right!"

When I'm done with my diatribe, I collapse into a chair—panting from exertion and euphoric with victory—like an underdog that has captured the leader of the pack. My efforts do not go unnoticed. Having spilled my guts all over his office, the boss commends me for my honesty and rewards me with a box of two-ply tissues. As I blow my nose and mop up my mess, he pats me on the shoulder and says, "I'm glad we had this little talk. I'll speak with your supervisor."

"Thank you," I sniffle, exiting his office and closing his door behind me. Nothing beats direct communication.

A little euphoria can work wonders. Over the next two weeks, my rage retreats and my mood lightens. My routine hasn't changed: I'm still working nine to five, going to therapy,

walking the dog, sleeping on weekends. But now I am feeling hopeful. Digging my way out of depression seems possible, until I get a phone call at work from my dad, and suddenly digging out seems pointless.

"Hi, Robyn. I've got some terrible news." His voice sounds hollow, lifeless.

"Oh, no. What's wrong?" My voice sounds shrill, fearful.

"It's Mom. She's in hospital with a collapsed lung."

"What happened? Is she going to be OK?"

"She was having a test done on her lungs, and during the procedure, something went wrong."

I listen in stunned silence as he explains the grim situation.

My mom is unluckily lucky. Sick but not sickly. Dying but not dead. She has just been diagnosed with stage-four inoperable lung cancer. It's in both of her lungs and has likely been there for years. It comes as a total shock—considering she feels perfectly healthy and has been as active as always: looking after my dad, walking five miles a day, playing golf, shopping at the mall, getting her hair and nails done, visiting grandchildren, playing bridge and mah-jongg, going out with friends. She would probably still be in the dark, had she not volunteered to participate in a hospital research study. They were looking at the incidence of cancer among aging ex-smokers, like her, particularly heavy smokers who puffed away the early half of their lives and then managed to kick the habit and live smoke-free for decades.

Fortunately, it's a slow-growing cancer, and for now she is asymptomatic. She doesn't feel pain from the cancer, just from her collapsed lung, which the doctors expect to heal quickly.

I hear unfamiliar voices muttering in the background, and my dad tells me the doctors have come to check up on my mom. So he will have to call me back later.

After I hang up, I sit shivering in my chair, waves of nausea rippling through my body, conflicting thoughts gripping my mind: compassion for my poor mother and anger at her for getting sick too—she's supposed to look after my dad; he's the sick one. I feel overwhelmed by despair—what's going to happen now?

Lost in thought, I hear the gentle voice of a colleague asking me, "Are you OK?"

"I don't know," I answer. I clutch my belly and bolt for the bathroom, where I disappear into a stall. All I know is that I need a break—from work, from family, from stress, from life. But how? Days later, I find out.

THE BOSS IS INSTRUMENTAL—in more ways than one. He invites me back into his office, this time for a private concert. He greets me at the door and hands me the event program: *Requiem for a Cry Lady's Obsolete Job.* As I take my seat across from his desk, a slow, mournful dirge fills the air and sets the tone for the show.

"I want you to know that this has nothing to do with you—or your work. Radio 3 is moving in a new direction, shifting focus away from radio to the web. Unfortunately, your job is being eliminated. We're giving you notice and severance pay. I'm really sorry."

Slowly, his words begin to sink in, and my eyes begin to sting. I think, if ever there was a perfect time to let a Cry Lady loose, this is it. I imagine the headline news: "Boss tragically drowns in disgruntled worker's tears. Foul play suspected."

But that's not what happens. Pride intervenes. And my Cry Lady remains composed until she's out of his sight.

My work ends in midsummer, on a warm, cloudy day. There is a farewell lunch and promises to keep in touch and bittersweet

good-byes. Heading home, I feel absolute relief in leaving this obsolete job behind. I am exhausted, in dire need of rest. My body has been growing old right before my very eyes. I shuffle when I walk. I have trouble getting out of chairs. My fingers have lost strength and tire quickly. My mind is muddled, and I'm still depressed. Advil no longer relieves my aches and pains. Even sleep has lost its luster—I can't seem to find a comfortable position anymore. I'm always tossing and turning, wondering where to place my arms. They feel remote and disconnected.

Severance pay provides the precious gift of time—the entire month of August to relax and unwind. A real holiday with Bergen and Naomi. And the opportunity to embark on a friendship pilgrimage—something I've been thinking about for a while. I really want to deepen my relationships with close girlfriends and special acquaintances, as well as reconnect with friends I haven't seen in years. If all goes according to plan, I will be better by September and then I'll start looking for work.

I begin my pilgrimage without even leaving home. My dear friend Mahima, who lives in Singapore, comes to visit. Ever observant, she looks me over and, with a puzzled expression on her face, asks, "Do you always hold your hands so delicately, like a dancer?"

I have no idea what she is talking about. "Like a dancer? What do you mean?" Now I'm the one wearing the puzzled expression.

"Like this," Mahima says, wrapping her outstretched arms around a giant invisible ball, then bending down into a plié. She holds this ballet position for several seconds and I laugh self-consciously, thinking, what if she's right?

All day long, I hear Mahima's voice, with its distinctive lilt, looping over and over in my mind asking, "Do you always hold your hands so delicately, like a dancer?" Later, while getting

ready for bed, I stand in front of the mirror and stare at my naked body. She's right. My arms are positioned in a dancer's pose, my hands graceful extensions. They are frozen in place. It's all so effortless, unintentional, alarming. And it's in this state of hyperawareness that I discover the most disconcerting thing: my left arm is not swinging while I walk. Instead, it remains fixed in place, stuck magnetically by my side. Suddenly I feel rigid and robotic and idiotic. How long has this been going on? Why have I never noticed this before? And why is it happening?

These questions spawn more questions: Why am I still so depressed? Why am I so tired all the time? Why am I not getting any better? Am I paranoid, or am I getting worse? My search for answers is short-lived. By early September, I hit rock bottom.

MY CRASH is silent and solitary. I land on the living room floor—an incoherent clump, clinging to the yoga mat, in a downward dead dog pose. The crushing weight of gravity makes it difficult to breath. And my limbs feel heavy and cold and useless. Somehow, I am sinking into a deep, dark hole, and I don't know why.

Bergen comes to my rescue, calm and unflinching, kneeling by my side: a heroic handyman with his tenderhearted toolkit, inspecting his broken wife. He wades through my silence and pries open my pain. I drift to the surface, hysterical.

"I need help," I cry. "Something is wrong... I don't know what... but I feel like I'm dying... like I want to die... I don't know what to do."

"I'll help you," he assures me. "I'll do anything for you. I'm right here. We'll figure this out together."

He gently lifts me to my feet, and we sit down on the couch. My body is shaking, my teeth chattering, my heart pounding away. I need warmth—he brings me tea and blankets. I need

peace and quiet—he walks on eggshells and coaxes Naomi and her friends to do the same. I need mindless distraction—he installs me in the TV room, where I lie lifeless on the couch, like a heap of wood for a funeral pyre. I need doctors—he takes me to appointments where I'm told I need a lot of other things too: antidepressants, sleeping pills, medical diagnostic tests, appointments with specialists, specialists with ointments.

Only a few people know that something is terribly wrong. Of course, Bergen and Naomi do—they're stuck in front-row seats at this horror show, every single day. There's also my G.P., Dr. Mintz, and my therapist, Theresa. And finally, my Toronto Trio: Ruthie, Bonnie, and Sweet Lisa. They call every day to talk to me, but because my Cry Lady is rude and unruly—always erupting into tears, interrupting conversations—I hardly get a word in edgewise. Fortunately, my friends are fluent in melancholy, so my sniffles and snorts make sense. They know this is no ordinary case of the blues. Whatever is bringing me down is serious and dangerous. I let their familiar voices assure me: "It's not your fault that you're sick." "You'll find out what's wrong." "You will feel better soon." "See Theresa as much as possible; no matter what it costs, you're worth it." And with their constant love and guidance, I take each day one moment at a time— while Bergen spends almost every moment of his time taking care of me.

2

Breaking News
Is Hard to Do

I DON'T WANT TO KILL MYSELF. I just want to be dead. Like the Lucky Ones in the obituaries. Every morning I greet them with green-eyed envy. Hello, Dearly Departed. Bonjour, Tragically Taken. Nice to meet you, Sorely Missed. Welcome, Gone But Not Forgotten. Breakfast just wouldn't be the same without their alphabetized, memorialized faces staring out at me from the newspaper. I always appreciate their company—they're such a breath of fresh death air.

I feel more at ease with these dead strangers than I do with my living loved ones. Dead strangers don't make messes or noises or demands. They don't notice if teeth need brushing or pajamas need washing. Best of all, they are immune to misery—which is a great relief for my guilty conscience.

I'm mortified by the insidious way my suffering has contaminated our home. It's been just one week since my crash, and already apprehension hangs in the air, sadness frames every doorway, stress creeps into each room. I blame myself

25

for dragging my family down, leading them to the edge of this dark hole—the portal to my depression. Where they watch me picking at my food, searching for my snapshot and Lucky One liberation. And where I watch them carry on.

Since I am out of commission, Bergen launches into rescue mode—taking care of everything and everyone but himself. My heart sinks as I catch glimpses of him rushing from room to room, up and down the stairs, in and out of the house. He's like a whirling dervish, spinning from chore to chore. Cooking meals. Washing laundry. Buying groceries. Walking Nellie. Cleaning the house. Helping Naomi. Saving me—or whoever I am now. I'm certainly not the wife I once was. Or the mother. The guilt is excruciating. I can barely make eye contact with Naomi. The poor kid. It's tough enough being thirteen and trying to fit in at high school while keeping her grades up. Now, in addition to all that, she has to endure living under the same roof with a catatonic Cry Lady and a frantic father who won't allow her to escape this nightmare and go live at a friend's house. Even though she has several invitations and her suitcase is packed.

I CONFESS: I'm one of those people who write lists. All types, from the classic to-do list to the clandestine ex-lovers list. And no matter how mundane or insane they seem, these inventories are useful devices. They help keep the fridge stocked, the house clean, the dreams wet, the bills paid. And I'm hoping that this list I'm about to write will help me make it through this bleak September day.

It's titled "One Hundred Reasons Not to Kill Myself." It's one of the many therapeutic exercises in this self-help book I'm reading. I've never written a list like this before. But I'm willing to give it a try, even if it means tossing out the other list

I've been secretly compiling. The one called "Bergen's New and Improved Wife." Already I've jotted down the names of several potential candidates to replace me when I'm gone. These women are all wonderful—I wouldn't care which one he chooses. The only thing I really care about is that Bergen find happiness in the arms of another woman—preferably someone with two swinging arms.

Turning my attention to this new list, I pick a fresh page in my journal so that there's plenty of space to jot down my one hundred reasons to stick around. I write the title at the top, numbers down the side, and begin. Within minutes, I sense the futility of compiling this list—I am, after all, feeling listless. Within an hour, I know I am not only depressed but am also demented. No matter how hard I concentrate, the same solitary reason keeps popping into my head. And it isn't profound or practical or religious or romantic—it isn't even hygienic. Reluctantly, I scribble it down: "Nellie licking my feet."

She loves to lick them, and they love being licked, but declaring my dog's tongue bathing my ticklish feet to be the only thing worth living for—well, that's just shameful. I'm sure I have more relevant reasons. I just have to think of them. Eventually, I come up with number 2: "The taste of dark chocolate." Now I am frantic. What about the people I love? My family? My friends? What if someone reads this list? What will they think?

In a state of panic, I pick up my pen and quickly add Naomi and Bergen to the list. I breathe a sigh of relief, having corrected my oversight. And then the panic returns as it dawns on me, I've just made the list even more deplorable. The sequencing is all wrong. What kind of person ranks a dog footbath higher than her own flesh and blood? Or her beloved spouse? Of course, I know the answer. That's why I scribble over the list and make an appointment to see Theresa later today.

THERESA'S OFFICE is small and cramped and shaped like the letter *L*. As usual, she sits in the swivel chair and I sit on the snivel couch, within arm's reach of a fresh box of tissues.

"How are you doing?" she gently asks, her blue eyes on red alert—scanning my horizon, watching my sun set, wondering if it will rise again. She knows how I am doing before I say a word. I just fill her in on the details—the crash, the calls, the list—while my Cry Lady sets the mood. Theresa listens intently. "It sounds like you're in a lot of pain."

"I just want someone to tell me what to do," I sob. "My doctor wants me to start antidepressants. But I don't know if it's the best thing. What do you think I should do?"

"Well, I can't make that decision for you. But I can tell you that sometimes, for some people with clinical depression, taking medication while continuing with therapy makes all the difference."

I consider this, as we breathe deeply in unison, in and out, in and out.

"What are you feeling now?" Theresa asks as I massage the back of my neck.

"It hurts. Everything hurts. I don't know how much more I can take. What if the medication doesn't help?"

"I understand," she says. "It's hard to imagine things getting better when you're feeling so awful. But they will."

"It's hard to feel hopeful when I just want to die."

"I know that you don't feel hopeful. But I do. And I'm going to hold on to your hope, for you, if that's OK."

I try to imagine the shape of my hope, cradled in Theresa's hands. But all I can see is emptiness.

I have to ask, "Have you ever felt like you wanted to die?"

Theresa's hands lift off her lap and slide down the sides of her neck. Then she presses them protectively against her chest.

"Years ago, I came very close to ending my life. I was extremely depressed."

"What happened?" I ask.

"Well, I found a great therapist, and with her help I made big changes in my life. I used to be a lawyer."

Suddenly, a wave of sadness sweeps through me. "I'm sorry for your suffering, and I'm so grateful that you're still here."

"Me too," she says. "I told you this not to make you sad but because I truly believe you can make it too. It's just going to take time."

"I have lots of time; I just don't have lots of money. Definitely not enough to see you regularly."

"That's not a problem," she says. "We can work something out. You can pay me later, sometime in the future, when you do have the money."

I don't know what to say. I just know how I feel: overwhelmed.

"Instead of running up a tab, would you consider a trade? One of my paintings?"

"That would be perfect." Theresa smiles.

At the end of the session, Theresa hands me a sheet of paper with two phone numbers: her cell and the suicide-prevention hotline.

"You can call either one, anytime. Just promise me you'll call if you need to talk." Nodding, I tuck the paper into my pocket and give Theresa a hug good-bye. I don't say it out loud, but I'm sure she hears my request: hold on tightly to my hope.

ALTHOUGH AN APPLE a day keeps the doctor away, no fruit has been discovered that keeps the patient away. This is good news for me, bad news for Dr. Mintz. He's my family physician. And I'm his boomerang patient: in one day, back the next. The waiting room regular in the coveted chair. What'll it be today?

The usual? Coming right up—one paper cup of filtered water, with a side order of two-ply facial tissues and all the issues of *National Geographic* I can read. Plenty to keep me occupied until it's my turn. Again.

I like Dr. Mintz. He's big hearted and dedicated. He moves with ease between life's comedies and tragedies. He's a real mensch—a person of integrity and honor. In the thirteen years I've known him, he's grown a little older and a little balder, but really, he hasn't changed much. Or at least that's what I thought. While he's always had a swagger in his step, lately it seems more exaggerated—especially when he moseys on over in his bowlegged jeans, alligator boots, and silver string tie. Something is definitely different about him. He looks more like a snazzy Jewish cowboy than a nice Jewish doctor. But it's more than how he's dressed. I can't exactly put my finger on it, but a change has occurred.

So far, Dr. Mintz is stumped. Whatever disease, disorder, or syndrome is causing my mishmash of symptoms—foot dragging, arm numbness and immobility, body aches and pains, muscle and joint stiffness, mind fuzziness—has not been detected by any of the many tests he's done. It's a mystery. And since mystery loves company, he calls up his colleague—the neurologist. I'm booked to see her soon. Meanwhile, Dr. Mintz urges me to take his advice and start the antidepressants he prescribed ages ago. He promises they'll help me feel better. He says they make everyone feel better, even him. He takes them to cope with his own depression, since being treated recently for prostate cancer. His disclosure explains his exaggerated swagger and strikes a hopeful chord. Maybe the meds will help a little; maybe they will help a lot. Maybe they will lift me out of this dark hole so that I can return to my life and my life can return to me. And then I won't have to see Dr. Mintz so often.

In mid-September, at the pinnacle of my clinical depression, I finally surrender into the arms of Big Pharma and her chemical concoctions. No one forces me to do this. It's my choice. It's my hand clawing its way up and out of the dark hole, placing the pill on the back of my tongue, pouring the water down my throat. Holy water that's been blessed by Dr. Mintz and Dr. Smyth (the neurologist he recommended), as well as Theresa, Bergen, and Sweet Lisa.

I swallow and wait—for side effects and for joy. But nothing happens that first day. Or the next. On the third day, mild nausea sets in and for a while I feel worse. And then, one October morning, the tiniest tinge of joy bubbles up inside me and I wake up, dry eyed, with a dash of happiness lifting the corners of my mouth, unearthing my long-lost smile. Only briefly. But long enough to prove that Dr. Mintz is right. These antidepressants do help. I'm feeling a little bit better, a little less depressed, a little more alive.

TWO SYLLABLES I keep repeating on this miserable November morning: "Don't go. Don't go. Don't go."

"I'll be back soon. You'll be OK," Bergen promises, pressing his lips against mine. Compared with what we're capable of, this good-bye kiss is downright dreary. There's no passion or pizzazz, no sneaking in tongues. Just the perfunctory locking of lips; that's all I can handle. Not that I'm disappointed—it's the hug I'm really after. I need a lot of hugs these days, and with Bergen going out of town on business, this one has got to last me a while. I also need someone to move in and watch over me while Bergen is away. I'm still that fragile.

A few hours after Bergen leaves for Carcross, Yukon, I head out to the airport to pick up Sweet Lisa, my substitute spouse. I spot her near the luggage carousel, holding her daughter's hand. Danielle is six years old—a miniature version of her mom, with

the same wild brown curly hair, the big toothy smile, and the talent to remain unruffled when I burst into tears while driving us home in the rain.

Soon after Lisa and Dani are settled, we take Nellie for a walk. It's a typical Vancouver autumn, just after Halloween. The rain has been relentless, and my neighborhood has turned to mush. Everywhere we go, there's muddy grass, dirty puddles, clumps of soggy leaves. The sidewalks are smeared with the trampled guts of reckless worms and suicidal slugs. Rotting pumpkins lie smashed to pieces in the streets. I feel compelled to apologize for this dismal weather and mucky mess. This is not Vancouver the beautiful. This is not Vancouver at its best. Mind you, I'm not at my best either. And yet, my dearest friend is here, with her girl, and they're both smiling at Nellie, wearing raincoats they brought from home. It's just like Lisa to come prepared for the weather. She's always planning ahead. But she could never have prepared for what is about to unfold. And for this, I am truly sorry.

Lisa proves to be an excellent surrogate spouse. I knew she would be. We used to live together in Toronto, back when we were university students. We were so compatible that we imagined building a life together. And had we not been such devout heterosexuals, we could have made a lovely lesbian couple: the short, sexy psychologist and the tall, curvaceous artist.

The first few days of their visit we play tourists on vacation: lunch at restaurants, a trip to the aquarium in Stanley Park, riding the gondola to the top of Grouse Mountain, grocery shopping at Granville Island. It's obvious to Lisa how hard I'm working to keep my spirits and energy up—even though she is cooking the dinners and cleaning up the house. And although I'm lethargic and clumsy and easily fatigued, she thinks I've got my life and parenting well in hand.

"You're doing great, Robbie. Making Naomi's lunches. Driving us around. Taking care of yourself. You're certainly better than I expected you to be."

"Really?"

"Yeah. Back in September, every time I called, you were in such anguish. Constantly crying. Wanting to die. I was really worried that you might not get through this."

"It's the drugs," I say. "I still feel depressed, but now it's like I'm wearing a life jacket and it's keeping my head above water."

"For sure the drugs are helping, but it's also you. Your life force is so strong."

Lisa gives me a hug and I begin to cry.

"But don't you think I've changed?"

She takes a deep breath, then says, "To me, you're still the same Robyn; you just seem diminished. You walk slower, talk softer. You're not as confident."

"But what about my left arm? Look. It barely moves."

"That's puzzling. But I treat many depressed clients in my practice. And I've seen how depression and medication can slow people down. It messes with their bodily mechanics. I really think that your body will get better as you adjust to the meds and your mood improves."

"I really hope so." I sigh.

"Me too."

THE NEXT DAY, Lisa accompanies me to the hospital, where I have an appointment to see the neurologist. When my name is called, Lisa stays with Dani in the waiting room. It's my second time seeing Dr. Smyth. The first was many weeks ago, when I nearly drowned her in a biblical flood of tears. Somehow, she managed to stay afloat and give me a full examination. But because I was so severely depressed, she couldn't distinguish

between symptoms caused by clinical depression and those perhaps caused by a neurological disorder. Unable to make a diagnosis at that time, she too prescribed antidepressants, a battery of blood tests, and a brain MRI and told me to come back to see her in a month.

When I step into her office today, we're both surprised by each other's physical appearance. Dr. Smyth remarks how much livelier I am now that I'm medicated and no longer crying constantly, just dripping sporadically. The reduced flow of tears might be why Dr. Smyth looks so different to me this time— I can see her clearly. I can't remember how she looked last time, but it wasn't like this. The woman I see today resembles a twenty-year-old Meg Ryan, with short, tousled blond hair and perfect skin. I say, "You don't look old enough to be a neurologist." "I know," she says. "Everybody tells me that. But I am."

She examines me, asks questions about my current state of health, and dims the lights. Apparently, it's show time. I turn to face her computer screen, and the moment she starts the MRI slide show I regret leaving Lisa out in the waiting room. She would have loved seeing this: my brain is a mind-boggling work of art. These technicolor magnetic resonance images are incredible. It's all digitized and computerized. Dr. Smyth zooms in and out, and psychedelic formations appear up close, then far away, like pulsating oceans, mountains, and volcanic rock viewed through Google Earth. I follow along as she points out the significance of different shapes and colors. Because of this, she rules out a stroke. Because of that, she rules out a brain tumor. All good news, so far. She also rules out MS—multiple sclerosis—her area of expertise. My relief is palpable. That's what I thought I had, MS, just like my dad's sister. She was diagnosed in her early teens. She'd have flare-ups the rest of her life, but it was breast cancer that killed her at age forty-nine. My poor auntie Glenda.

Dr. Smyth clicks on another image and zooms in tight.

"This region is your substantia nigra. It looks normal, but it's not. There's a problem."

"Problem? What problem?" I sputter.

She looks me straight in the eye and calmly drops the bomb. "You have Parkinson's disease. I'm sorry." She braces herself for another biblical flood of tears.

"How can you be sure?" I blubber.

"You present with many classic Parkinson's symptoms: muscle rigidity, slow body movements, flat facial expressions, depression."

"But you said that part of my brain looks normal."

"The only way to be 100 percent certain is by doing an autopsy of your brain. It's a little early for that."

"So you could be wrong?"

"I'd love to be wrong, but I don't think I am. You can get a second opinion."

At the end of this appointment, Dr. Smyth answers my questions and gathers together depressing handouts for me to read. I tell her I'm plagued by the letter *p*. PMS, premenopause, and now this—Parkinson's. She suddenly bursts into laughter and says, "And me. My first name is Penny." The absurdity of it all gets me laughing. But not for long. Heaving sobs return, and Dr. Smyth becomes solemn and says, "It's going to be OK. You'll see." And because Lisa is out in the waiting room, and Bergen is up in the Yukon, I ask Dr. Smyth for a hug. She walks over to me and opens her arms, and I pretend I'm embracing a beautiful young movie star, not a neurologist who has diagnosed me with an old person's disease.

BATHTUBS ARE VERSATILE VESSELS—just fill one up and pick a verb: soak, wash, relax, play, read, write, talk, sing, study, cry, celebrate, rejuvenate, meditate, masturbate, fornicate. I've done

it all. More than once. But tonight is different and requires different verbs. And so Lisa lights some candles, pours us a bath, and together we weep, grapple, question, despair, console, and deny the shocking news. And by the time we've toweled off and the bathwater has drained, the neurologist's devastating diagnosis feels right: I have early-onset Parkinson's disease. Just like Michael J. Fox. Of course, I'll get a second opinion from an expert in the field, to be absolutely sure. But my doubt has diminished. Just like me.

Later, when Bergen calls to say goodnight, my soft voice breaks the news. We fill the phone line with long vulnerable silences. Space to breathe. Space to cry. He'll be home soon, with his luggage and laptop and pent-up sorrow. And he'll tell me he loves me, still. And this is the first thing I want to believe this week.

I HAVE A CONFESSION: I married an older man. Three years older, to be exact. Mind you, that's in dog years. Multiply three by seven and you get the age difference in human years— something to really bark about. I never expected things to last. It was supposed to be just a summer fling—fun and fleeting. But come autumn, our hearts were entwined like two tangled dog leashes, and by winter we had begun to build a life together. That was sixteen years ago.

It's amazing how love bridges the generation gap between us. But it does nothing to ease my anxiety. Even though Bergen is in perfect health, possesses boundless energy, and looks much younger than most men his age, I always worry—a lot. I worry that he'll have a heart attack or stroke and die. Or that he'll have a heart attack or stroke and survive—living out the rest of his life in a vegetative state, leaving me stuck changing his diapers and spoon-feeding him mush. I even worry that I lack the moral fortitude to stick around if such a tragedy strikes.

All this worrying can land me in the doghouse. On the rare occasions I find Bergen napping midday, if I don't see his chest rising and falling, I work myself into a tizzy until I'm convinced that his slack jaw and limp body can only mean one thing: he's dead. Panic sweeps through me, followed by grief. All hope is lost. But on the off chance he's not dead, I yell out his name and give him what I call a "love shove" but what he calls a "paranoid punch." There's no point quibbling over words, especially since my arm movement either jolts him wide awake or brings him back from the beyond. All that really matters is he's alive and well, albeit a little groggy—leaving me giddy with relief.

My obsessive worrying is based on the belief that older husbands are more susceptible to disease than younger wives. Now I've blown that theory out of the water. And although I regret getting Parkinson's disease, I appreciate the irony of the situation: a future where it's possible, and even probable, that my senior-citizen husband will spend his golden years changing my diapers and spoon-feeding me mush. Will he stick around? Do I want to be a burden to him? Tough questions. Unknown answers. More doggone things to worry about.

THE MORNING AFTER Dr. Smyth's diagnosis, I lie in bed, stiff as a board, staring at the ceiling. Finding the motivation to get up isn't easy, considering this is the first day of the rest of my neurodegenerative life. There's so much to not look forward to: dry skin, dry scalp, dry eyes, incontinence, constipation, tremors, falling, freezing in place, stooped posture, involuntary movements, dementia. It's all listed in these helpful handouts Dr. Smyth gave me. But the thing I dread the most is telling Naomi. She doesn't know yet. I'm waiting until Bergen gets home so that we can break the news together. Tomorrow, after school. This gives me a bit of time to think things over. To

research and strategize. To come up with a plan. Thank goodness I have Sweet Lisa to talk to.

After breakfast, Naomi heads off to school, and Dani
watches cartoons on TV. Lisa and I sit at the table, sipping hot
lemon drinks. Neither of us slept very well last night, and it
shows—we both have bags under our eyes. We sit in silence
watching Nellie gulp down her bowl of food. When she's done,
she lets out an impressive burp. I usually laugh whenever she
does this, but not today. Instead, I dab my eyes with a tissue
and say, "I'm really scared to tell Naomi."

"Of course you're afraid. It's such a scary thing for you to
have to deal with and to have to tell your daughter. Do you
think you'll tell her on your own, or with Bergen?"

"With Bergen. I need him to be there with me."

"That sounds like a good plan."

"She's only thirteen. This is going to ruin her life," I say.

"No it's not. It's going to ruin her day, maybe even her week.
But not her entire life."

"Why do you say that?"

"She's a teenager. And the wonderful thing about teenagers
is that they are incredibly self-absorbed. She's not thinking long
term, just how it's going to impact her right now. She'll go back
to her life afterward."

I mull this over while Lisa peels us an apple.

"She's also your and Bergen's daughter. She's been around
adults all her life. And she's expressive, resourceful, intelligent,
and resilient. She'll be fine as long as she has the opportunity to
talk with people."

"But you know she's depressed."

"I do. But I don't think this is going to throw her into a deeper
depression. If anything, she might feel relieved, knowing the
reason you haven't been well these past years."

"How much information do you think I need to tell her?"

"I would try to keep it simple. Explain the biology. Answer all of her questions. And if she doesn't ask any, don't worry. She'll ask when she's ready to know."

"This is the hardest thing I've ever had to do in my life," I moan.

"I know it is."

"It's heartbreaking to imagine a daughter watching her mother disintegrate. You know the saddest thing of all?"

"What?"

"I'm afraid that Naomi's memories of me, back when I was vibrant and healthy, will be displaced by this disease. She'll forget who I used to be, what I used to do. I'll just be her sick mom."

"I hope she doesn't lose those memories. And if she does, we'll just have to remind her."

Later that day, I crawl under my covers and take a much-needed nap. By the time I wake up, Lisa and the girls are cooking dinner. I watch them taking turns stirring a pot and tossing a salad while they sing along to Feist: "1, 2, 3, 4, tell me that you love me more." Lisa looks my way and smiles. I try to smile back and enjoy the moment, but I'm too busy worrying about tomorrow. That's when Lisa leaves and Bergen comes home and I tell Naomi that I have Parkinson's. My sadness summons my Cry Lady, but I'm determined to give her the night off. So I pour myself a glass of wine, sit down at the table, and will my tears away. Nellie wanders over and curls up by my feet. The rain taps out a rhythm on the kitchen skylights, while I breathe in the mingled smells of wet dog and roasted vegetables. Not the most appetizing aroma, but better than roasted dog and wet vegetables.

After dinner, when the kitchen is cleaned up and homework is done, Lisa puts Dani to bed. Then Lisa, Naomi, and I cuddle

up on the couch and chat about high school, close friends, and dating. Lisa asks Naomi, "Do you know that your mom dated a movie star?" Naomi's eyes light up. "Really?"

"You mean you haven't told her?" Lisa gives me one of her mischievous smiles.

"Not yet," I admit.

"Well, what are you waiting for? Tonight's the night. Naomi, you're mom dated Dr. McDreamy, on *Grey's Anatomy.*"

"That was so many years ago," I say.

By the look on Naomi's face, I can tell she's impressed and bewildered.

She says, "I can't picture what he looks like."

So we Google him on the computer, and voilà, there he is, all grown up and gorgeous, a hot Hollywood star. I tell Naomi the sanitized version of the story.

"I was only twenty-one and still living in Toronto. I was working part-time at a trendy clothing store, downtown on Yonge Street. And one day, this tall, cute guy walks in and we start chatting and joking around. I remember he was quite funny. Anyway, I help him pick out a bunch of stuff to try on. Of course, everything looks great on him. And when he's done, he walks out of the change room, carrying this mountain of jeans and shirts, and says he'll take everything. I'm a bit shocked but try to stay cool as I ring up his bill. When I ask him how he wants to pay, he hands me a credit card. But he's got such an adorable baby face, I ask him, "Do you have a note from your mommy?" He laughs and tells me the credit card is his, not his mom's, and says he's an actor, performing the lead in *Brighton Beach Memoirs,* a Neil Simon play. And then he invites me to see the show. So I go. And that's how our brief summer romance began."

"How old was he?" Naomi asks.

"Around nineteen."

"Why didn't you tell me this before?"

"I guess I was waiting for the right time."

Naomi rolls her eyes at me, and I brace myself for more questions about my love life, but the phone rings and she spends the rest of the evening yakking to her friend. On my way upstairs, I overhear her talking about me. Not the usual bitching about her sick mother who's always crying and complaining and making her life miserable. Instead, I hear her gushing with pride and delight about my mysterious life—before marriage and motherhood—and about how much she misses being close to me. And for the first time in years, I sense the strength of our underlying love, and I allow myself to imagine us reconnecting and deepening that love.

The next day, I drive Lisa and Dani to the airport. Saying good-bye to my surrogate spouse isn't easy. For five days, I have feasted on her wisdom and love, spilled my sorrow into her heart, and taken refuge in her compassion. Now that she's gone, I feel exposed and vulnerable, like a desert flower caught in a sandstorm.

A few hours later, Bergen is back and I crumble into his arms.

"I'm sorry. I'm sorry. I'm sorry," tumbles from my mouth.

"I know. I'm sorry too."

By the time Naomi gets home from school, we have synchronized our sadness and are ready to reveal my diagnosis. Bergen makes a pot of tea and asks Naomi to join us in the living room. She takes a seat on the couch next to him and smiles nervously at me, sitting rigidly in the armchair.

"We have something to tell you," I say, holding a tissue in my hands.

Naomi waits in silence, looking down at the floor. Bergen clears his throat, then says, "You know that Robyn has not been feeling well for quite a while. And she's been going to different doctors, trying to find out what's wrong."

Naomi slowly nods her head and looks toward me.

I take a deep breath and say, "I now know what's wrong. I have Parkinson's disease."

For a moment, her eyes stare blankly into mine, as if my words are meaningless. Then a flash of comprehension contorts her face and triggers a landslide of primal emotion.

"Are you going to die?" Naomi weeps, swept away by fear and anguish into a motherless state.

It's the question I've been waiting for, preparing for. Tears stream down my cheeks as I recite a quote I read in one of Dr. Smyth's pamphlets:

"People don't die from Parkinson's. They die with Parkinson's."

Somehow, the way I say this sounds unintentionally light-hearted, like I'm only dating an incurable neurodegenerative disease, not married to one. My answer doesn't ease Naomi's mind. If anything, it agitates her. I get up out of my chair and sit next to her on the couch. Our hands clasp and she leans her head on my shoulder.

"When did you find out?" she asks.

"Back in September I went to see a neurologist and she suspected I had Parkinson's."

"Why didn't you tell me then?"

"Because the doctor wasn't absolutely positive. And I didn't want to worry you. Then, two days ago I went to see her again, and this time she was sure. She diagnosed me with early-onset Parkinson's."

I feel Naomi's body pressing against mine, I feel her need to be protected. Holding her tight, I offer a cliché to cling to—the same cliché Dr. Smyth gave me: "It's going to be OK."

Bergen offers one of his own, "We'll get through this together."

I'd like to believe this—that a family that clichés together stays together—but I'm not convinced. I'm sure Naomi isn't either. We're in the same sinking boat now: daughters coping

with parents who have Parkinson's. Under these circumstances, how can anything be OK? How can we get through this together, when I'm falling apart? Will she ever forgive me for getting sick? What if she's next? How could I ever forgive myself? My mind natters on and on. My worries are endless, and they all lead to dead ends. Naomi snuggles in closer while I stroke her head. I want to say something to reassure her, to reassure myself. But she beats me to it. "Maybe they'll find a cure."

We let these words sink in. And while there's plenty more to say, those other words will have to wait. We are busy contemplating and commiserating.

After dinner, we sit around the table, drinking tea and eating cookies. I feel emotionally drained but also relieved now that Naomi knows. She seems more relaxed, having had a few hours to absorb the shock and to realize that I'm not on my deathbed.

"How did you get Parkinson's?"

"I don't know. And I probably never will."

"Is it genetic?" she asks nervously.

"The doctor says it's unlikely."

"But Zaidie has it. And now you have it. That doesn't sound like a coincidence to me."

"I know. It's unbelievable."

"It's a brain disease, right?"

"Yeah. It's a neurodegenerative disease. It's also called a movement disorder, since it causes tremors, shaking, slow movement, things like that. People with Parkinson's don't have enough dopamine-producing brain cells. And without enough dopamine, our bodies can't move normally. My dopamine brain cells are dying."

"All of them?"

"No, not all of them. But lots of them. That's why I look like a zombie."

"No, you don't." Naomi smiles.

"Well, I feel like a zombie. I walk really slowly, and I have this creepy blank expression on my face."

"I know there's no cure. But isn't there medicine you can take, to make you feel better?"

"There is Parkinson's medication that helps improve body movements. And I'll need to take it someday. But for now, I'm taking antidepressants."

"Papa told me. Are they helping?"

"I think so. I'm not as depressed as I was before. Do you notice any difference?"

"Not really. You still seem pretty depressed. You still cry a lot."

Her words cue my Cry Lady, and I burst into tears. "I'm sorry," I sob. "I'm sorry for everything. For getting this disease. For not finding out sooner. But most of all, I'm sorry for how I've treated you and the suffering I've caused. I know I can never change the past, and I take full responsibility for the damage it's done to our relationship. But I want you to know that depression is one of the symptoms of Parkinson's. And the day someone is diagnosed isn't the first day of their disease. I've probably had Parkinson's for the past five years—that's how long I've been dealing with this awful depression and moodiness and anger. I've been sick. And I'm sorry. I love you so much. I never wanted to hurt you or push you away."

Naomi sits slumped in her chair, burying her head in her hands. She is crying quietly, processing everything I have said. I offer her a tissue and she wipes her face.

"Would you like a hug?" I ask.

She nods, and I go stand behind her, lean over the chair, and wrap my arms around her. She reaches up with her hands and weaves them into my embrace. Our embrace. Our new beginning—I hope.

NOW THAT LISA, Bergen, and Naomi know, it's time to tell my father.

When I was a little girl, everyone always told me, "You look just like your dad." Beaming with pride, my dad always responded, "I guess we'll just have to dress her well." Which my mother did. But much to my chagrin, nice clothes didn't quell the comparisons. Neither did puberty, pierced ears, or makeup.

While growing up, I just didn't see the strong resemblance. Sure, we both had big brown eyes, dark brown hair, and thick eyebrows. But so did lots of other people—including Groucho Marx, one of my father's favorite comedians. In fact, there was a time my dad grew this bushy mustache and actually looked a bit like Groucho when he tilted his head at a certain angle. The implications of this were horrifying: if people thought I looked liked my dad, and if I thought he looked like Groucho Marx, then I was in double trouble. It was in times of crisis, like this, when I needed reassuring proof that our father-daughter resemblance was exaggerated. Fortunately, all I had to do was peer out through my mass of Medusa curls and stare at his shiny balding head. Me, his spitting image? Not a chance.

There's no official date that marks the change in my perception. I didn't wake up one day and suddenly see my dad in the mirror. It happened gradually, incrementally, ironically. Errant eyebrow hairs began growing haywire—like his. Long curling toes started turning knobby—like his. Familiar gestures and facial expressions would catch me by surprise. And then came the clincher. It was last year. My parents were in Vancouver for a visit, and my dad and I were having lunch together. I can't remember what I ate, but I'll never forget what I saw: our left hands perfectly synchronized, lying rigidly on the table, in identical frozen positions. It was as if they were communicating with each other, like telepathic twin aliens.

Since my dad had recently been diagnosed with Parkinson's, the immobility of his left hand was understandable. But how to explain mine? It should have been obvious, but it never even crossed my mind. I simply chalked it up to subconscious mimicry and left it at that. But months later, it was clear that something was seriously wrong: my left arm wasn't swinging; my left leg was dragging; I was dropping things and tripping; plus, I was depressed. Still, I didn't make the connection. It was way too preposterous to believe—even when Dr. Smyth broke the news. Of course, my denial was short-lived: Parkinson's is like an uninvited guest who moves in with you, constantly demands attention, and is impossible to ignore. So this is yet another way I resemble my dad. I hope he doesn't mind. After all, imitation is the greatest form of flattery. And there's no one I'd rather resemble than my kind-hearted, compassionate, generous dad. But I'll soon find out how he really feels about sharing this disease—I'm telling him tonight.

I'D RATHER do this in person, not over the phone, but living three thousand miles away makes things complicated. I could fly to Toronto. But that would require cash and courage—two things I'm short of these days. So the phone it is.

"Are you sitting down?"

It's the cliché question that bad news is about to be conveyed. But considering my dad's health and state of mind, he shouldn't be standing up for this news.

"I'm sitting down now. Just give me a minute. Is everybody OK?"

I can feel his anxiety level rising.

"Dad, I have Parkinson's disease. I was just diagnosed the other day."

He takes a few deep breaths and then says, "And I thought

you were going to tell me something terrible. Parkinson's isn't so bad. We can help each other."

His pragmatism surprises me, makes me smile. Maybe Parkinson's isn't as bad as I thought it was.

After a short silence, he says, "Do you want to tell Mom? I can get her to pick up the phone."

"Can you break the news?" I ask, feeling weary and vulnerable.

"Sure, I'll tell her."

Now that I've told my dad—who is telling my mom—next on my list is my sister. Fern is three years younger than me. She's married to Bob, and they live in the burbs with their two young kids, Kayla and Josh. We get along much better now, living three thousand miles apart, than we did as girls sharing a bedroom. Back then, we did our best to bring out the worst in each other: taunting, teasing, insulting, ignoring. We were so good at fighting, we could start a war with just a dirty look. But usually we had legitimate reasons to tattletale on each other: "She was hogging the popcorn!" "She wouldn't let me watch my TV show!" "It was my turn to use the washroom!" "She was spying on me when I was making out with my boyfriend!"

Finding common ground wasn't easy. We were so different: I was the tall early bloomer, full of curves and cleavage; Fern was the petite late bloomer, all skinny and flat. I was painfully shy and kept my mouth shut; Fern was extroverted and mouthed off to anyone, even the school principal. I could hold a grudge longer; she could forgive faster. I was an A student, motivated by a neurotic fear of failure; she was an average student who didn't know the emotional price I paid for trying to be perfect.

I've since apologized to Fern for being such a mean big sister. And now that we're both moms, our sisterhood has slowly blossomed. No wonder, when I break the news about having

Parkinson's, it hits her hard. Twice. Not only is she devastated to hear I have this disease, but she's also shocked to find out that I'm even sick—have been sick for years. She had no idea. But how could she, when I haven't revealed my vulnerability to her or complained about my mysterious symptoms and depression? Instead, I have listened patiently to hours of her personal problems over the telephone. She says had she known what I was going through, she would never have burdened me with her complaints. She would have tried to help me. She's sorry. So am I. Living on the other side of Canada has made it easy to fool my family and myself, to hide my failing health, to pretend everything is OK. Even if it means sacrificing closeness to my sister.

My brother, Jonathan, is next. As with my sister, I've kept him in the dark. He is six years younger than me—an age gap that was wide enough to separate our egos and protect us from intense sibling rivalry. We still fought, but never as much as I fought with Fern or she fought with him.

I used to worry about my brother. When he was growing up, he was impulsive, unpredictable, and hard to tame—qualities that often landed him in trouble. But he was also charming, funny, and warm-hearted, and it was these qualities that eventually took center stage. The wild child was still there, waiting in the wings. All he needed was an invitation to lure him out.

One such invitation presented itself years ago, when Jonathan and I went out on a Saturday night. We ended up at a karaoke bar, and after a few drinks we struck up a conversation with the man sitting next to us, who happened to be a musicologist. And who happened to have written his master's thesis on one of Jonathan's all-time favorite Motown musicians: Marvin Gaye. Jonathan was ecstatic. He was also drunk. And soon he was clutching the microphone, channeling the late, great

Prince of Motown, belting out "I Heard It through the Grapevine" for everyone to hear. Only, he wasn't singing in tune or dancing in time, and the musicologist was not amused.

"Make him stop! He's killing the song!" the musicologist shouted.

But there was no stopping Jonathan.

"'I know that a man ain't supposed to cry, but these tears I can't hold inside.'"

"I'll pay him to shut up!" he shouted, pulling twenties from his wallet.

"Encore, you say?" Jonathan roared at the audience.

The musicologist didn't stick around for "Mercy Mercy Me."

Today, when I tell Jonathan my news, he is caught off guard. At first he thinks I'm joking. I assure him I'm not that funny—but someone up there sure is. Talk about a good cosmic joke: me being diagnosed with Parkinson's just months after my dad's diagnosis. Then he says, "You're going to beat this; don't you worry! You're going to get better, you'll see!"

Jonathan subscribes to the cheerleader style of moral support.

"But it's a degenerative disease. You don't get better; you get worse," I whine into the phone.

This causes him to drop his pom-poms—but only momentarily. He quickly scoops them back up and jumps into another cheer: "The doctor will give you medicine, and everything will be OK."

I know he's trying to be helpful; it's just that he's scared. He's recently married and a new dad—at a stage in life that should be full of blessings and joy. But our dad is sick, so is our mom, and now I am too. And these boo-boos can't be kissed better.

At the end of the day, the phone rings, and before I even pick it up I know who it is: my mom. "Daddy told me the news," she says, and then, without missing a beat, she launches her

inquisition: "Do you have a good doctor?" "What's his name?" "Are you sure it's Parkinson's?" "Did you get a second opinion?" "Do you want to fly in to see Daddy's doctor?" "When is your appointment with the specialist?" "Do you want Daddy's doctor to call the specialist?" "How special is your specialist?" On and on she goes until I can't take anymore. I know that bombarding me with these questions is her way of coping, of feeling like she's in control. I know she loves me and she means well and would do anything to help. But what I need from her right now is compassion, not the third degree. Hell, I'd settle for a pittance of pity—a "poor you" or "there, there" would do just fine. But that's not what she gives me. So before she can ask me anything else, before I lose my cool and say something I might regret, I say goodnight and abruptly hang up. And then I burst into tears. Where is *my* compassion?

Being my mother's daughter has never been easy. When I was young, I was too sensitive for the job. I never rolled with the punches. I couldn't sweep things under the carpet. I tended to brood. Had I been hardwired like her, things might have been different between the two of us. We might have been closer; I might have had more fun. She certainly never allowed misery to get in the way of her having a good time. She could switch from angry mode to party mode in the blink of an eye. Watching this transformation always amazed me.

I can remember family fights erupting while we were getting ready to go to a wedding or a bar mitzvah. By the time we were all dressed and heading out the door, we were in the mood to attend a funeral, not a celebration. But the moment my mom stepped out of the car, she leapt into her favorite role: the life of the party. Her attempts to coax me onto the dance floor were futile. I preferred sulking in a chair, where I'd catch glimpses of her bright red hair and glittery gown, twirling the night away.

She always loved being the center of attention. She still does. She's sixty-four years old and shamelessly dyes her shoulder-length hair Atomic Pink. Or High Octane Orange. Or Cherry Bomb Red. Colors that scream: *Look at me! Look at me!* According to my mom, the brighter, the better. The more flash, the more fun. And according to my dad, the more vibrant, the more visible. Years ago, while visiting the Vatican, they wandered off in different directions. My dad says it took him just thirty seconds to spot my mom in a crowd of fifteen thousand people. Another time, when they got separated at Disney World, he saw her riding a roller coaster five miles away.

After all these years, she's still a party girl at heart. She's still devouring distractions to feed her insatiable appetite for escape. And in my mind, she's still a fiery force to be reckoned with—particularly at this vulnerable time in my life. Maybe that's why it's hard for me to imagine anyone or anything powerful enough to extinguish her flame. Even inoperable lung cancer. But deep down, I know that she must be suffering. And I'm sorry I'm not the kind of daughter who makes motherhood easy for her, particularly at this vulnerable time in her life when no number of Hollywood movies or shopping sprees or travel adventures can drown out the sound of her ticking time bomb or hide the unsettling truth that her family is slowly self-destructing.

ANOTHER MORNING, another breakfast with the Lucky Ones. The way I'm feeling, I could easily squeeze in between Lessing and Lewington:

> Robyn Michele Levy passed away peacefully into her bowl of organic cornflakes. She leaves behind a ripe kiwi, a fistful of pills, her teenage daughter, and her devoted husband. In lieu of flowers, donations to her MasterCard account would be appreciated.

NOW THAT I'VE told my family, the fun of telling my friends begins. When I was in grade school, I always liked show and tell. There was something tantalizingly voyeuristic about inspecting other people's stuff: their treasured object, coveted collection, peculiar pet, extraordinary scar. Occasionally, a kid would even bring in a person and beam, "My dad, the dentist" or "My mom, the pastry chef." While we appreciated these guests and their gifts of toothbrushes and puff pastry, we secretly wished a student would bring in someone scary, someone sinister—"Meet my uncle, the axe murderer"—if only to see what kind of souvenirs he would hand out.

Parkinson's disease has rekindled my interest in playing show and tell with friends. And based on the "oohs" and "aahs" I'm getting, it's clear that we adults (at least the ones I hang out with) haven't outgrown this voyeuristic childhood activity. Especially when it appeals to our fascination with the grotesque—which I fear I am becoming.

"Watch this," I say, holding up my hands in front of my face, swiveling them side to side, as if I'm screwing in a pair of light bulbs. At first both hands are synchronized, but suddenly my left hand freezes in place, the built-up tension causing it to tremor and jolt. My right hand carries on, oblivious and obliging, until I will it to stop.

"I have Parkinson's disease. So far, only the left side of my body is affected."

At this point I ask, "Would you like me to show you more?"

And since no one has turned down this offer, I roll my left shoulder to demonstrate its clunky cogwheel motion, then I rotate my left foot in circles until it seizes up. My repertoire of symptoms doesn't end here—my voice has softened, my left arm doesn't swing when I walk and tremors when I extend it, my entire body is rigid and stiff, and my movements are slow

and strained—but since I don't want to appear boastful, I keep the show and tell short and sweet.

Once my friends overcome the initial shock, I explain what I know so far about this disease. Fifty percent or more of Parkinson's patients suffer from clinical depression. There is nothing wrong with my muscles—the problem is in my brain, specifically a depletion of dopamine. There are drugs to help ease some of my physical symptoms, but for now I'm focusing on dealing with the emotional. I sheepishly admit I'm on antidepressants, and much to my surprise one friend reveals she is taking them too. Then another friend mentions that several of her close pals are also on them. It's the same story with other friends, until pretty soon I realize that I'm just one glum soul among many. I find this both comforting and disconcerting—and I burst into ambivalent tears.

3

Ladies
in Waning

THESE DAYS, everyone is worried about me, even strangers—particularly impatient strangers at the grocery store, waiting in line behind me at the express checkout counter. Sometimes they are so worried that their eyeballs roll right out of their sockets as I slowly fumble through my purse to pay the clerk.

I'm worried too. Unsettling thoughts of drooling, diapers, and wheelchairs loom large. And so does death (hopefully before diapers). But these fears seem rather futile to fret about now, considering I'm just in the early stage of Parkinson's. This means I can focus my anxiety on concerns I face every day. For starters, there is my deteriorating walk, which I am very self-conscious about—particularly at the dog park. Let off leash, Nellie runs like the wind, as far away from me as possible. Then she conducts "canine crop circle" research, eventually marking the perfect celestial spot with a down-to-earth turd. Which I

must find and dispose of, in front of everyone. I lumber awkwardly across the grass, dodging dogs chasing tennis balls and squeaky toys, my left leg dragging behind, my crooked left arm frozen at my side, torso tilting too far forward, right arm swinging back and forth, back and forth, like a doggie poop divining rod, searching... until I strike gold.

My many other concerns are not as public. I'm having difficulty flossing my teeth, folding the laundry, chopping vegetables, vacuuming the floors, putting on my shoes, doing up zippers, typing on the keyboard. Little things only Bergen and Naomi notice when we're at home. And while they don't say it out loud, I know they both worry about me a lot. Most of the time I appreciate all this concern from everybody. But sometimes I find it difficult being the center of apprehension and long to escape the scrutiny.

That's where Nellie comes in handy. As far as I can tell, my dog hasn't the foggiest idea that I have a degenerative brain disease—or that I have a brain to degenerate. In her eyes, I'm just this omnipresent creature she adores, who fills her food bowl, takes her for walks, picks up her poop, scratches her belly, and reluctantly removes sticks protruding from her bum—the very sticks I am always telling her not to eat. And while she isn't the brightest dog in town, her ignorance often brings me bliss—rare moments when I forget that I have Parkinson's and that people worry about me.

WARNING: Habits may be habit forming. Habits may also be hilarious. Sometimes they can be both. Such as the habit I have of marching around inside my house, like a soldier in basic training. Every day. Rain or shine. Hup, two, three, four. Back and forth between the kitchen and the living room—with gusto. According to my physiotherapist, this marching drill should

help my rigid left arm swing back and forth and my limping left leg lift up and down, in smooth rhythmic motions that would make a sergeant major proud. That's what it should do. But I march to the beat of a disabled drummer. And no matter how hard I try, I lurch to the right like a spastic soldier—perky but jerky. I'd make a sergeant major cry.

The first time Naomi saw me marching, she laughed and then squealed, "I arrived just in time for the show!" I was flattered—teenagers are notoriously hard to impress.

"Welcome to Cirque d'Oy Vey," I said, putting more schlep into my step.

Luckily for her, I was at the beginning of my workout routine, cobbled together from physio, Pilates, and yoga exercises I'd learned over the years. There was plenty still to come. Leg kicks and figure eights. Arm flexing. Knee tapping. Stretches and lunges. Postural poses. And the showstopper: tripping over Nellie while walking backwards.

Naomi was entertained. She even got into the act by coaxing my left arm into positions it can no longer find on its own. She still occasionally does this, without hesitation or awkwardness and without the slightest indication that I embarrass her—even in front of her friends. I find this remarkable because I consider my body an embarrassment of glitches, which I'd do anything to fix.

Unfortunately, fixing things isn't my forte; I'm better at breaking things. Casualties include the garburator, the clothes dryer, the dishwasher, and, of course, the computer. I'm lucky that Bergen can fix almost anything—he's a handyman with a workshop full of tools and spare parts and an eclectic collection of you-never-know-when-this-might-come-in-handy junk. Which somehow always comes in handy for something, somewhere, sometime.

I'm secretly hoping someday he'll emerge from his work-shop with "The Lazarus"—a custom-built contraption that resurrects dead dopamine brain cells and cures Parkinson's. Of course, I'll bravely volunteer to be the first guinea pig to test it out. And I'll try not to flinch, even if he attaches a modified Ham radio with guitar-pick electrodes to my head. I realize there's bound to be some kinks to work out in the beginning, so I'll brace myself for possible side effects—nausea, chills, headache, double vision, multiple orgasms—I can handle almost anything if it leads to a fix.

Meanwhile, I'm collecting facts—searching the web, bor-rowing library books, learning the lingo. Apparently, so is Naomi. When I go to tuck her into bed tonight, I have to choke back my tears. Probably every kid in the world is reading the latest Harry Potter book, but not my daughter. She is flipping through the pages of an illustrated neurology textbook.

"Are you sure you want to read that stuff before bed?" I ask.

"Yeah. Look at these brains. This one is healthy. This other one has Parkinson's. And did you know that smoking may some-how protect the brain from getting Parkinson's disease?"

"I wish I'd known that years ago—I'd have started smoking."

Naomi asks, "Do you want to cuddle?"

"Of course I do. Move over," I say, squeezing in beside her. I wrap my arms around my girl while she leans her head on my shoulder. We hear Nellie jingling her way into the room and jumping up onto the bed. I'm in her spot, she whimpers. My head is on her pillow, she woofs.

"Don't go," Naomi whispers. "Stay."

So I stay, forcing Nellie to cancel her pillow reservations and curl up at Naomi's feet. The three of us close our eyes, but only the dog falls fast asleep. Together, Naomi and I luxuriate in this shared end-of-day stillness. Neither of us can remember the last time we cuddled like this, but our bodies remember.

Tentatively, our legs entwine and our arms overlap—reviving the affection I thought we'd lost, collateral damage from the Bad Old Days. Naomi yawns, pulls the covers close, and rests her head on my shoulder. We are tired, but we continue talking about brains and dogs, while invisible threads of trust begin mending our tattered love.

AS AUTUMN PREPARES to make way for winter, the neighborhood squirrels are busy collecting nuts. At the same time, I'm frantically foraging for help and hope. So far, I have collected nine health care professionals spanning the spectrum of the medical rainbow—five doctors (a general practitioner, a neurologist, a naturopath, a homeopath, and an acupuncturist), three therapists (a physiotherapist, a massage therapist, and a psychologist), and one beautician—all of whom I consider essential for tending to my calamity, my sanity, and my vanity.

The beautician's name is Diane. She's French, middle-aged, and well preserved. Her skin has a youthful glow, her hands are supple and manicured, and the pores on her face are never clogged. She radiates natural beauty, as if she doesn't need any of the expensive anti-aging, exfoliating, beautifying creams and lotions she recommends to her clients. She owns the beauty salon down the street. If it weren't for her, our neighborhood would be overrun by hirsute women with clogged pores, brittle nails, and unibrows. I'm one of her regulars. Every two weeks I show up for an electrolysis treatment, and each time Diane assures me that it's working. I want to believe her.

In the 1990s, I used to be a hirsute heroine. I credit my hairy legs, pits, and pubes for catapulting me to cult status. And not just at the local swimming pool, where I was affectionately nicknamed Chia Pet. No, my furry fame grew out all across Canada, the United States, and even Japan.

It all started with a cheeky cartoon of a happy, horny, hairy lady I named Libby Doe, who bore a striking resemblance to me in my birthday suit. After I drew her, I composed the following poem:

I AIN'T NO SHAVE SLAVE

I ain't no shave slave
no beauty queen
bikini waxes are not my scene
I ain't no shave slave
no centerfold
for every hair on this bod
there's a story to be told
I ain't no shave slave
no depilatory dream
electrolysis just makes me scream
I ain't no shave slave
no Jolen junkie
I trashed the tweezers
I'm furry and funky
I ain't no shave slave
no *Vogue* vixen
it ain't ingrown hairs that I'm itchin'
I ain't no shave slave
no Barbie doll
if you want me, darling
you've got to take it all!

On a whim, I printed greeting cards and T-shirts of Libby Doe and her poem—adding her to the other designs I was marketing through my art business. Of course, she stuck out like a sore nipple—shamelessly flaunting her tits, hairy pits, and private bits—and so I braced myself for a wide range of reactions. There were prudish pooh-poohs and testy tsk-tsks. But much to my delight, Libby Doe struck a positive chord. It seemed women from all walks of life could relate to her; they had a friend or a relative who didn't shave, they themselves didn't shave occasionally or at all, or they wished they had the courage to chuck the shaver and let it all hang out. And so, Libby Doe cards and T-shirts infiltrated multitudes of mailboxes, wardrobes, and, best of all, hearts. Teenagers would mail me fan letters and snapshots of them wearing the "I Ain't No Shave Slave" shirt. Businesswomen in pantsuits would bashfully flash me their unshaven legs and buy a stack of cards for friends. Lesbians and hippies adopted Libby Doe as one of their own. Even women repulsed by real body hair found the cartoon body hair hilarious.

And then Hollywood North came knocking. Penny Wheelwright, a Canadian documentary filmmaker, was working on *Hair, There and Everywhere,* a film exploring contemporary cultural attitudes toward body hair. She'd received one of my "I Ain't No Shave Slave" greeting cards and gave me a call. Would I be interested in doing animation for her film, featuring this hirsute cartoon? Would I consider teaming up with hip-hop artist Kinnie Starr, who was composing original music for the film and wanted to set "I Ain't No Shave Slave" to music? Would I like to be one of the hairy women interviewed in this film? I said yes to all three invitations.

The documentary debuted prime time on CBC TV. Many people must have watched it, because strangers would do

a double take when they saw me out in public, then give me that "Don't I know you from somewhere?" look. Sometimes they connected the dots on their own; other times they needed prompting. But either way, they'd invariably say something like, "Hey, aren't you that artist with the hairy armpits?"

It turns out they all remembered me and my hair but not the animation or the theme song. But those tufts of hair are not why I'm here at Diane's salon. All my life I have lived harmoniously with my minimustache, content to bleach it into peach-fuzz submission. But days after my diagnosis, a narcissistic neurosis infiltrated my mind. I'd look in the mirror and not only see an unsightly stash but also an unsightly future—where Parkinson's has demoted me to diapers and dementia, where my nimble fingers fail to function, and where I am oblivious that my neglected whiskers have grown into a hideous handlebar mustache, which the staff at the nursing home trim, wash, and wax regularly. And so, in an effort to avoid this hairy humiliation, I submit my upper lip to Diane's magical device—the Apilus Platinum—a needle-tipped pen she pokes into my hair follicles, then zaps with an electrical current. After this, she plucks out the damaged hairs with tweezers and triumphantly lays them to rest on a fresh tissue. Of course it hurts, leaves my skin red and inflamed for hours, and costs hundreds of dollars. But it's a small price to pay for dodging the dubious distinction of being the first woman to join the exclusive Handlebar Club.

Regrettably, electrolysis is not covered by my provincial health care plan. Neither are naturopathy, homeopathy, acupuncture, massage, physio, and counseling. This explains my dwindling bank balance and my wretched wardrobe. Who knew hope was so expensive? There are consultation fees, treatment charges, vitamins, purported remedies, specialty foods, blood tests, saliva analyses, exercise equipment,

self-help books—all sold in the spirit of healing and purchased in the pursuit of a miracle.

Still, there are unexpected perks to practically everything—even Parkinson's disease. One day I discover that my disease is helping my neighbor cope with hers. Susan is a chatty, hard-working chartered accountant, and while some might consider her profession hazardous to one's health, that's not her disease. It's breast cancer. She was diagnosed six months ago but never mentioned a word to me until yesterday, when I spilled the beans about my Parkinson's. How she managed to keep two lumpectomies, radiation treatment, chemotherapy, and a bald head secret is beyond me. But now that we've each flaunted our afflictions, the floodgates have opened wide. So today, while I am walking Nellie, Susan confides that in a few days she will be back under the knife, this time for a double mastectomy and reconstructive surgery.

"I've got the Dream Team," she says, "a fantastic surgeon to take them both off and a fantastic plastic surgeon to install two brand-new ones, right away."

It takes me a few seconds to process this admission, and before I have a chance to respond, Susan continues, "I have to tell you, for weeks I've been feeling really anxious about this operation, but not anymore. Last night I barely slept; I just kept thinking about *your* awful situation. Going over and over in my head what I'd do if I were you, forty-three years old, facing the future with a degenerative brain disease, raising a teenage daughter—these are such critical years when a girl needs her mother—and I did some research, found some good websites about Parkinson's, and I have to tell you that some of these sites say early-onset Parkinson's is more aggressive than the regular kind older people get. And the medication taken to deal with symptoms—it eventually stops working really well. So the big

question is, do you wait until you really need the medicine, which could be years from now, and meanwhile continue slowing down? Or do you start taking the meds right away so that you can go back to being as normal as possible—for Naomi's sake, at least until she graduates from high school? I don't know, Robyn. It's a tough call. You've got some hard choices to make. But it sure makes my situation seem easy."

Susan stops to take a breath, then dips her hand into her coat pocket. Feeling rattled and anxious, I fully expect her to whip out a spreadsheet charting the statistical potential outcomes of my bleak future, but it's only a tissue to wipe her nose. Nothing to worry about.

A few days later, early in the morning, Susan's husband drives her to the hospital. I hear their car pull out from the lane and I wave bye-bye to her "boobs gone bad." That's what she called them: boobs gone bad. Like Thelma and Louise, driving off a cliff—the final escape. By the time lunch rolls around, Susan is in recovery, tripping on morphine, sporting a pair of synthetic tits. And Bergen and I are thinking of her while we drive down the hill, toward the ocean, on our way to visit the Answer Lady.

Like many CBC fans, I first knew the Answer Lady as a feisty disembodied voice on Vicky Gabereau's afternoon radio show. Inquisitive listeners would mail in their quirky questions, and the Answer Lady, whose real name is Marg Meikle, would conduct exhaustive research on the various subjects. Then she'd triumphantly appear on the show, telling Vicky what she'd learned. The on-air banter between the two women was always entertaining and sometimes piss-your-pants funny. She went on to publish several books, and then, when Vicky's show ended, the Answer Lady fell off my radar.

A few years later, when I began freelancing at CBC, I wound up meeting Marg. She was doing some research for the

show I was assigned to and joined our morning story meeting. Although I'd never seen her before, I knew by the way she spoke and fidgeted in her chair that something was wrong with her. Later that day, I found out she had early-onset Parkinson's. Back then, I didn't know much about the disease, but I knew enough to feel sad for Marg's misfortune. And I knew that Parkinson's was one disease I never wanted to get.

Since that day, I've learned to be careful what I don't wish for. I've also learned that Marg and I have a lot in common: we're both artists, writers, and radio broadcasters. We're both married and raising one child. And we were both diagnosed with early-onset Parkinson's disease at age forty-three. If anyone could shed some light on life with this affliction, the Answer Lady could. But would she? I called her home to find out and spoke with her husband, Noel, who invited Bergen and me to drop by for a cup of tea and a chat later that week. And so here we are, knocking on the door of their heritage house, being welcomed by a bushy-bearded Noel. He leads us to the living room, and out of the corner of my eye I spot safety railings on the walls and along the staircase, a cane leaning against a door frame, and a metal walker next to a window. When I last saw Marg, six or seven years ago, she was managing quite well—walking unassisted, talking clearly, working on her projects. But I'd heard from mutual friends that her Parkinson's had become quite severe since then. She'd had experimental surgery—deep brain stimulation—to help ease her debilitating symptoms, however the surgery hadn't helped very much. So I had mentally prepared myself for this encounter. Or so I thought.

My heart begins breaking the moment we say hello.

"It's been a long time," Marg slurs quietly from an oversized chair.

"It sure has," I say, fighting back the panic rising in my throat as Marg fumbles with her personal remote control. When she

finally gets a good grip, she clumsily aims the remote at her chest, presses a button several times, then mumbles that she just sent a message to her brain via an implanted electronic device. I can feel my Cry Lady cringing inside, aching to crank out her tears. But somehow I stay calm, and the four of us start talking. There are so many questions I want to ask Marg, but first I need to make something clear.

"Even though one neurologist just diagnosed me with Parkinson's," I say, "I'm still not 100 percent convinced I have it. That's why I'm going to see another neurologist in a couple weeks; he specializes in Parkinson's. To get a second opinion, from an expert."

No one says anything for a few seconds, then Marg leans her rigid body forward in her chair, looks me straight in the eye, and slurs, "Oh, you got it, all right. You got it."

Her words sting like icicles plunging into my flesh. I desperately want to cling to my speck of doubt, but I can't escape this feeling that I am staring at my future and Marg is staring at her past.

"What makes you so sure?" I sputter.

"It's the eyes, how starey they are. And the face, hardly any expression. And the body, stiff, slow, and tight."

I try moving my mouth into a smiling shape, to politely mask my shock, but my face feels frozen, locked in place. At least I can blink. Yes, that I can still do.

But I can't stay here very long—for my sake or for Marg's. So I rattle off my questions, and within an hour, my mind is swimming in advice, opinions, facts: "Parkinson's affects everyone in the family." "Find a good neurologist who makes time to see you." "Support groups are depressing." "Your pharmacist is your best friend." "Qualifying for social assistance is difficult." "Massage therapy is a waste of money." "Parkinson's causes

constipation." "Clinical depression comes and goes; get help when it's severe."

Before we leave, Noel gives us a tour of their spectacular kitchen. A giant granite island sits smack dab in the middle of encircling custom cabinets, workstations, and appliances. French doors open onto the backyard garden. And next to the doors is a cozy sitting area, with couches and chairs and a compact computer nook. Perfect for entertaining. In fact, they are hosting a breakfast party in a couple weeks and would love us to drop in. It's a fundraiser called Porridge for Parkinson's. They do it every year. And they've inspired other people across Canada and the United States to hold such an event. So far, they've helped raise over $500,000, money that goes directly to funding research into a cure for Parkinson's. We thank them for sharing their insights and experience with us and promise we'll drop by for a bowl of porridge.

Bergen and I are both silent during the drive home—thinking and trying not to think about all that was said. Especially Marg's pronouncement: "Oh, you got it, all right. You got it." Maybe not the warmest welcome into the Parkinson's community. But certainly an honest one, from a generous family, coping with a devastating disease.

THE EARLY-MORNING SKY is a silver-gray reservoir of rain. It straddles the city and sits tight, still, pensive. The forecast calls for showers, but it hasn't spilled a drop. It's considering its options—something I've been doing a lot lately too. For instance, should I keep struggling with these stupid shoelaces or invest in Velcro runners? Is it better to boycott buttons or ask Bergen to help me do them up? Should I learn voice-recognition software or carry on typing with only my right hand? If the second neurologist diagnoses me with Parkinson's, should I shoot

him or get a third opinion? These are some of the many options on my plate. What to do, what to do? I'm not usually so indecisive. But having only recently discovered that pride really is hard to swallow, I have lost my appetite for making decisions.

By midmorning, the sky is stalling—still considering its options. This monotone holding pattern feels familiar. I want to crawl back into bed, escape into sleep. Keep the world and its evil shoelaces and backstabbing buttons far, far away. And if it weren't for my grumbling tummy, that's exactly what I'd do. But apparently, I still have an appetite for food, and breakfast is beckoning.

I'M GETTING PICKY in my middle age: I like my cereal cold and crunchy, not hot and mushy; and I like my diseases curable and short-lived, not incurable and degenerative. So what am I doing here? This place will be teeming with steamy bowls of oatmeal and people doing the Parkinson's shuffle. Well, a promise is a promise. And besides, I'm in perfect shape to attend this Porridge for Parkinson's fundraiser—I didn't sleep very well last night, so my body is extra slow and extra stiff. I'll fit right in.

Bergen holds my hand as we walk tentatively toward Marg and Noel's front gate. The closer we get, the more uncertain we are of what awaits us. Smiling strangers welcome us into the garden, while other smiling strangers brush past us, carrying boxes and flowers and grocery bags. I don't feel much like smiling—I'm famished and anxious. What if I bump into someone I know? What if they find out I have Parkinson's? What if everyone finds out I have Parkinson's? I've only told family and close friends—I'm not ready to go public yet. And neither is this crowd—no one is wearing a personal floatation device. I'm such a sucker for sympathy, all it would take is one teensy-weensy whiff of compassion and my Cry Lady lament would wash them all out to sea.

Someone points toward the basement and says, "Make sure you check out the silent auction. It's down these steps." We thank him for the tip, then walk upstairs to the porch. As at our last visit, a bushy-bearded Noel greets us at the front door. He's wearing an apron and a chef's hat and smells of cinnamon. We follow him to the kitchen, where he resumes stirring a colossal pot of porridge.

"Help yourself." Noel gestures toward the spread laid out on the kitchen island. There are muffins and cookies, dried fruit poached in port compote, freshly brewed coffee, an assortment of teas and juice, porridge, of course, and, last but not least— the secret ingredient that makes this mush palatable—scotch whiskey. Not for drinking in a glass but for drizzling on top of the porridge.

After eating, I spot Marg. She's sitting on a chair by the door, waiting for us to say hello. As we walk toward her, I wonder: Can she smell my fear? Hear my heart racing? See my feet fight the urge to flee? I bend down and give her an awkward hug.

"You made it," Marg mumbles knowingly—she is still the Answer Lady, after all. She's also the bravest person I know— unabashedly welcoming hundreds of people into her home, year after degenerative year, where bowls of porridge are doled out, generous donations are drawn in, and the Pacific Parkinson's Research Centre gets closer to finding a cure. Marg truly believes it's going to happen in her lifetime. And when we add our check to the donation box, I tell Bergen, "I hope she's right."

Just like the disease, this fundraiser is a family affair. The house is packed with people of all ages, most of whom do not have Parkinson's. It's easy to spot those of us who do— our bodies broadcast the telltale symptoms: tremoring limbs, bobbing head, rigid muscles, poor balance, stooped posture, shuffling walk, slow movements, expressionless face, hushed voice. Not everyone experiences every symptom, especially in

the early stages, but there are enough of us here today to demonstrate each one.

Marg and Noel's son, Mac, is one of many kids roaming around. We could have brought Naomi; she was invited. But my Mama Bear instinct knew not to. It's only been a month since my diagnosis; it's much too early to expose her to what lies ahead. And judging from my escalating anxiety and Bergen's weary eyes, it's much too early for us too. We give each other "the look," and as we're on our way out, my old Pilates instructor recognizes me.

"Hey, what are you doing here?" Kit asks.

A wave of shame sweeps through me. I feel caught and exposed—and unbearably guilty—for developing this disease, for being embarrassed I have it, for wanting to keep it a secret, and for not being totally honest.

"I know Marg from my days at CBC. I'm here to show my support. And you?"

Kit's eyes quickly scan my flushed face, then my stiff-as-a-mannequin body.

"I give private Pilates lessons to Marg. Here's my card."

What does she mean by "Here's my card?" Can she tell I have Parkinson's? I don't stick around to find out. I shuffle out the door and catch up to Bergen, who is waiting outside. His hair matches the silver-gray sky, still holding back the rain. It's comforting, walking toward him, knowing that forecasts can be wrong.

4

Sex and Dogs
and Crowd Control

ACCORDING TO BERGEN, I am the sexiest female patient in this waiting room. Mind you, I am also the youngest female patient in this waiting room—decades younger than anyone else. Some might say this gives me an unfair advantage. And I would agree, if we were posing for *Playboy* magazine's "Naughty and Neurodegenerative Vixens" photo spread. But sadly, we're not. My cleavage has no clout at this clinic; my feminine charms beguile Bergen alone. So, just like these old ladies, I must wait my turn to see a Parkinson's specialist. But I don't mind. I've come prepared.

For I am a waiting room warrior—armed with snacks and water, diversions and distractions, a typed list of questions to ask the neurologist, and, most important, Bergen. He's sitting right beside me, getting his fix of black holes, genetic mutations, evolutionary theories, space exploration, dinosaur discoveries, and biochemical breakthroughs. He never leaves home without his *Scientific American*. I've always admired his thirst for this

knowledge—and now that my brain is malfunctioning, his scientific aptitude comes in handy.

I also brought along something to read—Michael J. Fox's autobiography, *A Lucky Man*. I flip it open and pick up where I left off, at his memories of the *Back to the Future* movies he starred in. Which gets me thinking of time machines and traveling back to my past to that magical day Bergen and I got married. And it's all so vivid; I can smell the flowers in my bouquet, I can see Bergen's hazel eyes welling up with tears, and I can hear his deep voice reciting his romantic wedding vows:

> I, Bergen, take you, Robyn, to be my young, nubile wife,
> to love, honor, and chauffeur to doctor appointments and
> medical laboratories, in sickness and in traffic, with you
> backseat-driving me crazy, until death do us part.

My heart bursts with love as I reach over and squeeze his hand, repeatedly. I can tell by the way his eyes eventually lift off the page to gaze into mine that he appreciates this interruption. As he lets out a long sigh—code for "Nothing is more important than you"—I know we are speaking that mysterious language reserved for lovers, a language composed of private gestures and pet names and secret desires. I am tempted to kiss him on the lips, or mouth the words *"Je t'aime,"* but both seem so clichéd. Instead, I whisper in his ear that flirtatious phrase, which he once heard me muttering in my sleep, a phrase that fused sex with science in the middle of the night: "Plate tectonics, baby, plate tectonics."

Finally, a nurse calls my name, and I am ushered into an examination room. Bergen comes along.

"The doctor will be with you shortly."

Her words go in one ear and down to my bladder. I have to pee. Urgently. Again.

"Where's the nearest washroom?" I ask.

She points down the hall, to the left. "Be quick," she says, smiling.

Did she just crack a Parkinson's joke? Or is she being sincere?

When I return, Bergen is reading his *Scientific American* with his eyes shut. I bet it's something he learned how to do from one of the physics articles. There's probably a technical term for this study technique—something really hard to pronounce. I'll have to ask him about it later, because someone's knocking on the door. A tall, dark, and handsome man enters the room. He introduces himself and explains that he is a visiting neurologist at the clinic.

"If it's OK with you, Miss, I'd like to conduct a preliminary examination."

I'm impressed: such nice manners; he even called me "Miss." If I am ever abducted by extraterrestrials, I hope they are this polite.

"That would be fine," I say. And so he begins. Probing question after probing question about my medical history and my family history. Physical tests. Reflex tests. Visual tests. Memory Tests. Psychological tests. He records each answer on a sheet of paper. He draws diagrams and charts and family trees. And when he's done, I realize I'm doomed: neurological diseases run rampant in my family. Alzheimer's, multiple sclerosis, Parkinson's. But before my Cry Lady crumples in a heap of tears, the Visiting Neurologist says, "Please excuse me. I must go tell Dr. Stoessl I am done, and we are now ready for him to exam you." I wipe away the tears dripping down my face and turn toward the sun-filled window. There's not a cloud in the sky. I tuck my tissue in my pocket and say to Bergen, "It's a beautiful day for a second opinion."

When the Visiting Neurologist returns, he is accompanied by Dr. Stoessl—director of the Pacific Parkinson's Research Centre and National Parkinson Foundation Centre of

Excellence and considered by many to be the best Parkinson's expert in town. He shakes our hands and takes a seat behind the corner desk. Bergen and I sit in chairs across from him, while the Visiting Neurologist remains standing. Dr. Stoessl's bearded face consults his computer; then he picks up his pen and gives it an orchestra conductor's wave. And right on cue, the Visiting Neurologist clears his throat and begins his diagnostic serenade:

"It's a tragic tale that I recount, of a dark-haired, middle-aged dame, whose ancestors were cursed and dutifully nursed because of their broken brains. And this dame did succumb to sensations numb, impaired movement, and melancholic pain. She's been told by one neurologist, Parkinson's is her nemesis, and comes to you, a second opinion to obtain."

"I see," says Dr. Stoessl, rising from his chair, staring in my direction. "Do you mind if I have a look?"

And so begins round two of the examination. More testing of motor function, reflex reaction, strength and balance, agility and flexibility, sensation and numbness, cognitive function, short-term and long-term memory. And then the verdict: "You have Parkinson's disease. Early-onset Parkinson's. You're in the early stage."

"Are you sure?" I ask, clinging to the finest thread of hope, tears streaming down my cheeks. "Could it be something else instead of Parkinson's?"

Dr. Stoessl hands me a box of tissues and says, "Why? Do you want it to be something else? If it were something else, it would be worse."

I can't imagine anything worse than this, but I'll take his word for it. He is the expert, after all.

The discussion turns from diagnosis to drugs. Dr. Stoessl tells me there are many options for treating Parkinson's. But

he won't prescribe any meds now; my symptoms are much too mild. Yes, I drag my left foot, my left arm doesn't swing, and my entire body has slowed down. But that's considered a cakewalk around here. In fact, he thinks I could run circles around his advanced patients. I know a challenge when I hear one, and if it weren't for my cranky Cry Lady bringing me down, I would get off my ass and race the old lady in the wheelchair I saw in the waiting room. I'd race her all the way down the hall and back. Just for fun. But sadly, I'm not in the mood. That's clear to everyone in this room—Dr. Stoessl, the Visiting Neurologist, and Bergen—that although I'm on antidepressants, I am still quite depressed. So he refers me to his colleague, Dr. Young, a psychiatrist who treats depressed Parkinson's patients. Like me. And when Bergen and I leave the clinic, sunshine escorts us to our car. And I think, it really is a beautiful day for a diagnosis. There'll be no third opinion, after all.

ANOTHER DAY, another appointment. This time with Dr. Young, the psychiatrist.

He's bald and British and bombards me with questions about my depression, my family, my childhood, my body, my work, even my dog. He is so thorough, and I am so thoroughly bored.

Blah blah black sheep of my family... have I any woe?

Yes sir, yes sir... time to go.

I leave with a prescription for the same antidepressant I've been taking, just a higher dose, which, hopefully, will elevate my mood. I also receive a card indicating the date of my next appointment, four weeks from now. I can hardly wait.

THIS MORNING'S BREAKFAST is dedicated to Dawn Marie Jones (née Kelly), AKA Cupcake the Party Clown. After a courageous battle with cancer, Dawn joined the Lucky Ones. She

is survived by her soulmate, Andrea; her two children, George and Sharayah; her parents, Christopher and Teresa; her siblings, Christopher, Robert, and Tina; her many friends, and fans; and her performing partner, Dougie the Duck. So, in lieu of boring cornflakes, I'm having something fun—chocolate pancakes with maple syrup. And sprinkles.

IT'S SNOWING IN VANCOUVER. It started last night. Just a civilized dusting of shimmering white—enough to add irony to the snowdrops already in bloom and plenty to turn sidewalks slushy and slick. But not nearly enough to answer Naomi's prayer that school will be canceled.

This morning at breakfast, Naomi complains, "Why can't we get walloped by snowstorms and blizzards, just like the rest of Canada?"

"Because winters on the west coast are wimpy."

My answer makes Naomi smile.

"Actually, we live in a temperate rain forest."

Naomi rolls her eyes at Bergen—code for "spare me the scientific lecture"—and gobbles up the rest of her cereal before heading off to school.

I look out the kitchen window at the parade of snowsuits, toboggans, and swirling snowflakes, enticing me to join the fun. Winter is such a flirt—and I've always fallen for its charm. But not anymore. Parkinson's has fogged up the view from my rose-colored glasses; it's made me clumsy and unstable and paranoid about slipping on the ice. If I didn't have a dog, I'd probably stay indoors on a snowy day like this. If I didn't have a dog.

After cleaning up the kitchen, Bergen and I take Nellie for her morning walk. At least, that's what we set out to do. But Nellie has other plans—and she does not want to be late. I do my best to pick up my pace without falling and breaking my

neck. For a snowy day, we make it to the dog park in record time. I unhook Nellie's leash, but instead of racing off as she usually does, she just stands there, knee deep in snow, stylish in her black fleece Dracula cape. She is poised and polite—graciously exchanging some courteous sniffs with some curious dogs—and then, as if on cue, she rubs her face in the snow, flashes us a toothy grin, and begins her one-canine show: the Abominable Snowdog Ballet.

She is riveting—I can't take my eyes off her, and neither can Bergen nor the curious dogs and their owners. I also can't stop laughing—Nellie is hilarious.

With the speed of a cheetah, and the craziness of a clown, Nellie carves concentric circles in the snow. Round and round and round she goes, a blur of fur, her cape aflutter, barking with delight.

"Look at me!" she yowls.

"Go Nellie!" we cheer.

She stops for a moment to catch her breath, then resumes her berserk ballet. Round and round again she goes, plowing through the snow, a little more slowly with every pass, her cape coming undone. And when at last she flops to the ground, rolling on her back, her belly fur is covered with clumps of snow—like dangling Ping-Pong balls. Over she rolls and up she stands. She's ready to romp again. But her poor little legs are encased in snow—all the way from her paws to her paunch—and she walks like John Wayne wearing a diaper. It's the funniest thing to see.

Bewildered, she trudges toward us, and with blinking eyes and snowy face, she lets out a little yelp—"I'm ready to go home". The show is over. The crowd applauds. Nellie curtseys as she pees. There will be no encore. No Q & A. No autographs to sign. Just a warm bath to melt her clumps, a towel to pat her

dry, and a photo of Nellie dancing the Abominable Snowdog Ballet on the mantel to remind me of the fleeting joy I felt that snowy day.

VALENTINE'S DAY. The forecast calls for heavy menstrual flow with a chance of leakage, low-pressure back pain, and scattered showers of tears. Expect gusty mood swings and libido temperatures well below zero. Non-flirting advisory in effect.

Bergen gives me a lovely bouquet of flowers anyway. I give him a morning hug, then dissolve into tears.

"I'm sorry," I cry. "I'm so sorry for getting sick."

This has been my mantra for months. He's grown accustomed to these apologetic eruptions, the spewed-out remorse and regret. Just as he's grown accustomed to my downhill slide—from wife to washout, from co-parent to couch potato. He is overworked and overwhelmed, juggling consulting contracts and home renovations while doing all of the chores we used to share—housecleaning, grocery shopping, cooking, and parenting. I marvel at his vitality and his lack of complaining. And even though he would welcome me back to the team, he supports my temporary reassignment to another department. My new business card reads:

ROBYN MICHELE LEVY
Off-duty Wife and Mother
Convalescence Specialist: Department of Doldrums
and Conundrums

I take this new job seriously. So do Bergen, Naomi, and my growing collection of health care professionals. It's a collaborative process. And it's working.

IT'S TAKEN A WHILE, but my denial has almost disappeared. I just find fragments in the mornings, in a semiconscious state,

while I'm waking but still tethered to a dream. Sometimes I am flying or dancing or lying in bed with Leonard Cohen touching my perfect body with his mind. My perfectly healthy body—with two swinging arms and two steady legs and a brain brimming with dopamine. That's the body I have beneath these sheets. Before I'm wide awake. Before remembering wrecks everything.

NAOMI'S FOURTEENTH BIRTHDAY. The evening forecast calls for scattered shoes stinking up the hallway, couches crawling with hungry, hormonal teenagers, and a steady stream of screams and laughter. Expect messes and mayhem and all-night horror movies. There is a risk of heavy petting.

I have been dreading this party for weeks. Back when I caved in to Naomi's request, I had high hopes that Big Pharma and her chemical concoctions would deliver a knockout punch to my depression and anxiety so that by the time Naomi's birthday rolled around, I would be well enough to welcome twenty teenage boys and girls into our home. But no such luck. I'm not ready to sacrifice my sanctuary. Ready or not, here they come.

They arrive ravenous. Snacks are devoured. Drinks are gulped down. The noise level is deafening. And the more chaotic the kitchen gets, the more neurotic I become. "Don't worry," Bergen says, "I'm on clean-up duty. You can just relax." That's easier said than done—my mind is racing, my muscles are tense, and my Cry Lady can't stand kids. So I take Nellie for a walk, then retreat to our bedroom. Small doses; that's my survival strategy. I pop in and out of the party—for homemade pizza, birthday cake, the opening of gifts, and the exodus of the boys—but mostly I hide away. And when the girls get ready for the sleepover, I crack open a brand-new pair of earplugs and climb into bed.

Miraculously, I get some sleep. In the morning, I tiptoe downstairs to the living room, which is strewn with mattresses and pillows and girls in pajamas—some sleeping, some whispering. Nellie is curled up beside a tangle of feet. One pair belongs to Naomi; the other pair belongs to one of her friends. Together, the girls stir beneath a blanket, then drift back to their dreams.

Compared with the racket last night, the house is incredibly quiet. So quiet I have space to think. Two thoughts pop into my head. I definitely prefer teenagers when they are asleep. Better yet, I prefer other people's teenagers sleeping over at other people's homes—not mine. Is that too much to ask? A wave of guilt washes over me. Poor Naomi. What kind of a stick-in-the-mud mother have I become? These kids are terrific. I should feel lucky that they feel comfortable enough to make themselves at home—raiding our refrigerator, dropping their clothes on the floor, yelling at the top of their lungs. And for a moment, I do. But then one of them farts. And another one starts laughing. And pretty soon all the girls are awake, transforming my quiet morning into a chaotic chorus of girls brushing their teeth, toilets flushing, cell phones ringing, music playing, and girls gossiping, while I silently repeat over and over in my head, "Go home. Everyone, go home."

MUCH TO MY CHAGRIN, neurodegenerative diseases don't dilly-dally—there's always more damage to be done. The latest casualty is my left baby toe, oddly jutting out straight to the side. Every day this little piggy moves farther away from the little piggies living next door. I'm afraid if it moves any farther, it's going to fall right off my foot. Losing a toe wouldn't be the end of the world, but it could set a dangerous precedent. What if more toes jump ship? And my left foot falls off? And then other left-side parts depart? I feel my blood pressure rising while

I'm catastrophizing. This paranoia has got to stop. Clearly, my imagination is progressing more quickly than the disease. So I take slow, deep breaths, in and out, until I'm feeling calm. Nothing is falling off or jumping ship—this little piggy is staying home.

GOOD HELP IS HARD TO FIND, unless you happen to live next door to Will and Helen, the most helpful neighbors in town. Pull up with a carload of groceries and poof!—Will magically appears to help carry everything inside. Find yourself in need of parenting advice and voilà!—Helen shares her time-tested techniques. Over the years, they've also walked Nellie, washed our car, collected our newspapers and mail, spotted Bergen on the ladder, helped build a trellis, rescued me when my car broke down, and offered a shoulder to cry on. Will, who happens to be a dentist, has also provided emergency dental examinations.

Giving *them* a helping hand is not easy. Usually they turn down our offers of assistance. And so we reciprocate with plates of homemade banana bread, cookies, lemon meringue pie, as well as a supply of homegrown kiwis and homemade jam. They always appreciate these offerings, even though their three teenage daughters (or their daughters' boyfriends) sometimes get to the food first.

For obvious reasons, my baking—and their partaking—of these treats has temporarily stopped. I'm sure they understand—they know about my diagnosis. But what they don't know, and I'm only just beginning to comprehend, is how much my identity and self-worth are wrapped up in cracking eggs, mixing in honey, oil, and flour, popping this concoction into the oven, and then sharing the results with family and friends. It's as if, on an existential level, *I bake; therefore I am.* No wonder I'm feeling so lost and inconsequential—I haven't baked anything in months.

BERGEN WAS RIGHT. Back when my biological cuckoo clock was ticking, every hour I would chime, "Let's have a baby together." And without missing a beat, Bergen would respond, "You mean, let's have a teenager together." Of course, that's not what I meant, but that's what we got, rather quickly. A teenager with all the typical bells and whistles—including acne and angst and attitude—and sexual desire.

Having been one horny teenager myself, albeit thirty years ago, I believe teen sexuality is natural, beautiful, and inevitable. That's why there's only one rule about sex in our house: no one is allowed to have more fun than Bergen and me. I realize this may put a damper on Naomi's fun—considering that Parkinson's has parked my libido—and my only interest in sex is putting a checkmark in the female gender box when filling out health forms. But a rule is a rule.

Meanwhile, I'm trying not to worry. My desire has ebbed and flowed all my life, depending on health and circumstances. For instance, after giving birth to Naomi, my sex drive drove off with the placenta. But it came back, eventually. Just as it has other times in my life. So I am hopeful, and so is Bergen, that it will return again, soon.

I'm also trying not to worry obsessively about Naomi. As unique as she is, she resembles both Bergen and me: she got his feet, my eyes, his smile, my shape, his sociability, my artistic disposition. And if she got all that, what if I have unwittingly passed on Parkinson's? Even though the jury's out on whether to blame coincidence or inheritance for my dad's and my misfortune, I can't help but feel genetically responsible for putting her future health at risk. I would do anything to protect her from succumbing to this disease. Unfortunately, there's no vaccine or panacea to offer her. At least not yet.

So my worry continues and wanders about until it latches on to manageable risks. We give her vitamins and vegetables,

math tutors and car rides. We give her a cell phone to keep her connected. And we give her plenty of eye-roll-inducing parental advice. Including my "one drop" talk. As in, all it takes is "one drop" to get a girl pregnant. And it can happen when "one drop" drops in the vicinity of a vagina. This was news to her, but since she had a boyfriend at the time, I thought she should know.

Yesterday, Naomi took her turn, sharing news she thought we should know. Personal news that took incredible courage to convey. We listened intently to her three-word proclamation that confirmed our hunch:

"I am bisexual."

We marveled at how effortlessly these words slipped out of her mouth. Such honesty at age fourteen. And as we talked about her world and how she sees herself fitting in, everything and nothing had changed. And when I tucked her into bed that night, my worry turned to wonder.

IN THE MEANTIME, I'm keeping my rendezvous with Dr. Young. By my third appointment, I'm getting used to the drill—it's like playing psychological Ping-Pong. He serves me a question; I fire back an answer. We volley back and forth until he knows how I'm feeling, sleeping, doing, coping, adjusting to the meds, and even how my family is. Clearly, Dr. Young is winning: he knows all about me, I know nothing about him. Except that he's British, balding, and married. Suddenly, my competitive streak kicks in.

"That's quite the collection you've got," I say, pointing to a mess of tangled name tags hanging from a hook on his office door.

Dr. Young lets out a sigh of resignation. "Those are from all the conferences I've attended this year."

"Do you enjoy going to these?"

"To be honest, I hate traveling. I don't usually mind the conferences, though they can be boring. But it's part of my job."

We stare at the dozens of dangling, dejected name tags, each one bearing his credentials and conference location. And I think to myself, if you hate traveling so much, why on earth do you display these travel mementos, here, in your office, where you are forced to face them every day at work? If you ask me, this behavior smacks of masochism. I bet it's even listed in the *Diagnostic and Statistical Manual of Mental Disorders*: Self-Torture Travel Disorder. Poor Dr. Young. I think he may need professional help.

He turns his attention to his notes, glances at his watch, then asks the usual end-of-session question:

"Is there anything else you'd like to tell me?"

I hate this question. It always makes me feel guilty, as if he suspects that I've been intentionally withholding vital information and now is my chance to come clean. To spit it out. To reveal my deepest, darkest secret. Which I have absolutely no intention of sharing with him.

"Nope," I say.

"Very well then. Let's book you in for your next appointment. How does six weeks from now sound."

"That would be fine."

I mark the date in my calendar, and as we say good-bye it occurs to me—we all have our collections. Some of them dangle. Some of them don't. But they all remind us of something—sometimes even the things we'd rather forget.

MY LEFT HAND is on hiatus; its fingers have turned to stone. They look like frozen french fries, ready to be cooked. The very sight of them makes my Cry Lady weep. "Farewell, manual dexterity," she moans. I sympathize with her sorrow, but she's overreacting—my right hand is still nimble fingered. I remind her of that and of how lucky I am—so far only the left side

of my body is affected. It could be years before Parkinson's migrates. Plus, I'm not taking any medication yet. This consoles my Cry Lady, for now, but I can tell that she's still shaken up.

Compared with her, I'm adjusting remarkably well to the new and worsening me. It turns out, most activities I do can be done with one hand: emptying the dishwasher, working on the computer, doing the laundry, shampooing my hair. Even walking the dog. And when I need a helping hand with chores—chopping vegetables or folding towels—I just wave my tragic wand and poof!—Bergen turns into my sous chef, and Naomi my girl Friday. They are so loving and so loyal—they'd be crushed to find out that I am even thinking of asking our neighbor for help. But in the bathroom, I have heard the sound of one hand flossing, and it's not pretty. Neither is the spell it has cast on my sexual fantasies.

It's late at night. I'm lying in bed, sliding my tongue back and forth—slowly, smoothly—across my teeth. Bergen is next to me, sound asleep. My tongue stumbles on something stuck between my molars. A kernel of corn? A smidgen of chicken? I can't be sure, but whatever it is, it must be removed. So I slither silently out of bed, creep down the stairs, and slip out the front door. My Victoria's Secret nightgown flutters in the wind. Bursting with desire, I limp lasciviously across the street. A tiny gasp escapes my lips. There he is—my neighbor, Will, the dentist. I can feel my heart throbbing, and my knees go weak. We stand beneath the full moon and glittering stars, staring deeply into each other's teeth, until finally I whisper, "Floss me, Will, floss me." And he does.

5

Lost
and Found

A MONTH HAS PASSED SINCE that first moonlit flossing. For a while, I couldn't stop thinking about it. But now I have other things on my mind.

Today Nellie found a ten-dollar bill. It was folded in half, lounging on a patch of grass near the park. I'm not sure if it was the sweet smell of money or the stench of well-anointed grass, but when she caught a whiff she woofed, then launched into a sniffing frenzy. Sensing the inevitable, I limped into action and rescued the cash before Nellie had a chance to squat and squirt all over it.

This was the first time she found money. I wish she'd find more of it, instead of all those pointy sticks, food scraps, icky insects, and used tissues I dig out of her mouth. But who am I to talk? I can't even remember the last time I came across a nickel, let alone a ten-dollar bill. But I did find something of significance the other day.

I wish it were something joyful, like my elusive G-spot, or something musical, like Naomi's lost iPod. Instead, I'm afraid it's rather dismal: two lumps in my right breast. The small one feels like a pebble—hard and round. The larger one feels formless and spongy. And even though they are practically neighbors, just inches apart, they have never been formally introduced. Being the hostess and all, I got the ball rolling by asking their names.

"I'm Little Lump," chirped the small one, curled up by my sternum.

"And I'm Big Blob," bellowed the other.

He had set up camp behind my nipple, in the shade of my areola. Compared with Little Lump, he was huge.

At first, I was worried that they wouldn't get along. After all, one is timid; the other is aggressive. The last thing I needed was a bra-room brawl. So I read the riot act to each of them, in private, and they both assured me they won't pick a fight. But Little Lump was still scared.

"Why should I trust him?" she asked.

"Because Blob's your uncle," I said.

Ever since my auntie Glenda died of breast cancer, I've kept close tabs on my tits. I'm always on the lookout for lumps or bumps and other ominous signs. By now, I know them inside out. So does Dr. Mintz. When you have breast tissue as lumpy as mine, medical exams and mammograms are essential for peace of mind. And that's exactly why I'm here, again, in Dr. Mintz's office. For peace of mind. While Dr. Mintz examines my breast lumps, I study the expression on his face. I'm looking for clues and cues: should I or shouldn't I panic?

"It's probably nothing," he says, "but I'd like to get you in for a mammogram. Just to be sure."

The tone of his voice pushes my panic button.

"Do you think it's cancer?" I ask.

"I don't think so," he says. But what I hear is, "Maybe."

When I get home, I tell Bergen about Little Lump and Big Blob. He stays calm and reassures me. "You know, there's no point worrying, until we know what it is."

"I know. That's why I don't want to tell Naomi."

But I do call Lisa.

She says, "It's good that you're getting it checked out, Robbie, but it's probably nothing to worry about."

Sweet Lisa, the eternal optimist.

ONE DAY I save an earthworm. Not in any evangelical way—I only proselytize to praying mantises. I simply save this worm from imminent death. While taking Nellie for a walk, I spot the wiggling creature, smack dab in the middle of the sidewalk. Baking in the hot sun.

"Look, Nellie," I say.

She gives it a sniff, then watches me slip my hand into an empty poop bag and gingerly pick it up. I carry it away from the concrete, to a nearby garden, and place it in a shady patch of grass.

"Take care, little worm," I whisper.

Then Nellie barks at it three times—sage advice that I translate for the benefit of that critter: "Location. Location. Location."

This is the first time I have ever saved a worm. This must be what happens to people who spend too much time looking down at the ground. People like me who don't have a job, who are clinically depressed, who do the Parkinson's shuffle while walking a dog that loves to swallow sticks. People who know that one day they could be the wiggling creature—lying smack dab in the middle of the sidewalk, baking in the hot sun—in need of saving.

OVER THE YEARS, I've bartered my art for many things: photo sessions, dental work, toy boats, handmade dolls, clothing, hats, jewelry. But this is the first time I've bartered for therapy. When I arrive for my session with Theresa, I present her with a large rectangle wrapped in brown paper. Theresa smiles and says, "Is this my painting?"

"If you like it," I say.

"I'm sure I will. May I see it?"

Together we unwrap the package, revealing a colorful collage of three childlike figures holding hands, next to a cat, on a tree-lined street. The sky is filled with swirling dots. The trees are overflowing with hundreds of tiny cutout painted leaves. The houses are simplified boxes with lace windows. I lean the framed artwork against the wall and say, "The title is *Down the Street, Hand in Hand*."

"It's beautiful. There is so much joy—I love it."

"One reason I chose this one is because it has a lot of purple in it, and you wear a lot of purple. It's also one of my 'Dancers' series. When you looked through my portfolio, you liked that style."

"Thank you, Robyn. I can't wait to find a place for it in my home."

I curl up on the couch while Theresa sits down on her chair. We allow our breathing to synchronize, letting our shoulders relax and our heads roll slowly from side to side. And then Theresa gently asks, "How are you?"

"I'm not sure," I answer, pressing my right hand against my tightening chest. "I found two lumps in my breast. I've started picking up worms off the sidewalk. And I'm fantasizing about getting flossed by my neighbor."

Theresa's face turns serious. "Have you gone to your doctor about the lumps?"

"Yep. I'm booked for a mammogram and ultrasound soon. But I'm worried."

We talk about the challenges of waiting—for the examinations and for the results. We explore the best- and worst-case scenarios, as I imagine how they might unfold. We review techniques to help me cope with my tendency to catastrophize. And when I'm all lumped out, we talk about my newfound affinity for worms and Will the dentist and my deteriorating manual dexterity—all within sight of my painting, leaning against the wall, reminding me that I haven't painted in a very long time.

Soon after my session with Theresa, Bergen and Naomi abandon me to go on a road trip, up to Williams Lake, in northern British Columbia, to visit Bergen's cousin and go to the Williams Lake Stampede and Rodeo. They left this morning, the first day of Naomi's summer vacation. I was invited to join them. But we all knew I'd say no. Considering my low energy, and my daily nap and exercise routine, I decided to stay in my comfort zone—at home with Nellie. They'll be gone for two weeks—long enough to soak up some traveling adventures and to get a much-needed break from me. I get the house to myself for a couple of days, and then the visitors arrive. First Ruthie. Then my dad.

When Ruthie arrives, she is in demand. She has friends all over the world, many of them right here in Vancouver. We all want a piece of her, so she is parceling out her time judiciously. Today is my day.

She arrives bearing gifts, and I welcome her with tears. Nellie starts licking her pedicured toes.

"You call this a dog?" Ruthie laughs, leaning down to rub her belly.

"I know—she's a crouton compared with your pooch."

Maya. The massive Great Dane.

"How is Maya doing?" I ask.

"Getting old. She has arthritis. She's staying with friends, the ones who always look after her while I'm away."

Good friends, no doubt. Because Ruthie is away a lot. She loves to travel. And she looks the part: exotic, voluptuous, comfortable in her sun-kissed skin. I feel like a gargoyle in the presence of a goddess.

I've known her since high school, where we became instant friends. Together we pursued typical teenage obsessions: sex, drugs, and rock 'n' roll, and moving out of our parents' homes. But I quickly learned there was nothing typical about Ruthie— she was an overachiever. At sixteen, while I was still planning my escape, she had her own apartment and a full-time job and had boldly upgraded from boys to men. At eighteen, while I was still living at home, she was traveling overseas. When Ruthie returned home, seven years later, the world had penetrated her heart. She was fulfilled and ready to settle down, for a while. She started a small business—a mobile juice bar—that grew into a chain of vegetarian restaurants called Fresh. While she had been traveling, I had finally made several escapes—from my parents' house, from university, from Toronto. I was by then living in Vancouver, establishing my art career. In so many ways, our lives had changed, are still changing. But our sisterly love has remained constant.

"What's up with you?" she asks. "Lisa mentioned you're getting some tests."

"I'm scheduled for a mammogram next week. I found two lumps. What if it's cancer? What'll I do?" Tears stream down my face.

"You'll fight. That's what you'll do. Right? You'll fight."

But I'm not so sure. Part of me thinks breast cancer would be a blessing, a morbid means of escape from Parkinson's.

"What would you do?" I ask her.

And without hesitation, Ruthie says, "Whatever it takes to beat it."

She stares at me with those green eyes, then she issues her command: "You'll fight. And we'll be there to help you."

My tears come and go for the rest of the day. While we walk Nellie. While we go out for lunch. While we drink tea and talk about her travels, her man, her miscarriage. And before you know it, our visit is over—time flies when you're having phlegm. I wipe my nose; we hug good-bye; I escort her to the door. Then the gargoyle blows the goddess a kiss, and she drives off in her rental car.

MY DAD TRAVELS light but always packs dozens of jokes and one-liners. Never newish, mostly Jewish, borrowed from the best: Henny Youngman, Groucho Marx, Jackie Mason, Rodney Dangerfield, Woody Allen. I've heard them all a million times, but I don't mind hearing them again. I know that the more jokes he cracks, the happier he is. When we get home from the airport, I can tell he is no longer depressed.

"Are you tired?" I ask.

"I was born tired," he replies.

When he's settled in the guest room, I ask, "Are you comfortable?"

"I make a living," he quips.

When he winces while getting up from the couch, I ask, "Are you all right?"

"I told my doctor my back hurts whenever I stand up, so the doctor told me, 'Then don't stand up,'" he laughs. He's seventy years old and still remembers them all.

This is the first time in years that my dad has visited me on his own, without my mom. She stayed in Toronto, to help look after my brother's and sister's kids. She likes to be where the action is—and it sure isn't here. Left to our own devices,

my dad and I devolve: we are two peas in a Parkinson's pod. Moving in slow motion. Lounging on the couch. Reading the newspaper. Taking midday naps. We're both perfectly content to hang out at home. And when we do venture out, it's to walk the dog or buy groceries or go out for dinner.

"I feel like I'm on holiday," my dad confesses after waking up from a snooze. He is so easy to please.

I have arranged a special surprise for him. It's opalescent blue and seats two. It pulls up to the curb—curvaceous, flirtatious—be still my beeping horn.

"Hop in!" says Will the dentist. "I'll take you for a spin."

My dad is smitten. He loves Jaguars, and this one is vintage: a 1967 convertible. He slides into the passenger seat. Will's nimble fingers grip the wheel. Then the purring engine lets out a roar, and off they drive into the sunset.

Will's wife, Helen, is standing beside me. She's so happy to wave them off.

"That's one less car ride for me. I wish your dad would stick around so that I wouldn't have to be Will's only sidekick."

Then she smiles and says, "You should get Will to take you for a ride."

The thought had crossed my mind, but only if he can floss and drive at the same time. "Maybe I will, one of these days."

My dad flies home this afternoon. There's only one thing left to do. So I set up my mini-disc recorder and microphone and begin. Over the years, he's told me his stories, the details of his life, but I have forgotten key facts and mixed up dates and even remembered things that never happened. This is my chance to set the record straight. I ask him about his childhood, the jobs he had as a kid, his business, the charitable work he's done.

I want to remember my father. I want something to remind me of him—something quintessential and sentimental—if he

dies before I do. I've given this a lot of thought, and there's only one thing that fits the bill. I work up the courage to make my request:

"Can you bequeath your hairbrush to me?"

He lets out a laugh and gives me that "you can't be serious" look. But I assure him that I am dead serious. This hairbrush is an heirloom; it's half a century old and is as bald as his head. He paid five bucks for it when he was nineteen. Back then, they were both young and invincible, brimming with bristles, oblivious to the perils of male-pattern baldness and repetitive use. And while my dad had the means to buy a new hairbrush every day, he remained loyal and devoted to this one.

"Well, I could even leave it for you today, if it means that much to you. Nobody else has ever asked for it."

This doesn't surprise me. "No, I just want you to will it to me," I reply.

"Consider it done," he says.

IT'S QUIET WITHOUT my dad in the house. But I'm not lonely or alone—I've got Nellie to keep me company. And Little Lump and Big Blob. It turns out that these two are quite mischievous. Yesterday during my mammogram, they played hide and seek so well that no one could find them. But the ultrasound blew their cover. Now they want to do a biopsy on Big Blob to see what he's made of. Something tells me it ain't sugar and spice and everything nice.

Today is Big Blob's biopsy. The forecast calls for morbid jokes from a middle-aged dame, with periods of emotional turbulence and disbelief. Expect hovering doctor with long, pointy needles and hand-holding nurse with soothing voice. There is a slight chance of internal bruising. Apply-pressure advisory in effect.

I'm half-naked, flat on my back, scared stiff—in a room so small and so cramped, surrounded by blinking, beeping, humming high-tech machines, that I feel like I'm in a medical cockpit:

"This is your doctor speaking. We'll be cleared for your core needle biopsy shortly. Kindly unfasten your hospital gown and remain in a reclining position."

Up until now, I have been amusing the doctor and nurse with my lie-down comedy routine. Joke after joke after joke. But the minute the doctor tells me, "Hold perfectly still," the kidding stops and the tears start flowing.

"Does something hurt?" she asks, pointing this menacing needle at my nipple.

"No," I whimper, "my defense mechanism just broke down. This isn't funny anymore."

"I know. It's scary. But I need you to hold perfectly still, OK?"

"OK."

"You'll feel some pressure."

And I did.

"You'll hear a loud clicking sound."

And I did.

"Now let's do this again . . . and again."

Three samples, and it's over. I feel rattled and relieved. I'm glad I followed Susan's advice and let her accompany me to this appointment instead of waiting a week until Bergen gets home. By the time he's back, we should know exactly what Big Blob is made of.

MY TRAVELERS come home with stories and photos and gifts and laundry. Naomi looks taller. Bergen looks tanned. They say I look rested and Nellie looks scruffy—but it's probably the other way around. Life returns to normal for five summer days.

The house goes from clean to cluttered; the telephone rings and rings; there are family walks and visits with friends. And then normal disappears.

When I call the doctor's office this morning, my biopsy report has finally arrived.

"Can you tell me the results over the phone?" I ask.

"No, I can't do that," the assistant, Peggy, says. "You have to make an appointment with Dr. Mintz."

"Well, then, can you tell me if I should bring Bergen along, to cry on his shoulder? Or should I just come on my own."

"Better bring Bergen."

Behind every great man, there's a great woman. And at Dr. Mintz's office, it's Peggy. She's been his loyal assistant for twenty years. Her work never ends: schmoozing with patients, answering the phone, arranging referrals, collecting specimens, managing files, booking appointments, keeping Dr. Mintz well fed. These last two tasks go hand in hand and often lead to mouthwatering delights that magically appear just in time for lunch. Here's how it works: with a little luck and some culinary cunning, Peggy cooks up the perfect storm by scheduling certain patients' appointments between noon and one o'clock. These certain patients tend to be Greek grandmothers—AKA Yayas—or East Indian women, with the usual aches and pains but also with heartfelt appreciation. They adore Dr. Mintz, and they know what he adores. So along with their bodily complaints, they bring him homemade spanakopita, samosas, baklava, ouzo, and wine. And every second Friday, butter chicken.

Today when we arrive, the waiting room smells like cinnamon.

"Someone baked us coffee cake," Peggy says. "You can head into Dr. Mintz's office; he's expecting you."

Bergen takes my hand and leads me into the room, where two empty chairs await. Everything feels surreal and distant—as

if I'm in the theater of the absurd. I watch myself sitting down. I see Dr. Mintz moving his mouth. But the words I hear him say get mangled in my mind.

"We caught it early bird." "I know an excellent circus." "Paging invasive ductal carcinoma. Please meet your party at stage one."

On our way out, Peggy hands me a slip of paper.

"I got you an appointment—for tomorrow—with Dr. Chung. She did my surgeries. I told her it was urgent, and she squeezed you in."

Good old Peggy. I'd forgotten that she's had two bouts of breast cancer. How lucky for me that she's well connected to this surgeon.

"What's she like?" I ask.

"She's one of the best and busiest surgeons in town. Look at me, I'm still here."

"Is she nice?"

"She's serious. When you meet her, you'll understand."

A wave of relief sweeps over me and I think, it's terrible to have such a critical disease, but wonderful to receive such urgent attention.

TODAY'S APPOINTMENT with the surgeon is scheduled for late afternoon. Happy hour. If I were a drinker, I'd cheer myself up and calm Big Blob's nerves with a few cocktails. But I'm no drinker—I'm a walker. That's how I clear my head. And there's just enough time to take Nellie out for a stroll.

We wind our way through the neighborhood, dodging lawn mowers, barking at kids, rescuing worms. When we reach the top of the hill, we turn left onto Dunbar Street—the business section. A few stores down from Diane's beauty salon is an art school for young children. I walk by it all the time, admiring the cheerful paintings displayed in the storefront window. There's always a theme. A few days ago it was Vincent Van

Gogh's *Sunflowers*. Before that it was Claude Monet's *Water Lilies*. And before that, Leonardo da Vinci's *Mona Lisa*. These pipsqueak forgeries of masterpieces always make me smile, but today's new display—various versions of Edvard Munch's *The Scream*—not only makes me smile but also sends shivers down my spine. All the elements of the original artwork are simplified and cartoonlike—the helpless hands against the skeletal head, the turbulent orange sky, the ominous bridge over murky water. Yet the essence of emotional suffering comes through loud and clear. I can hear the shrill screams escaping the gaping mouths. These childlike paintings are hilarious and horrific, just like my life. The perfect backdrop for my happy hour meeting with the surgeon.

This is the saddest waiting room I've ever seen. There must be twenty chairs in tidy rows, all of them occupied by breast cancer patients and their loved ones. When more people arrive, it's standing room only. There is a three- to four-hour wait to see the surgeon. The décor is dismal. We are surrounded by floor-to-ceiling filing cabinets, overflowing with thousands of multicolored folders. I wonder what color my file will be. Red for right breast? Blue for Big Blob?

Three and a half hours later I find out: it's white with red and yellow tabs. Dr. Chung apologizes for the long wait. She says, "You are my last appointment of the day. I'm going on vacation tomorrow; there were a lot of patients to squeeze in." Bergen and I give her understanding looks and sit quietly while she reviews my file. I watch her delicate fingers slide across the pages while her dark eyes dart back and forth. She looks poised and petite while sitting down. She glances up from the file and says matter-of-factly, "You were diagnosed with Parkinson's disease eight months ago. And you have just been diagnosed with breast cancer."

"At least I don't have testicular cancer," I reply.

"What's that supposed to mean?" she asks.

Obviously she didn't get the joke. But Bergen did, and now he's giving me a disapproving look, while mouthing the words "Not now" and pretending to slice his neck with his hand—code for "Cut out the morbid jokes."

Then he says, "Robyn has a black sense of humor, especially when she gets nervous."

This seems to patch up any damage done to Dr. Chung's sensibilities, and we move on to the physical exam.

Dr. Chung's hands are intuitive instruments—they press and plunge and squeeze and dig and oscillate and calibrate every nook and cranny of my breasts, my chest, my underarms, my neck. I have never been palpated like this before. She is very concerned about the size of Big Blob. And flabbergasted that Little Lump was not biopsied.

"That should have been done at the same time," she huffs, reaching for her pad of requisition forms. "I'll set up an appointment to have this biopsy taken right away. And also an MRI of both your breasts. Depending on the lab results of this second lump, you will need either a lumpectomy or a mastectomy. Plus some lymph nodes removed. How does three weeks from today sound?"

It sounds inconceivable, hilarious, horrific. Too soon. Too real. It also sounds inevitable.

"Three weeks from now would be fine," I say.

She marks my name down in her calendar; then I add, "My auntie Glenda died from breast cancer. Could this be genetic?"

"Are you Jewish?"

"Yes. Why do you ask?"

"There is a higher incidence rate of breast cancer among certain Jewish women. Your ancestry—are you Ashkenazi or Sephardic?"

I know the answer. But I can't seem to locate it in my mind.

So I hesitate and guess. "Sephardic. My grandparents were from Eastern Europe."

"Then you are Ashkenazi," Dr. Chung says, laughing. "Now that's funny. You didn't know which one you were."

I start laughing too, then Bergen joins in.

At the end of the appointment, Dr. Chung hands me a thick folder. "This is for you to keep," she says. "There's lots of useful information in there."

In other words—homework. When Bergen and I get to the car, I look in the folder and find brochures and a book titled *The Intelligent Patient's Guide to Breast Cancer*. Stupidly, I start reading the chapter on mastectomies—detailed descriptions of surgical procedures, potential health complications, photographs of mastectomy scars. It's all so graphic and gruesome. I feel sick with worry about this pending surgery. I may have signed up, but do I have the balls to show up?

IT'S A WARM sunny day. Bergen, Naomi, and I take a drive to Commercial Drive and eat lunch on the patio of a favorite restaurant. The little hand on my watch is pointing at Naomi, and the big hand is pointing at my breast. Tick. Talk. Tick. Talk. It's time to tell Naomi. Before dessert, I casually say, "I have some news."

She looks at me, then Bergen, then down at her hands, and shuffles nervously in her chair.

"I've just been diagnosed with breast cancer."

I watch her face flutter with surprise.

"You have that too?" she moans. Her question is so sad and so funny—she's my daughter, through and through—that we all start laughing and crying, at the same time.

"I'm lucky, I caught it early. I'm going to be OK. So don't worry, all right?"

"Why didn't you tell me before?"

"I just found out two days ago. You've been so busy with your friends these past few days; I've hardly seen you. That's why we arranged this lunch." There are plenty more questions to ask and answer, but first there's pie and cake to share. A little sweetness to add to the sorrow.

That night, lying in bed with Bergen, words are whispered, then brushed aside by searching fingers and aching flesh. His touch distracts me from my bewilderment at having two diseases and all that entails. But not for long. My muddled mind interrupts with questions: How can Bergen still find me desirable as Parkinson's distorts my body? How will he react when my breast is gone? What will I look like? How will I feel? Who will I be? Tears stream down my face and dampen his shoulder.

"Do you hate me?" I ask.

"I love it when you say that. It brings us closer together," he laughs.

Then he wraps his arms around me and says, "I'm lucky to be with you. You're very sexy, you know."

"I don't feel very sexy."

"Oh, but you are very sexy," he says in a Scottish accent.

"You won't be saying that when I only have one tit."

"Oh, yes, I will. You will always be my bonnie lass."

We kiss. I veer my mind away from my worries, toward the possibility of pleasure. After all these years, our bodies still transport us to electric places. Even now. Maybe even after my breast surgery.

A few days later, I have an appointment with Theresa. She has a new office; I have a new disease. Both take some getting used to. This office is bigger and brighter than her previous one, and this new disease is more deadly than my first. Both feel foreign—discombobulating. But Theresa's my anchor. I tell her about the diagnosis.

"I'm so sorry, Robyn," she says. "You seem remarkably calm, considering what you are dealing with."

I suppose it's possible to confuse a stunned "deer in the headlights" demeanor with calmness, but I know that's not what she means. ·

"I know. It's so strange. It's as if my Cry Lady is incognito, keeping a low profile. Sure, there have been tears—but nothing melodramatic. I almost feel numb."

"It must be quite a shock," Theresa says.

"Yeah. But it's also a kick in the pants. There's so much to do before the surgery."

"Like what?"

"Get all these tests done, the second biopsy, the MRI, X-rays, blood work. Tell my family and friends. Finish my will and find and burn my old diaries."

"Your old diaries?"

"Yeah. From my university days. If I die in surgery, the last thing I want is Naomi rummaging through my stuff, reading about my sexual adventures."

Theresa laughs.

"What if I die in surgery?" I wonder out loud.

"It's highly unlikely, but it's possible."

"Lots of women die from breast cancer."

"That's true. And lots of women survive."

"When I first found the lumps and was waiting for the biopsy results, part of me thought I'd be lucky to die this way—I wouldn't have to worry about Parkinson's anymore. I also wouldn't be a burden to my family. But now that I know I have cancer, I realize I don't want to die. Not yet. I want to live."

The moment I say this, my chest tightens and I feel like I can't breathe—I'm having an anxiety attack. Theresa remains calm and focused.

"Try doing this," she says, placing her hands on her chest, taking deep breaths in, exhaling loudly. I copy her motions and feel the panic subside a bit.

"That's good," she nods. "It's OK to feel scared. I'm right here."

And with that, my body surrenders to some primordial force. I'm Gug the Cavewoman, quaking like thunder, weeping with abandon, summoning the gods. The sky is falling, and I am falling apart. Finally.

BONNIE IS COMING to visit me. She got a deal on a last-minute flight. By the time her plane arrives, I've recovered from yesterday's therapy session. My plan is to pick her up at the airport, be cheerful and chatty, then break the news when we get home. In other words, avoid a public display of affliction. I spot her by the luggage carousel looking tanned and trim.

"Beachface!" I shout.

Several people turn their heads in my direction, but only one person answers to that nickname. Bonnie smiles, grabs her bags, and walks over.

"Hi, Robbie," she says, giving me a great big hug.

That's my cue to be cordial, to stick to the plan and say, "Hi, Bonnie. Did you have a good flight?" But as our bodies meld, my plan is hijacked by a sudden surge of emotion ripping through me. Oh, God—here it comes—premature revelation!

"I have breast cancer," I blurt out, exploding into tears—right here, at YVR domestic arrivals.

Once we've loaded the luggage into the trunk, we hop into the car. There's a gift waiting for Bonnie inside.

"Go ahead and open it," I say. "It's for you."

She unwraps the package and finds a shiny red plastic case, decorated with a cartoon of a little boy dressed up as a doctor.

"A toy medical kit?" she asks, opening the lid.

"I have a few appointments this week—some blood tests, X-rays, a biopsy. I was hoping you'd come along; you could be my make-believe nurse. I know you loved volunteering at the leper colony in Calcutta years ago. I'm sure it won't be as exciting as cleaning festering wounds, but it could still be fun."

"Of course I'll go with you," Bonnie says. "I just want to hang out with you. It doesn't matter where."

ANOTHER DAY, another waiting room. I've got the right person for the right job. Nurse Bonnie, oblivious to the watchful eyes around us, is busy checking my vitals—taking my temperature with the yellow toy thermometer, listening to my heart with the blue stethoscope, checking my blood pressure with the tiny inflatable armband.

"There. Everything seems normal," she smiles, packing away her medical instruments.

Normal? If only that were true. What a difference a lump makes. Or two.

When my name is finally called, I leave my purse with Bonnie, change into a hospital gown, and wait in an examination room. My fingers slide along the right side of my collarbone, then travel down my ribs until they bump into Little Lump. Woe is we—me and my lump—waiting for this second biopsy is more nerve-racking than it was waiting for the first one—now that we know exactly what to expect. But when the doctor arrives and preps us for the procedure, it turns out all that worry was for nothing. Little Lump is located too close to my chest wall.

"Instead of a core needle biopsy, you need an excise biopsy," the doctor explains.

"Does that require a priest?" I ask, recalling *The Exorcist,* where Linda Blair plays the devil-possessed girl whose spinning head spews vomit and vulgarities.

The doctor either didn't hear my question or just ignores it. "You'll need to call your surgeon. She'll probably do the biopsy for you."

"LET'S GO to the Naam for lunch," Bonnie says.

It's her favorite vegetarian restaurant in Vancouver. Mine too. The service can be slow, but the food is always great. And today, as far as I'm concerned, they can take their sweet time filling our orders—Bonnie and I have lots of catching up to do. I want to hear all about her two young boys, her husband, and the amazing lighting designs she is creating for theatrical productions around the world.

I've known Bonnie since high school, but it wasn't until after graduation that our lives intersected, at the corner of Yonge and Bloor, in downtown Toronto. It was summer, and we were both street vending our handcrafted jewelry. Bonnie's earrings were elegant, made of shiny silver and shimmering beads. Pretty enough to wear to a wedding. My earrings were not elegant or pretty. They were called "cute" and "weird" and "rude" and "funny." I sculpted teeny-weeny people from special Plasticine— some wearing bathing suits, others wearing birthday suits. These sold steadily, but it was my Gumby knockoffs that killed. That retro green clay toy figure was making a pop-cultural comeback at the time, and I couldn't keep up with demand. I churned out thousands of these mini-Gumbies, most of them modest in boxers and bikinis. But I also cranked out nude versions that were anatomically correct.

Bonnie and I would often set up our displays next to each other. We'd spell each other off for bathroom and lunch breaks. And between sales, we'd talk. By the end of the summer, we were friends. And then Bonnie moved out west to study theatrical lighting design at the University of British Columbia.

We didn't reconnect until the following summer when I transferred from psychology at the University of Toronto into fine arts at UBC. I was driving my car across Canada with my soon-to-be ex-boyfriend and his buddy. We broke up along the way—somewhere in the Prairies, just off the Trans-Canada Highway, in the parking lot of some coffee shop, in the pouring rain. I wish it had been one of those mutual "let's just be friends" endings. But it wasn't. I broke his heart. And then he lost his left boot, his appetite, and his interest in bathing. So by the time we showed up at Bonnie's house in Vancouver—which she was renting with several other students—my ex was an existential, one-booted mess. In spite of the awkwardness of the situation, Bonnie's compassion prevailed, and with my acquiescence, she let my ex stay a couple days until he found other accommodations.

Although this was not planned, I moved in, first into Bonnie's room and then into my own room when one of the roommates moved out.

By the end of the school year, our lives were intertwined and forever changed. We were soul sisters. Bonnie moved again—to take a job in Halifax. I also moved—into an apartment of my own, in Vancouver. But this time we kept in touch. There were long-distance phone calls and cross-Canada visits. And always Bonnie's presence in my life—her steady, fearless love that whispered, "No matter what happens, or where you go, I will be there for you." Like she is now, here with me in Cancerland. And like she would be, if I were to wind up in a leper colony.

I HAVE A CONFESSION: I'm seeing another man. Almost every night. He has baby blue eyes and manly tattoos, and when he talks, I glisten. He's charming and funny and sexy and smart.

He's married. But so am I. He's smutty and I am smitten. It took me by surprise.

It was my dad who introduced me to him, while Bergen and Naomi were away. We were watching the evening news. Then my dad changed channels and there he was—gazing into my eyes, extending his arms, smiling seductively.

"Welcome to *The Late Late Show*. I'm your host, TV's Craig Ferguson."

His mellifluous voice melted my heart—I'm a sucker for Scottish brogues. He had my vagina with his monologue. And then he had the rest of me when he pulled out his puppets.

"It's a great day for America!" Craig teases me each night, arousing my adulterous desire. This unrequited lust can't last forever, but it sure feels good for now. And so I wait with bated breasts for Craig to cross my border and plunge his patriotic flagpole into my foreign soil—hopefully before my surgery.

And when he does, I'll say, "It's a great day for Canada!"

IT'S TIME to climb back on the bad-news bandwagon—I've delayed it long enough. There are people I have to tell. I've been dreading all these phone calls I'm about to make. If only there were an easier way...

For Immediate Release

Middle-Aged Dame Diversifies Disease Portfolio

Vancouver, B.C., July 2008—Robyn Michele Levy has diversified her disease portfolio with the unexpected acquisition of breast cancer. This follows hot on the heels of her recent partnership acquisition of Parkinson's "R" Us, formerly a sole proprietorship owned by her father, Gordon Levy.

> As part of her strategy to survive, she is planning
> to postpone her summer vacation, lop off her right tit,
> and try not to wallow in self-pity.
>
> Robyn deeply regrets any distress this may cause
> family, friends, and pets.
>
> Robyn's right breast deeply regrets any distress
> this may cause brassieres, plunging necklines, and
> ex-boyfriends.

THE DEED IS DONE—well done. It's left me medium rare. Marinating in other people's calamitous tears. I now have a cache of their concerns, unsolicited advice, and heartfelt offers of help.

My poor father—he's been down this road before. It was a dead-end street for his sister, Glenda. Neither of us mention her name while we talk on the phone. We cradle our memories of her in our silence.

"I want to be there for the operation. I'll fly out," he says, pushing through fear, grasping for hope.

I am hesitant to say yes, for both of our sakes. "Let me think about it, OK?"

"What about Mom? I know she'll want to come help you too."

His question lands in my lap like a hot potato. After all these years, my dad is still trying to bring my mom and me closer. I don't blame him. He's only doing what he thinks is best. But considering how scared and vulnerable I feel now—just imagining the horror of possibly having a mastectomy—I expect to feel worse after my breast has been amputated. And in this fragile state of recovery, I'll need plenty of rest and nurturing. Sadly, just thinking about my mom visiting me under these circumstances makes me feel anxious. My decision is difficult to make and even more difficult to convey to my dad. But the more we talk, the more sympathetic he is to my wishes and the deeper I

understand why he needs to be by my side. So I say yes to him and no to my mom. We agree that he will fly back here in two weeks—the day before my surgery.

In the meantime, Bonnie has gone home. She left her toy medical kit behind.

She said, "You should keep it. It might come in handy."

It's got the cutest little yellow plastic scalpel. I was going to take the kit along to today's biopsy—it's Little Lump's unlucky day—but Bergen thought it best to leave it at home. He's probably right. I wouldn't want to give Dr. Chung the wrong impression (again). She might think I need a lobotomy in addition to a biopsy.

I ask Bergen to come along to help keep me calm. Of course, he says yes. He would never turn down an opportunity to accomplish more than one thing at a time. He could be helpful by providing moral support, while stimulating his scientific curiosity by watching a surgical procedure.

Soon after we arrive at the hospital, Dr. Chung's face says, "Hello." That's the only part of her petite body we can see. Everything else is shrouded in green hospital scrubs and latex gloves and hair net and booties. On all the other surgeons and nurses, this outfit looks sloppy and bland. But on Dr. Chung, it looks elegant and chic; she could be a doctor on call at a cocktail party.

"Hors d'oeuvre? Champagne? Bilateral mastectomy?"

In the operating room, we chat, and I'm struck by her radiant smile and the excitement in her eyes. It's obvious that she is raring to go. I watch her flip through some paperwork, nod to her nurse, then announce, "We're ready to begin."

The operating room is bright and cold. Bergen's hand is strong and warm.

"Do you enjoy performing surgery?" I ask Dr. Chung's hovering head.

"It's my favorite part," she says from behind her mask, while painting antiseptic on my exposed skin.

"I'm going to give you some local freezing now, so I need you to lie perfectly still."

"I have Parkinson's. That won't be a problem."

I am awake the entire time, squeezing Bergen's hand. I purposely don't watch her making the incision or scraping away my flesh. I'm afraid if I did, my reaction might be impolite or foolish—I tend to fart or faint under extreme pressure. So to prevent any one of us from needing resuscitation, I keep my eyes on Bergen, sitting quietly in his facemask by my side, and together we calmly breathe the antiseptic air in and out.

Meanwhile, Dr. Chung keeps on digging, prodding, swabbing, dabbing. When she finally extracts Little Lump from my anesthetized breast, she holds it out for me to see. And there it is, glistening between the tweezers, no larger than a pea, looking more boogerlike than bogeyman.

"This doesn't look like cancer," she says. "But we have to know for sure." That's why Little Lump is sent off to Biopsy Land in the bottom of a sterilized jar. And I am sent off to Worryville to wait for test results that will determine the fate of my right breast.

THERE'S NO REST for the weary, or the teary. My Cry Lady and I were swamped. We had ten days to get this pre-surgery to-do list done. It was daunting but doable, provided we took one Parkinson's shuffle at a time.

The items on the list fell into three familiar categories: calamity, sanity, and vanity.

My calamity checklist looked like this:

· Go to the cancer agency to get an MRI of both breasts.

- Go to the local health clinic to get a preoperative blood test.
- Attend an urgent meeting with my neurologist, Dr. Stoessl, to discuss specific medications and anesthetics that should not be administered to Parkinson's patients during surgery and recovery.
- Attend a follow-up meeting with my surgeon, Dr. Chung, to hear results of Little Lump's biopsy report and MRI, as well as her recommendation for either a lumpectomy or mastectomy.
- Go to the hospital for a preoperative meeting with the anesthesiologist.
- The day before surgery, go to the hospital for a nuclear medicine injection for sentinel node biopsy.

The good news is I managed to get all these things done, and I didn't panic in the MRI (I just focused on John Lennon's soothing voice in my headphones), I didn't faint during the blood test, I didn't need to worry about the drugs (Dr. Stoessl knew exactly what to avoid), I didn't joke with Dr. Chung, I didn't sleep with the anesthesiologist, and I didn't glow in the dark after the nuclear medicine injection—though in my mind, these were all distinct possibilities.

The bad news is that Little Lump is also cancerous: invasive ductal carcinoma Grade 3. Although she may be smaller than Big Blob, she's more deadly. Now the writing is on the chest wall: hello, mastectomy; good-bye, boob gone bad.

My sanity checklist was smaller:

- Book a massage with Jessica.
- Schedule a session with Theresa.
- Hire a part-time housekeeper.

Jessica is a registered massage therapist. Week after week, I venture downtown to lie prostrate in her presence. Blessed with strong peasant fingers and athletic prowess, she coaxes my rigid muscles to relax. This is no easy task for either one of us. It's demanding physical work: pressing, being pressed; pulling, being pulled; kneading, being kneaded. And I need her now more than ever—she's a necessity in my life.

"Oh, dear," she uttered, when I told her my breast was doomed. She offered to make postsurgery house calls if required. And then she silently deployed her healing fingers into my mournful flesh, expanding time and extracting tears.

I finally found someone to help clean the house. Her name is Lourdes, and she comes highly recommended. She'll schedule us in every other Monday, but she'll pray for me every day.

How can my tit be so sick when it doesn't even hurt? How is it something so small can be so catastrophic? Fear and grief and disbelief—these are the dominant themes of my bon-voyage-breast session with Theresa.

And finally, my vanity list:

· Get legs waxed.
· Get mustache zapped.
· Get a haircut and color touch-up.

So that if I die in surgery, I'll die smooth and coiffed.

6

Kissing
My Cleavage Good-bye

IT'S THE EVE OF my mastectomy. The forecast calls for heavy gusts of trepidation amid a downpour of telephone calls from family and friends. Expect seasonal escape for daughter at overnight summer camp, treat-filled vacation for family dog at neighbor's house, and laid-back night with husband, father, and sexy TV host. There is a 5 percent chance of my cracking a smile.

In the hullabaloo of rushing to appointments and making necessary arrangements, I had forgotten one key thing that I had intended to do—find a meaningful way to honor my right breast while she was still attached.

The last time I honored one of my body parts was fourteen years ago. I was pregnant with Naomi, due to give birth any day, and I had opted out of having a traditional baby shower. Instead, I threw myself a Bless My Vagina party. This was far more practical. Who needs gifts like receiving blankets and baby booties when your vagina is in imminent danger? What I needed was a posse of pussies praying for my private parts.

And so, my local girlfriends gathered at my home for a magical night of drumming and incantation. It worked. My baby arrived; my vagina survived.

It is far too late to organize a Bless My Breast party—with gourmet victuals and rituals and wine. Even if it had been planned, I would have canceled—my mood is more funereal than celebratory. So after a simple home-cooked meal with Bergen and my dad, several more ideas surface:

· gold-plated trophy of a solitary tit with
  "In Appreciation of Thirty-Four Years of Loyalty"
· Bronzing my first training bra
· Ceremonially burning my 36 C bras

Nothing is feasible or appropriate. And as the evening wears on, I am overtaken by the past three weeks' worth of worrying and fatigue. There will be no tributes or ceremonial gifts. Just a silent surrendering to fate, with Bergen's arms wrapped around my bosom and our tears a prelude to sleep.

I wake up in the middle of the night to pee and to ponder. If it's possible to die of a broken heart, then it's plausible to die of an amputated tit. In the event that I join the Lucky Ones, as a courtesy to my grieving family, I have composed the following obituary:

ROBYN MICHELE LEVY
In the early morning of August 6, 2008, TV host Craig Ferguson (CBS) lost his biggest fan. Surrounded by her surgeon, anesthesiologist, and nurses, Robyn took her final breath as her right breast took her final bow. She leaves behind the remote control and the corner seat of the couch. In lieu of flowers, donations can be made to Craig Ferguson's snake-mug replacement fund, should his current snake mug ever break.

IN THE MORNING, Bergen and my dad take me to the hospital. When I check in at the reception desk, I see my name printed in capital letters on the surgery whiteboard:

ROBYN LEVY 7:45 AM

But I know that nothing is permanent around here. Just like my right breast, my name will be taken off later this morning.

I follow a nurse down the hall to the preoperative area.

"We'll get you ready in here," she says, drawing the curtains around a hospital bed and the two of us. She helps me get changed into a flimsy hospital gown while filling an oversized plastic bag with the clothes I struggled to dress myself in this morning. When I'm tucked under the sheets, Bergen and my Dad squeeze into this makeshift room. Having them here with me is as bittersweet as getting a mastectomy—their presence is both life saving and heart wrenching.

The nurse opens the curtains and explains, "Someone will be by in a few minutes with your chart."

And with that, she heads off toward a group mingling by a door.

Soon another nurse arrives with supplies. And questions. I tell her that everything is empty: my stomach, my bladder, my bowels. This news delights her and is noted on my chart. So are my vitals—temperature, blood pressure, heart rate; existing medical condition: Parkinson's. Her face betrays a hint of surprise, then quickly returns to her neutral nurse expression. Thankfully, I can't see my own facial expression. It would be too jarring, like looking into the eyes of a death-row prisoner about to be executed.

"The doctor's on her way," the nurse says, drawing the curtains.

My dad steps out and waits in the hall. Bergen stays by my side. Still, I feel lost and alone.

Dr. Chung glides toward me, looking elegant in green scrubs. A smile swoops across her face and lands gently on her cheeks. Her dark eyes say, "Trust me," with the unflinching gaze of a warrior. And I do. I must.

"It's almost time," she tells me, peeling back the sheet, opening up my gown, and exposing my chest. Then she uncaps a red marker and starts scribbling curvy lines and decorative dots and dashes. When she is done, my right breast resembles a preschooler's drawing, the kind proud parents display on their fridge. It's that good.

Dr. Chung covers us up—me and the masterpiece—then looks at the clock and says, "Any final questions?"

My mind is swirling. Final questions? I'm flooded with final questions. Especially those morbid ones that drown out hope and are best not asked when you're lying on a gurney, staring at your surgeon, bracing yourself for a mastectomy.

And so I pose this question instead: "I'm sure I don't want reconstructive surgery, but what if I change my mind years from now—would an implant still be an option?"

Dr. Chung looks surprised. "Didn't you read chapter 34 in *The Intelligent Patient's Guide to Breast Cancer?* I gave you a copy of the book."

I sheepishly admit that I'd skipped over this chapter—after all, I'm not planning to get a replacement. She gives me the look that teachers give students whose dog ate their homework. Then she glances at the time again and quickly explains that to keep this option open, she'd have to leave a flap of loose, dangly skin next to the scar. That's instead of a smooth, flat chest.

It's time to wheel me to the OR—I've got seconds to decide. I think, even if I never get reconstruction, that flap could come in handy. For what, I don't know. But it's always good to keep your options open, right? Then I look at Bergen for guidance,

and instantly I know: I don't want any more surgery after this ordeal, not even to install a brand-new breast. So what's the use of saving something I don't intend to use? If I want loose and dangly, I know where to get it. Decision made: forgo the flap and stick with the smooth. Dr. Chung nods to the nurses, and then I'm rolling slowly down a hallway, toward a set of swinging doors, my husband's and father's faces dissolving in my tears. On this early summer morning, my mourning has begun— before the anesthetic, before the first incision, before the great collector takes my masterpiece away.

I WAKE UP horrified and hazy amid a commotion of concern. Everything hurts. Something is missing. Bergen will help me find it later. First I have to pee. A dark-haired woman leans too close into my face and starts talking, "Easy does it, now. There's no rush." She's obviously speaking to me. Wherever I am.

Now Bergen is leaning into my face. "Hello, sweetheart."

Then my dad, who just smiles. They're both blurry. I hope they're OK. I hope I'm OK. I feel terrible. Nausea. Headache. Unbelievable pressure on my chest. I don't know why. I struggle to sit up, and the dark-haired woman rushes to my side. She's dressed as a nurse.

"Are we going to try walking to the bathroom?"

There's something about the tone of her voice that tips me off—this is not just a question, this is also a warning that some-how involves her.

"Nice and slowly. Let's scoot your bottom toward the edge of the bed."

Bed? Another clue. That's where I am, in a bed with beep-ing noises and long tubes attached to my arm.

The trip to the bathroom is harrowing, even with the nurse by my side. The combination of shock, anesthetic, and

painkillers has exacerbated my Parkinson's symptoms. I am so stiff and so slow that I feel like the Tin Man from *The Wizard of Oz*, all rusted and immobile, bladder about to burst, being coaxed along by doting Dorothy to follow the yellow brick road. "You can do it. We're almost there."

Miraculously, I make it just in time to pee and to pass out. When I come to, flashes of lucidity break through my delirium. I now know that I am breastless in hospital. And I know the reason the yellow brick road was yellow.

I AM TOO afraid to look. The nurses who change the dressing on my vacant lot assure me this is normal. I'll look when I'm ready, they say. Dr. Chung drops by at the end of her shift to check up on me. She proudly reports that my surgery went well and everything has been sent to the lab for analysis.

"You mean my breast is on some stranger's desk?"

Dr. Chung smiles. "Theoretically, yes. But removing a breast is complicated. It doesn't pop off all in one piece, you know."

I imagine my subdivided breast, sprawled out on a countertop in some cancer laboratory—just one of the many condemned properties Dr. Chung knocks down. Some vacant lots will be rebuilt. Others, like mine, will remain empty. Either way, the view from this prime real estate will be different. One of these days, I'm going to muster up the courage to have a look.

Dr. Chung is reading my chart. "Your blood pressure is quite low. How are you feeling?"

"Wiped out. Dizzy when I stand up."

"I'd like to keep you in hospital an extra day, just to make sure your blood pressure returns to normal, before sending you home."

"That would be great," I say. The prospect of going home the day after surgery seems reckless.

"I'll be back tomorrow morning to check up on you again, before my first operation."

My remaining time in hospital is spent under the spell of morphine. Or as I like to call it, "More Please." It takes the edge off the pain, making it easier for me to sleep. Whenever I wake up, either Bergen or my dad is by my side. Sometimes both. When my dad isn't around, he's either napping in the waiting room or out shopping for my comfort foods: freshly squeezed veggie juice, ginger rice muffins, and an assortment of fruits and vegetables. Bergen is busy stickhandling the details of my follow-up homecare, which will include daily visits from a community nurse and occasional visits from homecare assistants. Something tells me I'm going to need all the help I can get. Both of my arms are disabled—the left one from Parkinson's, the right one from having eleven lymph nodes surgically removed.

Just two days after the mastectomy, my morphine supply is cut off, and I am released from hospital—a one-breasted shadow of my former self. While I am convalescing at home, nothing feels comfortable. Not my pajamas. Not my bed. Not the couch. Not even my name. I long to belong to a culture that honors life transitions, where shamans or elders bestow new reverential names that embody change, that reveal powers, that summon ancestors. I wonder what I would be called.

Somewhere deep inside, I feel a stirring. I let out a grunt, and suddenly I am Gug the Cavewoman again, clutching my empty chest, encircled by chanting clan members singing my praises. For the gods have accepted my sacrificial breast, and I have survived this gruesome test. Together we celebrate this rite of passage with song and dance in my honor as I await the unveiling of my new name. The eldest of the elders approaches, her ancient eyes twinkling, her toothless mouth issuing guttural grunts and groans that epitomize my pitiful condition. And then the elder declares, "Eee-Oooh-Huuh." My new name, which means "One-Good-Tit." It fits, at least for now.

BEFORE THE OPERATION, Bergen bought me an MP3 player and loaded it with some of my favorite music. It came in handy while I occupied room 438, drowning out irritating hospital noises with the sweet, soaring voices of Feist, Joni Mitchell, and k.d. lang. Had it been wintertime with the windows sealed tight, I'm sure I would have continued listening to the device when I relocated to my own bedroom. But it was summer, and the windows were open, inviting cool breezes and a cacophony of lawn mowers, barking dogs, crying children, and roaring car engines. And somewhere in the space between the noises and fresh air came the sounds of pounding drums, electric guitars, melodic keyboards, and powerhouse vocals from a neighborhood band belting out a live soundtrack to my first day home: "Brown Sugar," "Mustang Sally," "Back in the USSR," "Hot Blooded," "All Right Now," and many more covers of classic rock 'n' roll songs.

Sprawled out on my bed and loaded with painkillers, I had no idea which neighbor's house or garage this music was coming from. All I knew was that the band was hot, and, like it or not, I was probably their only one-breasted groupie on the block. Everything else about them was left up to my imagination. So I pictured cute guys in their early twenties—indie rockers with bed-head hair and bad-ass attitudes, wearing jeans and T-shirts, rehearsing in a semifinished basement strewn with empty pizza boxes and beer bottles, and making ends meet by playing cover tunes at weddings and bar mitzvahs. Little did they know that they were serenading a middle-aged dame's postmastectomy homecoming.

MY MENSERVANTS, Beck and Call, bear a striking resemblance to my father and my husband. Beck is the tall, bald jokester, who brings me freshly squeezed juices and take-out treats

and *New York Times* bestsellers I've been dying to read. Call is the silver-haired juggler, who dazzles me with his dexterity, functioning as my short-order cook, housekeeper, confidant, chauffeur, secretary, social filter, dog walker, and nurse.

Beck and Call are a good team, but their days of working together are numbered. Beck is booked to fly home later this afternoon. He makes one last trip to the health food store, and when he returns he packs his suitcase and sets it beside the door. There's still time to be helpful. So he looks around and sees a basket filled with clean laundry.

Meanwhile, I am in bed, propped up by pillows, reading one of my new books. As I'm turning a page, I look up and see a shiny bald head hovering above a stack of floating folded towels, slowly, cautiously ascending the top stairs.

"Where do these go?" Beck asks.

"They go downstairs," I say, laughing for the first time in days.

I'm sure going to miss Beck when he goes.

The next day, Naomi comes home from camp covered in mosquito bites and bursting with stories. We don't say it out loud, but we both know it was good she was away while I was in hospital. It allowed her to keep her spirits up and me to let my guard down. She had called Bergen a few times to find out how I was doing. He assured her that the operation had gone well and that I was OK and explained what to expect at this point in my recovery. So by the time she sees me, she is prepared. She doesn't even flinch.

I have Nora to thank for making me presentable that day. She's a home caregiver, originally from the Philippines, with a bachelor of science degree. She's half my size and double my strength—and unbelievably efficient. In just one hour, she washes and styles my hair, gives me a sponge bath, moisturizes

my skin, helps me get dressed, makes my bed, does a load of laundry, tidies up the bathroom, takes Nellie for a walk, and cheers me up enough to laugh at the irony of the neighborhood band singing "Pretty Woman" over and over again until they get it right.

Later on, I give Susan a call. Even though she has spoken with Bergen since I got home, she is relieved to hear my voice. I thank her for the funny get well card, and she asks if I'm up for a visit.

"I was thinking of getting a bit of fresh air. Would you like to take me for a walk?" I ask.

"I'll be right over," she says.

We eventually make it halfway down the block, and then I burst into tears.

"I hate this fucking disease!"

"I know," she says. "It's awful. Which disease do you mean?"

"Breast cancer," I moan.

"It's inhumane—chopping off tits."

Suddenly I feel faint and crouch down on the grass. Some walk—I'm not even moving fast enough to call it a shuffle or a creep.

"You're body's been through a lot." Susan crouches down beside me.

"This is probably far enough for today. Every day you'll get a little bit stronger and walk a little bit farther. You'll see. Let's get you home."

RECOVERING FROM a mastectomy is draining. Literally—I've got a god-awful drain dangling from my side. Apparently, if Dr. Chung hadn't installed it after removing lymph nodes from my armpit, a lot of bodily fluids would have nowhere to go. I'm sure this tubular contraption is better than having my arm balloon up. Still, I can't stand the sight of it. Which is why I have

obstructed the view of its bloody contents by slipping a sock on top of it. Out of sight, but not out of mind—the container needs monitoring, so I have to sneak a peek every few hours. The container also needs emptying, and the liquid needs measuring—jobs the homecare nurses really enjoy.

The nurses come in all shapes and sizes and have names like Debbie and Shawna and Barbara. They don't wear nurse uniforms or scrubs. Instead, they dress in comfortable summer outfits—usually capris and a short-sleeved blouse. Each day, one of them drops by the house with her medical kit and supplies to check up on me, change the dressing on the Steri-Strips, and tend to my drain. There's a lot of leaning over and hovering above me. The view peering down those billowy blouses is much more titillating than glancing down at my own vacant lot. So I am always happy to see them, even though their visits remind me of what I no longer have.

Plenty of others are around to help me too. My neighbor Helen makes me a beautiful fruit salad. Full of seasonal berries, peaches, pineapple, grapes, apples, and pears. Everything is chopped up into such tiny delicate pieces that each spoonful tastes delightfully different. I used to be able to chop like that.

A few days later, she pops by to say hello. I thank her for the salad, tell her I am feeling better every day—eating healthy food, taking long naps.

"I hope Will isn't keeping you awake," she says, rolling her eyes and feigning exasperation.

My heart skips a beat; my cheeks flush with guilt. Does Helen know that her husband is flossing me in my fantasies? And if so, how did she find out? Not knowing what to say, I just stand there in silence.

Then she adds, "I haven't seen Will this happy in years. I don't even mind that the band has taken over our living room."

"The band? Will is in that band?"

"Oh yeah, he plays drums." Helen smiles. "You should see them. They're all dentists, around Will's age, almost ready to retire. Everyone in the band is faculty at UBC's Department of Dentistry, except for the singer. She works in faculty administration."

I try to picture mild-mannered Will going wild on the drum kit with his balding buddies riffing on electric guitars and keys, climbing the crescendo of Led Zeppelin's "Stairway to Heaven." But my mind can't sustain this incongruous image—one minute I flash back to the cute indie rockers I dreamed up while lying in bed; the next minute I flash forward to imagine one of the aging dentists keeling over from a heart attack and Will saving him with an electric-guitar defibrillator. I am tempted to tell Helen what I am imagining, but in the end I hold back—I'm not sure how she would react. The last thing I want is to piss her off. In case I have more body parts removed, I wouldn't mind another one of her fruit salads.

Then there are my girlfriends. I'd be lost without each one of them. Especially now. They're like GPS for my soul, helping me navigate through this uncharted territory of disease and detours and dead ends. My Toronto Trio calls me frequently, as does my sister. And my Vancouver friends drop by: Diana, Betina, Joey, Gillian, Linda, Yvonne. Gloria would be here too if she were in town, but she's spending the summer in Spain.

And then there's Hildi, my oldest, funniest, most gullible friend. We met in grade 6, when she was honing her skills as class clown—a job she took more seriously than her studies. I was new to the school, and she terrified me so much that I befriended her.

We often played practical jokes on each other, and to this day we still talk about the best one I ever pulled on her. She had asked me when my birthday was, and I told her I celebrate my birthday for eight days—beginning March 29 and going

through April 5—because it took me eight days to complete the journey out of my mother's vagina. First my head, then my neck, and so on until finally my feet flopped out and the doctor cut my umbilical cord. It was the best lie I'd ever told, and Hildi believed me. Mind you, we were only eleven years old at the time, but I must have been extremely convincing and she must have been extremely naïve.

For years, we were inseparable. Best friends. And then our worlds shifted and gaps grew between us until we no longer played leading roles in each other's lives. Still, we kept in touch through occasional phone calls and visits whenever I was in Toronto. When Hildi heard I had breast cancer, she called me up and made me an offer I didn't refuse—to fly out and take care of me after my mastectomy.

The minute Hildi walks into our house, she takes charge of everything and everyone. Hildi is good at that. She takes charge of everything and everyone at work. (She's an interior designer and contractor.) She takes charge of everything and everyone at home (her husband, their three daughters, one nanny, two dogs, one guinea pig, and a chinchilla). And after she gives me a big hug, she sends Bergen out grocery shopping, tells Lourdes what chores to do, prepares an enormous salad for our lunch, bakes chocolate chip cookies for Naomi and her friends, makes a pot of chicken soup that will be ready for dinner, cleans my refrigerator and kitchen drawers, and then persuades Bergen to take a break from looking after me—his first break in days. He goes for a run in the forest, does some errands, and works in his office. When dinnertime rolls around, he is refreshed and relaxed.

After dinner, Hildi makes tea, and the two of us lounge on the couch in the living room. The balcony door is open, and she is massaging my feet while "Hey Jude" drifts in.

"Where's the music coming from?" Hildi asks, her hands momentarily abandoning my feet for her BlackBerry.

"My neighbor across the street has a band. They're all dentists. I don't even know the band's name, so I have decided to call them the Overbites."

"They're really good," Hildi says, resuming my foot massage. A grimace spreads across her face.

"What's wrong?" I ask.

She drags her hand along my stubbly leg hair and says, "If you want, I can shave your legs for you."

Another offer I can't refuse—especially if I want any more of her foot massages.

Naomi is enjoying having Hildi around—and not just because she baked her cookies. Hildi is a woman of contradictions—stylish yet original, unpredictable yet reliable, manic yet composed, hilarious yet philosophical. She is also a woman who never forgets—at least when it comes to other people's sex lives. It occurs to me that burning my old diaries—if I ever find them—wouldn't be enough to prevent Naomi from learning about my past. Hildi's brain contains a top-secret list of who-I-did-what-with-when-and-where. Which is why I'm a little worried. Nevertheless, everyone should have a Hildi.

I'VE ONLY BEEN home one week and already I have dozens of thank-you notes to write to family and friends. My missing tit would be tickled by this outpouring of support: exotic flowers and gift baskets, books and CDs, pajamas and slippers and hats and scarves, home-cooked meals, antioxidant juices, homeopathic remedies, gift certificates, massages. There were also generous donations to breast cancer research on my behalf and in memory of my auntie Glenda.

This showering of gifts is both overwhelming and comforting. But I couldn't help recalling that it barely drizzled when I was diagnosed with Parkinson's. Clearly, in a popularity contest,

breast cancer would win a landslide victory over Parkinson's. The headline would read: "Tit trumps brain cells: Sympathy gifts for middle-aged dame's diseases skewed."

I'm not complaining. I'm just pointing out the obvious. It's easier for people to relate to breast cancer. Breasts are sexy, symbolic, and tangible. They stick out for all the world to see. And because breast cancer is so common and affects so many people, it has become a popular cause to support. Brain cells, in contrast, go about their mysterious business in the dark. And Parkinson's is a mysterious and frightening disease, gnawing away at our gray matter, hidden from sight.

It's always harder to relate to the unknown, let alone shop for it. So, to provide a service to the unafflicted, I compiled a list of gift ideas for someone who has just been diagnosed with Parkinson's—especially the early-onset variety. Here are some presents I would have appreciated at the time:

- flannel pajamas with built-in three-ply Kleenex dispenser
- a rearview mirror inscribed with the words "Warning! Abject woman in mirror is sicker than she appears."
- a DIY suicide kit with fill-in-the-blank suicide notes and obituaries, plus no-nonsense noose with lifetime guarantee

Simple gifts, really. But all I got were shoulders to cry on— which probably saved me.

I FEEL LIKE I've joined the circus, and I'm waiting in the wings for my cue. The ringmaster shouts, "Ladies and Gentlemen, welcome to Cirque d'Oy Vey. Get out your hankies for today's opening act—presenting Robyn the Wretched. She will bravely attempt looking in the mirror at her naked chest for the very

first time—a dangerous stunt requiring a safety net. Remember, Ladies and Gentlemen—it ain't over till the flat lady cries."

Thank goodness for Hildi. She catches me before I plummet to the ground and enfolds me in her arms. And when the ringmaster waves good-bye, she gives him the one-finger salute.

Had Hildi not saved me, I might have become one of the Lucky Ones:

> After a tragic fall under the big top, Robyn the Wretched joined the Celestial Circus in the Sky. She leaves behind her old diaries, a stack of unfinished thank-you notes, and her unfulfilled dream of going to the Overbites' upcoming gig.
>
> She will be dearly missed by family, friends, neighbors, and pets.
>
> In lieu of flowers, donations to her favorite charity, Naomi's Soy Latte Trust Fund, would be appreciated.

HAVING BRAVELY VIEWED my vacant lot, I'm prepared for the next day's showing at a follow-up appointment with Dr. Chung. Bergen and I are waiting for her in the examination room. Soon there's a knock on the door, and she walks in. She parks her clipboard on the sink counter, greets me with a smile, and says, "Your breast pathology report arrived. It's good news."

"Great," I say, thinking back to my school report cards that were loaded with A's and accolades. I imagine my breast pathology report card:

> It was a pleasure having Robyn's right breast in my laboratory. I'm delighted to report that it excelled in all areas of testing. Most notably, it distinguished itself from the other specimens by developing two unique cancers in separate locations. The large tumor exceeded all size expectations, proving to be bigger than initial estimates.

Both tumors demonstrated superb communication skills by constructing a cancerous highway between them. They were also tidy and considerate tumors, refraining from spreading their disease to any of the eleven lymph nodes that were surgically removed. In light of these accomplishments, Robyn's right breast has deservedly earned A+ in the following subjects—individuality, ambition, communication, and organization—and hereby graduates with top honors.

Bergen squeezes my hand, and together we let out sighs of relief. Dr. Chung beams with pride and says, "It's good we removed your entire breast. Let's have a look at how you're doing."

I maneuver myself up onto the examination table and sit on the edge with my legs dangling down. Dr. Chung moves in closely, gently removes the gauze dressing covering my vacant lot, and begins her inspection. Her delicate fingers trace the periphery of my scar, hiding beneath the white Steri-Strips.

"No swelling at all, no sign of infection. This looks great," she says, moving on to the drain tube jutting out from my side. "This also looks great. You're healing up quickly. How's your arm?"

"Painful and tight," I answer, struggling to lift it up to shoulder height—as far as it can move. Dr. Chung touches my arm and asks "Are you doing the exercises from the book?"

"Several times, every day."

"That's good. Keep it up. The mobility will improve."

When the exam is over, Dr. Chung asks, "How is your daughter doing?"

I tell her that Naomi is coping quite well and fortunately has been out of town for much of the summer. And then Dr. Chung smiles and closes my file. It's time to go, and I give her a thank-you card, a jar of Bergen's homemade kiwi jam, and an A+ for likely saving my life.

MY PHONE RINGS, and as usual, Bergen answers it.

"It's Gloria. She's back from Spain. Do you want to talk to her?" he asks. I think, of course I want to talk to her, but not over the phone.

"Can you talk to her? Just fill her in, I'm sure she'll want to drop by for a visit."

Boy, is she in for a shock. The last time I saw her was six weeks ago—the day before she left for Spain—and just a few days before my diagnosis. We were out for brunch and I didn't mention my lumps. The timing wasn't right. Imagine saying, "By the way, I found two lumps in my breast that may be cancerous. I hope you have a wonderful holiday with your family in Spain. Have fun! See you next month."

When the doorbell rings, I know it's Gloria. Bergen and Nellie greet her at the door while I shuffle to the front hall. The moment she sees me, she comes undone—tears cascading down her cheeks, arms crushing me close to her chest, deep sighs spilling from her mouth. For a moment, she loosens her grip and I think I will be released from this agonizing tableau with my remaining tit intact. But then she looks me in the eyes, shakes her head in disbelief, and mutters, "Oh, Robyn" several times before she pulls me and my left breast back into her arms. This time my drain gets wedged between our ribs, and I have to wiggle myself free.

She wipes away her tears, then semi-smiles.

"These are for you," she says, handing me a bouquet of flowers she'd been clutching during the hug. Dahlias and freesias and gerberas.

"They're beautiful. Thank you."

A few more drops trickle from Gloria's eyes, and I wonder—where are my tears? It feels strange to be the dry-eyed witness and not the weeper.

"Come meet my friend Hildi. She's visiting from Toronto."

We head into the TV room, where Hildi is stretched out on a couch. She wiggles her toes hello. And soon, the three of us are chatting away, barefoot on the couch while Nellie lounges on my lap.

The conversation turns to how Gloria and I met. We take turns telling Hildi the story.

"It was almost twenty years ago," Gloria starts, "before we had husbands and kids."

"That was so long ago."

My voice startles Nellie, and she scoots off my lap, curls up by Gloria's feet, and starts licking her pedicured toes. I can't remember when this first started, but every time she comes over, Nellie goes for her feet.

"Anyway," Gloria continues, her eyelids beginning to flutter, her mouth growing slack, "I was on a lunch break, at Granville Island. And the moment I saw Robyn's artwork on display, I knew one of her paintings would make a perfect wedding gift for some friends of mine."

"So Gloria commissioned me to make a custom painting for the couple."

"Who aren't even married anymore," Gloria laughs.

"Who got the painting when they split up?" Hildi asks.

"She did," Gloria says, wiggling her wet toes.

"And then Gloria invited me out for lunch."

"We had so much fun consulting about this project," Gloria smiles, "I wanted us to be friends."

By now, all three of us are watching Nellie—her little furry head bobbing up and down at Gloria's feet. It's hard to tell who is having more fun—my dog or my friend.

"This feels so good!" Gloria sighs, unabashedly stretching out her legs and arching her back, as if she's on the verge of an orgasm.

My own toes are tingling with vicarious pleasure, taking my mind off my sore chest and arm. That's when I realize my friendship pilgrimage is back on track. My friends are coming to me. They're meeting one another. And I am luxuriating in their love.

THE NIGHT BEFORE Hildi leaves, we take her out for dinner at an Indian restaurant. The place is packed with families and couples. We are seated at an empty booth at the front. Bergen, Naomi, and I go for the all-you-can-eat vegetarian buffet. Hildi orders butter chicken off the menu. The food is delicious, especially my favorites—dal and basmati rice. I make several trips to the buffet at the back of the room, and each time I am delightfully surprised by how polite and considerate the other customers in line are toward me. They smile and let me go ahead of them—some of them even insist. Then they wait until I've finished filling up my plate before they approach the bar and begin serving themselves.

When we're done, a waitress clears our plates and Bergen pays the bill. As I slide out of the booth and sling my purse over my shoulder, the strap catches on my surgical drain, which is pinned to the outside of my shirt. A wave of shame envelops me—I'd forgotten to tuck it out of sight or at least cover it with a sock. What an eyesore! I've been parading around the restaurant with this blood-filled contraption dangling in full view. No wonder those strangers at the buffet were so nice to me.

On the drive home, my embarrassment subsides and soon I'm feeling smug. For I have discovered the secret to getting front-of-the-line treatment—the bloody surgical drain.

Back at the house, both Hildi and Naomi haul out their suitcases and start packing. Tomorrow they fly to Toronto—on different flights, for different reasons. Hildi is returning home

to her family and work. Naomi is going on vacation, to visit family and friends. Originally, I was booked to go with Naomi. Then along came cancerus interruptus, and I had to cancel my flight. But Naomi still wanted to go. This will be the first time she travels on her own.

Once they're finished packing, we all sit around the dining table sipping tea and nibbling on fresh fruit. The kitchen looks sparkling clean, and the flower arrangements look stylish—thanks to Hildi's professional interior designer touch. It's been a long, busy day, and just as I'm about to suggest we all watch some Craig Ferguson to unwind, Hildi leaps up from the table and declares, "I need chocolate." She starts pacing back and forth, running her hand along the counter and asks, "Has anyone seen that container of gourmet hot chocolate?"

"You mean the chocolate mix from that beautiful gift basket my cousins sent me?" I ask.

"Yeah. That stuff. I could have sworn I put it away in this drawer," Hildi says, exasperated, digging through jars and bags of baking supplies.

"It's not in here. Shit. Where the hell is it?" she yells, slamming a bottle of vanilla on the counter, tossing bags of sunflower and pumpkin seeds beside it.

Of course, if anyone should know the whereabouts of this chocolate, it should be Hildi. Just two days ago, she reorganized everything in our kitchen, from baking supplies to cans of tuna to boxes of cereal. She may very well never forget other people's sexual secrets, but obviously her exceptional memory skills don't apply to food. There's no point telling her this—or anything at all—given the frenzied state she is in. Bergen gets up to help her look, but Hildi is determined to find it on her own.

And so instead of the *Late Late Show* with Craig Ferguson, we watch the *Obsessive-Compulsive Show* starring Hildi—as

she frantically searches the cupboards and drawers until the counters are cluttered with everything but that elusive container of gourmet hot chocolate.

"I hate it when something special goes missing," Hildi moans.

"Me too," I say. But it's not chocolate I'm thinking about.

I'M NOT GOOD at good-byes, especially when they involve boarding an airplane, which may or may not be doomed. My fear of flying generously extends to family and friends, so today, with Hildi and Naomi flying to Toronto, I'm a nervous wreck. Standing on the sidewalk, they give me reassuring hugs and kisses, I give them anxious ones in return. Bergen loads their luggage into the trunk. Then there's a flurry of hands waving from car windows, and for the first time in weeks I'm left all alone—abandoned by the curb, wiping away my tears, silently screaming, "Don't leave me! Don't crash! Don't die! Call me when you land!"

I shuffle through the remaining weeks of summer, vulnerable and moody. On good days, I feel like a wilting flower springing back to life. On bad days, I feel like the compost, putrid and decaying. My right arm is slowly healing, but I still need Nora's help washing my hair and helping with chores.

The nurses continue their daily visits. They're pleased to see that my leakage is tapering off and promise that my bloody drain will be removed soon. When that day arrives, the nurse lays a towel across my bed and I nervously lie down on top of it. She spreads out her medical tools and offers these words of comfort: "Don't watch me do what I'm about to do." To further put me at ease, she assures me, "This is going to feel strange." Then she starts tugging at the tube inserted into my side and eventually pries it loose from what I assume is surrounding skin. But I can't be sure; my eyes are squeezed tightly shut. And

then she stops doing whatever it was that she was doing and starts doing something else. A wave of nausea ripples through me, as an alien slowly snakes its way through my innards and out my ribcage.

"There, it's all out," she says. "Now you can look."

I tilt my head in her direction, and my body shudders with disgust.

"That tube is incredibly long. I can't believe it was actually inside me," I say.

"It sure was," she says, smiling, coiling it up, and stuffing it into a garbage bag. Then she bandages up the hole and says, "I told you it would feel strange."

A steady stream of friends continues dropping by. Betina from Argentina, who became my long-lost sister the moment we met eleven years ago. Diana brings me bottles of mangosteen juice, books on breast cancer, and beautiful blouses. The librarians, Brian and Gillian, bring us home-cooked meals and travel stories. Then Gillian takes me shopping for my first falsie. It's a little foam insert that slides into a soft cotton camisole. Under loose-fitting shirts it adds dimension, but when worn under something tight it looks weird—like an oversized hard-boiled egg that's been cut in half. It also moves around, shifting to the left or the right or sometimes straight up, as if trying to escape. I don't blame it—my vacant lot is not the most hospitable of places.

I HAVE BECOME a morbid measuring stick. When I ask, "How are you doing?" people reply, "Compared with you, I'm doing great."

And when I ask, "How are you feeling?" they shrug and say, "I've got nothing to complain about, considering what you're going through."

I'm tempted to retort, "But what about your loveless marriage? Or your debilitating debt? Your sciatica? Your hemorrhoids? Or your beloved dying pet? Your lack of employment? Your loss of enjoyment? Your mysterious aches and pains? Your whiplash? Your mustache? Your varicose veins?"

But instead I bite my tongue and crank out my new business cards:

ROBYN MICHELE LEVY
Morbid Measuring Stick
Certified "Sight for Sore Eyes" Specialist
Department of Poor Health and Comparative Happiness

I HAVEN'T SEEN Marg in months, but we keep in touch through e-mail. The last time she wrote, she invited me over for tea. Better late than never, I'm responding today:

Dear Marg,

FYI, I have discovered a fail-proof distraction from Parkinson's disease—a distraction I don't recommend. Breast cancer. I was diagnosed mid-July, right tit lopped off early August, and now I am in recovery mode waiting to find out if I need chemo or radiation or both or none. It sure has taken my mind off my PD. In fact, I'm surprised I haven't lost my mind, but strangely enough part of me finds this all wickedly hilarious. What else can one do but see the humor, albeit black humor, in life?

I'm still up for a cup of tea . . . but just one cup, since that's all I now require.

Be well,
Robyn

Dear Robyn,

What a blow—and an insult. I'm so sorry about your
cancer and mad too...

Tea soon,
Marg

7

In Search
of Kick-Ass Clarity

I<small>T'S</small> **SEPTEMBER.** The forecast calls for heavy showers of
advice from oncologists and a flood of anxiety. Expect seasonal support from breast cancer survivors. There is an 80
percent chance of scattered thoughts and indecision.

It sure is handy living in the same neighborhood as Susan.
Not only is she a breast cancer survivor, but she's also a breast
cancer encyclopedia. Consequently, our daily walks with Nellie serve as peripatetic tutorials in chemotherapy, radiation, and
hormone treatment—all of which may be prescribed when I
meet my oncologist.

There's a lot to learn, and none of it is pleasant. Today I take
mental notes while Susan talks chemo:

"I have to tell you, if you have to do chemo, make sure you
take those antinausea pills before your treatment. The best
ones cost one hundred dollars a pop, but they're worth it. Otherwise you're gonna feel like you're dying. Actually, you're gonna
feel like you're dying regardless, but the pills will take the edge

off. And drink lots of water before and after each session; you want that poison out of your system as quickly as possible— it's hell on the organs, especially the liver. And buy yourself a nightcap, because you'll be surprised at how cold it is, sleeping with a bald head. Of course, your immune system is going to be trashed. So, if I were you, I'd ask Naomi not to bring her friends home while you're getting treatment. Kids always have germs. The last thing you need is to catch a nasty cold or flu."

"You mean I'd have a legitimate reason to keep the teenagers away? Why didn't you say that in the first place?"

Naomi's at a new school, in a literary arts program she really likes. But more importantly, she loves her new friends. They drop by after school. Some stay for dinner. Some sleep over on weekends. The same girl shows up every morning before school. Together they turn the upstairs bathroom into a beauty salon, transforming their sleepy faces with cover-up, eyeliner, eye shadow, and mascara. Then they rifle through Naomi's wardrobe until they agree on the perfect T-shirt to match Naomi's jeans, leaving the rejected shirts in crumpled clumps on the floor.

I do my best to stay in bed and out of the way, for their sake and for mine. The last thing they need is a one-breasted curmudgeon breathing morning breath down their backs. And the last thing I need is to become one.

It's always a scramble, Bergen getting the girls out of the house in time to catch the bus. Or Bergen corralling them into the car and driving them to school. But once I hear that front door slam, I take a bow for pulling off yet another one of my self-preserving parent-disappearing acts and emerge from my bedroom, ready to begin my day.

WHEN I WAS LITTLE, I had a hunch that change was inevitable. Feet outgrow shoes. Plants outgrow pots. Families outgrow

homes. And eventually, children outgrow childhood. I didn't understand exactly how this happens, but I figured it had something to do with that annoying question adults always ask: "What do you want to be when you grow up?" It certainly got me thinking. So did other kids' predictable answers: firefighter, ballerina, astronaut, teacher, doctor, nurse, pilot, movie star. There was a definite formula to follow, and so I memorized a handful of stock answers—painter, poet, songwriter, or art teacher—all of which appealed to me. But that's not what I really wanted.

Secretly, I dreamed of growing up and becoming someone else, anyone else, other than me. The logistics of this were baffling, but I'd watched enough Disney movies to convince myself that this could, and would, happen. After all, mistakes need fixing, and everything about me was wrong. My hair was too thick and curly and required hours of tedious blow-drying to straighten it during the day and an army of metal hair clips to clamp it down at night—forcing me to sleep on what felt like a pillow of nails. My pubescent body was foreign and dangerous, each budding breast a bull's-eye target for men to ogle. And my talent with words was useless. What good was writing love poems when I couldn't discern sexual innuendo? I still blush when I think back to that snowy winter day when a strange man stopped and asked me, "How much do you charge for a blow job?" Not knowing what he meant, I replied, "I don't know, but I can shovel your driveway for five dollars." By far, my worst defect was my debilitating shyness. I hated how shy I was. I was trapped—there was no escape. Not only did it prevent me from living life to the fullest, but it also prevented me from loving myself. For all these reasons, I wanted to be someone else.

I think about this unfulfilled dream a lot these days. Perhaps it's not so far-fetched after all. It seems I'm well on my way

to becoming someone else, anyone else but me—already I don't want to recognize myself in the mirror. How long before I actually can't?

Sometimes I don't even want friends recognizing me. Especially when I'm not in the mood to be boo-hooed or when I'm weary of wearing my health on my sleeve. These can be lonely times indeed. Thank goodness for strangers—they break the ice of my isolation with their liberating ignorance of who I used to be. When they meet me for the first time, my current condition is the baseline, the ground zero of who they think I am. There are no comparisons. No remember whens. Just a fresh and friendly start. But my encounters with strangers can also be frustrating. People make all sorts of assumptions and judgments based on how one looks and talks and walks. They may not say anything, but I can see it on their faces. On such occasions, I would like to hand these people a "perception correction" card:

For Your Information:

This slow, limping, one-breasted, middle-aged dame
was once a vibrant, healthy, and energetic woman.

I miss that woman I used to be, and I wonder who I am becoming.

STRIKING. EXOTIC. BEAUTIFUL. These are words people use to describe Naomi. As I stand next to her at the bathroom sink, she is all that and more. Creative. Insightful. Compassionate. Playful. And something new: confident. My heart soars with delight as she gazes at her reflection in the mirror, brushes her teeth, watches me brushing mine. This self-assurance suits her—she stands taller and smiles more often. I have never seen her so comfortable in her own skin.

We head downstairs in our pajamas. Bergen is multitasking in the kitchen: making pancakes, coffee, and fruit salad for our breakfast while reading the Saturday paper and listening to the BBC TV news with special headphones my father sent him that allows him to rush back and forth between flipping pancakes and watching compelling images on the TV. I've learned from experience that getting too close to Bergen in the morning while he's wearing these headphones is hazardous to my health. Once bumped, twice shy—I wait for him to take them off before we kiss.

After breakfast, we all relax in the living room. Naomi curls up on the couch with a book, I do my stretches on the floor, and Bergen sits in a chair with Nellie on his lap. We talk about Naomi's new teachers, her weekend homework, and, of course, her new friends. She is keen to inform us which of them are straight or gay or bi.

Then she says, "Remember when I told you I was bisexual? I only said that because I was afraid of your reaction if I told you the truth, that I'm gay."

Without missing a beat, Bergen exclaims, "Great!"

Then I say, "Straight, bisexual, or gay—it doesn't change anything. We love you."

Naomi looks at us with a serene expression on her face, hugs Bergen and then me.

We didn't tell her that we've known this for some time and were waiting for her to share "the news" when she was ready.

"I'm out to all my friends," she smiles, "and I've joined the GSA."

"What's that?" I ask.

"The Gay-Straight Alliance. It's a club at school. All high schools have one."

We talk some more about sexual orientation and about our own friends and colleagues who are gay. It brings us all closer

together. It also brings me to the brink of tears. Naomi and I are at such different phases of life—her sexuality is blossoming, while mine is being dismantled.

MY PANIC ALARM is broken and I can't turn it off. The dread drones on and on—when I sleep, when I wake, when I read or eat or walk. Even when I dial the phone.

I call an old acquaintance I haven't seen in years—Cicely, the breast cancer oncologist. She knows all about panic buttons and, though recently retired, offered to help me prepare for my oncologist appointment at the BC Cancer Agency. So on a quiet Sunday morning, Bergen and I go to her house with my file and a long list of questions: What are the risks and benefits of chemo and radiation treatment? Can chemo exacerbate Parkinson's disease? Does the fact that none of my removed lymph nodes were cancerous affect what treatment is recommended? What are my risks of cancer recurring with or without chemo or radiation? Since Little Lump and Big Blob were both estrogen positive, what hormone therapy options are available? What are the benefits and risks of hormone therapy? Are there certain estrogen-containing foods I should avoid? What if I want a second opinion?

Cicely answers all my questions with patience and precision. She explains the treatments my oncologist would likely offer me: chemo, radiation, Tamoxifen hormone therapy, and induced menopause (through chemo, medication, or surgery). She also reminds me that whatever is recommended, ultimately it is my choice. I can accept or decline any or all treatments. And having worked at the cancer agency, she shares some insider information: every Friday afternoon, a group of oncologists convene to discuss their unusual or challenging files. This is called a case conference. Given that I have Parkinson's and

my tumors were at different stages, I can ask for a case conference and get an enhanced second opinion.

At the end of the visit, we thank Cicely for this oncological
dress rehearsal and tell her what a difference it makes to our
comfort level. With a clearer idea of what to expect during my
upcoming meeting with the oncologist, my overwhelming panic
has downgraded to manageable anxiety. We hug good-bye, and
she wishes me well, handing me the notes she's made from
reading my file. And as we drive away, I watch her standing on
the front porch, one hand waving, the other hand holding a jar
of Bergen's homemade kiwi jam.

THE NIGHT BEFORE my appointment with the oncologist, I am
wound up with worry and in desperate need of distraction. Bergen suggests we escape to the movies for some comic relief.
"How about Woody Allen's new film, *Vicky Christina Barcelona?*"

"That means I'd have to get out of these pajamas and put on
some real clothes," I whine.

"That's right. I'll help you,"

Soon I'm wearing what will become my post-mastectomy
uniform—jeans and a loose-fitting blouse with a scarf strategically draped around my collar to conceal my vacant lot.

This is our first evening out since my surgery—just the two
of us. Once we've bought our tickets, the mouthwatering aroma
of popcorn lures us into the lobby, where I immediately have
second thoughts. What am I doing here? This is crazy! People and popcorn stream by. I snuggle up close to Bergen, not
because I'm feeling romantic, but because I'm feeling neurotic
and self-conscious. What if someone accidentally elbows me in
the chest? What if I bump into someone I know and my Cry
Lady makes a scene? I don't tell Bergen what I'm thinking, but
he knows that I'm nervous.

"Don't worry," he says. "Everything's going to be OK." I take a deep breath, and while exhaling I spot Michelle and Honey. They're old friends of Bergen's, and judging by the expressions on their faces, they are surprised to see me alive. There's a round of hugs and hellos, and then Bergen says, "I'll be right back," and heads to the washroom, leaving us ladies alone to chat.

Michelle stuffs her hands in her pockets, gives me a nervous smile, then bravely asks, "How are you? I heard about your diagnosis."

"I'm doing OK," I say, aware of a slight tingling sensation in my eyes.

"When was your surgery?" Honey wants to know.

"About a month and a half ago. The beginning of August," I say, determined not to cry.

"Wow! You look great," Michelle says.

"Thanks," I reply, strategizing how best to keep those unwanted tears at bay. Poke my eyes out? Pass. Let out a primal scream? Not in the mood. Play a practical joke? It's worth a try.

I spot Bergen in the distance. "Here he comes," I say.

We all turn our heads toward the rear of the lobby and watch him weave through the crowd toward us.

"Do me a favor," I whisper, keeping a straight face. "Please don't mention my mastectomy to Bergen. I haven't told him yet."

Michelle and Honey freeze in place, their eyes bulging out at me, then at each other, then back at me. I can almost hear their voices inside their heads: "Why hasn't she told him? What kind of husband doesn't notice a missing breast?" These precious fleeting seconds of deception fill me with joy—it's comforting to know that my hoodwinking habit still works as well as it did when I had two tits. When Bergen rejoins our group, there's an awkward silence. And then I start to laugh.

"What's so funny?" he wants to know.

"Robyn is," Michelle answers, laughing along with Honey, "but you probably already know that."

ENTERING THE SLIDING GLASS doors of the BC Cancer Agency is like being swallowed by a benevolent monster: terrifying and comforting at the same time. Its cavernous belly is filled with cheerful volunteers welcoming everyone, while hand-sanitizing stations wage war with everyone's germs. I smile at the smiling receptionist sitting behind the smile-shaped information desk and ask her, "What floor is Dr. Lohrisch on?"

"Second floor," she says, pointing to a crowd of patients and their entourages, waiting for an elevator.

Bergen and I join the group, and I try to pick out the people plagued with cancer. Some are easier to spot than others. Wheelchairs, bald heads, intravenous units—these are all dead giveaways. So far, I count four cancer patients. But I'm sure there are more. They just blend in with the healthy ones.

The elevator arrives, and a volunteer holds the doors open while everyone crams inside. When the doors close, we all retreat into our solitudes, avoiding eye contact, preserving our privacy—or what's left of it since cancer invaded our lives and led us to this public place. Most of us get off at the second floor, register at the front desk, then take a seat in what resembles a small airport waiting room. For every name that is called, I imagine a different plane taking off in a different direction, and I feel the shared emotional turbulence of suffering, fear, and hope.

An elderly woman pushing a stainless steel refreshment trolley is slowly making her way toward us. The coffee and tea are complimentary. The snacks are by donation. When she pulls up beside us, Bergen puts down his *Scientific American*

and gets a coffee. I don't want anything; I packed my own snacks from home. My appointment is at 8:15 AM, and already it's after 8:30. I dip into my supply of raisins and flip through a magazine. Soon, a nurse holding a clipboard calls out my name. I give her a wave, and Bergen and I pack up our stuff and follow her to an examination room, where I change into the flimsy hospital gown folded on the table. It's a good thing I didn't shave my legs or my pits for this appointment—it's so chilly in here; if it weren't for my hairy insulation, I'd freeze my tit off.

We wait some more until another nurse arrives. This one measures my height and weight, takes my blood pressure, checks my heart rate, and asks basic questions about my current state of health. Apparently, I am now ready for the oncologist.

A tall, dark-haired, two-breasted, arm-swinging woman in a fancy dress suit and leather pumps introduces herself: "Hi, I'm Dr. Lohrisch."

"I'm Gug the Cavewoman," I imagine saying, "and this is my husband, Bergen."

There is a round of civilized handshakes, and then Dr. Lohrisch examines my vacant lot and remaining breast. When she's done, she says, "You can get dressed in your clothes now. I'll be back in a few minutes."

The remaining time is spent reviewing my case history—which Dr. Lohrisch has memorized—and discussing treatments that increase the probability of a cure and may prevent breast cancer from recurring.

"Here's what I recommend," she says, placing a clipboard on her lap and jotting down notes as she talks. "First, chemotherapy. Then hormone therapy, including Tamoxifen and ovarian suppression. The chemo may actually induce

menopause. But if it doesn't, then there are three other ways to do this: radiation of the ovaries, monthly injections of a special hormone-suppressing drug, or surgical removal of the ovaries."

Despite the topic of discussion, I feel remarkably calm and focused, thanks to the preparatory consultation with Cicely. There are no surprises—this protocol is almost identical to what Cicely predicted. Except for one thing.

"Why don't you recommend radiation for my chest?" I ask.

"Because when your breast was removed, the margins, those areas surrounding the tumors, were all clear of any traces of cancer. And so were your lymph nodes. In my opinion, radiation is not needed."

Bergen and I sift through the information, asking questions, expressing concerns, particularly about the negative impact chemo may have on my ailing body and my quality of life. Before being diagnosed with cancer, I was going to start Parkinson's medication this fall, but I decided to wait until these treatments were over. I tell Dr. Lohrisch that I have no reservations about taking Tamoxifen and suppressing my ovaries, but I have mixed feelings about chemotherapy.

"What would you do, if you were in my shoes?" I ask her.

"I'd start chemo. You might not have such bad side effects. And you can stop taking it anytime."

"When would I have to start?" I ask, hesitantly.

"In a few weeks."

"I understand we can ask for a case conference, to get some more opinions from a team of oncologists," Bergen says.

"I think that's a great idea. I'll set that up," Dr. Lohrisch smiles. "In the meantime, why don't I set things up for you to start chemo in three weeks? Book you in for some tests, arrange for you to get a port implant in your vein, and I can write a prescription for antinausea medication."

On our way out, just thinking about chemo makes me nauseous.

Back in the lobby, we squeeze through a fresh supply of cancer patients and their entourages, waiting their turn to be swallowed.

MY STREET has been designated a bicycle commuter route, and construction is underway. Nellie and I watch the city workers installing traffic-calming circles in the middle of intersections. They measure and map, dig up asphalt, pour concrete, and in the end plant simple round gardens, smack dab in the center of each one. A few green-thumb neighbors have adopted a circle to call their own. We think these are the most alluring gardens.

I'm considering adopting a circle, the one closest to my house, where I'd plant towering sunflowers that dance with the wind, where my remains could be buried on a moonlit night, and where Nellie could pee on my plaque:

> Here lies most of Robyn Michele Levy
> Beloved wife, mother, daughter, sister, friend
>
> May she rest in piss
>
> Amen

I'VE JOINED a women's cancer support group. We meet Monday afternoons at two o'clock. Eight of us attend regularly. Most of us have breast cancer, including the group leader, Chantal. She is in her early forties but could pass for twenty-five. She was first diagnosed years ago, underwent surgery and treatment, and after years of remission has been dealing with metastatic cancer. Looking at her, you'd never know it. She is beautiful and vibrant, full of life. She leads with a gentle touch. So gentle that our first session makes me question her approach.

It starts off well, as we take turns introducing ourselves and our afflictions, while respecting the don't-interrupt rule. But soon our sacred circle begins to collapse, as Cantankerous Woman keeps shooting off her mouth at inappropriate times. And just when Chantal's softhearted reminders not to interrupt have the desired effect, Cantankerous Woman's whining is replaced by the stammering voice of Little Old Lady, who, up until a moment ago, has been fast asleep in her chair. In a medicated mist, she rambles her way through what seems to be a barely comprehensible book report, which has no relationship whatsoever to the topic of discussion or Cantankerous Woman's gripes. There is no stopping her until she eventually nods off to sleep again. I have to stop myself from laughing. Chantal regains control for a while until Cantankerous Woman gets all worked up again and wakes up Little Old Lady, who picks up where she left off until she finally conks out for the rest of the afternoon.

Despite the screwball comedy of that first day, I feel an undercurrent of connectivity between some of the women. Particularly Sue and Cheryl—who, like me, are undergoing treatment for recently diagnosed breast cancer. Sue is athletic, adventurous, and indomitable. As far as she is concerned, her cancer—which has spread to her ribs—doesn't stand a chance. She sailed through chemo and is preparing for radiation, the removal of her ovaries, and a double mastectomy to be followed by reconstructive surgery. Cheryl is a hard-working, hard-playing social worker who is undergoing radiation treatment and will soon have a single mastectomy and reconstruction. The three of us exchange e-mails, and sometimes we go out for a bite. Through them, and the support group, I am discovering that not only is there strength in numbers, but there is also hope.

In the meantime, however, I'm having a mid-disease crisis, and my panic has returned with a vengeance. The very word

"chemotherapy" sends shivers down my spine. Who knows what it will do to my body? Who knows what it will do to my brain? This fear of the unknown is unnerving; I've only been terrified like this once before. It was when I was eight months' pregnant and about to face giving birth. I did a lot of research and started interviewing all the mothers I knew and even some I didn't. I was scared and unprepared, so I gave them each a minute to tell me how it really felt—I simply had to hear all the gory details so I could face my fear. Most mothers were obliging. Some grimaced. Some gloated.

I kept a written record and quote from those notes:

"It felt like a tornado was twisting in my gut."

"It felt like my baby squeezed right out of my butt."

"It felt like Tiger Balm had been rubbed you-know-where."

"It felt like a bomb went off in my underwear."

"It felt like my vagina was committing suicide."

"It felt like my period, except I almost died."

"Don't worry; you'll do fine. Have you written out your will?"

"Why don't you learn to meditate, 'cause it's going to

fucking kill!"

Thanks to my investigative research, and a prenatal class Bergen and I attended, when I went into labor I was no longer afraid of the unknown. Instead, I was terrified of what I knew about: pain and suffering and possible death. But at least I could make informed decisions. And since I was afraid I would be the one woman in a million to wind up permanently paralyzed by an epidural, I chose not to have this pain-blocking procedure.

Although fear of the unknown is at the heart of both my past and present crises, there are significant differences between the two. For one thing, there is the issue of choice. Once I was pregnant, giving birth was unavoidable, whereas chemotherapy is avoidable. For another, there is the research

factor. When I was pregnant, my body was strong and healthy, and my mind was focused and alert; I was a research whiz. But that was then—before Parkinson's scattered my thinking and skewed my moods and tampered with my body. Now my capacity to conduct extensive research is compromised. Everything takes more time and more effort—surfing the web, finding sources, collecting studies, compiling notes, comparing facts, processing information. And with less than three weeks to go before my first dose of chemo, I'm feeling overwhelmed and underqualified to thoroughly investigate all the risks associated with chemotherapy and Parkinson's disease. Could chemo exacerbate my current symptoms? Could it trigger the onset of other symptoms? Could it accelerate the progression of Parkinson's? Could it interfere with the effectiveness of Parkinson's medication?

I obviously need help. So I pick up the phone and call an expert.

"Hello, Zoë? It's Robyn," I say, my voice tinged with shyness and urgency.

"Hi, Robyn. What a surprise. How are you?" she asks.

It's been years since we last connected, our busy lives having pulled us in different directions. But now I'm heading into her terrain.

"Actually, I'm not doing great. Do you have time to talk?"

She assures me she does, so I bring her up to speed and she is shocked and genuinely sorry.

I've known Zoë for fourteen years. When our kids were little, she invited Bergen, Naomi, and me into her community of young families that gathered for potluck dinners and moral support. She was one of those rare mothers, blessed with not only natural parenting instincts but also the guts to follow them. She was also blessed with a voracious appetite and talent for acquiring and sharing knowledge about raising

kids. And then a few years into our friendship, Zoë was diagnosed with metastatic breast cancer and used her phenomenal research skills to determine her strategy to quash the cancer. She chose to have a mastectomy and radiation, as well as alternative healing treatments, and thankfully her cancer went into remission.

When I tell her about my chemo conundrum, she is sympathetic. And when I ask her to disclose her secret research tips, she says, "Would you allow me to do this research for you? It sounds like you could use some help."

"Really?" I ask, tears streaming down my face.

"Really," Zoë says with conviction.

I take a deep breath and feel my panic beginning to subside, like a slowly deflating balloon. "That would be incredibly helpful," I say. And then I realize that we haven't talked about her yet.

"How are you doing?" I ask. "How are your kids?"

She tells me about her teenage son and preteen daughter. Then she is silent for a moment and reluctantly says, "My cancer is back. And I'm back in treatment."

This news cuts me to the core. "I don't think it's a good idea for you to do my research," I say. "You need to look after yourself."

"But I'm so tired of being so focused on me all the time. This is exactly what I need right now—something to distract me and help me feel useful. I really want to do this for you and for me."

There is no point arguing; Zoë has made up her mind. And so I graciously accept her offer.

"I'll e-mail you my report in a few days."

"Thank you, Zoë. Let's go for a walk with our dogs sometime soon," I say.

"I'd like that," Zoë says. So would our dogs.

A few days later, Zoë's e-mail arrives:

Hi Robyn,

I sure wish we had reconnected under wildly different circumstances, but I'm really glad that you called me. I went
online after we spoke and quickly found out that that
wasn't going to be a useful route. I then e-mailed some
of my contacts, including my naturopath.

One contact, who just started work at the College of
Physicians and Surgeons, tried to find out how chemo
might affect Parkinson's symptoms. Unfortunately, she
couldn't find any research on this subject. But she suggested you could go to the library at the BC Cancer
Agency and ask them to do a search for you.

My naturopath said hard data will be hard to find.
He suggests asking your oncologist about complementary
therapies that might be neuroprotective and consider glu-
tathione IV, an excellent antioxidant.

I'm sorry to not have anything solid to offer you at this
point. I'm thinking of you and am sending you kick-ass
clarity to help make the incredibly hard decisions you
are being asked to make.

Your friend,
Zoë

Hi Zoë.

Thank you thank you thank you.

I too wish we had reconnected under wildly different circumstances, and I am so sorry about your health
situation.

I really appreciate your time and energy spent
researching on my behalf.

Let's walk our dogs one day soon,

Love, Robyn

ALL LEADS have proven fruitless—it seems no research exists about chemotherapy's detrimental effect on Parkinson's disease. So without damning proof, I am still on the hook for making a decision. With less than two weeks to go before my first round of chemo, I am desperate for some kick-ass clarity.

Then Bergen and I attend Chemo 101 at the cancer agency—a private crash course taught by a nurse. At least, that's who she says she is. But she doesn't fool me with her little nurse disguise. Right away, I smell a rat. And as she walks us through the nasty nuances of this toxic concoction, I catch a glimpse of her true identity—Grim Reaper Sales Representative. I hope she isn't working on commission, because she does a lousy job selling me on any of the sinister side effects she rattles off. And much to her dismay, I don't fall for her promise of silky smooth legs, a clear-cut crotch, and bald pits. This road to no hair terrifies me.

At the end of the class, I am convinced that chemo is not for me. But I hold off making my final decision—I am still waiting to hear back from Dr. Lohrisch and to hear what the other oncologists at the case conference recommend.

I HAVEN'T SEEN Theresa in months, though I did leave her a phone message after my mastectomy to let her know that I'd survived. I haven't been avoiding therapy; I just haven't felt the need. Until now. When she sees me, Theresa says, "Thank you for calling after your surgery. I was so relieved to hear your voice and to know that you were OK."

"You're welcome." I'm sitting cross-legged in the chair, watching her watching me.

I say, "I don't know why, but you look different. I must look different too."

"A little," she says with a smile.

"It's gone." I point at my vacant lot. "The dingo ate my baby."

"I know. I'm sorry." I watch her smile drift away as she takes a long, deep breath.

"How are you?" she asks.

"Sad. And still in shock," I answer, as my Cry Lady reaches for a tissue.

We wind our way through my grief at the loss of my right breast, the fear that I might pass breast cancer to Naomi as well as Parkinson's, my chemo conundrum, my continuing Parkinson's degeneration. I point out the scenic highlights along the way: harmony at home, my father's visit, my friendship pilgrimage. By the end of our session, I am still sitting on that chemotherapy fence. But now I accept that there is no right choice—there is just a decision that works best for me.

"Is there anything else you want to say or need from me before you leave?" Theresa asks.

"I don't think so."

"Then I have something to tell you—I'm pregnant. I'm due in five months."

"That's why you look different," I laugh. "I thought you had gained a little weight. How are you feeling?"

"Much better these days. I was quite sick in the first trimester."

We sit quietly for a while, and then Theresa adds, "I'll be going on mat leave in a few months. I've just started telling my clients. I want you to know that even though I won't be coming to the clinic, you can call me on the phone at home if you want to talk. I'd also be happy to recommend another therapist who does similar work."

I feel a rush of excitement for her and sadness for myself. Theresa has played such a pivotal role in my life this past year, helping me cope with so many challenges. I can't imagine

finding a replacement, but I'm not sure that I need to. I feel our work is almost complete. Knowing now that she's having a baby, I am happy that the painting I gave her in exchange for all these sessions would be perfect for a child's room.

Several days later, on a Friday afternoon, I get a call from Dr. Lohrisch. "I have some news regarding your case conference."

"OK," I say nervously, feeling my anxiety level rising. What advice will her colleagues give me, and will I heed this advice?

"At this morning's meeting, we discussed your treatment options, and it turns out that the majority of oncologists are not recommending chemotherapy for you."

"The majority?" I feel stunned and relieved, like a death-row prisoner who has just been granted clemency.

"That's right," she says.

"Do you still recommend chemo?"

"I do. But it's your choice. You've still got some time to decide."

"I need to talk it over with my husband. Can I call you back tomorrow?"

"Actually, I'm going on vacation for a couple weeks. So once you've made up your mind, call my assistant and let her know. OK?"

"OK," I say. "Thanks for calling. And enjoy your vacation."

Once I hang up the phone, I rush downstairs to Bergen's office and tell him the news. He is delighted and curious. "So, what did Dr. Lohrisch say were the reasons for not doing chemo?"

"She didn't say," I reply sheepishly.

"You mean you didn't ask?" Bergen laughs.

"I forgot. But I wish I'd asked. It would help us make the final decision."

"Well, I'm sure you can call her back."

"Nope. She's gone on vacation."

"Then here's what I suggest. On Monday, we'll call the cancer agency and see if we can speak with one of the oncologists who was at the case conference."

"That's a good idea. Let's think of any other questions we might have, OK?"

Over dinner, we jot down the following: What are the reasons for not recommending chemo? Did my having Parkinson's influence the recommendations? What's the latest research on breast cancer survivors who don't get chemo?

When Monday morning rolls around, I call Dr. Lohrisch's office. The assistant squeezes me in for an appointment that same afternoon with the oncologist who chaired my case conference.

After lunch, Bergen and I drive to the cancer agency. A nurse leads us into an examining room. Eventually, there's a knock on the semiclosed door, followed by a handsome head with sparkling blue eyes peering into the room.

"I'm sorry to have kept you waiting. I'm Dr. Kennecke."

Then the rest of him—dressed impeccably in a tailored suit and dashing tie—steps inside and shakes our hands. For a moment, I imagine we are at a fashion photo shoot, not a cancer consultation.

"I understand you have some questions about your case conference," he says, sitting down across from us. I catch a glimpse of his colorful patterned socks and beautiful leather shoes.

"I really didn't want chemotherapy, and I'm very happy that you and the other oncologists don't recommend it. Is this because I have Parkinson's?"

"Actually, no. This decision was based on the fact that your cancer was caught early, you've had a mastectomy, there were no traces of cancer in your lymph nodes, and your cancer is estrogen positive. Based on the most recent research, we felt

that ovarian suppression and Tamoxifen hormone therapy alone would suffice. In other words, there would be no advantage in your case to adding chemotherapy."

We talk further about ovarian suppression, and I say I would prefer surgery to remove my ovaries instead of shutting them down over several years with monthly chemical injections. I agree to start Tamoxifen right away.

Next, Dr. Kennecke examines my chest, armpits, and lymph nodes. Palpating the skin surrounding my scar, he asks, "Have you thought about taking the other one off?"

Flattered by his compliment, I reply, "No, actually you're the first one to mention it. Should I be thinking of this?"

"It's something to consider down the road."

As I get dressed, Bergen asks Dr. Kennecke, "Any significant breakthroughs in the latest breast cancer research?"

Dr. Kennecke smiles and describes some promising studies in Europe that he's following and tells us that he also does research here at the agency. I am impressed and ask, "Would you be my oncologist?"

He smiles politely and assures me that would be fine.

"I was supposed to start chemo next week."

"I'll cancel your chemo appointments for you."

Over the next few days, I tell family and friends the good news that the majority of oncologists don't recommend chemo and I am following their advice. The only person who questions my decision is my dad. I can hear him thinking over the phone line, and then he says, "Are you sure? Everybody's doing it." And for him, this is true—many older relatives and his friends in Toronto are undergoing chemo treatment. So I explain the reasons behind this decision, and in the end he understands. And if he still has doubts that I'm making the best choice, he keeps them to himself.

8

Travels
with Dolores

BACK WHEN I HAD TWO, it never occurred to me to give my breasts special names. I simply referred to them as "right one" and "left one." But now that I only have "left one" left, I regret this omission. It's not that I'm feeling sentimental. Or morbid. I just think that well-chosen names would better convey my deep love and appreciation for my bosom buddies. After all, as a team they were precocious (early bloomers), ambitious (outgrowing cup size after cup size), flirtatious (ooh-la-la), vivacious (putting *wow!* into my womanhood), industrious (nursing my baby), suspicious (nipple radar, detecting danger a mile away), and, of course, courageous (battling cancer). Now that the two are separated, I am compelled to honor them properly by renaming them. But so far the perfect words elude me.

In the meantime, my first falsie, the one I bought right after my mastectomy, has worn out its welcome. I'm ready to upgrade from an egg-shaped escape artist to a breast-shaped impersonator.

The saleswoman at the lingerie shop assures me that fitting survivors with natural-looking prostheses is her specialty. "Would you mind if I take a look at your breast?" she asks.

We step inside a change room, and I remove my top. She bends down to nipple level, studies my tit from different angles and exclaims, "I know exactly what you need."

She heads to the stockroom and returns with a square box and several styles of post-mastectomy bras. The prosthesis is fleshy-pink and spongy, with a slight protruding nipple for effect. It weighs about as much as my real breast and slips into a built-in pocket in the bra cup. Soon I am standing in front of a three-way mirror, wearing the impostor underneath my shirt and enjoying the illusion of having two tits. So is the saleslady.

"It's a perfect match," she declares.

And I agree. This illusion costs an arm and a leg, but I don't blink an eye as I hand over my credit card with a smile. Money can't buy happiness. But it can sure buy breast prostheses.

I never intended to name this plastic impostor. It just sort of happened. I was talking on the phone to Lisa, telling her about my new purchase, and she said, "I knew this woman who also had a mastectomy. She would wear her prosthesis when she was out in public, but when she got home, she would take it off and leave it somewhere in the house. And whenever she was getting dressed to go out, she would frantically search her home for her mislaid prosthesis, shouting out, "Dolores, Dolores, where are you?" This story made me laugh, something I hadn't done in a while.

I took this as a sign and began calling my own prosthesis Dolores. The name fits, and I like the way it rolls off my tongue. Dolores. It sounds contemplative. Dolores. It sounds musical. And just the other day our friend Hank, who is coincidentally married to a woman named Dolores, told me that Dolores

means "sorrowful" in Spanish. Which I am—and so is the "left one" left behind. He also gave me his blessing to name a second prosthesis—should I ever require one—after him. Touched by his thoughtfulness, I gave Hank a hug and promised to put his name at the top of my list.

I DECIDE IT'S TIME to go to Toronto to visit family and friends. I can't arrive empty-handed or empty-chested, so I'm bringing along gifts and Dolores. Before I board the plane, all these items must be checked off the list:

· Have session with psychiatrist, Dr. Young.
· Get radioactive bone scan at cancer agency.
· Attend cancer support group meeting.
· Meet with surgeon re: prophylactic removal of my ovaries.
· Get massage with Jessica.
· Have session with Theresa.
· Get mustache zapped.
· Get haircut and color touch-up.

I manage to get everything done so that if I die in a plane crash, I'll die medicated, mollified, mustache-free, relaxed, radioactive, proactive, and coiffed.

It turns out that Dolores loves to fly. Preparing for departure, she's as bubbly as champagne, whereas I am queasy and convinced we're going to crash.

"Don't be silly," Dolores giggles as the plane taxis down the runway, "I predict a perfect takeoff."

As the engine starts its roar, the cabin shakes and the flight attendants take their seats. Any minute now we'll be airborne: exactly how, I haven't a clue. But I know words like "thrust" and "throttle" play a role. If Bergen were here, he'd explain the physics of flight, and I'd pretend to understand. Then he'd

pretend that he believes me and recommend an article in his latest *Scientific American*. But it's just Dolores and me and a barf bag and my stash of Ativan ascending into the cumulus clouds.

Once we reach our cruising altitude, the ride smoothes out and I finally relax. Hunger displaces nausea, and I nibble on some snacks while Dolores takes a nap. I catch up on some reading, then watch satellite TV.

The pilot interrupts and says, "Good evening, Ladies and Gentlemen. This is your captain speaking. We're heading into some turbulence, and for your safety we ask that you return to your seats and kindly fasten your seatbelts."

Then I think I hear him say, "And if your name is Robyn Michele Levy, we ask that you take an Ativan right about now."

So I do. There's a chorus of clicks as passengers buckle up. Mine is already on, but I double check to be sure. And then we start to rock and roll. Drinks are sloshing, pretzels are rolling, overhead compartments are flipping open, lights are flickering off and on. This is it; we're going down. I nervously bite my lip and rub my fingers over my chin.

Dolores wakes up and calmly says, "Don't worry. This will pass. I predict a safe flight."

What does she know? Who does she think she is? A prophetic prosthetic tit? That's when my fingers find it—a stubbly hair at the base of my chin. Damn! My beautician missed this one. I don't want to die with a starter beard. Suddenly the turbulence stops and the seatbelt light turns off. Soon we begin our descent.

"Don't tell me," I say to Dolores, "you predict a smooth landing."

My dad picks me up at the airport. "You look great," he says, giving me a hug and kiss hello.

"So do you," I tell him as he elbows me out of the way, insisting that he push the luggage cart to the car. When he opens the trunk, all hell breaks loose—it's a Parkinsonian free-for-all.

"Ladies and Gentlemen, welcome to the Battle of the Bag. Introducing...first...near the left taillight...weighing 155 pounds...turning seventy years old...sporting a frozen shoulder and a sciatic leg... rated as the best luggage schlepper of the last decade... the one and only Daddy Gordoon. And his opponent...near the right taillight...weighing 125 pounds... clocking in at a mere forty-four years of age...sporting one tit and two ovaries slated for surgical removal...rated as the worst luggage schlepper in the family...the one and only Disintegrating Daughter. On your mark...get set...go slow!"

My dad and I duke it out, sluggishly, but in the end it takes two of us to lift my heavy suitcase and heave it into the trunk. For now, it's a tie. But I'm sure we'll battle again when he drops me off at Lisa's.

LISA'S HOME is my home away from home. It's where I stay whenever I come to town. When we pull into the driveway, she bursts out the front door, her curly hair dancing around the collar of her shirt. It's raining lightly, just like it is back in Vancouver, but here it's colder and more convincing that winter is on its way. She gives me a big shivery hug, and my chin disappears in a clump of frizzy curls.

"You're still short," I mumble into the top of her head.

"Yep, I still am." She laughs.

Then she gives me a final squeeze before turning to greet my dad—my dear, competitive dad, who was taking advantage of our distraction to sneak my suitcase out of the car by himself (pre-empting the repeat tug-of-war I was expecting). It's late in the evening, and he is anxious to get home.

"Call me in the morning," he says.

Lisa helps me get settled in the guest room. While I get ready for bed, she brings us tea, and we begin our long-awaited face-to-face chat. Although my pajama top is loose fitting, the altered landscape of my chest is detectable. Sliding my hand over my vacant lot, I watch Lisa's eyes take in their first viewing. I answer her questions about how I'm healing and dealing with the loss. Then, looking around, she asks, "Where is Dolores?"

I point to a shelf next to the bed. "Shhhh. Dolores is already asleep," I say, lifting the lid on her box so Lisa can peek inside. She leans over and takes a look.

"Sweet dreams, Dolores," she whispers. "You too, Robbie. See you in the morning."

FRUGALITY IS NOT my mother's forte. She's generous to a fault, especially when it comes to entertaining. She doesn't just cook up a storm; she cooks up an entire weather system. For dinner one night she serves teriyaki salmon, sweet and sour meatballs, braised beef ribs, roasted potatoes and vegetables, rice pilaf, lasagna, chicken noodle soup, noodle pudding, breaded chicken, steamed broccoli and cauliflower, two salads, and, for dessert, chocolate cake, blueberry pie, and fruit salad. All this for only seven of us: my sister, her husband, their two kids, my dad, my mom, and me. As much as we all ate, we barely made a dent. There are enough leftovers to feed all the starving people in Toronto.

So far, things are going better than I expected. Everyone is making nice. In fact, the only tension I feel is within myself. I've been worried my family might recoil in fear when they see the new and worsening me. But everyone is so busy and preoccupied—cleaning up, playing with toys, watching TV—I realize it would take more than a limp and a missing tit to get noticed

around here. And nobody talks about the elephant in the room: the fact that my mom, my dad, and I all have medical problems.

My dad says, "I just realized that you've lived exactly half your life here and the other half in Vancouver."

"Really?" I do the math in my head: born in 1964, moved in 1986, and now its 2008. "You're right. Twenty-two years in each city."

"It's a long time to be away," my dad sighs.

"I know."

Being a long-distance daughter—sister, auntie, friend—has never been easy, and as the years have gone by it has taken its toll. There's an ache in my heart for missing memories.

I devote the next day to my brother and sister. Getting together with them in person is a rare treat. It only happens when I come to town—once or twice a year. In a way, it's like cramming for an exam as I try to deepen our connections and learn as much as possible about their lives and their children in such a short span of time.

I spend the afternoon at Jonathan's home. His wife, Ariella, makes the lunch, and Gabby makes the mess. He's two years old and melts my heart with hugs and kisses and an uncanny resemblance to Jonathan when he was that age. He has the same big brown eyes, shape of mouth, curly head of hair, and hearty appetite. Stuffed from a feast of sushi and salads, we relax in the living room, listening to the Grateful Dead. Gabby hunts down the remote control and cranks up the volume, and soon he and Jonathan are dancing wildly on the carpet, spinning and gyrating and bobbing their heads.

Ariella laughs and says, "They always do this. Gabby loves dancing."

When the show is over, Ariella makes a pot of tea and sets out a fruit platter. Gabby stuffs his mouth with strawberries

while he and I construct colorful towers with his stacking blocks. They don't last long—Gabby knocks most of them down with his strawberry-stained hands. After every successful demolition, his face lights up while he points at the scattered blocks he wants me to pick up.

Eventually Gabby tires of this game, and I join Jonathan on the couch. He leans over, gives me a kiss on the cheek, and starts rubbing my shoulders and neck.

"Are your muscles always this tight?"

"Unfortunately, yes. That feels nice," I mumble.

"It's great having you here, hanging out with us."

"I'm happy to be here."

"You sure seem a lot happier than the last time you came over."

"I am. Thank goodness for antidepressants. I probably should have started taking them years ago."

He continues massaging my neck and says, "It's so weird that you and Dad both have Parkinson's."

"I know." What I don't say, but what I'm sure he's thinking, is that I hope he isn't next in line. Of course, he's already coping with this disease indirectly. He works with my dad in the insurance business, and although they each have their own clients, Jonathan now has the added responsibility of tending to my father's files as his health declines.

"How's work going for you these days?" I ask.

"I'm swamped. Sometimes I don't get home until ten o'clock."

"That's sounds stressful. Is that because you're helping Dad with his work?"

"That's part of it. But sometimes, when Dad comes into the office, he gets all anxious and needs my support. I spend hours just helping him calm down. Then I drive him home or arrange for someone else to take him home. It's tough. I'm happy to help him anytime. But it really cuts into my productivity."

"No doubt. You've got a lot going on."

"We all do."

Ariella joins the conversation, and we talk about Gabby and their challenges of balancing family and work, and about my life in Vancouver with Bergen and Naomi. By the end of the afternoon, I feel content and fulfilled—as a sister, a sister-in-law, and an aunt. I'm ready for round two, and after I hug Ariella and Gabby good-bye, Jonathan drops me off at Fern's house.

Fern greets me at the door and gives me a big hug, then yells, "Look who's here, you guys!"

Kayla and Josh come running down the hall.

"Hi, Auntie Robyn."

"We've been waiting for you."

I get more hugs and kisses, then Josh asks, "Do you want me to show you VY Canis Majoris? It's a red hypergiant star!"

"Do we get to take a space shuttle?"

Josh gives me a strange look, and Fern assures him, "Auntie Robyn's just joking, Joshy." Then she looks at me and explains, "He doesn't appreciate jokes about astronomy. He takes it very seriously."

"So do you want to see VY Canis Majoris?" Josh asks again.

"Absolutely!"

He takes my hand and leads me to the computer in the living room. He's only four years old and knows more about the solar system and black holes than Bergen. In a few clicks, Josh takes us to the official NASA website, and there it is, a bright burst of white surrounded in a foggy rainbow of light.

"See, Auntie Robyn! This is what the star looks like. It's about 5,000 light-years away from Earth. And it's the biggest star! Between 600 and 2,100 times the size of our sun!"

"Wow! Amazing!" I say, referring to both the star and my nephew—the budding astronomer.

"Did you know that vy Canis Majoris is very unstable and will probably be destroyed, as a supernova, in less than 100,000 years?"

"I didn't know that," I say. "In fact, I don't even understand that."

Undeterred by my ignorance, Josh pulls out one of his drawings, which shows the comparative sizes of planets and stars.

"This is Europa; this is Titan; this is Dione. Of course, this is Earth."

When he gets to Mars, Kayla comes over and asks, "Can I show you something now?"

"Josh, do you mind if we take a break? I'd like to see what Kayla wants to show me."

"Sure," he says.

Kayla and I sit on the floor, leaning against the couch. She opens her notebook and says, "I wrote all these stories."

"Did you draw the pictures too?"

"Yep. I want to be an author and illustrator when I grow up."

"I'm sure you will be. Especially if you keep writing stories. Can you read me something?"

"OK."

Kayla begins with a story about a grade 2 teacher who apparently spends all of her teaching time explaining elaborate school rules to her students. One day, the teacher surprises the children by announcing that there will be a joke contest. The kids get all excited, but then the teacher spends the entire day explaining all of the rules of this contest.

"Is your school like this?" I ask.

"No," Kayla assures me.

When Fern's husband, Bob, gets home, Fern and I go out to dinner together.

At the restaurant, we are seated at a table in a quiet section, which suits me fine.

"I'm glad it's not so noisy here," I say. "We can actually carry on a conversation without shouting."

"And without being interrupted by kids," Ferns adds. "So are you having a good visit with everyone?"

"Yeah. Much better than I expected. I was really nervous about how everyone would react when they saw me."

"Why?"

"Because . . . is that a fire alarm?"

"Sounds like it," Fern yells over the shrill ringing.

We cover our ears and look around. No sign of smoke. No sign of firefighters. In fact, no sign of any emergency. Just business as usual: hostesses smiling, servers serving, customers consuming.

"Do you think we should be worried?" I shout.

"I'll go find out," Fern yells, getting up from the table.

A few minutes later, she's back, "There's no fire. Apparently the alarm system has been malfunctioning."

"Apparently."

"Do you want to leave?"

"Nah. I like things that malfunction, makes me feel right at home. Besides, I'm sure by the time we get our food, the alarm will be off."

Wishful thinking. The alarm drones on for half an hour. When it's finally turned off, we are partway through dinner.

Fern picks up where we left off. "So why were you nervous to see everyone?"

"Because of how different I look: all stiff and robotic and missing a breast."

"I don't think you look that different. You look beautiful. And you can't even tell that you've had surgery."

"Thanks to Dolores," I smile, patting my imposter.

"Dolores?"

"That's what I call my prosthesis."

Fern laughs and grabs her belly roll between her fingers and gives it a squeeze. "I call this Yum Yuck, because of all the Tim Hortons breakfast sandwiches I eat. See, my stomach looks like an English muffin!"

"Cute. Do you want to see my party tricks?" I ask.

"Sure."

"Watch this," I say, twisting my hands as if screwing in light bulbs. Very quickly, my left hand freezes in place, while my right hand continues twisting.

"I don't like that party trick," Fern says.

"Then how about this one?" I stretch out my left arm and wait until it begins to tremor.

"Don't like that one either," she says.

"OK. Last one. This is my future." I pick up my glass of water and try taking a sip with my hand shaking wildly, water splashing everywhere.

"That's not funny," she says with tears in her eyes.

"If I don't laugh about it, I'll cry."

"Can we talk about something else?" Fern dabs at her eyes with a tissue.

And so we end the evening talking about our kids and husbands, our parents and brother. And by the time I'm back at Lisa's, I'm exhausted and ready for sleep. So is Dolores.

LISA LOVES SHOPPING, and Lisa loves me. And she wants to buy me a gift. So we're going to a clothing sample sale downtown. When we arrive at the warehouse, the place is packed with women rifling through racks and racks of clothes: shirts, skirts, sweaters, pants, jackets, scarves. Standing by the door, I watch the action. At first, everything looks chaotic. But then patterns emerge. There are the zigzaggers who go diagonally

from one rack to another. There are the wallflowers who prefer the tables near the walls. There are the groupies who dress the same and move in clumps. And there are the soloists who drift in and out with samples draped over one arm.

I look at Lisa. Her face is covered in tiny beads of sweat; her eyes are wild with hunger.

"Ready?" she asks.

I nod my head yes, despite my Tin Man body's protests. I can't remember the last time I went shopping for clothes. However, I do remember the last purchase I made: Dolores. Who, by the way, is delirious with joy to be in the company of so many breasts.

Lisa leads the way. I shuffle behind, reluctantly joining the jostling crowd, gathering shirts and sweaters to try on. There are no private change rooms. Instead, there is one large communal changing area. And it's crammed with women stripped down to their thongs and bras (heaven for Dolores, hell for me). Lisa quickly peels off her clothes, while I struggle to unbutton my blouse. By the time I'm finally ready to try on one of the sample shirts, Lisa has already tried on several. She's watching me out of the corner of her eye as I slip my right arm into one sleeve and make several pathetic failed attempts to insert my frozen left arm into the other sleeve. I can feel her hesitation; she's wondering if she should or shouldn't help me. But by the time she lends a hand, it's too late—I'm gone.

Poor Lisa. She thought she was taking *me* shopping, not my Cry Lady.

"Do you want to go home now?" she asks.

It's a perfectly reasonable question, and my Cry Lady has a perfectly unreasonable answer: "No."

And so Lisa digs through her purse for some tissues, and taking control of the frozen left arm, she discovers that dressing my Cry Lady is like dressing a waterlogged

mannequin—one that squirts and drips tears and snot. She mops up the mess and folds up the clothes that don't fit, while my Cry Lady says, "I like this one," admiring the big-buttoned sweater.

"Me too," Lisa says. "It looks great. Let's buy it."

I used to think shopping and crying were never a good mix, unless you're a child whining for candy or toys.

MY TORONTO TRIO and I join a cult. Just for the weekend. We are all wearing the cult uniform: a plush white terrycloth robe and plastic reflexology sandals. We are naked underneath. So are all these subdued strangers milling about this place. This was Ruthie's idea. She always has good ideas.

We drove up this morning, north on Highway 400, into cottage country. The Muskokas. The spa is called Taboo. With a name like that, I was expecting kinky treatments such as "The Dominatrix Deep Tissue Tease" or "No-Hands Foot Fetish Pedicure" or "Sperm of the Moment Facial." But everything on their menu is tame. Both Ruthie and Lisa are getting hot stone massages. Ruthie is also booked for a white mud toning wrap, and Lisa a traditional pedicure. Bonnie ordered an aromatherapy massage plus a cocoa butter wrap. And I am having a reflexology treatment plus a traditional pedicure.

We are expected at the lounge—our spa treatments start soon. So the four of us meet outside our rooms, in robes and sandals, with the intention of walking down the hallway together. And that's exactly how we start off—together. But soon, Ruthie, Lisa, and Bonnie are way ahead of me. Damn them and their arm-swinging prowess! I used to be the fast walker, leaving *them* in the dust. Now they're waiting for me to catch up; Ruthie's holding the door open.

"I think these sandals are broken," I shout.

They watch me limping toward them, my left toes constantly sliding out of the top of the sandal, then inching their way back where they belong. It's a losing amusing battle. Before I accidentally trip, I kick them off and walk barefoot.

"I'll swap them for a new pair later on."

The lounge is spacious and inviting. We wait on the couch. Then one by one, our names are called out, and we follow our leaders to private rooms. My leader is a young beautician, straight out of beauty school. She helps me get settled on the massage table and then begins my treatment.

"Have you ever had reflexology before?" she asks.

"No, never."

She smiles and tells me, "You're going to really enjoy this."

And then she starts pressing her fingers into my aching feet while providing a play-by-play commentary, which includes reciting textbook definitions she must have memorized for her final beauty exam. Her chatter nullifies whatever pleasure I derive from her touch. She never shuts up. Of course, it occurs to me I could ask her to stop talking. Or I could scare her into silence by flashing my mastectomy scar. But I'm not in the mood to be rude or assertive. I'd rather just try to tune her out.

When the treatment is finished, I am delighted. She escorts me to the pedicure room and says, "I really enjoyed treating you today. Isn't reflexology great?"

I nod, and as she walks out the room, I can still hear her voice yakking away in my head.

Lisa shows up a few minutes later, looking relaxed from her hot stone massage. She sits next to me, plunges her feet into a warm footbath, leans back, and closes her eyes. My feet are already soaking. While we wait in silence for our pedicurists to arrive, I pray for a mute pedicurist. My prayer is partially answered; she barely talks.

One by one, we reconvene in the lounge, sipping herbal tea and lemon water. Then we make our way to the dining room for lunch. The room is packed with pampered people wearing only white terrycloth robes. The hostess leads us to our table, and I sink self-consciously into the chair, feeling vulnerable and nearly naked: the gargoyle among the goddesses.

LISA AND RUTHIE are sharing a room. Bonnie and I are in the other. After my shower, Bonnie nonchalantly asks, "How is your scar?"

I smile, thinking to myself: you can take the girl out of the leper colony, but you can't take the leper colony out of the girl.

"Do you want to see it?" I ask, knowing she does.

"If you want to show me," she says.

I drop my towel and Bonnie's eyes light up. "Oh, Robbie. Your scar is really nice. It's not terrible at all."

"You think?"

"I do. I've seen lots of scars, and yours is lovely."

A wave of pride washes over me, and my eyes begin to tear. I feel as if Bonnie has placed a tiara on my head and I've just been crowned Ms. Mastectomy. I imagine stepping up to the microphone and giving my acceptance speech:

"Oh my God. This is amazing. I never imagined in my wildest dreams that I'd end up here. This is so exciting. I want to thank Dr. Chung, my brilliant surgeon, for her steady hands and exceptional technique..."

My speech is cut short by the ringing of the phone.

"Hi. It's Ruthie. Just wanted to let you know I made dinner reservations for us at eight."

"Perfect," I lie.

By that time of night, I'm ready to flake out on the couch or crawl into bed. Fortunately, there's plenty of time to take a nap.

MENUS ARE MEANT to be enticing, and this one doesn't disappoint. The four of us are salivating. The appetizers sound scrumptious; the entrees sound superb. We tell our waitress we need a bit more time to decide. I've never met the chef, but his victuals are revealing. I can tell he likes to garnish with fruit. There's grilled peach beside the duck, sautéed grapes on the lobster ravioli, and blueberry sauce drizzled over the bison. The menu also suggests that he's a hands-on kind of guy. His creations are hand rolled, hand snipped, handmade, hand picked, hand shaved. I imagine he is a compulsive hand washer.

By the time we place our order, we've polished off one bottle of wine. We're well into the second when the appetizers arrive. We share plates of pepper-seared Ahi tuna, risotto of woodland mushrooms, pastrami of magret duck, and red romaine with warm maple shallot dressing. The food is delicious, the company divine. And I am drunk and desperately have to pee. Soon. So I hold on to the table edge and hoist my body up from the chair.

Bonnie asks, "Are you OK?"

I'm not exactly sure, so I don't respond. Instead, I focus my attention on keeping my balance. The combination of alcohol and staying up late has exacerbated my Parkinson's symptoms: my limbs are extra rigid; my back is extra tight; my neck is fused in place. I feel like a frozen sapling, at the mercy of the wind. I take a few wobbly steps and wonder—if a tree falls in a restaurant, does anybody hear? Thankfully, I don't find out. Bonnie accompanies me to the ladies' room and back. Then there's more food and more wine and more trips to the washroom. Our voices grow louder and louder. When my Cry Lady makes a special appearance, my Toronto Trio knows it's time to go. We are the very last party to leave.

My last few days in Toronto are divided between visits with family and friends. There's lunch with my brother at a sushi bar,

dinner at a deli with my parents and aunties, lunch at my cousin's, and an evening with Hildi at her home. The night before I leave, Lisa throws me a farewell dinner party. This is apropos, since I am living in a perpetual state of farewell: first brain cells, then breast, and coming out soon in an operating theater near me, my ovaries and fallopian tubes.

There are eight of us gathered around the table: me, Lisa, Bonnie, Ruthie, Fern, Diane, Kimmie, and Donna. We're all over forty, well into the season of aches and pains. Words like "bursitis" and "arthritis" pop up in conversations. And so do the phrases "in vitro fertilization" and "dilation and curettage." But I am the first one to throw "cancer" and "neurodegenerative disease" into the mix. In other words, I'm the life of the party.

It's rare that we all get together like this—it only happens when I come to town. "You are a social magnet," Lisa always says. But now I am more than that. My revised business card reads:

ROBYN MICHELE LEVY
Social Magnet & Mortality Mentor
Helping Middle-Aged Dames Wake Up
and Face the Music

It's a grim job, but somebody's got to ruin it for everybody. We're all going to die sooner or later, faster or slower, intact or in pieces.

TEN DAYS is a long time to be away from home. Too long, according to Bergen. Although we spoke on the phone everyday, he still missed me. So did Naomi. They both give me warm hugs and kisses—a homecoming that's hard to beat. And then along comes Nellie, putting them to shame.

She is ecstatic to see me (she must think I've risen from the dead). I crouch down to give her a belly rub. And then suddenly

it's show time! and Nellie is channeling Liza Minnelli—tap dancing down the staircase, pirouetting in the hall, barking her heart out. I feel loved and adored and happy to be home. Today, life *is* a cabaret.

The rest of the week is filled with appointments. There's a follow-up meeting with Dr. Kennecke, who is pleased to report that my bone scan results look good—there is no indication that the cancer has spread to my bones. I go for a massage with Jessica and electrolysis with Diane. I have a pre-admission meeting over the phone about my upcoming surgery to remove my ovaries. And I attend another session with my cancer support group.

The ladies are happy to see me, and I'm happy to see them—even Cantankerous Woman, who seems to be mellowing out as weeks go by (perhaps this is because Little Old Lady has dropped out of the group). Chantal is as radiant and patient as always, and this time she brings her guitar. She leads us in a musical meditation, her voice so sweet and healing. And then we form our circle and one by one take turns talking.

We are all on the same journey but at different stages. Our concerns range from coping with chemo to preparing loved ones for our demise. Somehow we always end up talking about food—recipes, nutrition, cooking, gardening. I think it's our way to nurture hope.

9

The Comeback
Mama

DECEMBER IS OVER. The forecast calls for flurries of sawdust and trips to the hardware store. Expect low-pressure visits with friends followed by unsettling postponements of surgery. There is a 50 percent chance of going to the Overbites' debut performance. Flossing advisory in effect.

Holiday celebrations fell through the cracks this year. There was no Christmas tree or Hanukkah menorah, no roasted turkey or potato latkes. And instead of buying each other gifts, we agreed to splurge on one family present: a big-screen TV. This sounds deceptively simple, but it wasn't. And it's all because of Hildi.

When she was here in the summer, Bergen asked for her professional opinion about our unfinished family room. In a matter of seconds, Hildi told him what to do: "First, rotate the couches 180 degrees, so they face the fireplace, not the back

wall. Then renovate the hideous fireplace. Make it simple and classy. And install a flat-screen TV above it."

Bergen's face lit up with joy—Hildi's advice was more than music to his handyman ears; it was the authoritative voice of an angel commanding him, "Go forth and renovate."

He started the very next day and has been at it for months. Tearing out the ugly old bricks. Building a custom cedar mantel with shelves. Installing sleek black tiles. Insulating the wall. Doing the electrical wiring. Shopping for a TV. Installing it above the fireplace. It's not even finished, and it looks fabulous. So does Craig Ferguson on a fifty-inch screen.

The day before my surgery, the hospital calls. Apparently, I've been bumped. They reschedule me for the following week, and I get bumped again. Now I have to wait another three weeks. I feel as fragile as the eggs in my ovaries. I wish the surgery was over easy.

The next three weeks I try to keep busy. There's shopping with Gloria; dinner with Linda one night and Brian and Gillian another; lunch with Joey; visits with Diana and Betina. There's also massages with Jessica, electrolysis treatments with Diane, a checkup with Dr. Mintz, a follow-up with Dr. Chung, and an appointment with Dr. Young, my psychiatrist. I see him every two months or so—not for therapy—just to monitor my mood and prescribe my antidepressants.

When I arrive at his building, I experience elevator amnesia. I go up and down so many elevators I can't remember which floor he's on. The office directory is in the lobby, mounted on a wall. It's a large silver metal board, and all the names and organizations are stenciled in black. At the top I spot the first three letters of his name: Dr. You. Fourth floor.

"How's Robyn today?" he asks.

"I'm doing OK," I answer. "How are You?"

"Fine, thank you."

"I see you've changed your name."

"How so?"

"You've lost your *N* and *G* on the building directory. It says Dr. You."

"Oh, that," he sighs. "Someone picked off the letters."

"Are you going to replace them?" I ask.

"Nah, why bother?" He sighs once more. "Someone will only pick them off again."

I'm about to say, "That's the saddest thing I've heard all day," but he changes the subject. "How have things been going since I saw you last?" So I brief him about the delayed surgery, my trip to Toronto, and Dolores. And we talk about my moods and my meds. When it's time to go, he hands me a refill prescription, and I take the elevator down. Poor Dr. You, I say to myself, walking past the directory. Maybe next time I'll bring him the letters *N* and *G*.

EVEN THOUGH BERGEN and I live in the same house, sleep in the same bed, listen to the same radio programs, and read the same newspaper, sometimes it feels as if we're living in different worlds—physically, mentally, and emotionally. While this isn't surprising (I have Parkinson's disease, after all), it is still shocking to discover new barriers that restrict my access to his world—the world we once shared.

The latest barrier appeared the other day. Bergen had gone shopping and came home with a brand-new set of matching plastic food containers. It was the industrial design of the lids that sold him: hinged flaps on all four sides, guaranteed to lock in freshness and prevent leaks. We used them for the first time after dinner. While he filled one of the containers with leftover pasta, I filled another one with leftover broccoli. He

closed his lid, and I attempted to close mine. But my fingers couldn't exert enough pressure, let alone find the right position, to force down the flaps.

Trying to be helpful, Bergen offered me advice on how to use my mechanical advantage. Trying to be hopeful, I followed his advice, clumsily grasped the lid, and fumbled some more. Then I did what any self-respecting forty-five-year-old woman would do—I burst into tears.

"There, there," Bergen consoled me, hugging me tight.

"You forgot about my fingers," I sobbed.

"I know. I'm sorry."

"Me too," I said, glaring down at the open drawer of perfectly stacked matching containers. "I hate this fucking disease! And I hate these fucking containers!" I kicked the drawer shut with my good leg, then stepped into the bathroom and blew my nose. To my horror, high-pitched *honks* wailed out of my nostrils, as loud and obnoxious as those noisemakers people toot on New Year's Eve.

"What was that sound?" Bergen called out.

"Me," I answered, looking at myself in the bathroom mirror, tears streaming down my face. "It's my Tupperware party and I'll cry if I want to."

VALENTINE'S DAY is fast approaching, and if everything goes according to plan, I know exactly what I'm getting. Nothing predictable like decadent chocolates or slinky lingerie. And nothing pampering like a day at a swanky spa. Nope. This Valentine's day I get "bed rest and morphine." That's because on February 12 a surgeon will remove my ovaries and fallopian tubes. A procedure I'm told is quick and easy and safe, highly unlikely to result in any accidental damage to my adjacent vital organs (listed in the hospital waiver I signed in triplicate).

The clinical term for this operation is "oopherectomy," but it sounds really sexy when you pronounce it with a heavy French accent, as in "OOff-urr-eck-tum-mee." Of course this leads to instant menopause, but that's sexy too, right?

I have three friends who have survived this life-altering operation. The first is Zoë. When I asked her how this surgery affected her, she said life in the instant menopause lane was hell for about three years. Sue is the second friend, and she, like me, was diagnosed with estrogen positive breast cancer last year. She had her oopherectomy one month ago. Sue told me the operation went well—that is, until the surgeon inadvertently nicked her bladder. Fortunately, she recovered not only from this surgery (and fluke accident) but also from a double mastectomy a couple of weeks later.

At this point, it would only be natural to be filled with trepidation. But thanks to my third friend, who happens to be my spayed dog, Nellie, I'm feeling optimistic. Not only did she survive an oopherectomy and a hysterectomy, but she also survived an entire week of public humiliation wearing one of those obnoxious plastic lampshade cones around her head. Something I hope to avoid. After all, unlike my dog, I will promise my doctor not to lick my stitches.

But life doesn't always go according to plan. My surgery date might get bumped for the third time, thereby leaving my reproductive organs intact a little longer. Or Dr. Gregory House might reach out from our fifty-inch plasma TV screen, pull me into his cantankerous diagnostic world, and perform my oopherectomy strung out on Vicodin, after which we go limping off together into the high-definition Hollywood sunset. Either way, one thing's for sure: compared with coping with Parkinson's disease and breast cancer, instant menopause is sure to be a breeze.

THE HOSPITAL didn't bump me. It's all systems go. I know the preoperative drill: put on the gown; get poked, prodded, and primed; remind Bergen of my final wish.

"If I die, promise me you'll burn my old diaries—if you find them."

"I promise," he says, squeezing my hand. "And you're not going to die."

My Cry Lady is on standby; she's waiting for her cue, holding a white tissue in her hand. She waves it in surrender when a dark-haired doctor walks in.

"Hello, I'm Dr. Mazgani. I'll be performing your surgery."

"Hi," I say. "You've done this before, I hope."

"Many times," she assures me with a quick smile.

Her face is round and friendly. Her hospital scrubs fit like pajamas.

She touches my shoulder, looks me in the eyes, and says, "We're almost ready to begin."

A hospital orderly appears by my bed and unlocks the wheels one by one, and then I'm rolling slowly away with Bergen's kiss, down a corridor, into an operating room. Au revoir, ovaries... Farewell, fallopian tubes... Parting—with more parts—is such sweet sorrow.

I WAKE UP groggy and sore and stiff as a board, with nurses on one side and Dr. Mazgani on the other. She leans over me and says, "Hi, Robyn. Everything went really well."

"Great," I groan, feeling slightly nauseated.

"Where's Bergen?"

"He's on his way," she assures me.

I drift in and out of consciousness, catching snippets of conversation. Something about someone with low blood pressure. At some point I open my eyes and see Bergen smiling. "I told you that you wouldn't die."

What a relief—I'm not only alive, I'm still recognizable.

"How do I look, now that I'm down to one tit and a uterus?"

"Beautiful," Bergen says.

Compared with a mastectomy, an oopherectomy is minimally invasive. I imagine it's like being probed by aliens. A tiny wandlike camera—called a laparoscope—is inserted into the abdomen through tiny incisions, and then the ovaries and fallopian tubes are fished out. This procedure is considered day surgery, and patients are generally sent home a couple of hours after recovery. But not me. My blood pressure is quite low, so they keep me in hospital until it rises enough that I don't faint when standing up. It's the end of the day when I'm finally discharged.

WE'VE ARRANGED for Naomi to sleep at a friend's house tonight to spare her from seeing me in this decrepit state: Tin Man stiff, depressed as hell, watching TV while waiting for the painkillers to kick in. Bergen is cooking dinner for just the two of us. When it's ready, he helps me walk upstairs—I'm still dizzy and shaky on my feet.

"Oh, the table looks beautiful," I say.

He's lit candles and plated the food. He's even set out napkins with the cutlery. All that's missing is a violinist. Without a doubt, this is the most romantic postsurgery dinner I've ever had.

I take a bite of broccoli and a forkful of rice. Bergen does the same. And then suddenly I am hit by a tsunami of emotion and burst into uncontrollable tears. Heaving sobs ripple through me. I can barely catch my breath.

"I don't know why I'm crying," I sputter, hoping Bergen will say something soothing to calm me down.

But then his lip begins to quiver, he slumps back in his chair, and he starts crying too. Whatever I've got must be contagious.

Then along comes Nellie, her big brown eyes darting back and forth, her pink tongue panting rhythmically, her stubby tail wagging with delight. The crying continues; the food grows cold; Nellie disappears. Then we hear a stream of squeaks and squawks under the table. It's Nellie—accompanying our duet, improvising on her squeaky toy, chomping it in her mouth. The more we cry, the faster she squeaks, until we are sobbing and laughing hysterically at the same time, releasing weeks of pent-up tension and stress. Eventually Nellie drops her toy and curls up by our feet, quiet and content—our cue to settle down and finish dinner.

RECOVERING FROM this latest surgery is easier than last time—at least for me. But not for Bergen. Even though there's no massive scar, no bloody drain, and no new damage to my limbs, my body feels battered and fatigued. So I spend most of my time resting and requesting. There's no shortage of things to ask for: scrambled eggs, almond butter on toast, chicken noodle soup, home fries, roasted chicken, beans and rice, salad and fruit, juice and tea and water. I keep Bergen busy beyond belief. And not just in the kitchen. The phone has been ringing off the hook, and Bergen is my answering machine. He's also my doorman—welcoming visitors, accepting deliveries of flowers, gift baskets, and books.

I am so grateful for Bergen's support. I always say please and thank you. But he deserves much more than that. In fact, had I known my expunged organs would lead to another generous shower of presents, I would have signed up at Home Depot's gift registry. So instead of sending me "get well" roses or "speedy recovery" gourmet snacks, family and friends could have sent him "we appreciate you" power tools or rechargeable batteries or an assortment of nails and screws—anything a handyman

might desire when he's not tending to what's left of his wife. It's too late to register now, but if I ever require more of me removed, that's exactly what I'll do.

MY NEIGHBOR HELEN drops by this morning with another one of her beautiful fruit salads.

"Thank you so much," I say, admiring the colorful mix of delicately chopped apples, pears, pineapple, banana, grapes, and strawberries.

I can see a pattern emerging: the more body parts I lose, the more fruit salads Helen gives. I'd hate to jinx this winning streak, so I make a mental note: exempt Helen from the Home Depot gift registry notification plan.

"How are you feeling?" she asks.

"Pretty good, my energy is coming back slowly."

"Did you know that Will's band is performing next week? It's a Battle of the Bands fundraiser for the dentistry school student yearbook society."

"Who are they competing against?"

"Oh, this band of young dentistry students. It should be fun."

"I'd love to come out to the show."

"Maybe you'll be feeling better by then," Helen smiles.

"I hope so," I say. Every band needs a one-breasted groupie.

EVERYONE WANTS to know how I'm doing—I've got a glut of e-mails and phone calls to return. I just don't have the energy to reply to each relative and friend individually. So I e-mail them this update:

Hi everyone.

I survived my oopherectomy and learned some valuable lessons:

194 MOST OF ME

1   That old expression "Never trust a stranger" doesn't apply
to surgeons. Because early Thursday morning I met Dr.
Mazgani, and within one hour I let this perfect stranger
(albeit a qualified one) poke holes in my abdomen and yank
out my ovaries and fallopian tubes.

2   Contrary to rumors I'd heard down at the cancer agency,
there is no Ovary Fairy! I know this for a fact because I
tucked my organs under my pillow the other night, and
when I woke up in the morning, they were still there. (I
was secretly hoping I'd strike it rich, because last summer
the Breast Fairy was very generous after my mastectomy.)

3   So far, instant menopause isn't so bad—a hot flash here, a
mood swing there—here a beard, there a mustache, everywhere extra hair...

4   I've kept the promise I made to my surgeon—that I
wouldn't lick my stitches—but maybe I should have promised that my stitches wouldn't be licked. By anyone. Or
anything. Anyway, I forgive my dog, Nellie, and have
warned her if she does it again, I'll take that obnoxious
plastic lampshade cone off *my* head and make *her* wear it.

5   Generally speaking, I believe in free speech. But for the
foreseeable future, I've banned that three-letter word that
chickens lay from being spoken in our house. Bergen and
Naomi are happy to comply, if it makes me feel better.
Which goes to show there's a sunny side up to everything.
Even censorship.

6   This is my first year celebrating Valentine's Day as a breast
cancer survivor. And even though I only have one breast
left, I'm grateful to still be here in this downsized body of
mine, surrounded by so much love and compassion. Makes
me want to stick around for more.

THE GOOD THING about having two simultaneous diseases is I'm spared from wallowing in either one too long. Following the rhythm of doctor appointments and surgical procedures, I swing back and forth between breast cancer and Parkinson's disease.

Today I have a follow-up appointment with my neurologist, Dr. Stoessl. It was booked six months ago, and yesterday his secretary called to remind me.

"Remember," she said, "don't be late or Dr. Stoessl won't see you."

And I thought, imagine that, a doctor who goes blind when his patients are late. Poor thing. So I assured her I'd be on time, and in fact I arrive early.

Even though there are no decorations or balloons or cake and ice cream, meetings with my neurologist remind me of a child's birthday party. That's because there are plenty of games and activities—and I get to be the center of attention! We play "tap the patient's impaired reflexes" and "try to move the patient's rigid left arm." Then we play hand-eye coordination games such as "try to touch the doctor's moving finger" and "copy the doctor's well-rehearsed intricate hand movements." At this point, the partylike atmosphere turns a little sour, since I always lose and my neurologist always wins these contests. But pretty soon things brighten up thanks to the Beck Depression Inventory. Here's a sample from this uplifting multiple-choice questionnaire:

Choose one statement from among the group of four statements that best describes how you have been feeling during the past few days:

☐ I do not feel like a failure.
☐ I feel I have failed more than the average person.
☐ As I look back on my life, all I can see is a lot of failure.
☐ I feel I am a complete failure as a person.

For the final games, we walk out into the public hallway. "Scrutinize the patient's lopsided walk" is almost as much fun as "make the patient lose her balance but catch her before she falls." As we return to the examination room, Dr. Stoessl smiles proudly. "You weren't expecting me to pull you backwards so violently, were you?"

Sadly, the party is over. Instead of a grab bag, Dr. Stoessl hands me a prescription. He assures me my quality of life will improve by treating my symptoms. This will be the first Parkinson's medication I try. Exhausted but hopeful, I pick up my winter coat and begin the slow struggle of threading my arms through the sleeves. Dr. Stoessl tries to help. This is no easy task, because my left arm is now stuck in the folds of the fabric and twisted behind my arched back. I'm feeling awkward and spastic (and a little mischievous) as my chivalrous neurologist tugs at my sleeve. Suddenly my left arm jolts violently against Dr. Stoessl's body. Then it happens again, and again. By the time my coat is on properly, I've "accidentally" punched him several times. Dr. Stoessl smiles proudly again, and for the first time that day I do not feel like a complete failure.

The next day, while walking Nellie, I bump into Helen outside her house. She looks exhausted and green around the gills.

"Are you OK?" I ask her. "You don't look so well."

"I'm not," she groans. "Last night was the big show. Battle of the Bands."

"I know. I wanted to go, but I was too tired."

"You're lucky. I wish I had stayed home."

"Why? What happened?" I ask.

"The music was so loud, it actually made me sick."

"Oh, no. That's awful. How's Will doing?"

"He's deaf," she says under her breath.

"He's deaf?" I repeat, wondering if I'd heard her correctly.

"When he woke up this morning, he couldn't hear a thing."

"That's not good," I say. "How are his hands?" I ask, hoping he hasn't lost his ability to floss.

"Oh, they're fine. At least his band won," Helen mutters. "And the girls had a blast. They made special T-shirts that said: 'My Dad's In The Band.'"

"That's so sweet," I say, picturing their two-breasted, arm-swinging teenage daughters prancing around the dance floor in the shirts. Having fun, no doubt. But the medium is the message after all, and with all that wiggling and jiggling going on, I can't imagine anyone was actually able to read the words. Which is a crying shame. If I had been there, my shirt would have read: "My Neighbor's In The Band & In My Dreams." And I would have stood as still as a billboard, in front of the stage, all night long, making it easy for everyone to read me. And while some might have thought I was crazy—that I'd gone overboard for the Overbites—I wouldn't have cared. Because that's the price you pay when you're a one-breasted dopamine-depleted groupie.

IT'S OFFICIAL—I'm a pill popper. Every day I dip into my geriatric pill dispenser and swallow a fistful of vitamins, supplements, and prescription drugs. There are antidepressants, anti-estrogens, antioxidants, anti-inflammatories, and now anti-Parkinson's. These little white tablets pack a punch. Classified as a "dopamine agonist," they conjure up images of a pharmaceutical superhero:

Look! Up in the sky! It's a bird. It's a plane. It's Dopamine Agonist!

Built to restore the brain's depleted dopamine signals, this childproof-capped crusader fights the never-ending battle for improved coordination, mobility, and speed. And after just

three weeks of taking this stuff, I'm starting to believe in its superpowers. Miraculously, my left shoulder is no longer frozen, and I have a bit more control of my limping leg. Sadly, my left hand remains stuck in an awkward "hand job" position. I'm aware some might consider this a windfall, depending on one's profession. But since my pole-dancing days are over, I'm hoping Dopamine Agonist will help relax my curling fingers, making my life a little easier (and a lot less embarrassing).

Of course, every superhero has a dark side. And Dopamine Agonist is no exception. When prescribing this medication, Dr. Stoessl listed the common side effects I might expect: nausea (tapering off), hallucinations (not yet), drowsiness (definitely), twitching (occasionally), and lightheadedness, especially when standing up (sometimes). He also took great pains to warn me of several unusual adverse effects of this drug including compulsive gambling, excessive shopping, overeating, cross-dressing, and hypersexuality. I assured Dr. Stoessl that I'd be on the lookout for the slightest sign of trouble, and if something strange happened I'd call his office immediately. But would I? Some of these side effects sound so exciting. And considering all I've been through, don't I deserve just a little fun? Especially the kind I can blame on my medication...

ZOË AND I make plans to get together at the dog park close to her house. These days, we e-mail regularly, but it's been years since we actually saw each other. I have a feeling we're both in for a shock.

Nellie and I arrive first, and we meander about. Then, off in the distance, I see a dog chasing after a ball and a person trailing behind. A hand is waving back and forth in the air. That must be Zoë. I wave back and whistle for Nellie. She runs to my side, and we walk toward Zoë and her dog. Then we hug hello, while our dogs get acquainted.

"This is Sadie. She's very gentle," Zoë says, bending down to pat Nellie. Not quite convinced, Nellie looks over her haunch at Sadie sniffing at her tail.

"She's a bit nervous. Big dogs intimidate her," I explain.

"That's understandable," Zoë says, scratching my pooch's head.

Zoë throws the ball, and much to Nellie's relief, Sadie stops sniffing her and runs off. Nellie sticks close to me, while Zoë and I swap war stories: She tells me about her metastasized cancer, continuing chemo treatments, side effects, and personal challenges; I tell her about my Parkinson's symptoms and medication, my oopherectomy and instant menopause.

As we talk, I am painfully aware of how thin and frail Zoë is—the chemo has whittled her down to skin and bones and fleeced the hair off her head. I am also aware that Zoë is observing me—and my own physical failings.

When Zoë is ready to head home, we hug once more and call out for our dogs. They come trotting back together, like old friends. Saying good-bye, I am struck by how easy it is to reconnect with Zoë after all these years. We've always appreciated each other, but our connection is deeper and more visceral now that both of our strong, healthy bodies have been snatched away.

THESE DAYS, everything is growing: the stacks of health books on my bedside table; the delicate snowdrops and crocuses dotting neighbors' yards, and the sexy black hairs on my unshaven legs. Even my comfort level with my missing breast is changing. She departed August 6, 2008, almost eight months ago. All I have left of her is a sloping horizontal scar across the right side of my chest. It horrified me in the beginning. Catching an accidental glimpse of my scar in the mirror, as if it were a stretched-out sealed mouth, muffling screams of terror, would

reignite my depression. But today things are different. Horror has subsided. And the scar, which now resembles the rim of a giant eyelid, triumphantly winks at me when I undress. Sometimes I wink back, tentatively. Sometimes I don't. Always I wonder about other breast cancer survivors and what they see in their mirrors.

I know many breast cancer survivors now. Most of them have had, or plan to have, reconstruction surgery. But there are other women with vacant lots, just like Zoë and me. There's even one in our neighborhood. Susan introduced me to her when we were walking Nellie one day. Her name is Corry, and she's a retired kindergarten teacher who loves to garden and travel. As we chatted away, it occurred to me that between the three of us, only two tits remain intact. That's two out of six. One is mine, the other is Corry's. She had her mastectomy ten years ago and never wanted reconstructive surgery. Soon after recovery, she got fitted for her very own Dolores, but eventually she got fed up wearing the prosthesis. So she embraced life as a conspicuous "one-boob woman." Life embraced her back. Family, friends, and colleagues grew accustomed to her asymmetric landscape. And she grew more grateful and compassionate.

I admire Corry. She is one of my "breast whisperers," a wise guide along this emotional path of loss, mourning, and acceptance, welcoming me into the alternate "one-boob" universe.

Such a peculiar place... unexpected... imperfect... lopsided... surreal... Home.

LIKE IT OR LUMP IT, I limp. A lot. In fact, I'm so used to limping, I often forget I'm doing it. Luckily, people remind me—mostly strangers, sometimes friends who haven't seen me in a while. They ask polite questions such as, "Twist your ankle or something?" or "What's wrong with your leg?" I have my arsenal of

answers. Depending on my mood, I might go for accurately mysterious: "I have an incurable neurodegenerative brain disease. Guess which one." Or mysteriously accurate: "My substantia nigra is depleted of dopamine." Or I might cut to the chase and declare, "I have Parkinson's disease."

You'd be surprised how people react when they hear that. I get everything from "But you're way too young to get Parkinson's!" (I'll be sure to inform my neurologist) to "What a shame, I'd hate to have that." More sensitive remarks include "That's a good way to get out of doing housework." Or "You must have done something really bad in a previous life to deserve this." The worst is over-the-top compassion from old friends or colleagues. They seem so devastated by my news that I end up consoling them.

"There, there. It's not as bad as it seems. There are worse diseases to get. At least it's not ALS or flesh-eating disease or late-stage leprosy."

This usually cheers them up, but not me. That's because I know how easy it is to diversify one's disease portfolio.

At the dog park the other day, a gentleman shuffled toward me and said, "I just had a hip replacement, how 'bout you?"

Feeling evasive, I told him, "I'm training for the O-limp-ics."

He gave me a puzzled look, so I repeated, "The O-limp-ics."

"Ah, I get it," he smiled, rubbing his sore hip.

Another question that people frequently ask me is, "How did you get Parkinson's?" Variations on this theme include, "Is it genetic?" or "Was it something you ate?" or "Is it caused by a virus?" or "Were you overexposed to pesticides or senior citizens?" All excellent questions—in fact, these are questions I've asked myself and my doctors too. Unfortunately, I have what is known as idiopathic Parkinson's disease. And although getting this disease at my age is idiotic, "idiopathic" simply means

the cause of the disease is of uncertain or unknown origin. In other words, "I don't know." Not a very satisfying answer, which is why I sometimes say, "I got Parkinson's disease from walking my dog in the park." Or "Parallel parking gave me Parkinson's." Either answer is a crowd pleaser. But more important, it changes the topic of conversation to something other than my health.

SPRINGTIME IS BIRTHDAY season in our house: first Naomi's, then mine, then Bergen's. Naomi celebrates her fifteenth birthday with a small gathering of friends. They cook dinner and clean up, then watch horror movies. Thankfully, most of them go back to their own homes to sleep. The remaining few spend the night here. It's all very civilized.

A few weeks later, Bergen and I throw ourselves a birthday party, celebrating our combined age—one-hundred and eleven years old. Miraculously, neither one of us is wearing dentures or diapers. This is a great relief to our friends. Not that they were necessarily expecting more misery to be visited on our family, but it wouldn't have surprised them either. When they ask me how I'm doing, I see them brace themselves for the worst. So I assure them that I don't have any new diseases or the need to have more body parts removed. Thankfully, they seem to believe this—more than I believe it myself.

When everyone has left, Bergen and I begin cleaning up the mess.

"I'm glad we had this party," I say. "It was fun."

"Me too. We used to have lots of parties."

"I used to have lots of brain cells. And more energy."

"You did great today. Why don't you go relax? Let me do the rest."

And with that, I head off to the family room and turn on the TV, just in time to catch Craig Ferguson's opening monologue.

MY FRIENDS CONTINUE to sustain me with their regular phone calls and visits. One day, Gloria arrives to take me to the spa. No matter where we go or what we do, going out with Gloria is always fun. She is playful and passionate—the life of the party. And she has a knack for knocking on opportunity's door. She once turned a girls' night out into a VIP adventure that kicked off with six of us sipping champagne in a stretch limousine while we rode through Stanley Park and ended up at her friend's upscale French bistro, where the food and wine were exquisite—and on the house.

Her optimism is irrepressible. While walking through a rough neighborhood that was on the verge of gentrification, she nonchalantly stepped over a puddle of vomit while extolling the virtues of a beautiful dress in a shop window.

She is also kindhearted and goes out of her way to put everyone at ease. Even Nellie, who goes bonkers whenever the doorbell rings. On this day, when I answer the door and Gloria steps inside, she gives me a warm hug and Nellie a warm foot. To lick. It works like a charm—instantly, the barking stops and Gloria's eyes glaze over.

Eventually, I say, "What time are the appointments?"

Gloria sighs. "In half an hour. I guess we should get going, huh?"

And with that, she reluctantly pulls her damp foot away from Nellie's pink tongue. "Now I'm really ready for a pedicure," she says.

We drive downtown to her friend's spa and sign in at the reception desk. I present the gift certificate that Gloria gave me for my birthday, and the hostess hands each of us the standard cult outfit: a plush white terrycloth robe and plastic reflexology sandals.

The change room is downstairs. Our lockers are side by side. I feel terribly self-conscious while we undress.

"You haven't seen my scar yet, have you?"

Gloria shakes her head no, and my eyes well up with tears.

"You don't have to look, if you don't want to," I tell her, unhooking my mastectomy bra, where Dolores resides. "It's quite shocking."

"I don't mind. It's just a scar," she says.

I catch a glimpse of Gloria, in one of the mirrors, viewing my vacant lot. "I warned you—it's not very pretty," I say. "It's so strange, only having one breast."

Unflinching, she gazes down at my chest, then looks me straight in the eye and announces, "Your left breast is pretty enough for the two of them."

"Thank you," I whisper, doing up my robe, repeating her words over in my head. She says it with such conviction that I want to believe her. So does my left breast. And so we do, all day long. And when I come home, I feel pretty—from my toes to my tit.

I also meet Sue and Cheryl for dinner at a local restaurant. Dining out with breast cancer survivors is not for the squeamish. When I arrive, the hostess says, "Your friends are already seated. Follow me."

As we snake our way through the room, I notice two women waving at me from a corner booth in the back. As I get closer, their bald heads come into focus, and I feel thankful I dodged the chemo bullet.

It has been a while since we'd last seen one another, so we have a lot of catching up to do. We kick off the evening with polite hellos and casual chitchat about parking spots, hairdos, holidays, and work. Then our conversation shifts from the mundane to the morbid, transforming the elegant ambiance of our dinner table into the clinical atmosphere of an operating room. The kind of circumstance you'd think would ruin most people's

appetites. But not ours. We are seasoned survivors, instilled with an insider's knowledge of medical treatments, comfortable in our modified bodies, which at the moment happen to be very hungry.

Between bites of salad, sips of soup, and nibbles of grilled chicken and tiger prawns, we yak our way through the following: double and single mastectomies, the distress of having internal surgical drains removed, breast-reconstruction procedures, surgical removal of ovaries and fallopian tubes, excised lymph nodes. In graphic detail, we cover all these topics and more, while our friendly young waitress refills our water glasses, repeatedly asking us if we are enjoying our meals. I am tempted to ask her if she is enjoying overheard snippets of our conversation. Perhaps she's caught wind of Sue's descriptions of the art of tattooing a new areola, or the incremental process of inflating breast expanders. Or maybe Cheryl's confession about the sexy side effect of chemo—a waxless Brazilian. But when our waitress flashes us a smile, revealing shiny dental braces, I am struck by her innocence. I even feel protective of it and refrain from asking her anything.

As our conversation turns to nipple reconstruction techniques, I wonder to what extent she has grasped fragments of our talk and what kind of people she thinks we are. I'd like to think her mind is so preoccupied with fantasies of some sexy movie star that she only registers enough to cast us as middle-aged, somewhat vulgar but amusing ladies, swapping operation stories. I'm sure it never crosses her mind that she might one day find herself in similar circumstances. I certainly didn't see breast cancer in my future when I was her age. And neither did my two friends.

As dinner comes to an end and our plates are cleared and the bill is paid, I silently wish that this dreadful disease never

visits our young waitress. But if it does, may she catch it early so that she too can be a survivor—blessed with the company of brave and inspiring women, like Sue and Cheryl, talking candidly about breast cancer, while eating a delicious dinner in a restaurant.

NOT ALL OF my excursions out of the house take me to spas or restaurants. Today, my left breast has an appointment at the cancer agency. She is scheduled for a mammogram and then an ultrasound. Routine tests, just to check that everything is OK. On the car ride there, I can tell she is anxious—beads of sweat dampen her underside, plus she isn't humming along to her favorite song on the radio: Beyonce's "Single Ladies (Put A Ring On It)." We drive in silence. I am thinking I should have worn Dolores so she'd have company. But we were in a rush, and putting on my special mastectomy bra—with Dolores tucked inside the prosthetic pocket—takes me forever. So I gave it a miss.

We arrive a few minutes early and take a seat in the waiting room. The technicians are running an hour and a half late, giving my left breast plenty of time to work herself up into even more of a tizzy. I don't blame her for panicking, for wanting to escape. This is her first experience going solo—the previous times my right breast always went first. But as scared as she is, I have faith in my left breast's ability to conquer her fears, especially since I slipped her a mild sedative in the change room. It's working like a charm, and she breezes through the flesh-compressing mammogram without complaint.

Next up is the ultrasound. The technician is a sweet-natured middle-aged man, who puts my left breast at ease by apologizing, in advance, for any pain or discomfort he might cause her. As we lie waiting on the examination table, he adjusts computer

equipment settings, then picks up the ultrasound wand and the bottle of gel. When he leans over my left breast, she braces herself for a chilly blast. He squeezes the bottle—and to her delight, she feels an unexpected warm gush of goop.

"Mine is never cold!" he says with a smile.

Once the ultrasound is over, we mop up, get dressed, and head home. It will be a couple weeks before the test results are in, and already my left breast is worrying about lumps and lymph nodes and latent cancer cells. She definitely needs cheering up, but I don't dare crack any of my jokes. Instead, I go into my closet, and in record time I am wearing my mastectomy bra, listening to Dolores and my left breast giggling away. I don't know what is so funny, but something is. And that's all that really matters.

IT HAPPENS to so many couples—you live together long enough and you wind up finishing each other's sentences or wearing matching jackets or growing identical mustaches. So after seventeen years of togetherness, I knew it was bound to happen to Bergen and me. But not quite like this.

After breakfast one day Bergen says, "I've been meaning to tell you something. It's a little embarrassing, but over the past few days I've found myself dragging my left leg when I walk, just like you."

"That's strange. I haven't noticed. Did you hurt your leg or foot?"

"Not at all."

"Maybe you're training for the O-limp-ics, like me?"

"Maybe. But I'm probably just subconsciously mirroring you, because once I'm aware that I'm dragging my leg, I can stop it and walk properly."

"Lucky you," I say.

Later on, we take Nellie for a walk. Sure enough, every now and then Bergen and I are limp-synching along the sidewalk until he corrects his gait for a little while, only to revert back to dragging his left foot, like me.

It's all very amusing and disconcerting at the same time. But at least we don't have matching handlebar mustaches.

SLOWLY BUT SURELY, I'm making a comeback. The anti-Parkinson's medication has really kicked in—boosting my energy level, decreasing my rigidity, increasing my mobility, and, best of all, defogging my mind. I'm much more alert and productive. I've started helping with some chores, and I've dipped my toe back into the parenting pond.

Some mornings I crawl out of bed early enough to help Naomi get ready for school. Long gone are the days of brushing her teeth or braiding her hair. The role I play now is less hands-on but no less useful, considering my contribution can set the tone for her day. For instance, when she is leaning over the sink, gazing into the mirror, making herself gorgeous, I nuzzle up beside her, give her a morning hug, and ask, "Are you ready?"

She smiles and together we look at my hilarious bed-head hairstyle: where some clumps of brown curls lie flattened against my head, and other clumps of curls stick out like corkscrews.

I'll say, "I've turned into Kramer from *Seinfeld*," or "I was electrocuted in my sleep."

And Naomi will say, "There's always a punch line when you look in the mirror."

And then we'll laugh.

Other mornings when I wake up, she's already eating breakfast. So I'll walk downstairs and announce, "And now, for your viewing pleasure, the Albert Einstein hairdo."

Naomi always looks up from the comics she's reading and grins and groans for the show. So does her girlfriend if she's there too. These are moments I know Naomi will treasure forever. Or not. But I certainly will. Her smiles and laughter reassure us both—that my playfulness has returned, and I'm still here. Her comeback Mama.

I've also started cooking and baking a little and have perfected the coconut macaroon: golden mounds of moist sweetness drizzled with melted dark chocolate. I've lost count of how many batches I've baked these past few weeks or how many times Bergen has asked me, "Are you saving any of these for our family, or are you giving them all away?"

It's usually a combination. While I love to bake, I love sharing the treats even more. So far, my macaroon taste testers include Bergen, Naomi, Susan, Helen and Will, Zoë and her kids, Gloria, Jessica, and Naomi's friends.

The latest batch is for Marg and her family. The cookies are still warm when I arrive at her house for tea. A caregiver greets me at the door and leads me to the kitchen.

"Look who's come to visit you," she says.

Marg is sitting in a chair wearing a helmet (to protect her head in case she falls), while her writhing legs perform an involuntary spastic tap dance.

"Hi, Marg," I say, leaning over to give her a hug.

"Hi, Robyn," she mumbles back.

"I brought you some freshly baked macaroons."

"Thank you. I love macaroons" is what I think she mumbles in response.

I sit down beside her at the kitchen island. She is gripping an open bag of graham crackers in one gnarled hand, while her other hand fumbles clumsily about, trying to fish out individual crackers. After many fruitless attempts, she finally manages to

grab hold of one and yank it out. A corner of the cracker breaks off and lands on her lap. I watch her rigid arm jerking erratically in the air until her fingers release the cracker, aiming for the baking pan in front of her. She misses, and it lands on the counter.

I've been resisting the urge to jump in and help, but I can't just sit here and watch Marg struggle. So I pick up the cracker and place it on the bottom of the pan. And together we line the pan with more of them. Her caregiver is standing across from us, stirring a pot on the stove. She says, "Are you done with the crackers? Ready for the next step?" She walks over to us, sets down a bag of chocolate chips, and resumes stirring her pot. I think I detect a faint burning smell.

Meanwhile, Marg crams her hand into the bag and pulls out a fistful of chocolate chips.

"Do these go on top?" I ask her.

"Uh-huh," she answers, concentrating on the task.

I watch her hand hovering over the pan, preparing to release the load. But as her fist unfurls, her arm jerks suddenly and the chocolate chips scatter like confetti. I leap into action, picking up the morsels that fell on the floor, on Marg, and on the counter. Then I sprinkle them over the layer of crackers.

Marg mumbles something I can't quite make out, but her caregiver understands and replies, "Yes. I think I burned the dessert topping. Sorry."

Marg rolls her eyes and mumbles, "She can't bake."

Her caregiver pours the burned mixture into the pan and pops it into the oven. Then she helps Marg over to the couch, takes off her helmet, and serves us tea and my macaroons. Her legs are still tap dancing, and I ask, "Is this the side effect of your medication?"

"Yeah. Dyskinesia," I think I hear her say. Involuntary movements.

We talk about our neurologists, our children, and our summer plans. I have a difficult time understanding her slurred speech and frequently ask her to repeat herself. I offer her another macaroon, and as she reaches out I notice that her hand is covered in melted chocolate. She clutches the second one, raises it to her mouth, and takes a bite. Now her lips and chin are also smeared with melted chocolate. When she's finished eating, I wipe her face and hands with a napkin and ask how her husband, Noel, is doing. Without missing a beat, Marg looks me in the eye and says, "Noel is really hard to live with."

She is dead serious, which adds to the hilarity of this declaration. This could be me, years from now down the neuro-degenerative road. I want to laugh. I want to cry. For her, for me, for every person with Parkinson's.

Before leaving, I head to the bathroom to pee and breathe deeply. When I walk back toward Marg, she mumbles, "You don't limp so bad."

I smile and say, "I'm in the honeymoon phase of this disease, aren't I?"

Staring blankly at me, she slurs, "Yeah. Honeymoon phase."

I wonder how long it will last.

10

Some Don't
Like It Hot

LAST SUMMER is a hard act I don't want to follow. So planning
this year's summer holiday requires a leap of faith (or in my
case, a limp of faith) that I will not diversify my disease portfolio or discover metastatic cancer or succumb to anything tragic.
If all goes well, we will entertain out-of-town guests, relax at our
cabin on Saturna Island, go to some festivals in Vancouver, and
visit family and friends back east.

So far, the season is off to a good start. Naomi has attended
Camp fYrefly—a groundbreaking national leadership retreat
for sexual minority and gender variant youth. Or as she calls it,
Gay Camp. She had a fantastic time. I'm not surprised. For the
first time in her life, she took a hiatus from being an outsider in
the heterosexual world and discovered life as an insider in the
LGBTIQQA2SA alternative universe. When she rattles off that
acronym, I test my knowledge and say, "Lesbian, gay, bisexual,
transgender. I don't know what the other letters stand for."

In one breath, she blurts out, "Lesbian, gay, bisexual, transgender, intersexual, queer, questioning, asexual, two-spirited, autosexual/ally."

"Now I know."

"That's not including pansexual."

"Let me guess—people who like to cook and make love at the same time?"

"Very funny. But no. Pansexual is when a person chooses to be with someone because of who they are, not their gender or orientation."

"That makes sense," I say. It's comforting to know that when it comes to sexual identity, there are so many options, so many descriptors. I bet there's even a word to describe someone like me. And if there isn't, I'll invent it.

THROUGHOUT MY LIFE, I've pursued many artistic endeavors: sketching, painting, animation, jewelry, collage, printmaking, sculpture, poetry, theater, stand-up comedy, freelance writing, and radio broadcasting. Not surprisingly, my creativity came to a screeching halt when I crashed. But ever since my ovaries came out, and I went on Parkinson's meds, my creativity has been reignited.

Writing has become my outlet—though Bergen calls it my obsession. I carry my notebook everywhere I go. And every week or so, I've been cheering up family and friends by e-mailing them a story about my diseases. They, in turn, cheer me up by writing back. Here is the most recent missive, followed by a friend's heartwarming response:

Hello everyone:

I'm feeling popular these days. Dare I say—in demand. Just this past week, I have received three special invi-

tations in the mail. Not to anything fancy, like swanky summer weddings or elegant cocktail parties—events where I'd get all gussied up in a sexy dress, paint my toenails, braid my armpits. The invitations I have are to more sterile affairs. Where the dress code is scrubs, lab coats, and hospital gowns, and the only alcohol being served is isopropyl. I'm talking about clinical research studies. And apparently, scientists consider me a hot commodity because I've got, or at least had, something of great value: breast cancer.

Partly out of curiosity, and partly because I have time on my hands, I accepted all three invitations. So far, I've undergone testing for the first research study, where I am affectionately known as #109. The nurses kept me busy with computer questionnaires, face-to-face interviews, and biospecimen collection. While donating a bucket of blood, I discovered an alternative to fainting—I just whined like my dog. This really amused Nurse #1, who was drawing my blood.

The other one, Nurse #2, did not find me so amusing. Nurse #2 measured my bone density and administered numerous other tests, including the "Tanita Body Composition Analyzer." She had me stand, barefoot, on this electronic scale-like machine, with my hands gripping spongy detachable handles. When she instructed me to squeeze hard, it occurred to me that since she is a practical nurse, she might appreciate a practical joke. So while squeezing the handles, I pretended I was being electrocuted, rigidly shaking while making this awful sputtering buzzing noise. She jumped out of her chair. Then, realizing she'd been fooled, she smiled in my direction. But not a friendly smile. It was one of those wide menacing smiles, where teeth look sharp and dangerous and poised to bite.

After a few more tests, my first volunteer session was over. I was surprised how quickly two hours had flown by. As a token of appreciation for participating in this breast cancer study, the nurses presented me with a ten-dollar gift card to a grocery store, which I graciously accepted.

When I got home, I was greeted with an invitation to participate in yet another clinical research study. The covering letter stated: "Thank you in advance for helping us in our continuing effort to understand the causes of breast disease. A tea bag is enclosed in the study package. Please accept this gift as a token of our appreciation." This made me laugh out loud.

Swayed by the solitary tea bag, I signed up right away for this study and resolved to sign up for any more that come my way. Donating my time, biospecimens and high jinks to science is a token of *my* appreciation—that I'm still here, lucky to be playing a small part in the search for a cure.

And now, my dear old camp friend's reply:

Dear Volunteer,

Very good of you to offer up your body for science.
I can remember a time when your body was in hot demand.

It was looked at, squeezed until juices were flying, and, in the end, much by way of clinical research was learned.

I am so proud that you are keeping up with science and lending your parts.

They are lucky to have you.

I am most proud of your antics, keep them on their toes. Good for you.

xox Susie

FIVE MONTHS HAVE PASSED since my surgical initiation into instant menopause, and surprisingly, nothing terrible has happened. Quite frankly, I was worried my vagina—who I have always considered to have a mind of her own—would be grief stricken over the loss of her ovarian and fallopian friends. So I've been watching over her, in case she did something drastic—like go out on a limb and start binge douching or sport fucking. Anything to fill the void. But so far, despite a few lonely tears and melancholic moments, she's kept a stiff upper lip, stayed upbeat, and maintained her composure. Talk about resilience and inner strength!

Unlike my valiant vagina, I've turned into a whining wimp. A whining wimp with a limp who sweats like a pig. Not all the time, thank goodness. Just during hot flashes—say, twenty, thirty, forty times a day. It's all so unpredictable. No matter what I'm doing, where I am, or who I'm with, at any given moment I'll be suddenly ambushed by a stupendous surge of heat deep within my core. This heat quickly radiates throughout my body, and soon I feel like an egg roll cooking in a deep fryer: boiling hot, greasy with sweat, begging for mercy.

Regrettably, I'm not witty when I whine. I make whimpering noises while mopping up beads of sweat with dinner napkins or facial tissues, even toilet paper, my hand swabbing discreetly under my shirt, aiming for armpits and phantom cleavage. I suppose I could dig out my stash of super-absorbent sanitary napkins and tampons. But after consulting my vagina, who endured thirty-five years of menstruating, we agreed to never use feminine hygiene products again—not even for unconventional purposes.

We would make one tiny exception—if Hollywood came knocking and paid me big bucks to star in my own reality TV show. It would be called *Hot Flash Hell*. And it would chronicle

my hilarious journey through instant menopause. There'd be close-ups of me sweating buckets while out shopping, fanning myself furiously with a menu at a restaurant, and even time-lapse photography of me sprouting sexy new chin hairs.

As my fantasy unfolds, the director takes me aside, whispers in my ear, then shouts, "Lights—camera—action!"

And right on cue, all flushed and soggy, I rattle off an original one-liner: "I'm melting, I'm melting!"

Then I unwrap a sanitary napkin, unfurl its wings, and mop up my sweat. When I'm done, the director praises my performance and calls a short break. To cool down, I sip an icy mint mojito while lounging in my air-conditioned dressing room and prepare for my next scene—the one where I try to convince viewers that I am not crazy and that millions of other menopausal women are not crazy either. We're just hot and bothered and fixated on finding some relief, even if it means letting our imagination run wild.

WHEN GERMAN PHILOSOPHER Friedrich Nietzsche coined the phrase "What doesn't kill you makes you stronger," he obviously didn't have Parkinson's disease and breast cancer—at the same time. Because if he had, he would have written this instead: "What doesn't kill you makes you stranger." I should know; I'm getting stranger every day. One disease makes me move weirdly. The other disease makes me look lopsided. And they both make me feel self-consciously conspicuous, like walking around with a ready-to-pop pimple on your nose on prom night. And that's on good days, when I'm well rested and I've remembered to take my Parkinson's medication.

I'm supposed to take this medication three times a day, with breakfast, lunch, and dinner. But sometimes I get distracted and forget to take a dose. That's when I get even stranger. The

first time this happened, I was standing by the stove, cooking pasta. The pot needed stirring, and as I went to pick up the spoon, my hand could barely move. After a few more unsuccessful attempts, I discovered my hand wasn't the only immobile part of me. My entire body seemed stuck. There I was, standing rigidly erect, head cocked, arms stiff, muscles tight, heart pounding against flushed skin. And even though I don't actually own one, I've seen enough of them to realize what I resembled: a giant penis with a robust erection. And if I didn't take my medicine soon, I feared I might wind up like those unlucky men with long-lasting Viagra-induced erections, in need of medical attention. Not a pretty sight. But one that leaves a lasting impression.

No doubt I left a lasting impression with Dr. Mazgani, the surgeon who performed my oopherectomy six months ago. Because she recognizes me out of context—here at the grocery store, standing beside the green beans, wearing street clothes— not in an operating room, lying down on a gurney, wearing a hospital gown. She smiles and asks how I am doing. While we chat, a wave of embarrassment sweeps over me, as I imagine how strange I must have looked at the hospital: I wasn't on Parkinson's meds yet, so my body was constantly rigid and stiff.

There's a lull in our conversation, and she wishes me well and says good-bye. Then, right on cue, a hot flash flares up, and I'm sweating like a pig, watching my surgeon disappear down the street. She seems like a nice woman, that Dr. Mazgani, even if she does have a strange job—yanking out ovaries and fallopian tubes, launching ladies into instant menopausal hell.

SOME DAYS SLIP by without a focus, but these days a definite theme is emerging. Since I bumped into Dr. Mazgani yesterday and am scheduled for a follow-up with Dr. Chung this afternoon,

I am officially declaring this week to be Surgeon Appreciation Week. The timing is perfect. My macaroon-baking phase has fizzled out. Now I'm cranking out banana breads. No one is complaining about this switch, though Bergen stills asks, "Is this for our family, or are you giving it away?"

Today I tell him, "I'm baking this cake for Dr. Chung."

"Didn't you bring her some banana bread last time?" he asks.

"Yep. But just a piece."

"Are you sure she liked it?"

"She mailed me a thank-you letter! For a *piece* of cake," I beam.

"Makes you wonder how she'll respond when you give her a whole cake."

I soon find out.

When I arrive for my appointment, the waiting room is packed. I carry the cake to the reception, to ask where it should go, but no one is at the desk. So I set it down on a table in the hall. It looks festive, covered in chocolate frosting and sprinkles. A few minutes later, the assistant returns, I give her my name, and she says, "Please have a seat, there are two people ahead of you."

A while later, I hear a door open, and a solemn couple leaves the office. Dr. Chung's voice rings out, "Where did this come from?"

"Where did what come from?" her assistant asks.

"This. A cake."

I twist in my chair and watch Dr. Chung suspiciously inspecting my offering, as if it might contain a bomb.

"I don't know where it came from," her assistant confesses.

"Cakes don't just appear out of nowhere," Dr. Chung huffs, lifting one side of the serving platter up, causing the cake to tip.

Afraid it might slide right off, I wave at her and say, "Hi, Dr. Chung. I brought the cake."

She looks over at me, and her face relaxes. "You did? Thank you."

Then she takes her next patient.

When it's my turn, Dr. Chung greets me with a great big smile.

"Thank you so much for the cake; it's very nice of you."

"You're welcome."

She conducts her usual exam and assures me everything feels and looks normal.

Then I ask her, "Do you bake?"

Dr. Chung smiles sheepishly and says, "Not very often."

This doesn't surprise me—she works such long hours, even on weekends. She once called me on a Sunday morning to tell me the results of my mammogram. I figure, for every cake she doesn't bake, she probably saves one woman's life.

Next up is a visit with Zoë. The forecast calls for devastating deterioration and the brutal reality of breast cancer. Expect shortness of breath, shattered hopes, and gusts of grief. There is a 100 percent chance of palliative care.

We are two one-breasted friends, sitting at her kitchen table on a Sunday afternoon. Zoë is wearing long pants and a sweater, a colorful knitted hat, matching gloves and socks, and her trademark smile. She is trying to stay warm, even in this hot weather. I wish I could harness the heat from my hot flashes and offer it to her. I also wish I had cooked her something useful—like oxygen soup or lung-inflating flan or miracle remission cookies—instead of banana bread and black bean stew. She's having trouble breathing. Her cancer—or as she calls it, her "mets"—has spread to various parts of her body, including her lungs. One has partially collapsed. But she doesn't dwell on this for long. She is still Zoë, after all, and nothing can quash her curiosity. So, while speaking is hard for her, not speaking is even harder.

She wants to know the latest news about me, Bergen, Naomi, and Nellie. I fill her in about my superhero drug, Dopamine Agonist, good old Dolores, instant menopause, volunteering in breast cancer research studies, and my rekindled passion for writing. I tell her that my family is doing well and we are enjoying our summer. When I ask about her son and daughter, her face intermittently lights up and clouds over—every story and thought and feeling she shares about them is imbued with fierce love and the torment of leaving.

Zoë's pain medication is wearing off, and her thin, frail body needs to rest. As tired as she is, she walks me to the door. We hug good-bye, and our vacant lots momentarily fuse.

"You are such a wonderful mother," I hear myself say.

These unplanned words pierce her heart, then ricochet into mine. We are stunned into silence. And then swept away by the past tense:

You were . . . she was . . . they had . . . they will miss . . .

Our good-bye drowns in grief.

I'M DREAMING OF WINTER. All the typical things: snow-storms . . . icicles . . . sub-zero temperatures . . . extramarital affairs with snowmen. Anything to turn down the heat of these hot flashes. They're brutal in the summer. And to think I used to love this season. Not anymore. Now I shun the sun and hate the heat. Menopause has changed me—right down to the molecular level.

Feeling sexy is not easy to do with just one breast, especially in cleavage-flaunting weather, but wearing my plastic prosthesis in sweltering heat is not exactly titillating—and it might not even be safe. With all that trapped hot air, it becomes a fiery furnace raging within my sizzling bra. And I imagine all it would take is one menopausal hot flash to set off a chain reaction, and BOOM—another case of spontaneous human combustion.

Of course, I'm doing what I can to prevent this calamity. Besides dreaming of winter, I'm also avoiding the sun, guzzling ice water, and taking cold showers.

Every little bit helps. Which is why Dolores doesn't mind staying tucked away in a shady drawer until autumn arrives. If only I could do the same. Together we'd escape this hellish summer and re-emerge when cooler temperatures, glorious gusts of wind, and tight-fitting sweaters prevail. Perfect conditions for us to make our sexy comeback.

WHEN I WAS A KID, my favorite thing to do at the park was play on the swing set. I would fly back and forth, back and forth, back and forth—pumping my legs vigorously, feeling the rhythmic rise and fall of invisible arcs etched in midair. It was never boredom that made me dismount. Only a full bladder could do that. Or someone else's meddling mother determined to let her whining child have a turn.

Eventually, I outgrew this childhood pastime. But since the Parkinson's diagnosis, my preoccupation with swinging has swung back into my life—with a vengeance. And in the most peculiar way. No, I'm not the crazy lady hogging the best swing at the local playground. Not yet. For the time being, I'm the limping lady who doesn't swing her left arm while out walking her dog. It's not that I don't try. Because I do. I've tried everything to get my stubborn appendage to budge.

So far, pep talks and affirmations have flopped. Apparently, motivational phrases such as, "You can do it, oh powerful one; swing your arm like a pendulum" aren't powerful enough to override the faulty wiring in my brain. Neither are guided meditations and visualizations—which I like to call naps. For a while I tried acupuncture and homeopathy. But the only upper-limb movement these treatments triggered was my good arm digging my wallet out of my purse and forking over way too much cash.

Both physiotherapy and massage seemed promising, since treatments relax my tight muscles and reduce rigidity. And if you saw me walking down the street after one of these therapeutic sessions, you might notice my left arm getting into the swing of things. But that's because I'm cheating. While my stiff arm is temporarily floppy like a rubber chicken, my right arm reaches across my chest and gives it the occasional push—giving the impression that it is swinging to and fro.

There was a time I believed Nordic walking poles would be my savior. I imagined they were equipped with a high-tech mechanism that positions and propels arms to swing in perfect repetitive formation—right arm forward, left arm back, left arm forward, right arm back. I'd seen people gliding by me at the park, their hands gripping these lightweight poles, their arms swinging sweetly, steadily, inspirationally. So the other day, I bought myself a pair. I tested the right pole first, and to my delight, it worked like a charm. My right arm swung upwards, bending at the elbow, then stretched out, planting the pole firmly on the ground. The left pole was next. Gripping the handle, I expected it to propel my left arm through the same movement sequence. But instead, the pointy stick clumsily flailed about, randomly whacking at objects, pets, and people, including me. Heartbroken, I realized that one of us was defective. So I returned my Nordic savior back to the store for a full refund.

It's quite discouraging—no matter what I try, nothing gets my left arm swinging. Not even my Parkinson's medication. But since I'm off to Toronto for a couple weeks, I'm hoping to try something on the wild side: a night out with my friend Belinda and her husband, at their swingers club. Because I hear anything can happen there—anything at all.

Naomi and I are going to Toronto together. I have been looking forward to the two of us spending some time together. Away

from the routine distractions of home. A chance to reconnect, build mother-daughter memories, discover common ground.

Bergen drives us to the airport and says, "I'm missing you both already." We give him good-bye hugs and kisses, then check our luggage and get our boarding passes.

There is a long lineup at Security. This gives me plenty of time to practice looking innocent while hot flashes rage through my body and sweat pours down my flushed face. When it's our turn, I watch our carry-on bags pass through the X-ray machine, while Naomi glides gracefully through the metal detector. The security guard gives me the nod, and as I walk toward him, he says, "Please remove your scarf."

"Welcome to the one-boob universe," I mumble under my breath, remembering that I'd packed Dolores. I pass the test and go to collect my carry-on bag.

"Is this yours?" a female guard asks, looking suspiciously at my knapsack.

"Yes," I answer.

"Can you open it for me?"

"Sure," I say, unzipping the bag.

The guard starts rummaging through my stuff, and when she finds a square box she grins. I say, "That's Dolores."

"Who?" she asks, opening the lid.

"Dolores. My prosthesis. I have only one breast." I point to my vacant lot.

"OK. You can go."

I pack up my bag and walk over to where Naomi has been waiting.

"Well, that was fun," I say.

She smirks and says, "The security guard tried to pick me up. He asked for my passport, boarding pass, and phone number."

"Lucky you. The only number I get asked for is my health card number."

We laugh and walk to the waiting area. We may be going in the same direction, geographically, but we are clearly living in different time zones.

WHENEVER I GO to Toronto, my dad always picks me up at the airport. Sometimes my mom comes along. But not this time— tonight he has passed the torch to my brother-in-law, Bob.

We throw our luggage into the car and drive to my parents' house. When my mom greets us at the front door, her electric-pink hair, jangling jewelry, sparkly outfit, floral perfume, and high-pitched squeals send me into sensory overload. This always happens when I haven't seen her in a long time. But within a few minutes, I acclimatize to her stimulating presence.

I wonder if she is also adjusting to mine. It might be just as jarring for her to see my deconstructed body, with its vacant lot and menopausal perspiration. If it is, she doesn't let on. Instead, she does what she does best—puts on a brave, smiling face and launches into party-girl mode, squeezing out every ounce of fun she possibly can. And why not? Naomi and I are in town!

My sister and her kids are in the family room. I give Fern a hug, while Kayla and Josh's sweet voices ring out in unison: "Hi, Auntie Robyn." I bend down for more hugs and kisses and marvel at how much they've grown. Kayla is now eight and Josh is five. Naomi walks into the room, and then it's her turn to be embraced.

"Where's Dad?" I ask my mom.

"He was resting in the bedroom. He should be on his way down."

I step back into the hallway, and sure enough, there he is, slowly, cautiously, walking down the stairs.

"Hi, Dad."

"Hi, Robyn. Stick around; I'll be there in a minute."

A Parkinson's minute, I think. When he finally reaches the bottom, our hug transcends "hello" and conveys a depth of understanding and compassion that comes from being held captive by this cruel coincidence—a father and daughter, decades apart, united by dying neurons.

"How was your flight?" he asks.

"It was good. No turbulence," I say.

My dad smiles and asks, "Where's Naomi?"

Right on cue, she pops up by his side.

"Hi, Zaidie," she says, wrapping her arms around his stooped shoulders and giving him a kiss on his cheek.

Parkinson's is often called a designer disease. This sounds glamorous and chic—like a fashionable affliction you catch from wearing expensive clothes. But it's not. There is nothing glamorous or chic about my wardrobe. Or the sickness. It turns out "designer disease" refers to the uniqueness of every patient's affliction—from onset and variety of symptoms to the severity and rate of progression to the response and tolerance to medication.

So while my dad and I have some similar symptoms, we are at different stages in the disease and respond differently to drug therapy. So far, I have been lucky. My antidepressants work wonders, and I tolerate Dopamine Agonist. My father is not as lucky. It took a while for him to find the right antidepressant. And since he had an adverse reaction to Dopamine Agonist, his neurologist prescribed Sinemet—the gold-standard medication (something I will require in the future).

For a while, his meds kept him in good spirits and mobile enough to go to the office regularly, socialize with family and friends, play golf, travel with and without my mom, and enjoy life. But lately, his depression is creeping back, and his physical symptoms are getting worse. I'm saddened to see the extent of his decline tonight.

"Who's hungry?" my mom roars from the kitchen.

"I hope Mom made enough food for all of us," my dad jokes.

We sit down at the table, and Naomi asks, "Where's Uncle Jonathan, Auntie Ariella, and Gabby?"

"They couldn't make it tonight. But we'll see them tomorrow," my mom assures her while uncovering the serving platters and bowls. Then she kicks off dinner with rapid-fire questions: "Who wants some teriyaki salmon? Honey garlic ribs? Mashed potatoes? How about roasted vegetables? Corn on the cob? Rice? Kayla, I made you your favorite—spaghetti. There's also sweet and sour chicken balls. Josh, I boiled you some plain hot dogs. Have some salad, Naomi. Robyn—you love my teriyaki salmon. Gord? Can you get some ginger ales from the fridge? Kayla and Josh—there's no chocolate cake unless you eat your dinner."

We eat and talk and nibble some more. As usual, my mom doesn't allow anyone in her kitchen—not even to help her clean up—so Naomi and I join Fern, Bob, and their kids in the family room. Together, we read books and draw pictures, while my mom tidies up and my dad dozes on the couch. Just like old times. It's comforting to see that some things haven't changed in the midst of so much that has.

In the morning, we go out for breakfast to my dad's favorite Jewish restaurant, Bagel World. The minute we walk in the door, my parents recognize half the people in the room. Everyone recognizes my mom and her hair. Some wave; others come over to say hello.

"You remember my daughter Robyn? And this is our favorite oldest granddaughter, Naomi," my parents beam.

"The granddaughter from Vancouver?" they all ask.

"Oy, is she gorgeous!" some add.

The waitress seats us in a corner booth. Naomi and I look

at the menu, but my parents don't bother—they already know what they want. We order our breakfasts—bagels, omelets, grilled cheese sandwiches, fruit salad, juice, and coffee.

"When did *you* start drinking coffee?" my mom asks Naomi.

"This year," she says, her fingers wrapped around her cup.

As she takes a sip, I watch both my parents smile. They have just learned something new about their long-distance grand-daughter, the one they long to know more about.

"Tell us about some of your friends," my mom says.

"What did you ask? I can't hear you," my dad blurts out.

"I asked about her friends," my mom says.

He leans forward, hoping to hear the conversation.

"The crowd I hang out with is really diverse," Naomi answers. "I have one friend who is transitioning."

"Transitioning from what? High school to university?" my mom asks.

"High school to *what?*" My dad is struggling to catch every word.

"University," she repeats.

"Transitioning from female to male," Naomi corrects.

I casually glance at my mom's face, expecting to see a puzzled expression, but she is smiling and nodding her head. My dad is also smiling ever so slightly as he leans back in his seat.

"Some of my friends are bisexual, gay, and lesbian."

I sit quietly beside her, resisting the impulse to laugh. My brave daughter is testing the water. On the plane, she told me she was considering coming out to my parents. She is tired of them always asking her if she has a boyfriend. Perhaps now is her chance.

My mom's face slides into neutral, as she mulls over Naomi's words. And then she says, "That's nice. I'm glad you are accepting of people that are different from you."

Moments later, the waitress delivers our meals. And before we have a chance to start eating, an old friend of my parents walks over to our table.

"I just had to come say hello."

My parents are happily chatting away with this heavyset bejeweled woman. My dad introduces us his usual way, "You remember my daughter Robyn? And this is our favorite oldest granddaughter, Naomi."

"How old are you, Naomi?" the woman asks.

"Fifteen." Naomi smiles politely.

"Oy, have I got a boy for you!" the woman announces.

Naomi and I glance at each other quickly, rolling our eyes.

"That's what they all say," I smile.

Later on, my dad drives us to his massage clinic. He booked Naomi and me for treatments with Julie, his massage therapist. When he walks us to the lobby, he looks exhausted and stressed.

"Why don't you take my appointment, Dad? You could use a massage more than me."

"No, thanks. I don't want a massage right now."

"How about sitting down and resting for a while?" I ask, pointing to a chair.

"I just want to go home."

"Are you OK to drive?" I ask.

My mom has been quiet all this time. "Do you want me to drive you home, Gord?" she asks.

"No. I can drive myself. But how are all of you going to get home?"

"Don't worry. We'll figure it out."

And with that, Naomi heads into the room for her massage, and my mom and I walk my dad to the car. As he drives away, I look at my watch and tell myself, it's only a fifteen-minute drive. He'll be all right. But really, I'm not so sure. My sense is that

his driving days are numbered. Twenty minutes later, I call him on his cell and breathe a sigh of relief that he made it home, safe and sound.

The next few days, Naomi and I make the rounds: visits at my brother's home, my sister's home, my aunt and uncle's, my cousin's. My mom takes Naomi shopping for back-to-school clothes. And in between the visits, I keep my dad company at the house—rubbing his feet, massaging his head, sitting quietly by his side—doing what I can to ease his anxiety. And mine.

I hate this fucking disease.

OUR TRIP TO TORONTO has an intermission—a four-day get-away plan. Out of the city. Into the woods. With my Toronto Trio. It's another one of Ruthie's good ideas. She has rented a lovely cottage on a private lake in the Muskokas and invited Lisa, Bonnie, and me to visit. She also invited our kids. In total there will be four adults, two seven-year-olds, one teenager, and a dog.

Naomi and I drive up north with Bonnie and Oliver. It's raining lightly. As the scenery changes from concrete and glass to trees and farms, my worries about my dad start to recede. While Naomi and Olie chat away in the back, Bonnie asks me, "Did you read Naomi's latest Facebook status?"

"Nope, I'm not her friend."

"Really? I am."

"What did she write?"

"Something like: Naomi is going to a cottage with two little kids and a bunch of middle-aged women."

"That's hilarious!" I say. "I think that's the first time I've been called middle-aged by someone else."

"Oh, I've been called it a few times. But it still takes getting used to."

After nearly three hours and several Tim Hortons pit stops, we finally pass through the town of Bracebridge. According to Ruthie's directions, we are almost there. Soon, we turn onto a bumpy dirt road that snakes its way through a pine forest and ends abruptly at a cottage.

"Hi, guys!" Ruthie yells out from the top of the porch stairs. "Stay here, Maya," she instructs her arthritic Great Dane.

"Hi, Ruthie!" we all shout.

She hops down the stairs, sweeping her long wavy hair from her face.

"Sorry about the rainy weather," our hostess smiles, giving us hugs. "It's supposed to clear up and get sunny in a couple days."

"That would be nice," I say, swatting at mosquitoes and black flies, waiting for nipple-sized itchy red welts to appear on my exposed flesh.

"I forgot you're afraid of bugs," Ruthie says.

"I wish they were afraid of me. But they find me irresistible."

We see Lisa's car pulling up and her and Dani waving.

Then there's a round of hugs, bags to carry in, groceries to unpack, and four glorious days to treasure with my daughter, my soul sisters, and their youngest kids.

Once we sort out the sleeping arrangements, we head downstairs. Since every kitchen needs a chef, and our hostess happens to be an award-winning restaurateur, Ruthie assumes this role. She also assumes we know The Rule. But we don't. At least not at first. Fortunately, we are fast learners. All it takes is one "Hey! Who changed the music?" admonishment from Ruthie, waving her chopping knife, to realize the chef controls the iPod. And apparently she hasn't had enough of Michael Jackson or his song "Don't Stop 'til You Get Enough." She resets the playlist, and the song starts over. When it's finished, the recently deceased King of Pop serenades us with more '80s hits: "Billie Jean," "The Way You Make Me Feel,"

"Beat It," "Thriller," "Bad," and "Man in the Mirror." I feel like I'm back in high school.

There's only one contender for the job of bartender, and that's Sweet Lisa, AKA Ms. Margarita. She unpacks her blender, bottles of tequila and triple sec, limes, and sugar and gets to work. In case things get out of hand, Bonnie is the designated bouncer. Blessed with exceptional bladder control—even after two babies—she happily bounces up and down for hours on the trampoline with Olie and Dani. And my job? I'm the floater, pitching in wherever help is needed: prepping food, washing dishes, shopping for groceries, hunting for mosquitoes.

THE DAYS UNFOLD in a slow, steady rhythm: Eating. Reading. Yoga. Swimming. Bouncing. Baking. Cooking. Eating. Drinking. Cleaning. More eating. Sleeping. I even squeeze in some writing when inspiration strikes. And I marvel at Naomi, as she flows effortlessly between children's games and adult conversations. Watching her interact with my girlfriends and their kids, I catch glimpses of the young woman she is becoming—resilient, outspoken, compassionate, independent, and fun.

One sunny afternoon, she surprises me. We are all down by the water, and she offers to take seven-year-old Oliver out for a canoe ride—revealing an adventurous side I've never seen before in her. Bonnie gives her permission, and the two of them strap on life jackets and get in the boat—Naomi in the stern, Olie in the bow, paddles in hand. It occurs to me that Naomi's canoeing skills may not be as proficient as she imagines they are. Then again, I could be wrong. I keep my eyes on them as they paddle away from shore. Either they are not interested in synchronizing their strokes, or any attempts to do so fail.

Bonnie asks, "Do you think Naomi knows what she's doing?"

"Yeah. Floundering," I say, my heart beating rapidly as we watch her struggling to turn the canoe around.

"I'm going to get them," Bonnie announces, plunging naked into the water. Mama Bear to the rescue. We watch her swim out into the middle of the lake and slowly swim back, the canoe and the kids in tow.

"The current surprised me—it was stronger than I expected," Naomi says. "Thanks, Bonnie."

"No problem," Bonnie smiles, toweling off.

With Naomi and Olie safe and sound, I announce, "I'm going inside. These black flies are brutal." Walking toward the cottage, I hear Naomi ask, "Who wants to go for a ride on the inflatable raft?"

Not me, I think, curling up on the couch, opening my journal to a blank page. Absorbed in my writing, I lose track of time until the sounds of footsteps and voices break my concentration. One by one, the gang walks through the door. Dani is laughing hysterically, and says, "Hey, Robyn. You missed another rescue!"

"Really?"

"This time my mom swam out to help Naomi, me, and Olie get the raft back to shore."

I look over at Naomi, who is smiling sheepishly by the door. I smile back and say, "Why am I not surprised?"

TODAY'S THE DAY we head back to the city. We spend the morning cleaning up, doing laundry, making the beds, and packing our bags while k.d. lang belts out spine-tingling cover songs: Joni Mitchell's "A Case of You," Neil Young's "Helpless," and Leonard Cohen's "Hallelujah." Her voice fills me with melancholy and longing and gratitude. I can feel my Cry Lady beginning to stir. Resting on the couch, I take a deep breath and close my eyes. When I open them, Lisa is sitting next to me.

"Hi, Robbie," she says.

"Hi, Sweet Lisa," I reply, wiping away my tears.

· "Are you sad?"

"Not exactly. More like relieved."

"Relieved about what?"

"It's so strange. I feel like I've had a holiday from my diseases. You've all been acting as if I'm still the same old me. Treating me as if I'm normal."

"Aren't you normal?"

"No. I'm abnormal."

Lisa looks at me strangely, while I conduct a silent inventory of all my defects: my limping leg, my dearly departed breast, my missing ovaries, my stilted arm, my dopamine-deprived brain.

"Abnormal?" Lisa exclaims. "Gosh. I wish you'd told me earlier. If I had known you were abnormal, I would have treated you abnormally. And that would have been way more fun!" She laughs. So do I.

Lisa gets up and joins Ruthie and Bonnie in the kitchen. I watch my Toronto Trio chatting away. These women are my best friends, my soul sisters. Maybe they know something I don't? I find this both comforting and confusing, especially since my social interactions are often tinged with pity—usually other people's, sometimes my own. As far as I can tell, there's not a drop of it to be found here. Of course, over the years, we've all had our share of heartaches and crises. There have been miscarriages, sick children, dying pets, cheating husbands, cash crunches, marital strife, ailing parents, work woes, and pesky aches and pains. And now there's Parkinson's and cancer thrown into the mix. Plenty to complain about, which we sometimes do. But pity? Not a chance. We are resourceful, we are resilient, and when in one another's company, we are resplendent. Even if we are middle-aged.

NAOMI AND I drive back to Toronto with Bonnie. The closer we get to the city, the more her BlackBerry buzzes, and the more

excited I am to go home. I miss Bergen. I miss Nellie. I miss my Vancouver life.

When we turn onto the 401, I ask Bonnie, "Do you ever miss living in Vancouver?"

"No. I love living in Toronto. But I love working on shows in Vancouver. So I get to visit you."

"When are you coming to town next?"

"No plans yet. But I'll let you know as soon as I get a contract. Hey, did I tell you that I bought critical care insurance?"

"No. Isn't that really expensive?"

"Really expensive. But you inspired me."

"Really?"

"When you were diagnosed with Parkinson's, I realized that I needed to protect my self and my family, in case I get sick and can't work. So I splurged."

"It's a good idea. I wish I had thought of that."

We spend our last few days in Toronto with family. My dad seems even more fragile, more anxious than he was before my trip to the cottage. It's heartbreaking to watch him suffer with this body-snatching disease. Before Naomi and I leave for the airport, I massage his feet while he rests in bed. I can feel his legs relax a little. I can hear him breathing more calmly.

"Can you rest your arms and hands on the bed?" I ask.

He glances down at his rigid limbs levitating a couple inches above the covers.

"I'll try," he says quietly.

I watch him bending his stiff arms and wiggling his frozen fingers.

"Is this better?" he asks.

"A little," I lie. "Let me help."

One at a time, I massage his floating arms, coaxing the tight muscles to relax. Eventually, his left arm surrenders and

flops down by his side. Then the right arm begins to relax too. As I set it down on the bed, his left arm rises up—as if an invisible pulley connects the appendages. I can't help smiling. And I can't resist the urge to see what will happen next. I grasp his left arm again, and sure enough, as I settle it back down on the bed, his right arm lifts up into the air. This time I laugh.

"What's so funny?" my dad asks.

I don't have the heart to tell him about his levitating arms. So I resume rubbing his feet and say, "Our disease. If I don't laugh about it, I'll cry."

A while later I hear my mom's voice announcing, "Robyn. Naomi. The taxi's here."

My dad has drifted off to sleep. I lean over and give him a kiss on his forehead and whisper, "Bye, Dad. I'll see you soon. I love you."

His eyes flutter open and he gives me a smile. "Are you leaving?"

"Yeah. Our ride is here. I'm going to miss you."

"I'm going to miss you too."

I head downstairs, hug my mom good-bye, and join Naomi in the car. My Cry Lady has been patiently waiting, and as we pull out of the driveway, the tears begin.

BERGEN PICKS us up at the airport.

"How was the plane ride?" he asks.

"It was a one-Ativan flight," I say, feeling a little woozy.

"In other words, Mama thought we were going to crash," Naomi says.

When we get home, I have just enough energy to give Nellie a belly rub and get myself ready for bed. Then I conk out for the night.

TWO DAYS LATER, I have a follow-up appointment with Dr. Chung. When she's finished examining me, I say, "I'm sorry I didn't bake you a cake this time, considering it's our anniversary."

She smiles. "Our anniversary?"

"Exactly one year ago today, you did my mastectomy."

"Well then, congratulations."

"Congratulations to you too." I look down at my chest. "Anything to worry about?"

"Everything looks and feels normal," Dr. Chung reassures me.

"That's a relief." And there's that word again: "normal."

"Do you want to continue coming to see me for your six-month checkups? Because your family doctor can do that for you, if you prefer. I don't know how far you have to travel to get to my office."

"Not far at all. And if it's OK with you, I'd like to continue coming to see you. I really trust your expertise."

"That's perfectly fine," Dr. Chung smiles.

I CALMLY LIMP through the remaining weeks of summer. There are dinners with friends, walks with Susan, massages with Jessica, and family time at our cabin. As September approaches, breast cancer steps out of the spotlight and Parkinson's takes center stage. It's been six months since I started taking Dopamine Agonist. It has certainly improved my bodily function and quality of life. But Dr. Stoessl warned me that this drug's superpowers would eventually fade and I'd need to augment my drug therapy regime with Sinemet. He was right; all summer long I've been experiencing a slow and steady decline of my mobility and dexterity. My body is slowing down again. My fingers are beginning to malfunction, making it difficult to chop vegetables,

type at the computer, and floss my teeth. It's all rather depressing, though I'm not depressed. Yet. However, I am anxious and worried that my symptoms will get worse and I will become a zombie again—just like I was before taking medication. I feel determined not to let that happen ever again. So now that I'm clear of cancer and have had all the surgeries I need, I decide it's time to start taking Sinemet.

If Dopamine Agonist is a superhero, then Sinemet is a supergod. Within days of starting this medication, I feel reborn. My rigid left arm is beginning to swing. My left leg is losing its limp. But best of all, the fog is lifting in my brain. After just one week on this drug, I say to Bergen, "I haven't felt this clarity of mind in years."

"That's fantastic!" Bergen says.

"It's unbelievable. It's like a switch has been turned on in my brain."

Which in a way, it has. I remember Dr. Stoessl explaining to me how Sinemet works—but back then I didn't grasp the concept. I do now: People with Parkinson's need dopamine. However, you can't actually give them straight dopamine, since it can't cross the blood-brain barrier to reach the brain. So Sinemet is the next best thing. It contains levodopa, which is the precursor of dopamine. And the levodopa crosses the blood-brain barrier and is transformed into dopamine in the brain.

"Is this the medication that Dr. Stoessl didn't want you take in the beginning?"

"Yep. He wanted me to wait until I really needed it. It can cause dyskenesia. But that may be three, four, five years down the road. I'm not going to worry about it now."

"Good idea," Bergen smiles, giving me a hug.

As the weeks go by and my dosage of Sinemet increases, so does my vitality. Friends who haven't seen me in a while

are stunned, "You look fantastic! Totally different." The more I hear this, the more I realize I must have looked like hell. Which makes perfect sense, considering all I've been through these past few years. More than my share of misery. Misery I regret sharing—particularly with Naomi and Bergen. How they endured my moods and melancholy during the Bad Old Days is beyond me. I know it wasn't easy for them. It took enormous courage and compassion, and in Naomi's case it also required her to grow up in a hurry.

Sometimes we talk about those days and the impact it's had on her. Today, when I ask her what she remembers thinking when I first told her about my Parkinson's diagnosis, she says, "I think I thought: Oh. It's a brain disease; it just affects the movement. So maybe there's something really wrong with me that makes you angry. That was my biggest thing. For me, you getting sick was just another reason why I had to be perfect and I couldn't do anything wrong to upset you. Because then you'd break down. And then it was like I was the mother and you were the kid."

"That's when I checked out of being a parent," I say, watching her eyes tear up.

"Did you think I was going to die?" I ask.

Naomi looks down and starts to cry. "When you told me the diagnosis, I thought, so it's *not* going to kill you?" She hangs her head in shame, having just spoken the unspeakable.

"It's OK to have wished that I was dead. It was a hard time for you. I'm sorry."

"It was really hard. And then you were diagnosed with breast cancer. In the summer! It was the worst possible timing ever."

"I know. I'm sorry."

We sit quietly together for a while, then I give her a hug. "I love you, Naomi. Thanks for being so honest."

"I love you too," she says.

OUR HOUSE has become a haven for teenagers. A place for Naomi's friends to drop by. They bake cookies, watch movies, play Scrabble, join us for dinner, and sleep over. This is a good thing. It means that Naomi is happy to be at home, and her friends are comfortable being here. It also means that I don't get as much privacy as I'd like. Around Bergen and Naomi, I am comfortable wearing clothes that reveal my vacant lot. But around all these kids, I feel conflicted. Not only am I self-conscious about my appearance, but also I'm worried about traumatizing her friends.

One day, while putting on Dolores, Naomi says, "You don't have to wear her. Nobody but you notices that you only have one breast."

"Oh, come on. Your friends must notice."

"Not really. And even if they do, so what?"

"I don't want to scare them away."

"You won't. You're a breast cancer survivor with one breast. That's an accomplishment! It's nothing to be ashamed of."

"How'd you get so smart?" I ask.

Naomi shrugs her shoulders. The doorbell rings and she heads downstairs to let her friends in. I've only been wearing Dolores a few minutes, and already I'm feeling uncomfortable and itchy. The truth is, I'd rather not wear her around the house. And so, guided by Naomi's words of wisdom, I remove my bra, tuck Dolores back in her drawer, and put on a T-shirt. It feels good to make my one-breasted self at home.

The following night, Naomi and her friends go to a party down the street. Bergen and I enjoy a quiet dinner together and then take Nellie for a long walk. When we get back, he asks, "What would you like to do tonight?"

"How about we go to bed early?"

He smiles. "Sure. Give me a few minutes to finish up in my office—I have an e-mail I promised to send someone."

I go upstairs to our bedroom, dim the lights, and freshen up in the washroom. Gazing at my asymmetric body in the mirror, I can't help noticing how sad and lonely my left breast looks next to my vacant lot. If only there was something I could say or do to make her feel better. Out of the corner of my eye, I glimpse Naomi's makeup bag lying on the counter, and inspiration strikes. I reach for a black pencil eyeliner, excited to do something I haven't done in a very long time: draw a picture. Why didn't I think of this before, considering the flat side of my chest is like a blank canvas?

Leaning toward the mirror, I uncap the pencil and scrawl a happy face over my mastectomy scar. It's a rush job, and the face turns out lopsided, the eyes a little too squinty. But the mouth is magnificent—a full throttle smile that is outrageous and contagious. Standing back from the counter, I stare at my masterpiece. Instantly, I know that this is the perfect companion for my solitary breast. I am giddy with delight.

I return to the bedroom and lie down across the sheets. There's no time to lose; I can hear Bergen climbing the stairs. When he arrives, my arms are tucked behind my head, my back is arched, my knees are bent. I feel like Marilyn Monroe posing for *Playboy*.

"What do you think?" I ask him playfully.

"About what?"

"This!" I exclaim, pointing to my creation.

He looks down at my chest. Then he bursts out laughing.

"I love it!" he says, bending over me and giving it a kiss.

"Maybe I'll get a tattoo."

"Really?" he asks.

"You never know."

All night long, I feel radiant and happy—as if equilibrium has been restored. Wrapped in Bergen's arms, I wonder if there

really is a tattoo in my future. And if there is, what other things might there be waiting for me to do, to see, to discover? Running my fingers along the contours of my happy face, I can't help thinking of Zoë and her mysterious tattoo, fading away together. Forever.

I feel a sudden sense of urgency deep within me. I close my eyes and imagine a lined sheet of paper. At the top, I write "To Do." And then I begin compiling my list: take piano lessons, learn computer animation, design postmastectomy clothes, take Naomi to San Francisco and New York, go on a honeymoon with Bergen, write books, travel to Toronto more often, get tickets to Craig Ferguson's *Late Late Show,* begin painting again, continue my friendship pilgrimage. I open my eyes and feel my horizons expanding. Who knows? There might be more of me, after all.

ROBYN MICHELE LEVY is a visual artist, radio broadcaster, and writer. Her paintings can be found in private and public collections around the world. Her radio work includes documentaries, commentaries, poetry, and sketch comedy for CBC Radio. Her writing has been published in the *Vancouver Sun* and the *Georgia Straight,* among other publications, and she has also dabbled in stand-up comedy and slam poetry. She lives with her family and her remaining body parts in Vancouver, British Columbia. www.robynlevygallery.wordpress.com